The Original

DOGS for Kids!

Everything You Need to Know About Dogs

By Kristin Mehus-Roe

Irvine, California

Karla Austin, *Business Operations Manager*
Nick Clemente, *Special Consultant*
Barbara Kimmel, *Managing Editor*
June Kikuchi, *Consulting Editor*
Jessica Knott, *Production Supervisor*
Amy Stirnkorb, *Design*
Indexed by Melody Englund

The dogs in this book are referred to as *she* and *he* in alternating chapter unless their sexes are apparent from the activity discussed.

BowTie Press®
A Division of BowTie, Inc.
3 Burroughs
Irvine, California 92618

Library of Congress Cataloging-in-Publication Data

Library of Congress Cataloging-in-Publication Data

Mehus-Roe, Kristin.
  Dogs for kids! / by Kristin Mehus-Roe.
     p. cm.
  Includes index.
  ISBN-13: 978-1-931993-83-8
  ISBN-10: 1-931993-83-1
  1. Dogs. 2. Children and animals. I. Title.

  SF426.M39 2007
  636.7—dc22
                              2006035434
Second printing in 2007:
10 09 08 07   2 3 4 5 6 7 8 9 10

Disclaimer
This book is intended to give general insight into the health and training of dogs. It should not substitute for the care and guidance of a veterinarian and professional trainer. Always seek professional help if your dog displays any type of medical or behavioral problem.

DEDICATION

For my dad, David Mehus,
and my son, Jack Chance Mehus Roe.

Contents

Acknowledgments		6
Introduction		7
Chapter 1:	The History of the Dog	8
Chapter 2:	Man's Best Friend	17
Chapter 3:	What Is a Dog?	33
Chapter 4:	It's a Dog's Life	47
Chapter 5:	Big Dogs, Little Dogs	56
Chapter 6:	Dogs and Responsibility	128
Chapter 7:	Choosing Your Dog	139
Chapter 8:	Preparing for Your Pup	153
Chapter 9:	Welcome Home, Pooch!	162
Chapter 10:	Sit, Stay, Good Dog!	171
Chapter 11:	Your Dog, the Social Butterfly	191
Chapter 12:	Food for Thought	201
Chapter 13:	Lovely Locks	211

Contents

Chapter 14: No Bites! — 225

Chapter 15: Healthy and Happy — 235

Chapter 16: Doggy Dilemmas — 260

Chapter 17: Doggy Sports — 274

Chapter 18: Doggy Games — 298

Chapter 19: Fun Away from Home — 323

Chapter 20: Helping Dogs in Big and Small Ways — 340

Chapter 21: Working with Dogs — 352

Conclusion — 367

Breed Pronunciation Guide — 368

Glossary — 369

Recommended Readings — 373

Photo Credits — 375

Index — 377

About the Author — 384

Acknowledgments

Although I've written about dogs for many years, nothing prepared me for writing a dog book for kids. This book is truly a culmination of advice, editing, and work from a huge number of people.

First, thanks to BowTie Press for allowing me to take on this project. Karla Austin, Heather Powers, April Balotro, Nick Clemente, Barbara Kimmel, Art Stickney, and Jarelle Stein were all wonderful sources of help and support. Special acknowledgment goes to Norman Ridker, who once again had faith in a giant book project and allowed me to run with it.

June Kikuchi and Roger Sipe of *Dogs for Kids* offered advice on both dogs and kids. Other advice from parents and kids, especially Robbie Bernstein, Chloe Da Silva, Mina Mehus Helbert, and Dean Styles Rutherford and their parents, was greatly appreciated.

Thanks also to Keith May for remaining calm during a long and chaotic photo shoot. Laurie O'Keefe, as always, inspired me with her wonderful illustrations. The Long Beach children's librarians were generous enough to allow me to sit in on one of their monthly meetings and graciously answered my questions. Thanks also to Bill Samuels at the ASPCA, Heidi O'Brien at NAHEE, Terry Long at DogPact, Dr. Tia Greenberg and Denise Bennett at Westminster Veterinary Group, and September Morn.

To Ruth Strother, her advice as a parent, a dog lover, and, of course, as my copy editor is always a tremendous boon. I can't imagine where this project would be without her.

I'm especially grateful to the dogs in my life (past and present): Desi and Muddy; Patsy and Molly; Tramp, Sunshine, and Muffin.

Finally, thank you to my amazing family who still listens to me talk endlessly about dogs and dog books and never seems to mind (or at least is nice enough not to show it). My most heartfelt gratitude and love go to my wonderful husband, Andrew, and my son, Jack.

Dogs! You can't live with them and you can't live without them! If you love dogs, you know that life is not the same without them. They play with you, cuddle with you, and keep your bed warm on cold winter nights.

But dogs are also a lot of work. You need to feed them, walk them, and pick up their poop. When they are sick, you need to take them to the veterinarian, and when they are naughty, you need to take them to doggy school and help train them.

Your work starts even before you bring your first dog home. You have to talk with your family about what kind of dog you all want. You must compromise if one of you wants a giant, shaggy Newfoundland and another wants a Chihuahua.

To raise a good dog, you need a lot of help. Friends and family can help you. So can doggy professionals, such as veterinarians, trainers, and groomers. Books like this one are great to read together with your family. Having a dog isn't easy, but it's definitely worth it!

Chapter 1

The History of the Dog

Dogs are our best friends. They play with us and relax with us. They cheer us up when we're sad and celebrate with us when we're happy. A world without dogs is hard to imagine.

Some scientists believe that dogs have been around for 135,000 years. But no one seems to know for sure. Scientists disagree on just about everything to do with dogs. They can't agree on how old they are. They don't know how long they have been kept as pets. They aren't even sure where they came from.

The first dogs may have been from the Middle East. That's where the earliest dog fossils were found. In Israel, a 12,000-year-old skeleton of a woman was found with a puppy in her arms. In Iraq, a doglike jawbone was found in a cave.

As you can see, there is wonderful variety in the world of dogs.

The Bering Land Bridge

Wherever the first dogs came from, they probably came to America at the same time that the first humans did, about 12,000 years ago. They came to America by walking over the Bering Land Bridge across a channel of water called the Bering Strait. The Bering Strait is about 55 miles wide and separates the continents of Europe and America. During the Ice Age, the sea level dropped by about 300 feet. It exposed the Bering Land Bridge—a swath of land connecting the continents at the Seward Peninsula in Northern Alaska and at Siberia in Northern Russia. It's not really fair to call it a bridge at all; the land was about 1,000 miles wide! The Land Bridge allowed humans and other animals to cross from one continent to another. When the Ice Age ended about 10,000 years ago, the sea rose and covered the land connecting the two continents.

It is probably about 12,000 years old, also. There are many fossils of dogs with people that are about 7,000 years old. Dogs were definitely part of human society by then.

What's in a Name?

Almost every animal has two names. The common name is the one used by us, and the scientific name is the one used by scientists to classify the animal. Scientific names are in Latin. The dog's scientific name is *Canis familiaris*. (See the box on page 12.)

The scientific name for an animal always has two parts, the genus and the species. The first part of the name, in this case *Canis*, is the dog's genus. The second part of the name, in this case *familiaris*, is the animal's specific name. The dog is the only animal who has this name. All animals with the same specific name are part of the same species. (The word *familiaris* means "someone who belongs to the household.")

Many people wonder if dogs descended, or came, from wolves. It's dramatic to imagine a fluffy Poodle as a descendant of a noble gray wolf. Dogs and wolves are very close relatives. In fact, their DNA makeup is about 99 percent the same. (DNA is basically the chemical map of an animal. DNA decides whether we have blue eyes or brown eyes or whether a dog has a short tail or a long tail.) Wolves are definitely dogs' closest relatives. Some scientists think that dogs came from different groups of wolves or from a canid that was related to both the wolf and the dog.

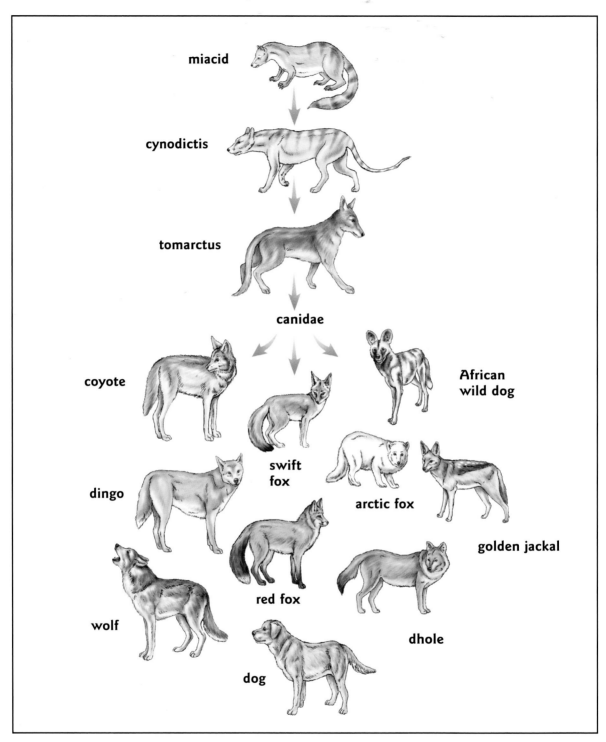

miacid

cynodictis

tomarctus

canidae

coyote

African wild dog

swift fox

dingo

arctic fox

golden jackal

wolf

red fox

dhole

dog

As this family tree of the domestic dog shows, all canids are closely related.

The African Wild Dog—Endangered!

African wild dogs (*Lycaon pictus*) live in Africa, south of the Sahara Desert. They have only four toes instead of the five the domestic dog and wolf have. They are especially known for their large round erect ears. The scientific name means "painted wolflike animal." The name is perfect for these dogs because their coat is made up of splotches of brown, black, yellow, white, and beige. It looks as if different colors of paint have been thrown at it. African wild dogs are like snowflakes—no two have the same coat.

African wild dogs live in savannas, or grasslands. They hunt zebras, impalas, gazelles, and other animals for food. They are pack animals: they live, hunt, and play together. The pack is usually made up of a male and female leader (called the alpha dogs) and their relatives. The packs used to be made up of one hundred or more dogs. Now, only about ten dogs are in each pack. There were once tens of thousands of African wild dogs. Now, only four or five thousand are left.

An African wild dog shows off his colors.

What's in a Breed?

What's the difference between a breed and a species? All dog breeds, from the tiniest lap dog to the biggest Mastiff, are part of the same dog species—*Canis familiaris*.

Because dogs are all the same species, that means they can mate and have puppies with one another. Dogs naturally mate with one another willy-nilly and don't favor one breed of dog over another. To them, a dog is a dog is a dog. If ten dogs of varying breeds were left to mate with each other on a desert island, after a few generations the puppies would look pretty much the same. They would probably be medium size with tan or brown fur.

Dog breeds were created by people, and people have created dogs who come in a whole range of shapes, sizes, and colors. Differences among dogs are more varied than in any other species in the animal kingdom. Although dog

breeds aren't species, they are different from one another. There is a small but real difference between each breed's DNA. The differences are so clear that a scientist can tell two breeds apart just by looking at their DNA. This tells us that the breeds have been kept separate over time.

In 2004, a study looked at the DNA of 414 dogs from 85 different breeds. The study found four types of dogs—guarding, hunting, herding, and ancient dogs. Ancient dogs are the closest relatives of the wolf. The DNA study showed which breeds are closely related and which aren't. Some were obvious. Greyhounds and

Dog Classification

Kingdom: Animalia
Phylum: Chordata
Class: Mammalia

Order: Carnivora
Family: Canidae
Genus: *Canis*

Species: *Canis familiaris* or subspecies: *Canis lupus familiaris*

All animals are part of the kingdom, Animalia. Mammalians (or mammals) are part of the phylum Chordata and the subphylum Vertebrata. The order Carnivora is under the class Mammalia. Carnivores (animals that usually eat meat) are all part of the order Carnivora. Canids are under the order Carnivora. Under the family Canidae is the genus *Canis* (canids). All of the animals that are part of the genus *Canis* are also part of the family Canidae, but not all animals that are part of the family Canidae are part of the genus *Canis*. Red foxes, for example, are part of the genus *Vulpes*.

The genus is a group of animals that have common characteristics. Domestic dogs are part of the genus *Canis*. Other animals that are part of the genus *Canis* are the wolf, the jackal, the coyote, and the dingo. Some animals are a subspecies of another species. A subspecies has three parts to its name—the genus name, the species name, and the subspecies name. Some scientists classify the dog as a subspecies of the wolf. The wolf's scientific name is *Canis lupus*, so these scientists call the dog *Canis lupus familiaris*.

Domestic dogs are part of the genus *Canis*.

Whippets are closely related. So are Siberian Huskies and Alaskan Malamutes. Some were unexpected. Basenjis and Pekingese are closely related. So are fluffy Saint Bernards and sleek Greyhounds.

Most breeds of dog were bred to do certain jobs. Some dogs, such as Border Collies and Welsh Corgis, were bred to herd. Other dogs, such as Mastiffs and Pyrenees Mountain Dogs, were bred to guard. Some dogs, such as Greyhounds, were bred to hunt with their eyes. Others, such as Beagles, were bred to hunt with their noses! Dogs look different and act differently depending on what job they were bred to do.

The Big and Small of It

The tallest dog breed is the Irish Wolfhound. Standing on his hind legs, an Irish Wolfhound can be up to 7 feet tall. That's about the same height as Shaquille O'Neal! The heaviest dog breed is the English Mastiff. The heaviest English Mastiff ever was a dog named Kell, who weighed 286 pounds.

The smallest dog breed in weight and height is the Chihuahua. The smallest living Chihuahua is named Danka. She's less than 7 inches in length and weighs 27 ounces. That's smaller than a large Slurpee!

Compared with dogs, there are mammals that are a lot bigger and a lot smaller. The largest mammal in the world is the blue whale. The blue whale is 110 feet long and weighs more than 190 tons. That's about as heavy as fifteen elephants and as long as two semitrucks! (That's about 3,330 English mastiffs!)

The smallest mammal is the Kitti's hog-nosed bat. The hog-nosed bat is 1.2 inches long and weighs .07 ounces. That's about the size of a paper clip! (And it would take about thirty-nine Kitti's hog-nosed bats to make one Chihuahua the size of Danka!)

The Irish Wolfhound is the tallest dog breed.

Dogs by Continent

NORTH AMERICA
- Newfoundland, from Newfoundland, Canada
- Boston Terrier, from United States
- Louisiana Catahoula Leopard Dog, from southern United States
- Xoloitzcuintli, from Mexico

SOUTH AMERICA
- Peruvian Inca Orchid, from Peru

ANTARCTICA
None

Newfoundland

Boston Terrier

Louisiana Catahoula Leopard Dog

Xoloitzcuintli

Peruvian Inca Orchid

Newfoundland, Canada

United States

Mexico

Peru

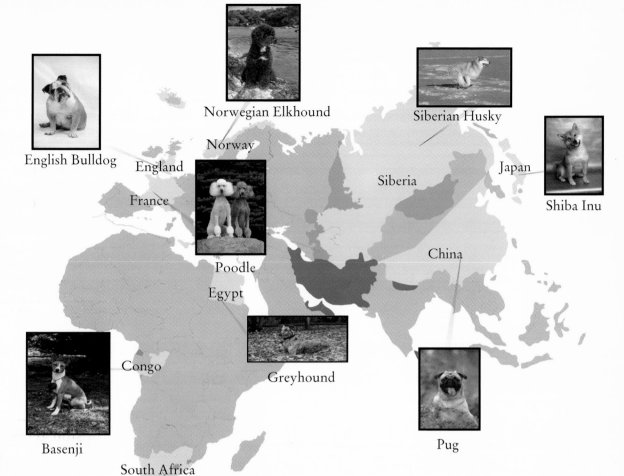

English Bulldog

Norwegian Elkhound

Siberian Husky

Shiba Inu

Norway

England

Japan

France

Siberia

China

Poodle

Egypt

Congo

Greyhound

Basenji

Pug

South Africa

Rhodesian Ridgeback

Australian Cattle Dog

Australian Kelpie

Australia

EUROPE
- English Bulldog, from England
- Poodle, from France
- Norwegian Elkhound, from Norway

AFRICA
- Greyhound, from Egypt
- Basenji, from Congo
- Rhodesian Ridgeback, from South Africa

ASIA
- Siberian Husky, from Siberia
- Shiba Inu, from Japan
- Pug, from China

AUSTRALIA
- Australian Cattle Dog, from Australia

True / False

Dogs are found on every continent in the world.

FALSE.

Antarctica is the one continent without dogs. However, dogs once played an important role on the continent. The first explorer to reach the South Pole, Norwegian Roald Amundsen, made the historic trip in 1911 with the help of ninety sled dogs. Only eleven dogs were alive by the end of the trek. Many people think that the only reason he was able to reach the South Pole was because of his sled dogs.

Sled dogs were used in Antarctica for transportation until the 1970s. Even after snowmobiles became common in Antarctica, there were still dogs. A small group of dogs stayed at a British research station as pets. In 1994, all nonnative wildlife was banned from Antarctica. The ban included the dogs. The last fourteen sled dogs left Antarctica in February 1994. The last of these dogs died in 2001.

Dogs of the World

Canids can be found on every continent except Antarctica. Dogs from certain regions look different from other dogs. Dogs from northern parts of the world—such as Japan, Siberia, Scandinavia, and Alaska—often have thick coats, triangular-shaped prick ears, and curled tails. Some people say they look foxy or wolflike. Can you think of dogs who look like this? One example of a dog with a foxy face is the Shiba Inu. Alaskan Malamutes and Siberian Huskies both look a lot like wolves. DNA research says these dogs are in fact closer relatives of the wolf than other dogs are.

Once you learn how dogs from different parts of the world look, it is easier to figure out where a breed is from. Look at the map and the dogs on pages 14 and 15. Do the dogs from the same areas look alike to you?

This Shiba Inu is a northern dog.

Chapter 2

Man's Best Friend

Like peanut butter and jelly, dogs and humans have been a great match for a very long time. We may have been fast friends for 10,000 years. We may have been friends for 135,000 years! Either way, it's been a wonderful relationship.

Dogs are domesticated animals. The word *domesticated* describes an animal that depends on people to survive. A tame animal is one that is comfortable with humans and will follow a human's commands. Cows, sheep, and dogs are domesticated. Lions, tigers, and bears are not. Dogs are the only species of the canid family who are domesticated. Sometimes people have dingoes and wolves as pets. They may be tame, but they are not domesticated.

Some scientists believe that humans took wolf pups and raised them within their homes. Over time, the descendants of these pups became tame. That's why dogs became domesticated. Other scientists believe that dogs came to humans on their own. Dogs' ancestors were wolves or wild dogs who scavenged from human dumps. People allowed them to do this because they barked at strangers and kept ver-

Humans and dogs probably first met when dogs crept into villages to steal food. They quickly began to depend on one another.

min, such as rats, away. Over time, people got to know the wild dogs and made them pets. At some point, dogs started to help humans hunt. They could track animals and even catch and kill them. Later, dogs were used by humans for all sorts of jobs, including herding, hauling, and protecting.

Some domesticated dogs continue to live a lot like wild animals. They are called pariah dogs. They live at the edges of cities and towns, and some live at dumps. They survive by scavenging, eating the garbage of humans. There are also some domesticated dogs who are feral. They no longer depend on people and have become wild. They hunt and kill smaller animals for food. In Australia, dingoes are domesticated dogs who became wild over time. They are probably the long lost relatives of Asian dogs who were on explorers' ships.

Dogs rely on us for food, water, shelter, and attention. We also rely on them. Dogs are our pets. They live with us and give us love and attention. They guard our homes and help keep us safe. Some dogs work with police or military or help blind people get around. We have what is called a mutually beneficial relationship. That means that both dogs and humans get something from our friendship.

Dogs and Their Jobs

Ever since dogs and humans first crossed paths, dogs have worked for us. We believe the first job dogs did for humans was to act as guards. This was mostly accidental. Dogs skulking around villages looking for food probably barked at people and other animals to protect their food source. The humans liked this because it kept invaders and dangerous animals away. The people probably gave the dogs extra

Is your dog descended from a wolf? Even if she is, this wolf has a very different life from hers.

food to reward them. Pretty soon, dogs were guarding people on purpose. The people became their food source! Many dogs guarded homes, but some dogs were also used to guard whole towns.

Hunting was another early job that dogs performed. Dogs helped humans track animals by sight, sound, and especially smell. They also helped catch and kill prey.

This is a search and rescue dog. Dogs have done many different jobs for humans, from sniffing out illegal substances to saving lives.

9/11 Dogs

On September 11, 2001, the World Trade Center in New York City was destroyed when two hijacked airliners rammed into it. The Pentagon in Washington, D.C., was also attacked. After the attacks on the World Trade Center, search and rescue dogs sprang into action. Dogs were sent from all over the United States to search the rubble. Nearly four hundred dogs worked at the site, and eighty of the dogs were FEMA certified. That means they

A dog searches for victims in New York.

were part of the Federal Emergency Management Administrations' Urban Search and Rescue Teams. FEMA dogs all must pass a difficult test every two years.

Most of the dogs who searched for people at the World Trade Center were family pets. They were trained by volunteers. The others were trained by firefighters or police officers.

The search and rescue dogs at the World Trade Center included Labrador Retrievers, German Shepherd Dogs, Rat Terriers, Portuguese Water Dogs, Golden Retrievers, Pointers, Border Collies, Australian Shepherds, and lots and lots of mixed breed dogs.

Once humans started keeping livestock, dogs were used to guard the livestock from wild animals and thieves. People also needed help to round up livestock and move them from one place to another. Dogs learned to herd, and they were good at it. Dogs were sometimes used to haul carts and wagons. They were even used as sort of animal motors: they paced on treadmills to run grain mills and spits that meat was cooked on.

Dogs have been used by the military and police for thousands of years. For instance, in ancient Rome, large Mastiff war dogs wore scary spiked collars into battle. The United States began using police dogs in the early 1900s. Now, most U.S. cities have dogs on the beat. Dogs help track and capture suspects, find lost people, and sniff out drugs and weapons. They also protect their human partners.

Poop Dogs

These dogs get the real poop—on wildlife! In Seattle, the Center for Conservation Biology at the University of Washington trains dogs to search for poop. Yep, that's right—poop! But it's not just any poop. These dogs are looking for the poop—or scat, as scientists call it—of endangered animals. They help biologists make sure that the populations of these animals aren't getting smaller. These specially trained dogs look for poop from grizzly bears, bobcats, and even Atlantic right whales. Whale poop floats on the surface of the water!

Well-trained working dogs do amazing things. Some can find trapped people after disasters such as earthquakes, bombings, and fires. Some dogs keep birds from landing on airport runways so planes won't run into them. Other dogs find termites in houses. There are dogs who scare bears away from neighborhoods and campgrounds. Dogs even can help endangered animals by sniffing out their poop! (See the Poop Dogs box to find out more.) Working dogs do these jobs cheaper, quicker, and better than humans or machines can.

Guide dogs have been used to help blind people

Dogs and World Events

This time line points out some of the important events that wouldn't have been the same without dogs.

4.5 billion BC
Earth Formed
No dogs (or people) yet!

135,000 BC
First Dogs?
Some scientists say that dogs date back to about this time, when Neanderthal humans existed. The Neanderthals were an early species of human that became extinct, but the first Homo sapiens (modern humans) had appeared in Africa at this time.

35,000 BC
Beginnings of a Great Relationship
At some point between this time and 13,000 BC, dogs became part of human lives. During this time, humans survived by hunting animals and gathering berries and other vegetation. Dogs began helping humans when they hunted.

13,000 BC
Bering Land Bridge
Humans crossed the Bering Land Bridge. These first migrants to the

American continent brought their dogs with them.

10,000 BC
First Permanent Villages
The first human towns were formed. Once humans settled down, they began raising livestock. Dogs were quickly trained to help herd and protect livestock.

This is one of the many dogs who work to help people with physical challenges.

for almost one hundred years. Dogs also help people who are paralyzed and those who cannot hear. Dogs can be trained to turn on lights, open doors, and pick up fallen objects. They let deaf people know when the doorbell or phone rings. Some dogs even know when their owner is about to have an epileptic seizure!

Dogs have also entertained people for a long time. We see dogs on TV shows and in movies. They have worked as circus dogs, riding horses and walking on their hind legs. Circus dogs were even trained to juggle!

One hundred years ago, most dogs

Dogs and World Events

3,000 BC   2,500 BC   2,000 BC   1,500 BC   1,000 BC

3,000 to 2,000 BC
Ancient Egypt

The ancient Egyptian civilizations began. Ruled by pharaohs, Egyptians worshipped many gods. Some of these gods, such as Anubis, looked like dogs. Egyptian dogs can be seen in hieroglyphics, on coins, and in art. They probably looked a lot like the Greyhounds and Salukis of today. It was probably in Egypt where dogs were first used for sport, for racing and fighting. They were also used in battle, as guards, to hunt, and to guard and herd livestock. And, they were kept as pets. Egyptians treasured their family dogs. When special family pets died, family members shaved their heads. There are even dog mummies. King Tutankhamen, or King Tut, had a faithful canine companion, Abuwitiyuw, who was mummified and buried with him.

3,000 to 300 BC
Ancient Greece

The Greeks were great thinkers, artists, and writers. Aristotle, Plato, Sophocles, Socrates, and Homer were all Greeks. Homer wrote about the loyal friendship of a dog. In *The Odyssey*, he wrote that the only family member to recognize Odysseus after his nineteen-year journey was his faithful dog, Argos. The Trojan and Peloponnesian wars were fought by the Greeks and by dogs. The Greeks took large, Mastiff-like dogs with them into battle.

1,500 BC
Moses Frees the Israelites

It's what dogs didn't do that is important when Moses freed the Israelites from Egypt. According to the Talmud, the book of Jewish law and tradition, the dogs of Egypt stayed silent while the Jews escaped from slavery.

Dogs are probably best known for their work as guide dogs, as shown here.

Dogs and World Events

1,500 BC   1,000 BC   750 BC   500 BC   250 BC

1,500 to 1,000 BC
Shang Dynasty
Chinese royalty of long ago loved their dogs. They were among the first to keep dogs just as pets. These dogs were called sleeve dogs because they were small enough to fit into the large sleeves of the royal robes. Some modern dogs, such as the Pug, were first seen during the Shang dynasty.

753 BC to AD 476
Roman Empire
Ancient Rome wasn't just the city of Rome, Italy, that we know today. It was a large kingdom that spread across western Europe, North Africa, and the Middle East. The Romans prized dogs for many reasons. They were war animals; large Mastiffs were equipped with spiked collars and sent into battle. They were also herders, guards, and pets. Some Roman dogs were used to pull wagons. The Romans loved blood sports, and they were the first to pit dogs against bears and against one another as a form of entertainment. (They also pitted people and other animals against one another. Not a friendly lot!) It's believed the Romans brought large Mastiff-type dogs with them when they invaded northern Europe.

300 to 251 BC
Mayan Calendar
The Mayans were an ancient people from the Yucatan Peninsula in Mexico. They were the first people to develop a real calendar. The calendar was based on 260 days per year. There were 20 day names, like our days of the week. One day was *ok*, or "dog." Mayans were quite familiar with dogs. But most Mayan dogs were kept for meat. Some were also kept for hunting and as pets.

did some sort of work for humans. They herded sheep or cattle on the farm, hunted animals for sport or for food, and protected the home. Now, most dogs in the United States are pets. We don't keep them to do a specific job, but they still help protect us and keep us company. And people with dogs tend to be healthier and have less stress than those without dogs.

Dogs in Human History

Did you know that dogs have been part of some of the most important events in human history? They can be found in Greek and Roman myths, and they are mentioned in the Bible and in the Koran. Dogs are also common in the religious stories of Buddhism, Hinduism, and Judaism. Dogs are a part of many cultures' folklore—

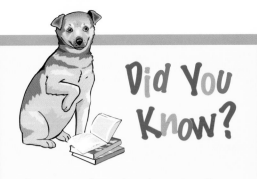

Did You Know?

The names of pet dogs in ancient Egypt always began or ended with abu or jwjw, meaning "bow-wow" and "howler." Some Egyptian dog names were Good Herdsman, Blackie, and Useless.

stories that people pass down for generations. They play a big role in the stories told by Native American tribes. Some ancient cultures

Dogs and World Events

250 BC   0   100   200   300

0
Christianity: The Birth of Christ
According to many cultures, dogs were among the animals in the stable the night Jesus was born. The shepherds are said to have brought their herding dogs with them. Next time you see a Nativity scene, see if dogs are included!

10 to 49
Buddhism to China
When Buddhism spread to China, the image of the Fo Dog changed from a doglike lion to a lionlike dog. Lions were unknown in East Asia, so the Chinese Buddhists adapted by breeding dogs who looked like lions. One of the Fo Dogs is the Pekingese.

79
Vesuvius Erupts
When Vesuvius erupted, a cloud of gas was released. The gas killed all the residents of the city of Pompeii— both human and animal. The city was buried in ash that formed a mold around the bodies. These molds still exist. One of the most famous is of a

dog. Dogs were common pets and guards in Pompeii.

300 to 349
Constantinople
Constantinople is the old name of the city that is now Istanbul, in Turkey. Constantinople was known as an important trade city and was the capital of the Eastern Roman Empire. The famed dogs of Constantinople were free and allowed to roam the city. They were given their freedom because they saved the town from invaders.

believed that dogs were created before humans. Some even believed that dogs created humans!

Many of the most important people in world history had dogs by their sides. King Tut had a dog, and so did George Washington and many other U.S. presidents. Soldiers during the American Revolution and the Civil War brought their hunting dogs with them into battle. During World War I and World War II, trained military dogs were used as messenger dogs and to keep guard.

Search and rescue dogs are dogs who are trained to find people who are trapped or lost.

Former President Harding and his dog Laddie play for the camera outside the White House.

Dogs and World Events

500   700   900   1100   1300

750 to 1000
Vikings
The Vikings were the people who lived in the regions that are now Sweden, Denmark, Norway, and Iceland. They are known for being pirates who plundered cities across Europe, but they were also explorers, fishermen, farmers, and tradespeople. The Vikings had many uses for dogs. They were used as hunters, herders, sled dogs, guards, and pets. Dogs were sometimes buried with important Vikings in burial ships. One modern breed

that was first bred by Vikings is the Swedish Vallhund.

1000 to 1532
Inca Empire
The Incas of South America kept dogs as pets. Hairless dogs were especially popular with Incan royalty. The Peruvian Inca Orchid was first bred by the Incas.

1254 to 1324
Marco Polo
The great adventurer Marco Polo was among the first Westerners to travel to the East, including China. He claimed to

have been a guest of the great Mongol leader Kublai Khan for seventeen years. In his book, *The Travels of Marco Polo*, he described many of the Asian dogs he encountered. He wrote that Khan employed 22,000 dog handlers!

1300 to 1700
Renaissance
The Renaissance was a time of great artistic and scientific advances in Europe. It was also a time of great power among nobility. During the Renaissance, the ownership of hunting, racing, and companion dogs became popular with the nobility. Only nobles were allowed to keep large dogs. During this time, English commoners began to breed small terriers for hunting.

They were used to save people during the worst tragedy of our country's history, the attacks on September 11, 2001.

Dogs have been every place humans have been. Dogs have been to both the North Pole and the South Pole. They have even been sent to outer space!

Dogs in Mythology

Myths are stories told by people of a culture to help them understand the world around them. The Greeks, Vikings, Romans, and Egyptians believed that there were many gods that ruled the sky, the earth, and the sea. And these gods are part of the myths.

In mythology, dogs have been viewed as both good and evil. In some cultures, dogs

Did You Know?

Search and rescue dogs have their own trading cards! Visit http://www.fema.gov/kids/games/heroes/hero_01.htm to print out the cards.

Dogs and World Events

1300   1400   1500   1600   1700

1347 to 1351
Black Death
The plague known as the black death killed a third of the population of Europe. Dogs and other animals were killed because people thought they carried the disease. When the plague struck again in London in 1665, 40,000 dogs were killed, but the real carriers were the fleas on rats.

1492
Columbus
When Columbus sailed to the New World on the *Niña*, the *Pinta*, and the *Santa Maria*, he had hunting dogs with him. In his journals, he wrote about the dogs he saw in the Americas. He wrote about seeing Mastiffs and dogs who didn't bark.

1554 to 1616
William Shakespeare
Shakespeare often wrote about dogs in his plays. *The Two Gentlemen of Verona* had a dog character named Crab.

1620
Pilgrims Land at Plymouth Rock
There were at least two dogs aboard the *Mayflower* when the pilgrims landed at Plymouth Rock. The dogs, a Mastiff and an English Springer Spaniel, were owned by John Goodman. Goodman didn't live through the first year in America, but it is unknown whether the dogs survived.

1775 to 1783
American Revolution
During the American Revolution, soldiers brought their hunting dogs to battle. At the Battle of Germantown in 1777, England's General Howe's Fox Terrier was captured by the American army! George Washington took care of the dog and eventually sent him back to General Howe as a truce.

represented gods. Sometimes dogs were gods! Other cultures saw dogs as bad omens. Black dogs, and especially black dogs with light markings over their eyes, have been considered evil in the past. Of course, we know now that no dog is evil, no matter what her eyebrows look like!

Dogs played a large role in Egyptian myths. There were dog gods, such as Anubis, who ruled the underworld. Anubis, called the dog god or jackal god, had a man's body and a dog's head. Sometimes he looked like a black dog or a jackal, a relative of wolves and dogs. His father was Osiris, god of death.

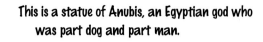

This is a statue of Anubis, an Egyptian god who was part dog and part man.

Osiris was sometimes represented as a dog, too.

The Greeks also tried to explain the world using gods and myths. Dogs were often part of these stories. Artemis, the goddess of the hunt, was always with her hunting dogs. Another hunter, Orion, had faithful hunting dogs, Canis Major and Canis Minor. According to myth, when Orion was killed, he and his dogs were placed in the sky as constellations. Sirius, the Dog Star, is found in

Dogs and World Events

1600 — 1650 — 1700 — 1750 — 1800

1769 to 1821
Napoleon Bonaparte

Napoleon was the Emperor of France and a great military leader. He was one of the first European generals to use dogs in battle. There are many stories about dogs and Napoleon. Supposedly, he was saved by a Newfoundland after almost drowning on his way to the Battle of Waterloo! Some say he hated his wife Josephine's Pug, Fortune. But he had a soft spot for his own dogs. After his death, his dog and horse were stuffed. The stuffed dog and horse can be found at the Musée de l'Armée in Paris.

1789
French Revolution (Louis XVI and Marie Antoinette)
Marie Antoinette was the queen of France when the monarchy was overthrown. She was famous for her lavish lifestyle. (Although historians now say that much of this was made up.) She adored her many dogs. Her favorite dog was Thisbee. It was said that when Marie Antoinette was beheaded, Thisbee killed herself by jumping into the Seine River.

1804
Lewis and Clark
Lewis and Clark led the team that explored the West. The journey began in St. Charles, Missouri, and ended at Fort Clatsop on the Pacific coast. Did you know a dog helped blaze the trail to the Pacific? Lewis and Clark began their journey with a Newfoundland named Seaman. (For many years, it was believed

that the Newfoundland was named Scannon because Lewis's messy writing was difficult to read!) Seaman had many adventures along the way. There are statues of Seaman at many of the historical Lewis and Clark sites.

Dogs in the Sky

Our ancestors spent a lot of time looking at the night sky. They didn't know what the stars were or how they got there. To explain the stars, they created elaborate stories about them. Many of the stories were about dogs.

Often the stories were about the Dog Star, Sirius. Sirius is the fifth nearest known star to Earth. The Egyptians called Sirius the Dog Star after their god Osiris. Osiris is a god who is sometimes shown with the body of a man and the head of a dog. In Latin, *sirius* means "glowing." Sirius is the brightest star in the constellation Canis Major (The Greater Dog). In the middle of the summer, between July 3 and August 11, Sirius and the sun rise at the same time. It is the hottest time of the summer in the Mediterranean. Our ancestors thought Sirius was responsible for the heat. Even today, this especially warm part of the summer is called the dog days of summer. You can see Sirius during the dog days of summer by looking just above the southeast horizon. The star looks white with a tinge of blue. The constellation Canis Major is next to another constellation, Canis Minor (the Lesser Dog). The Greeks believed that the dogs were the constellation Orion's hunting dogs.

Orion's hunting dogs are not the only dogs in the sky. There are also the Canes Venatici, the Hunting Dogs, who hunt alongside their master, Boötes. They are hunting for the bears, Ursa Major and Ursa Minor.

Dogs and World Events

1836
The Alamo
There were certainly a number of dogs at the Alamo. Early pioneers such as Jim Bowie, Davy Crockett, and William Travis—who all fought and died at the Alamo—usually traveled with their dogs. Dogs were guards and companions for the men of the new frontier. They were especially prized for their hunting ability.

1861 to 1865
American Civil War
Officially, neither the North nor the South used dogs in the Civil War. But there were many dogs on the battlefield. Soldiers took their own hunting dogs with them to war, where they helped keep guard at night and provided companionship.

1876
General George Custer and the Battle of Little Bighorn
George Custer is a legendary but controversial U.S. soldier. He always had a dog by his side, even on the battlefield. He fought in the Civil War but

became famous for fighting against Native Americans. Both Custer and his dog Tuck were killed at the Battle of Little Bighorn.

1877
First Westminster Show
The first Westminster Kennel Club Dog Show was held in Philadelphia in 1877. It moved to New York City the next year, where it continues to be held annually.

1891
First Crufts Show
Crufts, the world's largest dog show, was first held in 1891 in Islington, England.

the constellation Canis Major. It is the brightest star in the sky. An especially scary dog in Greek myths was the three-headed Cerberus. He guarded the gates to Hades, or the underworld. Even other gods were afraid of Cerberus.

The Vikings, who lived in the lands that are now called Norway, Denmark, Iceland, and Sweden during the eighth to the eleventh centuries, believed that dogs protected their most important god, Odin. The indigenous, or original, people of northern Scandinavia are called Sami. Old Sami myths say that people were created from either dogs or reindeer.

The Mongols in Asia believed that the first humans were created from dogs or created from a tree and then nursed by dogs. In Siberia, the Koryaks believed dogs were born from the creator, Eme'mqut, and his wife, Miti. When the two were apart, dogs served as their messengers.

Dogs in Religion

What's *dog* spelled backward? It's an old joke, but dogs have long been a part of religious traditions. Some of the ancient religions believed

Dogs and World Events

1898
Klondike Gold Rush
If it weren't for sled dogs, a lot less gold would have been found in Alaska! Gold prospectors had to take dog sleds to the site of the gold discovery at Yukon River in the Klondike Territory of Alaska. They also kept dogs as pets, guards, and hunters at their mining camps.

1911
Roald Amundsen reaches the South Pole
Roald Amundsen was an explorer. He was the first person to reach the South Pole. But without his sled dogs, Amundsen would have never made it to the South Pole. Robert

Scott was another explorer, who was racing Amundsen to the pole. Scott decided against using sled dogs. He died without reaching the pole.

1912
Titanic sinks
Three dogs are said to have survived the sinking of the *Titanic*—two Pomeranians and a Pekingese. A 1912 newspaper printed a story about a Newfoundland dog who saved a lifeboat of people from being rammed by the *Carpathian*, the ship that

rescued the *Titanic* survivors. Most historians think this story was made up by a reporter looking for a big scoop.

1914 to 1918
World War I
World War I is called the Great War. Much of World War I was fought in trenches in western Europe. It was the first European war since Roman times in which dogs were used in an organized way. They brought messages back and forth from one trench to another.

This is a Pekingese. This breed was originally developed in China to look like a Fo Dog, a doglike lion.

that dogs had something to do with creation. Dogs play a big role in modern religions, too.

You have probably seen nativity scenes. The three wise men and shepherds are shown visiting the newborn Jesus and his parents, Joseph and Mary, in a stable. Many of the animals that would have been typical to a Middle Eastern stable some two thousand years ago, such as donkeys, camels, sheep, and dogs, are also shown. Wait! Dogs? Since when have dogs been part of nativity scenes? Actually, many cultures believe dogs were with the shepherds who visited the baby Jesus. In Grenada, they even give the dogs names—Cibila, Lubina, and Malampo.

Many Christian saints had dogs. One of the most famous dogs is Grigio, also known as the gray mongrel. He was like a guardian

Dogs and World Events

1925
Sled Dogs to the Rescue
In January of 1925, Nome, Alaska, was hit with an outbreak of diphtheria, threatening to kill hundreds of children. The only vaccine available was almost 1,000 miles away, and there was no way to get it to Nome. In desperation, sled dogs were dispatched to bring the vaccine in a relay of twenty mushers (the drivers of the sled teams) and 150 sled dogs. They got the vaccine to Nome in only 5½ days, and the children were saved! The final relay team was led by a dog named Balto, who became a world-known hero. There is even a statue of Balto in New York City's Central Park.

1930
Presenting Pluto
Pluto, Mickey Mouse's favorite dog, made his first appearance in a Mickey Mouse cartoon called "The Chain Gang." In his first role, he was a Bloodhound hunting down escaped prisoner Mickey Mouse.

1938
Lassie Makes Her Mark
Lassie Come-Home, the classic dog book by Eric Knight, was first published in 1938. The movie based on the book was released in 1943.

1941
Pearl Harbor
The United States entered World War II after Pearl Harbor, in Hawaii, was attacked. It was the first war in which the United States used official war dogs. Americans were asked to donate their pet dogs to the war effort in a program called Dogs for Defense. There were many canine heroes during the war.

angel to Saint Giovanni Melchior, who was also known as Don Bosco, a priest in Turin, Italy, during the 1800s. Don Bosco devoted his life to helping the poor children of the city. Grigio appeared whenever Don Bosco was in trouble. One night, the gray mongrel protected Don Bosco from two thieves. Another night, the dog appeared at the saint's door and refused to let him leave. Later, Don Bosco learned that there was a plot against his life. In his memoirs, Don Bosco wrote that he never discovered who or what the mysterious dog was: "I never was able to find out who was his owner; I only know that the animal was truly providential for me

This is a Fo Dog.

on many occasions when I found myself in danger."

In India, Buddha, the founder of the religion called Buddhism, was said to have had a tame lion—so tame he was like a dog. This lion was called the Fo (meaning Buddha) Dog. Later, Buddhism spread to other parts of Asia where lions were unknown to most people, so Southeast Asian Buddhists bred dogs to look like lions—Fo Dogs! (You may see it written as Foo Dog.) That's how dogs like the Pekingese and Tibetan Spaniel get their lionlike looks. Southeast Asian Buddhists also used lionlike dogs in art. Large sculptures of Fo Dogs are often seen

Dogs and World Events

1940   *1945*   *1950*   *1955*   *1960*

1949
Communist China
In Communist China, pet dogs were banned. They were considered to represent the bourgeoisie, or middle class, which Communists considered to be their enemy.

1950
Snoopy's Debut
Snoopy, the canine star of the *Peanuts* comic strip drawn by Charles Schulz, made his first appearance.

1950 to 1953
The Korean War
The United States used military dogs to fight the Korean War. About one

thousand dogs served in the U.S. military in Korea.

1957 to 1969
The Space Age
During the 1950s and 1960s, the race to space was in full force. The United States and the Soviet Union (now Russia) competed against each other with space craft

that could go longer and farther. The race ended when the United States put the first human on the moon in 1969. There weren't just human astronauts during the Space Age. There were many brave dog astronauts, as well. The Soviet Union sent fourteen dogs into space. Five of them died. The most famous doggy astronaut was Laika. Laika was the first living creature to go into orbit. On November 3, 1957, she was blasted into space aboard the *Sputnik II*. The craft was not made to return to Earth. Laika died when her life support ended. Soviets and Americans were shocked to learn she died in orbit.

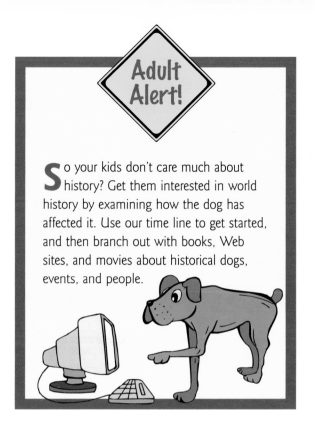

Adult Alert!

So your kids don't care much about history? Get them interested in world history by examining how the dog has affected it. Use our time line to get started, and then branch out with books, Web sites, and movies about historical dogs, events, and people.

outside Buddhist temples. On one side is the male Fo Dog. His right paw rests on a globe. On the other side is the female Fo Dog. Her left paw rests on the mouth of a cub.

Dogs also appear in Buddhist writings. In one story, a monk meditated in a cave for twelve years. When he left the cave, he came upon a dog who was dying and covered with maggots. The monk wanted to help the dog, but he didn't want to hurt the maggots, so he licked the maggots off the dog. Suddenly the dog turned into the Buddha of the future. The Buddha praised the monk for his compassion and agreed to become his teacher.

In Islam, dogs are thought to be unclean, but they also are used to teach people about kindness. Even though dogs are unclean, they

Dogs and World Events

1960   1965   1970   1975   1980

1962
Cuban Missile Crisis
The Cuban Missile Crisis was the closest the world has ever come to a nuclear war. So how on earth do dogs figure in here? Once tempers were soothed, Soviet president Khrushchev sent a peace offering in the form of a gift to President John F. Kennedy's

daughter, Caroline. The gift was a dog named Pushinka, the daughter of a Russian space dog. Pushinka went on to have a litter of puppies with the Kennedy's Welsh Terrier, Charlie. That's real diplomacy!

1968
Vietnam War
The Vietnam War was bad for America's military dogs. More than four thousand military dogs served in Vietnam. They were scouts, sentries, and messengers. Soldiers from the Vietnam War say that the dogs saved more than ten thousand lives. Despite their bravery, most war dogs were left behind when the United States pulled out. No one knows for sure what

happened to them. Only two hundred of the dogs were brought back to the United States by the military.

1974
Richard Nixon Resigns
President Richard Nixon was forced to resign, but he may never have become president if it were not for a dog named Checkers. Before he was president, Nixon was vice president to Gerald Ford. During the election, Nixon was accused of taking illegal gifts. In the Checkers speech, Nixon admitted getting one gift, a Cocker Spaniel named Checkers. He said he just couldn't say no to his daughters' appeal for the pup. The scandal blew over, and Nixon became president.

shouldn't be hurt because they are one of Allah's (God's) creations. They are also respected for their skills in hunting and herding. Mohammed, the founder of Islam, himself had a hunting dog.

In one story, a kind Muslim (a person who practices Islam) man gives water to a thirsty dog. His friends complain, saying that the is now impure because he touched a dog. Mohammed replies that the first man is a better man than the others because he is kind to animals.

Hindus also use dogs to teach people lessons about

kindness and loyalty. Gods sometimes take the form of a dog to test people. In one story, the Pandava brothers and a dog are on a journey to reach heaven, called Swarga. As they travel, they face many obstacles. Along the way, one by one the brothers die until only the dog and one brother are left. Suddenly, Indra, the ruler of Swarga, appears in a golden chariot. He offers the man a ride into Swarga but tells him the man cannot bring his dog. The man refuses because he will not leave his faithful companion. Suddenly, the dog turns into the god Dharma and blesses the man for his loyalty to his dog.

Dogs and World Events

1991
Persian Gulf War
As with every war since our nation began, dogs served in the Middle East during the Persian Gulf War.

1995
Oklahoma City Bombing
On April 19, 1995, the Alfred P. Murrah Federal Building was destroyed by a bomb. It was 9:02 a.m., and the building was full of people. One hundred sixty-eight people died, and hundreds more were injured. Search and rescue dogs showed up within hours. The last person pulled from the building alive was found by a Rottweiler named Bronte.

2001
World Trade Center Attack
On September 11, 2001, the World Trade Center was attacked. Hundreds of search and rescue dogs went to New York to search for survivors. The dogs worked tirelessly and were able to find the bodies of many people.

2005
Dog DNA
Maybe the most important contribution dogs have made is to just be dogs. Dogs' DNA is close to ours, and scientists have mapped it. They believe understanding dog DNA can help cure diseases in dogs and in people!

2007
War Dogs
Dogs continue to serve the U.S. military in Iraq and Afghanistan as guards and sniffer dogs, who find bombs and weapons. In war-torn countries, dogs work as mine-detection dogs, searching for explosives that are hidden under the ground and can hurt people.

Chapter 3

What Is  a Dog?

A dog is a dog is a dog. Or is it? In fact, there are many types of dogs, or breeds. There are more than 400 breeds in all. Some breeds, like the Labrador Retriever, are very common. More than 150,000 Labs are registered with the American Kennel Club in the United States (AKC). (Purebred dogs are often registered with the AKC or another breed registry so that breeders know each dog's family tree.) Other breeds, like the Lundehund, are very rare. There are fewer than 250 in the United States and only about 1,000 Lundehunds in the whole world.

There are also dogs who are a mixture of breeds. We sometimes call these dogs mutts or random-breds or even Heinz 57s, after the steak sauce that has fifty-seven ingredients. To many people, mutts are the ultimate American

This Lundehund is a very rare breed found in Norway.

dog. They are the country's most popular dog.

Breeds can be big, and they can be small. They can be curly haired or hairless. But what makes them all dogs? That's a question scientists have been scratching their heads about for some time.

There are a couple of traits that all dogs have in common. Every dog has forty-two teeth (except the Lundehund; for some reason, he has only forty!) and a gestation period (the number of days a mama dog is pregnant with her puppies) of about sixty-three days. It may seem hard to believe, but whether a dog is a four-pound Yorkie with tiny feet or a two hundred–pound Mastiff with huge paws the size of a whole Yorkie, all dogs are the same species.

Anatomy

Anatomy is an animal's basic makeup. A dog's anatomy is similar to that of all mammals, including people. The dog has musculoskeletal, nervous, digestive, cardiovascular, respiratory, reproductive, urinary, and immune systems. His skin is his largest organ and basically protects the rest of his body from the environment. It also makes sure he doesn't get either too hot or too cold.

The musculoskeletal system is made up of parts that allow the body to move and run. Its parts include bones, joints, cartilage, muscles, ligaments, and tendons. Although we think of bones as dead, they are living tissue with blood pumping throughout. The skeleton, made up of bones, is the framework for the body. The joints connect the bones and allow them to move. The tendons connect the bones to the muscles. The muscles are tissues that get bigger and smaller, causing motion.

The nervous system is what allows a dog to see a cat, decide to chase the cat, and then chase the cat! The nerves tell the brain what the dog's eye is seeing. The nerves then tell the muscles what the brain

Big dogs, little dogs—they're all just dogs!

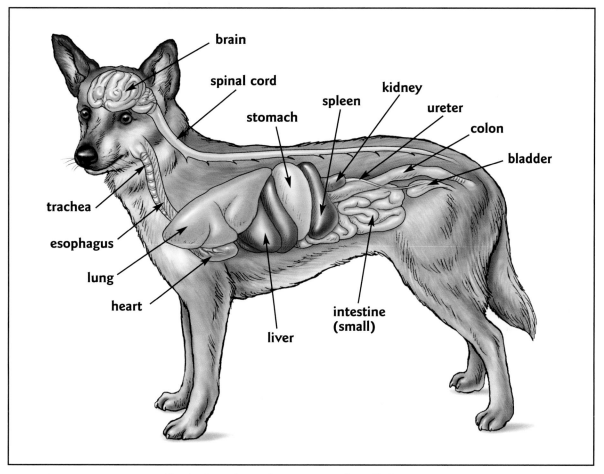

The dog is made up of many parts, all equally important.

wants them to do. The nervous system transfers all kinds of information throughout the animal's body.

The digestive system is what allows the food a dog eats to be turned into the energy he needs to run and play. The food a dog chews and swallows is first taken to the stomach. In the stomach, food is broken down and then moved into the small intestine. There, the food is turned into the energy the body needs to function—carbohydrates, amino acids, and fatty acids. What can't be used is moved into the large intestine. Here, the water is removed. The rest ends up as poop! The urinary system filters waste and makes sure that the body is getting enough water. The waste is pee.

The dog also has a cardiovascular system, which circulates blood through the body. The respiratory system brings oxygen to the blood. And the immune system fights all the nasty germs that get past the dog's protective layers of skin. The

Q. Can dogs really hear things that humans can't?

A. A dog's hearing ability is much better than ours. The highest pitch people can hear is 23,000 hertz. Dogs can hear up to 45,000 hertz! (Hertz measures how high a sound is—the higher the number, the higher the pitch.)

reproductive system is what allows dogs to breed and create new puppies and new doggy generations.

Dog Senses

A dog's senses are very important to him. He hears, smells (and tastes), sees, and feels the world. Each sense helps him navigate. Some of the dog's senses are very well developed. Others are less so. Dogs can hear and smell extremely well. They use their eyes but not as much as their noses and ears. Their sense of touch is not as good as ours.

Hearing

Dogs have great hearing. They can hear sounds from farther away than we can. They can also hear higher sounds than we can. They can hear some things that we can't hear at all! It's easy for a dog to tell where a sound is coming from. Dogs with erect, or prick, ears have better hearing than dogs with floppy ears. Have you ever seen a cartoon where a character holds a cone up to his or her ear to hear better? Prick ears act like cones. They catch sound so the dog can hear it better. Dogs with prick ears can even rotate their ears to catch the sound better! One ear can even move in one direction while the other ear moves in another direction! It's kind of like wiggling your ears, but harder.

Smell

The sense a dog uses the most is his sense of smell, which is an amazing 1,000 times better than a human's sense of smell. A dog's nose is specially made to trap smells and "read" them.

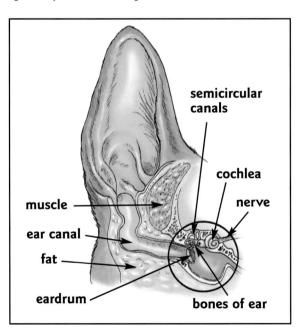

The dog's ear is specially designed to hear very high sounds from very far away.

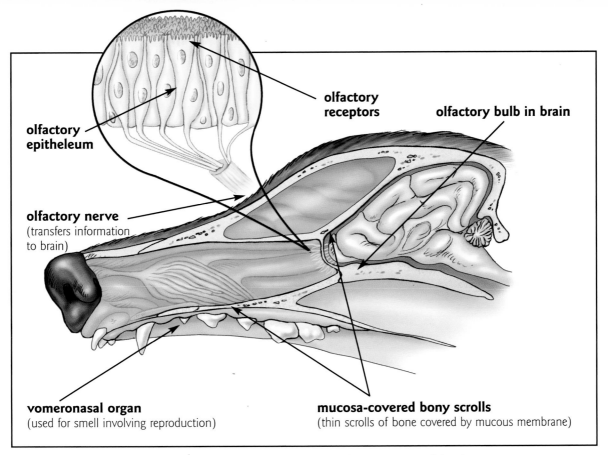

olfactory receptors

olfactory bulb in brain

olfactory epitheleum

olfactory nerve
(transfers information to brain)

vomeronasal organ
(used for smell involving reproduction)

mucosa-covered bony scrolls
(thin scrolls of bone covered by mucous membrane)

Dogs are super smellers. Their noses are their most powerful tools.

One reason a dog's nose is wet is that a wet nose traps smells better than a dry nose would. The inside of his nose is lined with mucous membranes. They are specially folded so they can trap as much odor as possible. The mucous membranes capture odor molecules, dissolve them into mucus (or what you may like to call snot!), and send them to olfactory, or smell, receptors, which is a fancy name for smell catchers. Humans have about 10 million olfactory receptors. Dogs have more than 220 million olfactory receptors! Smells are finally sent via the nerves to the olfactory lobe in the brain. The dog's olfactory lobe figures out what the smell is and where it

Did You Know?

Dogs have thirty sets of muscles for moving their ears! Humans have only six sets of muscles that move their ears.

comes from. It's the part of a dog's nose that allows a dog to find a person just by her smell!

A dog can sense smells at a concentration of 100 million times lower than humans can. Let's put this into real-life terms. Imagine a grain of sand. Imagine that this grain of sand smells like vanilla. Then imagine this grain of sand in a sand bucket with about 99 million other grains of sand. For a human to smell the vanilla, all the grains of sand would have to smell like vanilla. But a dog would be able to smell the one grain of sand that smells like vanilla, even in a bucket with 99 million other grains of sand that smell like, well, sand.

Another way to put it is when we smell a hamburger, we smell meat, pickles, ketchup, and maybe the bun. When a dog smells a hamburger, he smells the meat; any spices added to the meat; the grease the meat was cooked in; the sugar, flour, yeast, and sesame seeds in the bun; the tomatoes and vinegar in the ketchup; and the dill in the pickles. In other words, he smells all the separate ingredients. Plus, he smells the odor of the person who put the hamburger together, the pan where the meat was fried, even the perfume of the person who sliced the pickles! That's why dogs are often used to find people, drugs, bombs, and other things by sniffing them out.

Vision

Although dog vision is not as good as the other canine senses, it is a myth that dogs see only in black and white. They are basically like color-blind people and cannot tell the difference between greens and reds. The colors dogs see—grays, blues, and yellows—are

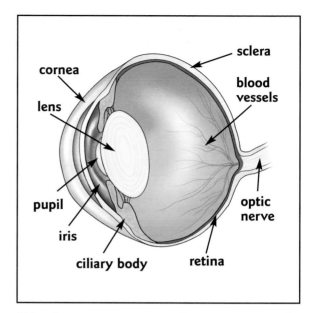

Although dogs cannot see as well as we can during the day, they can see better than we can at night.

not as bright as what we see. Dogs also have poor depth perception. That means it's hard for them to tell how far away something is. A human's perfect vision is 20/20. A dog's perfect vision is about 20/75. This means an object a person sees at seventy-five feet away, a dog won't see until he is twenty feet away.

Dogs do have excellent peripheral vision; they can see to either side of themselves much better than we can. They also see better at night than we do. That's because they have a special tissue called the tapetum lucidum (tah-PEE-tum loo-SID-um) behind the retina, the part of the eye that tells the brain what you are seeing. The tapetum lucidum traps and reflects light to the retina. This allows the eye to see images more clearly in the dark. It is also is why dogs' eyes glow at night!

When it works properly, the dog's body is amazingly athletic and full of energy.

Dogs see moving objects better than ones standing still. Have you ever noticed that your dog doesn't seem to recognize you from a distance? When you walk or wave, he suddenly knows it's you. He recognizes you when you are moving but not when you are still. Objects that don't move can be confusing for a dog. Lots of dogs have a hard time figuring out what a statue is. Sometimes dogs will even bark at statues!

Touch

Dogs use their sense of touch, but not quite in the way we do. They have heavy fur and thick pads on their feet, so they are less aware of whether things are smooth, rough, hot, or cold than we are. They don't use their paws to feel and sense things the way we use our hands. Sometimes they will use their noses and lips to investigate. These areas are more sensitive than the rest of a dog's body.

Like cats, dogs have whiskers that are very sensitive to touch. They may use their whiskers to sense wind direction when hunting. And if you touch a dog's whiskers, he'll probably pull away and close his eyes. (Nervous dogs may become frightened and even bite.)

Dogs use touch to talk with one another. Younger, polite dogs lick the mouths of their elders to show respect. Mama dogs teach puppies to play nicely by giving them gentle bites whenever they play too roughly.

As you can see, a dog's senses are very important to him. In the wild, they helped dogs find food and protect themselves. In our homes, the sense of hearing allows dogs to protect us. The sense of smell helps dogs find tasty treats or troublesome varmints in the garden. For working dogs, such as police dogs, search and rescue dogs, and guide dogs, senses are especially important. Dogs use them in combination every day!

The Whole Dog

All of a dog's anatomical features and senses come together when he is in action. Whether he is running after a ball or looking for food in the wild, he is using his eyes, ears, nose, and strong muscles and bones. His heart is pumping, his lungs are effectively filling with air, and his brain is working overtime—where is it, how far did it fly? Snap—he grabs the ball out of the air and on a dime turns to return it.

The complete dog body is a wonder. It is fast and efficient. Teeth are specially made for tearing and chewing. Eyes are specially formed to catch sight of fast-moving creatures, even those to the side and at night. Ears catch the quietest of sounds. The nose detects every new and unusual odor and can even find where the smells are coming from! Strong claws dig into the ground, and paw pads protect the feet. The tail helps with balance, and strong muscles in the thighs help the dog spring and jump.

Why Do Dogs Do That?

Some of the things that dogs do are kind of gross, but they're all very normal in dog society. Here are just a few of the icky things you may have seen dogs doing—and the real reasons they do them!

Scooting

Have you ever seen a dog scoot across the floor on his bottom? Why is he doing this? It's not very attractive, and it can be pretty embarrassing.

RIDDLE

Where does a dog go when he loses his tail?

A re-tail store!

True / False

Dogs' mouths are cleaner than people's mouths.

FALSE.

The bacteria in human mouths and dog mouths are pretty much the same. The difference in cleanliness is based on what we eat. People eat food. Dogs eat food plus garbage, dead animals, and poop. Who has the cleaner mouth?

That said, human bites are more dangerous than dog bites. Huh? Dogs have a lot of cruddy stuff floating around in their mouths, but so do humans. The cruddy stuff in a dog's mouth is mostly dangerous to other dogs. The cruddy stuff in a human's mouth is mostly dangerous to other humans.

How clean is this?

A dog scoots because his bottom hurts or itches. He may have worms, which can make him uncomfortable. It's more likely he is scooting because he is feeling some discomfort from his anal glands. His what? Anal glands, or sacs, are marble-size glands located on each side of the anus (butt hole). These glands are filled with a fluid, some of which comes out whenever a dog defecates, or poops. The smell of the fluid tells other dogs that he's been there.

Pet dogs eat food that is different from the food a dog in the wild would eat. A pet dog's diet usually produces poop that's too soft to push all the fluid out of the anal glands. Sometimes the glands get too full of the fluid. This makes the dog uncomfortable and makes him want to scratch his bottom.

To keep a dog's anal sacs from getting impacted (full), a veterinarian or groomer should empty them once in a while. She will squeeze the glands with her fingers, pushing the fluid out. It smells really, really bad.

Licking

Lots of dogs like to lick. They will lick your hand, the couch,

Pavlov's Dogs

Have you ever heard of Pavlov's dogs? Pavlov was a scientist during the late 1800s and early 1900s. He noticed that dogs drooled when they saw food coming. In his lab, he saw that the dogs also seemed to drool when they saw white coats. He wondered why they did this. He figured out that the dogs associated the white coats with the people who fed them.

He decided to try an experiment. He rang a bell each time a dog was given food. The dogs drooled. Then he rang the bell with no food in sight. The dogs still drooled!

You can try Pavlov's experiment with your own dog. For a few days, ring a bell each time you give him a treat. Then ring a bell without giving him a treat. Does he still drool? Does he look around for the food? You've just proved Pavlov's theory!

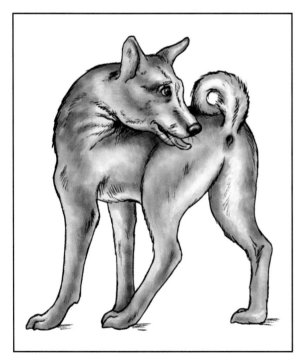

Dogs do a lot of licking. Usually, it's perfectly normal.

toys, and themselves. Dogs often lick us or each other to show affection. Sometimes they lick to find out more about an object. They sometimes lick because they are bored and it's just something to do. They may lick a cushion or a spot on the rug because something tasty was dropped there. Sometimes they lick and chew themselves in ways that seem disgusting to us. To a dog, it's perfectly natural!

Have you ever seen a dog licking his butt? He does this to keep clean. Dogs don't have hands so they can't scrub themselves clean the way a person does. Often, they'll lick themselves quickly after going poop. This is a dog's version of hygiene. But if a dog licks his bottom a lot, something may be wrong. He may have impacted anal glands, or he may have worms. His behind may be irritated if he has diarrhea or has swallowed something sharp (like a bone).

Dogs lick their private parts to keep clean, too. This is completely normal. If a dog licks more than a couple of times after peeing or licks his private parts constantly, something may be wrong.

Dogs also lick other parts of their body to keep clean. Sometimes they lick because they are nervous, and licking helps them calm down. Licking is normal, but if a dog is licking more than usual or if he is licking any area so much that he starts to lose hair or gets a sore, he needs to see a vet.

Drooling

Some dogs drool more than others. If you have a big Mastiff or a Newfoundland, you see a lot of drool every day. The reason these dogs drool so much is because the skin around their mouths is loose. The loose skin lets the drool run free. Short-nosed dogs, such as Pugs and English Bulldogs, also drool a lot because their small mouths can't hold all the drool in.

Just as people do, dogs produce saliva to help them eat food. The saliva wets the food so it can be swallowed more easily and starts the process of breaking down food for digestion. Saliva helps keep mouths clean, too. And for dogs, saliva helps keep them cool. Dogs can't sweat the way people do. Instead, they pant. When dogs pant, they exhale warm air across their wet tongues, the water evaporates, and that cools their bodies. Pretty clever, huh?

Dogs also drool when they are nervous, nauseous, excited, or, yes, hungry. You may notice a dog drool when there is a storm because he is afraid of the thunder. A dog may drool when he rides in a car because he feels carsick. And you may notice that dogs drool when their dinner is being prepared or when a snack packet is opened.

Eating Poop

Here is a doggy habit that drives people crazy. If you have a cat and a dog, your dog may find his way into the litter box to eat what he seems to think are tasty treats. Yuck! Outside, dogs may also eat cat poop, other dogs' poop, or even their own poop! Believe it or not, there's even a word for eating poop—*coprophagia* (kop-ruh-FAY-gee-uh).

A Rottweiler sees something tasty to drool over.

No one knows for sure why dogs do this. Some dogs may eat poop because they lack certain nutrients in their diet. Cat poop is full of things that dogs like and need. This doesn't explain why so many healthy dogs eat poop. They may just like the taste. Whatever the reason, eating poop is a pretty natural but totally gross thing for dogs to do. The problem is that we don't like it. We especially don't like being kissed by dogs who have just eaten poop. Can you think of anything ickier?

Smelling Butts

We may not think it's very polite to sniff one another's bottoms, but in dog society it is quite fine. In fact, dogs are being very polite when they sniff another dog's bottom and allow that dog to sniff theirs. It's the canine equivalent of a human handshake.

Dogs say a lot through their sense of smell. The same anal glands that sometimes cause dogs problems contain a lot of information about a dog, including sex, age, and health. By sniffing each other's bottoms, dogs sort out whether they want to be friends or not. After sniffing, they may begin to play, or they may just walk away from one another. When we stop dogs from sniffing one another, we're interrupting their greetings. Without a proper greeting, dogs may fight each other. The next time your dog meets another dog, let them sniff one another to their hearts' content.

Don't worry when your dog sniffs another dog's butt. He's just saying hi!

Eye Boogers

Dogs wake up some mornings with a crusty buildup at the inner corners of their eyes. You probably notice the same thing with your eyes! People call this crusty buildup a lot of different names, including sleep, eye boogers, or sleepy bugs.

Dogs' eyes make tears to wash away the gunk that gets into their eyes and to keep their eyes moist. Tears help fight infections, too. Tears are a combination of salty water, mucus, and oil. After washing the eyes, tears collect at the corners of the eyes and are carried down into the nasal cavity (that's why your nose drips when you cry). When a dog is sleeping, the tears sometimes dry out, leaving the gunk that they've collected at the corner of his eyes. Eye boogers are basically the trash that tears have collected from eyes during the night. They are pretty normal, but if more than just the corner of the eye is crusty, the dog needs to see a vet. He may have an eye infection.

True / False

Dogs eat grass because their stomachs hurt.

WHO KNOWS?

This is an unsolved doggy mystery. We all see our dogs eat grass. Sometimes we see our dogs throw up grass. But what comes first? Do our dogs eat grass because they feel sick? Or do our dogs get sick because they eat grass? Whatever the answer, eating grass is a harmless doggy habit that isn't going away.

Passing Gas

It's not unusual for a dog to be, shall we say, windy. Dogs sometimes suffer from gas because they eat too fast and gulp a large amount of air along with their food. They can also get gas if they have a food allergy or because they got into something they shouldn't have. The same foods that make us gassy, make dogs gassy—beans, cauliflower, soy, and cabbage are

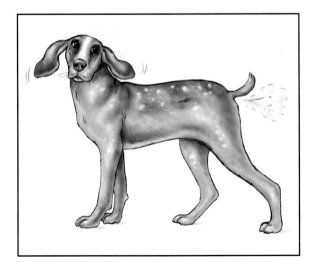

Sometimes dogs fart because they're sick or because they eat too fast.

all culprits. Some breeds are more likely to pass gas than others. Bulldogs, for example, are well known for what the English call trumping.

Passing gas, or flatulence, is caused by food not being broken down completely in the stomach and small intestine. Instead, it's broken down in the large intestine by bacteria that produce gases like methane and the smelly culprit hydrogen sulfide. Feeding a dog three small meals a day rather than two large ones may cut down on gas. Another trick is to put a large rock in the dog's food bowl. This will make him slow down when he eats. Dogs should also get a lot of exercise. Exercise moves gas through the system. If a dog doesn't respond to these solutions, he needs to see a vet. Smelly gas can mean a health problem.

Smelly Dog

Oh, smelly dog. There's nothing sadder than a smelly dog no one wants to pet. Some dogs seem to smell worse than others. And some people are more sensitive to doggy smells than others are.

FUN & GAMES

Matching Game

Do you recognize which picture goes with which breed of dog? Give it a try!

A.

B.

C.

D.

E.

1. Japanese Chin

2. Cavalier King Charles Spaniel

3. Poodle

4. American Staffordshire Terrier

5. Black and Tan Coonhound

Answers:
A: 3 B: 1 C: 4 D: 5 E: 2

Doggy smells can be caused by many things. Your basic stinky dog probably isn't bathed or brushed enough. A dog's skin produces oils that help protect him from the elements. Dogs constantly replace their old hair with new hair—that's what we call shedding. The buildup of oil and dead hair can get stinky. Dogs should be brushed daily or a few times weekly to distribute the oils throughout their fur and to pull out the dead hair. Monthly bathing will help keep them smelling fresh as a daisy.

If a dog is bathed and brushed regularly and he still smells, then there is probably something wrong. He may have an allergy to food, or he may have a skin infection. If a dog is getting bathed more than once a month, he may be getting too clean! Doggy skin requires oil to be healthy. Too much bathing can lead to dry skin, which can be stinky.

Doggy smells don't always come from their skin. Many dogs have bad breath. A lot of people think that just comes with doggy territory. It doesn't have to. Dogs need their teeth brushed, too. Brushing a dog's teeth daily will keep down the bad breath. Tooth decay can cause bad breath. So can digestive problems.

Some dogs have stinky ears. This is usually caused by an infection, which requires a trip to the vet. If a dog is bathed, is brushed, and has his teeth brushed regularly and he still smells bad, he needs to see a vet. A healthy, well-groomed dog doesn't smell. Really!

Chapter 4

It's a Dog's Life

Dogs go through many stages in their lives. They grow from tiny fetuses to feisty puppies to active adults and finally to senior dogs. As they grow, their bodies and minds change in many ways. Some are obvious, and others are subtle.

Before Your Puppy Is Born

Female dogs carry their babies for only about 63 days. How does that compare with other animals? Elephants carry their babies for 640 days. Humans carry them for 266 days. Dog litters may have just two puppies, or they may have as many as ten or twelve puppies. Usually,

Inside this mama, her puppies grow and prepare for life in the outside world.

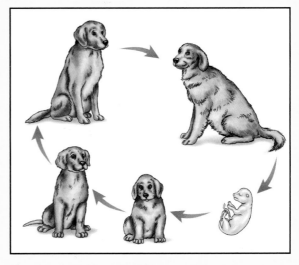

This is a dog's life cycle. Before you know it, your puppy will grow from a tiny ball of fluff to a gangly teen-ager to a raring-to-go adult.

small dogs have small litters, and large dogs have large litters. A puppy's size at birth will depend on the type of dog she is.

Puppyhood

When puppies are born, they are helpless. Their eyes are closed. Their ears are flat and closed. They have no teeth. They must depend on their moms for everything. They sleep almost

A Corgi mama nurses her pups.

constantly. When they are not sleeping, they are eating. They nurse (drink milk from their moms) every one to two hours during their first week of life. Puppies need to eat a lot so they can gain weight and become strong. Puppies double their weight during their first two weeks of life.

After about ten days, puppies begin to open their eyes and ears. They start to explore their new world. They are still very dependent on their moms, but they are beginning to grow up. Most pups get their baby teeth at around one month old. Soon, they can begin eating puppy food. They still eat more often

This newborn Australian Shepherd keeps her eyes sealed against the world.

than an adult. Puppies should eat at least four times a day until they are about eight weeks old, and three times a day until they are six months old. After they are six months old, they can switch to just two meals a day. By around six months old, puppy teeth fall out and are replaced by grown-up teeth.

During the first two weeks of life, a puppy's world is all about her mom and her sisters and brothers. After the first two weeks, she can start meeting friendly humans. It's important that she learns that people are positive parts of her life as soon as possible. A puppy who does not meet

The Growing Dog

One day old: When a puppy is born, her ears and eyes are shut. Her life is all about sleeping, eating, and cuddling with her mom.

Two weeks old: At two weeks old, a pup starts to explore the world a little. Her ears and eyes open. It's time to meet friendly humans and learn to play with her brothers and sisters.

Four weeks old: A pup's teeth are coming in. These tiny sharp teeth allow her to eat real food. She will begin to stop drinking milk from her mom. She continues to learn the doggy dos and don'ts from her mom and her littermates. Her human family exposes her to lots of fun and happy experiences.

At seven weeks old, this Beagle is almost ready to meet her new family.

Two months old: A two-month-old puppy is finally ready to go to her new home. Bye mom and littermates! The pup grows like a weed and wants to meet everyone and see everything. Because she needs lots of energy, she should be fed small meals three times each day. Keeping her safe and showing her lots of positive experiences are the jobs of the new dog owner.

Six months old: The pup is a teenager. She's gangly and a bit awkward. She's lost her baby teeth and has a whole new set of shiny adult teeth. Puppies at this age are ready to be altered (spayed or neutered) to keep them from having puppies. Female dogs are spayed and male dogs are neutered. It's important that a puppy is altered at this age so there are no accidental litters. It's also healthier for both girl and boy dogs to be altered when they are young instead of waiting until they are older.

One year old: The puppy may technically be an adult, but she doesn't always act like one! At this age, small dog breeds are as big as they are going to be. Large dog breeds may continue to grow over the next year. By this point, the pup can be fed adult food two times a day.

Two or three years old: Suddenly a dog looks like a grown-up! She isn't a skinny teenager anymore. She fills out and starts to act a bit more mature.

Seven years old: This is the official start of old age, but a dog this age may not act old. Old age depends a lot on the individual dog and the breed of dog. Older dogs usually slow down a bit. A raring-to-go Rover may be more of a take-it-easy Tiger now! Vets can give advice on ways to help keep an older dog healthy and comfortable.

Young Irish Setter pups drink milk from their mama.

humans when she is very young can become afraid of people. This can lead to her becoming very shy or even aggressive.

A puppy should stay with her mom and littermates until she is at least eight weeks old. During these eight weeks, she learns a lot about life! She learns how to play without hurting the other puppies. She learns to do what her mom tells her to. She learns to trust other doggies and how to "talk" to them. Dogs have special ways of talking to each other. A puppy who doesn't stay with her doggy family during her first eight weeks can have problems getting

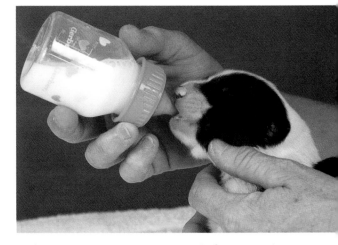

Sometimes puppies need extra milk from a bottle.

along with other dogs. She may become afraid of other dogs, or she may not understand what other dogs are telling her.

When a puppy is first born, she looks a lot like a guinea pig! She isn't the shape, size, or even color that she will be as an adult. Some dogs are one color when they are born and become another color as they age. For example, Dalmatians are born white but start to get their spots when they are about ten days old. Many dogs are born with blue eyes. Usually the eye color changes to brown or hazel after a few weeks. And many puppies have pink noses, eye rims, and paw pads. This coloring usually darkens as the puppies get older. All dogs have floppy ears when they are first born. Slowly, the ears may begin to stand up. Sometimes puppies have one ear up and one ear down for several months! Eventually, for dogs such as German Shepherd Dogs and Chihuahuas, both ears stand up completely.

Puppies grow by leaps and bounds over the first year of life. A puppy who is less than one pound at birth can grow to eighty or one hundred pounds by the end of her first year! Most dogs are considered adults at age one, but they may keep growing until they are two or three years old. Small dogs are usually at their full size by nine months

As your pup grows, she'll become more adventurous and playful.

to one year old. Giant breeds may not reach their full size until they are two years old. Many dogs fill out between ages one and three, getting to their full adult weight by the time they are three years old.

In one or two years, puppies basically grow as much as humans do in eighteen years. That's a lot of growing! Because they grow so fast, they need some extra special care from you. Puppy joints are under a lot of strain while they grow. Don't add to it by letting your pup get overweight. Giant dogs sometimes grow too fast if you feed them regular puppy food. Some vets recommend a special food. Puppies under one year old shouldn't jump or do

Most young adult dogs are full of energy from sunup to sundown.

really hard exercise. It can lead to bone and joint problems.

Puppies also need special care from their veterinarian. Just as babies should go to the doctor for well-baby visits, pups should go to the vet for well-puppy visits regularly. They need vaccinations, deworming, and regular physicals.

This is a play bow, showing you this dog is ready to play. Being an adult doesn't mean your dog is too grown up for fun and games.

Adulthood

When your pup has become a healthy adult, she is at the peak of her physical condition. Different dogs become adults at different ages. Remember that very small dogs may reach adulthood at one year old, but very large dogs may take two years. A dog's physical age is not always the same as her mental and emotional age. Most dogs act quite puppyish at two or three years old. Some dogs never seem to grow up!

Many dogs are lean, even skinny, until they reach three or four years of age, then they suddenly bulk up.

Unless your dog looks like a plump sausage, don't worry. Her new body image is all part of growing up. A healthy adult dog has a shiny coat; strong muscles; alert ears and tail; and shiny, curious eyes.

An adult dog continues to need yearly vet visits. She should eat a regular adult diet unless she has any special needs or problems. Two meals per day are fine for an adult dog. Be sure to give her plenty of water so she doesn't get dehydrated with all the running around she's probably doing.

Old Age

Dogs and dog breeds are all different. None enters old age at the same time. Giant breed dogs may be old at the age of seven. Very small dogs may not enter old age until twelve or thirteen! The signs of old age are both physical and mental. The first sign of aging in a dog is usually the white around a dog's muzzle. This white beard gives the dog a distinguished look. As she ages, the white will spread around her face. Even her eyebrows and the fur on her body can turn white.

One of the first things you will notice as your dog ages is a white muzzle, like this dog's.

As a dog ages, you may notice that the eyes start to become cloudy and even bluish. This looks alarming but is usually harmless. It is called lenticular sclerosis (len-TICK-ular skluh-RO-sis). It does not affect a dog's vision.

Q&A

Q. Is it true that every dog year equals seven human years?

A. Not exactly. Dogs grow very quickly at the beginning of their lives. Whereas a 1-year-old dog is an adult, a 7-year-old child most definitely isn't! Although many dogs reach 16, only a few humans have reached the age of 112. And the oldest dog ever recorded was 29 years old. No human has lived to the age of 203! Dog age also depends on the size and breed of the dog. Larger dogs age more quickly than smaller dogs. It's still an estimate, but here is a better comparison of dog and human years:

Dog	Human
3 months	5 years
1 year	15 years
2 years	24 years
3 years	28 years
5 years	36 years
10 years	56 years
15 years	76 years
20 years	91 to 96 years

Cataracts are another age-related eye change. Cataracts are white not blue, and they do affect a dog's vision.

Most dogs slow down as they age. They may not want to play as long or as hard as they used to. They may have a hard time catching a ball or chasing down a stick. Some choose to rest during much of the day. Unless this is a sudden change, it is just a normal part of aging.

Sometimes older dogs get stiff and sore, just as older people do. This is usually caused by arthritis. With arthritis, the joints, which connect the bones together, wear away, allowing the bones to rub together. Do you have a grandparent who uses a cane or needs some help out of a chair? Your dog is having the same feelings as grandpa or grandma! You may notice that your dog takes longer to stand up. She may seem stiff when she first gets up from a nap. She may be less eager to climb up onto furniture and up steep stairs.

Your veterinarian can help you figure out ways to make life easier for her.

Some dogs start to gain a lot of weight when they get older, partly because they are not as active as they used to be. You can switch your older dog to a special senior diet or just feed her less of her regular food.

Vets consider dogs to be seniors when they reach the age of seven. This is when the vet will start running special senior dog tests each year.

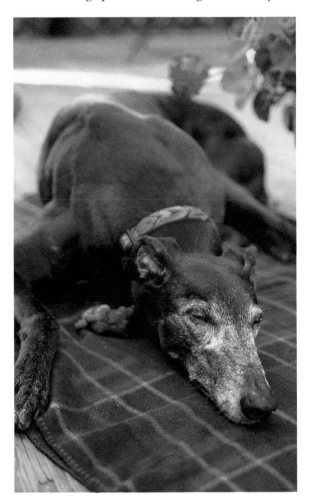

Older dogs may prefer a snooze on a warm bed to the rough-and-tumble games they used to enjoy.

These tests check to see if the dog has any problems with her heart, liver, or kidneys.

Just because your dog is getting older, there's no reason to end her fun activities. Many dogs play Frisbee or go jogging into their teens! They may not run as fast, but they'll still enjoy an outing as much as ever.

Sometimes older dogs get a little confused as they age. They may also begin to lose their hearing. It's important to keep your older dog on her leash or in a fenced area when she is outside. Otherwise, she may get confused and wander away. And then she may not be able to hear you if you call her name.

Older dogs sometimes get a little bit crotchety. Your dog may be startled when she is woken up suddenly or when someone comes up behind her. Some older dogs may even snap because they are sore or surprised. Be careful with your older dog, and make sure that really young kids do not play too roughly with her. A toddler can't understand that an older dog needs special care.

An older dog is a great companion. The once rambunctious pup is finally settling down and ready to live the good life. The older dog now enjoys lying next to you as you read a book. She's ready to stop and smell the roses.

Chapter 5

Big Dogs, Little Dogs

There are so many great dogs, where do we start? The world's tallest dog is the Irish Wolfhound. The smallest dog is the Chihuahua. And there are so many in between. There are big dogs like the Mastiff. There are little dogs like the Yorkshire Terrier. There are hairy dogs like the Old English Sheepdog.

There are hairless dogs like the Chinese Crested. There are yappy dogs like the Chihuahua. There are even yapless dogs like the Basenji (who yodels instead of barks).

There is a perfect type of person for every dog, and a perfect type of dog for every person. What kind of dog is perfect for you?

Here is the wonderful world of dogs in its full glory!

Rare Breeds

What is a rare breed? It is a breed that is uncommon. A breed may be uncommon just in the United States. Some types of dogs few of us have heard of are popular in other countries. For example, the Ainu is well known in Korea, but it is very rare here. Some rare breeds may be uncommon everywhere. For example, the Bleu de Gascogne is rare here *and* in its home country, France.

A great dog isn't determined by whether he comes from a rare or a popular breed. Sometimes breeds are rare because they were bred for a job that doesn't exist anymore. For example, American Bulldogs were originally bred to hold bulls for butchers. They were also used for bull baiting. This was a form of entertainment that is now illegal. Because their work is no longer being done, fewer American Bulldogs are being bred.

Some breeds are rare because they are mostly working dogs. One rare working breed is the Australian Kelpie, who was bred to herd sheep in Australia. A popular Australian saying is "Australia was built on the back of the Kelpie." That means that the Kelpie's work was very important to Australian farmers.

Some breeds stay rare because their fanciers want it that way. Fanciers are the people who are interested in a breed. Many people feel that it hurts a breed when it gets too popular. This happened to the Dalmatian, who became popular after the movie *101 Dalmatians*. People who knew

What kind of dog is right for you? This tiny Chihuahua or the energetic Border Collie?

nothing about breeding thought they could make a lot of money by breeding Dalmatians. Good breeders make sure the moms and dads are healthy before they let them have puppies. They find good homes for all their puppies and take very good care of them. But bad breeders don't do these things. Some bad Dalmatian breeders bred dogs without making sure the moms and dads were perfectly healthy. They sold the puppies to families who didn't know how much exercise Dalmatians need, and many ended up in animal shelters. So sometimes being rare is good.

Some of the rare breeds are very interesting. The Peruvian Inca Orchid is a breed from Peru. It has no hair except on the top of its head. It has huge prick ears and webbed feet. The skin color is usually black with pink spots. This breed not only looks unusual but also has a strange history. Inca nobility kept these dogs as pets and used them as bed warmers on cold nights! The tale goes, Spanish explorers found the dogs among orchid flowers. That's why they called it the Peruvian Inca Orchid.

Another unusual rare breed is the Lundehund, which originated on a small island in Norway. During World War II, many of these dogs died of distemper. Only five or six were left. All the Lundehunds now alive are related to those dogs. But that's not the only strange thing about the Lundehund. It was bred especially to hunt birds called puffins, which live on rocky cliffs. The Lundehund has six toes on each paw so it can climb better, and it can fold its ears shut to protect them from dirt. It also can turn its head completely upside down so it can work in the small spaces where puffins nest. Even the mouth is different from other dogs. It has only forty teeth. All other dogs have forty-two!

This Peruvian Inca Orchid is another breed that is rare, even in Peru!

Mutts

Mutts, mixed breeds, Heinz 57s, mongrels, random-breds, all-American dogs—call them what you want, we love them! There are more than 60 million pet dogs in the United States. More than half of them are mutts.

There are a million mutt combinations, including Labs mixed with Dachshunds, Corgis mixed with German Shepherd Dogs, Poodles mixed with Chihuahuas, Bullmastiffs mixed with Irish Setters. There are also many, many mutts mixed with mutts.

Some people think that mutts aren't as good as purebred dogs. That's not true. All dogs are basically the same type of animal. It doesn't matter what breed they are. They all have four legs, two ears, two eyes, one nose, and one wagging tail (although sometimes it's pretty short!). Mutts actually can be healthier than purebred dogs because they're less likely to pass on genetic diseases to their puppies. Genetic diseases are health problems that are passed from a parent to a baby.

Sometimes people cross breeds on purpose. They are trying to create new breeds. These new breeds are often called "designer dogs." Some popular designer dogs are Puggles (Poodles and Beagles), Cockapoos (Cocker Spaniels and Poodles), and Labradoodles (Labrador Retrievers and Poodles). Some purebred breeders feel strongly that new breeds shouldn't be created. However, every breed was a mixed breed once. The most important thing to know when choosing a dog is that the mom and dad are healthy and that the puppies are well cared for.

Purebreds and mutts are all just dogs—no better or worse. Every dog is unique, and any kind of dog can be your best friend.

A Guide to Popular Breeds

Many, many dog breeds exist—more than four hundred in total! Humans began creating breeds so they could have dogs with special skills. When Canadian hunters wanted a medium-size dog who loved water and had a great sense of smell, they bred Newfoundlands with small native dogs to create the Labrador Retriever. Some breeds are based on just one or two dogs who were really outstanding. The modern Border Collie was bred from two great herding dogs named Old Hemp and Old Kep.

For the most part, dogs weren't bred for looks but for ability. Old Hemp and Old Kep just happened to be fluffy black-and-white dogs. They passed these genes on to their descendants along with their herding talents.

The following breed guide (pages 62–127) includes more than 150 of the existing dog breeds. Most are registered with the American Kennel Club (AKC). Some, such as the American Pit Bull Terrier and the Rat Terrier, are popular breeds but are not recognized by the AKC.

In our breed descriptions, you will find some basic information: where the breed is

This Labradoodle is a popular "designer dog." People breed Labradors and Poodles together to get the best qualities of each breed.

from, a little of its history, and a general description of its looks and personality. (Remember that not all dogs of each breed act the same.) Each description also mentions whether this dog has a low, moderate, or high activity level.

Dogs with low activity levels are pretty mellow and would rather hang out on the couch than take long hikes and play hard. Dogs with moderate activity levels are the average. These dogs like to take walks and play, but they can chill out, too. Dogs with high activity levels need lots and lots of exercise. Then, we make some suggestions about the best kind of home for each breed. This is just a general guide. Every dog is an individual.

Each description also tells you what type of family is best for each breed of dog and what the breed's dream day would be. A list of each breed's pluses and minuses tell you what you're getting yourself into with that breed! Finally, every description has a fun fact—something you probably don't know about this dog.

If you are thinking of getting a dog, don't rely on one guide to find out about the breed. Talk to breeders and read books on the specific breed. Get to know a few dogs of the breed. Finally, look at your dog as an individual. You may have a Lab who hates water or an Australian Shepherd who is a couch potato. Love and accept your dog for who he is.

Breed Charts

There are many special words used to describe dog breeds. Some of these are very uncommon. Here are charts of terms for coat color, dog ear types, and dog tail types. You can look back at these charts when you come to a term you don't understand.

Coat Color Types

Coat Color	Description
ASCOB	any solid color other than black
Badger	a mix of brown, black, gray, and white hairs
Blaze	a strip of white down the center of the face
Belton	term used to describe spots of hair that are lighter or darker than the base color (ticking or roaning) in English Setters only
Blue	a grayish blue
Blue merle	black markings on a grayish blue background
Brindle	dark and light streaking that looks like tiger stripes
Café au lait	creamy brown
Chestnut	reddish brown
Chocolate	brown
Cream	off white
Dead grass	tan
Fawn	a reddish-brown yellow
Grizzle	mixture of white hairs with black or red hairs
Harlequin	patchy black or gray on white (this term is usually reserved for Great Danes)
Hound color (or marked)	white with tan and black patches
Landseer	black-and-white Newfoundland
Lemon	yellow
Lion color	reddish tan
Liver	deep reddish brown
Mahogany	dull reddish brown
Mask	dark color on the face
Merle	dark splotches against a lighter background of the same color
Mottled	dark, round splotches on a lighter background
Mustard	muted yellow
Parti-colored	patches of two colors or more
Piebald (or pied)	large splotches of two or more colors
Roan	mix of colored hairs with white hairs
Ruby	mahogany red
Rust	reddish brown
Sable	black-tipped silver, gold, gray, brown, or fawn hairs
Sandy	sand colored, tan
Seal	black with a reddish tint
Sedge	reddish yellow
Stag red (stag)	deep red with black hairs
Tawny	brownish orange
Ticking	little spots of color lighter or darker than the base color
Wheaten	wheat colored, tan

Dog Ear Types

Ear Type	Description
Bat ear	a large, rounded erect ear (example: French Bulldog)
Bell ear	a wide ear (example: Clumber Spaniel)
Button ear	an ear that folds forward and covers the inside of the ear (example: Jack (Parson) Russell Terrier)
Cropped ear	drop ear cut to stand erect (example: some Boxers)
Drop ear	an ear that hangs down instead of being erect; also called a pendant ear (example: Labrador Retriever)
Hound ear	a rounded drop ear (example: Basset Hound)
Natural ear	an ear that isn't cropped (example: Labrador Retriever)
Pendant ear	also called a drop ear
Prick ear	an ear that stands up; erect ear (example: German Shepherd Dog)
Rose	a small ear that folds over and back (example: American Pit Bull Terrier)
Semiprick ear	an erect ear with just the tips folding over (example: Collie)
Tulip ear	an erect ear with the edges curving in (example: Bull Terrier)

Dog Tail Types

Tail Type	Description
Bee-sting tail	a short, straight tapered tail (example: Pointer)
Brush tail	a bushy tail (example: Australian Cattle Dog)
Bobtail	naturally tailless (example: Australian Shepherd)
Carrot tail	a tail shaped like an upside-down carrot and carried straight up (example: West Highland White Terrier)
Corkscrew tail	a curled tail (example: Pug)
Crank tail	a tail that hangs down (example: Scottish Deerhound)
Curled tail	a tail that curls over the back (example: Alaskan Malamute)
Docked tail	a tail that is shortened by being cut (example: some Doberman Pinschers)
Double curl tail	a tail that curls twice over the back (example: Akita)
Flag tail	a long tail that is carried high with long silky hair on it (example: Irish Setter)
Gay tail	a tail carried higher than the back (example: Brussels Griffon)
Hook tail	a tail that hangs down and curves up at the bottom (example: Greyhound)
Horizontal tail	another term for a bee-sting tail
Otter tail	a long thick tail that is rounded (example: Labrador Retriever)
Plume tail	a tail with feathering (example: Gordon Setter)
Pump handle	a long tail that is carried up (example: Black and Tan Coonhound)
Rat tail	a long tail with curls of fur covering most of it but the tip, which is almost hairless (example: Irish Water Spaniel)
Ring tail	a tail carried up and curled almost in a circle (example: Afghan Hound)
Saber tail	a tail carried like a sword in a semicircle (example: Siberian Husky)
Screw tail	another term for a corkscrew tail
Sickle tail	another term for a saber tail
Whip tail	a tail carried straight out and pointed (example: Bull Terrier)

AFFENPINSCHER

Where They Are From:
Germany

History: Affenpinschers were originally bred to keep rodents out of houses and stables. Later, they were bred to be smaller and used to keep mice out of the home. The Affenpinscher is an old breed. It was developed in the seventeenth century—about four hundred years ago!

Looks: Affenpinschers are small and compact with monkeylike faces. Their ears may be drop, semi-erect, or erect. Sometimes they are cropped erect. They have shaggy short coats that may be black, silver, gray, black and tan, or red. Their hair is longer on the head, and they have bushy eyebrows and a beard. The tail is long, curling over the back, or docked short.

Height: 9 to 11.5 inches

Weight: 7 to 10 pounds

Personality: Affenpinschers are fun-loving, curious dogs. They can go from being quiet to being excited in an instant. They are very attached to their families.

Activity Level: Moderate

First Loves: Their families, chasing things

Best Families: Affenpinschers' best families are made up of people who are patient but who are able to tell them no when it's needed. Affenpinschers do well living in both the city and the country.

Pluses: Affectionate, always up for fun, good watchdogs, good with kids

Minuses: Can be unfriendly with strangers, hard to train, need to be groomed

Fun Fact: *Affenpinscher* means "monkey dog" in German. They were named after their monkeylike looks.

AFGHAN HOUND

Where They Are From: Afghanistan

History: No one knows for sure how old the breed is. Afghan Hounds may be from the seventeenth century. They were first used as hunting dogs by hunters on horseback. In the West, they are known as show dogs.

Looks: Afghan Hounds are large, elegant dogs. They have long heads with long drop ears. Their coats are long and silky except on the face and back. They can be any color. The tail is long and curved.

Height: 25 to 27 inches

Weight: 50 to 60 pounds

Personality: Afghan Hounds are independent. They can act a little stuck up, and they are stubborn. They love their families but are not very interested in meeting other people. They like other dogs but sometimes chase cats.

Activity Level: Moderate

First Loves: Running, their families

Best Families: Afghans' families understand that the dogs aren't always in the mood to play. Afghans don't mind living in the city or the country as long as their families have the time to train them.

Pluses: Gentle, good with kids and other dogs, playful with their families

Minuses: Chase cats, need to be groomed, need training, not really interested in new people, stubborn

Fun Fact: In Afghanistan, Afghan Hounds were originally trained to hunt with falcons.

AIREDALE TERRIER

Where They Are From: Great Britain

History: First bred in the early nineteenth century, Airedale Terriers were used to hunt small and large animals in Great Britain, Africa, India, and North America. More recently, they have also been police dogs and military dogs.

Looks: Airedales are large dogs with long heads. They have small dark eyes and V-shaped drop ears. They have thick, wiry coats, and they have beards and long whiskers. Their coats are tan and black. Their tails are naturally long but are often docked.

Height: 22 to 23 inches

Weight: 45 to 50 pounds

Personality: Airedales are brave, active dogs. They love to play more than anything else and will chase anything that runs. They are great with kids. They can be stubborn. They like meeting new people but take a little while to warm up to them.

Activity Level: High

First Loves: Running, chasing things, playing with their favorite people

Best Families: Airedales do best with older kids and

grown-ups who love to play. They do best in the country or in houses with big yards.

Pluses: Always up for a good time, brave, good watchdogs, good with kids

Minuses: Chase small animals, need lots of exercise, need to be groomed, need training, stubborn

Fun Fact: The Airedale is sometimes called the king of terriers.

AKITA

Where They Are From: Japan

History: The breed is about three hundred years old. Akitas have been used as guard dogs, for hunting, and for fighting. In Japan, the breed symbolizes good health. Statues of Akitas are sometimes given as good luck gifts.

Looks: Akitas are large, powerful dogs. They have triangular-shaped heads and small erect ears. Their bushy tails curl over their backs. Akitas can be any color but are often white with patches of color.

Height: 24 to 28 inches

Weight: 70 to 130 pounds

Personality: Akitas are brave and loyal to their people. They love their families but don't trust strangers very much. Some Akitas don't get along with other dogs.

Activity Level: Moderate

First Loves: Their families

Best Families: Akitas do well with active families who have had dogs before. They do best living in houses where there is room to run and play.

Pluses: Gentle and calm, loving with family, very good watchdogs

Minuses: Can be stubborn, can be territorial, shed, sometimes fight with other dogs, take a while to warm up to new people

Fun Fact: In Japan, the Akita is a national monument and a national treasure.

ALASKAN MALAMUTE

Where They Are From: Alaska

History: Malamutes were originally kept as sled dogs by the Mahlemuts, an Inuit tribe in western Alaska. They were used to pull heavy loads rather than to go fast.

Looks: Alaskan Malamutes are large, powerful dogs. Their heads are large and their bushy tails curl over their backs. They have heavy coats, and they have erect ears. Their coat color ranges from white to mixtures of gray, black,

sable, and red. They all have white markings and a white mask.

Height: 23 to 25 inches

Weight: 75 to 85 pounds

Personality: Malamutes are gentle, patient dogs. They are friendly, get along with almost everyone, and love to play. They can be a little stubborn.

Activity Level: High

First Loves: Snow, fun, family—in that order!

Best Families: Malamutes like families who have energy to spare. They do best in areas that get lots of snow. They need houses with yards to play in.

Pluses: Friendly, gentle, get along with other dogs, good dogs to do sports with, good with kids, love to play, smart

Minuses: Can be stubborn, hard to train, need a lot of exercise, shed

Fun Fact: Alaskan Malamutes were used as sled dogs by the U.S. military during World War II.

AMERICAN ESKIMO DOG

Where They Are From: United States

History: American Eskimo Dogs are related to German Spitz dogs (northern, wolfish-looking dogs) brought to the United States with German immigrants during the nineteenth century. They have been pets and watchdogs.

Looks: American Eskimo Dogs are small, compact dogs. They have heavy white coats. Their heads are wedge shaped, and their ears are erect. Their bushy tails curl over their backs. There are three recognized sizes of American Eskimo Dogs: toy, miniature, and standard.

Height: 9 to 12 inches (toy), 11 to 15 inches (miniature), 14 to 19 inches (standard)

Weight: No standard

Personality: American Eskimo Dogs are clever and full of pep. Sometimes they are even a little naughty. They adore their families and love to play with them. They don't always like strangers.

Activity Level: Moderate

First Loves: Family, fun

Best Families: American Eskimo Dogs' ideal families are as smart and as fun-loving as they are. They do well both in the city and in the country.

Pluses: Easy to train, friendly, good watchdogs, good with kids, good with other dogs

Minuses: Can be naughty, need lots of attention, shed

Fun Fact: American Eskimo Dogs were once popular circus performers!

AMERICAN FOXHOUND

Where They Are From: United States

History: American Foxhounds were bred from European foxhounds. Foxhounds were brought to the United States in the 1700s. As their name says, they were bred to hunt fox.

Looks: American Foxhounds are large dogs with big heads and drop ears. Their very short coats can be any color. They have long curved tails.

Height: 21 to 25 inches

Weight: No standard

Personality: American Foxhounds are easygoing dogs. They love to play but also enjoy just hanging out. They love everyone, especially kids and other dogs. They can be a bit stubborn.

Activity Level: Moderate

First Loves: People, playing, other dogs

Best Families: Most American Foxhounds live well with kids who have time for them. They need houses with big fenced yards.

Pluses: Easy to groom, friendly, good with kids and other dogs

Minuses: Hard to train, stubborn, will wander

Fun Fact: George Washington, the father of our country, was also the father of American Foxhounds. He was the first to breed them!

(See the charts on pages 60–61 for term definitions.)

AMERICAN PIT BULL TERRIER (APBT)

Where They Are From: United States

History: In the 1900s, English immigrants brought crosses of Bulldogs and terriers to the United States. American Pit Bull Terriers are one of the breeds that were developed from these crosses. They were used as cattle catchers and as pets. They

were also used for pit fighting, a cruel sport that is now illegal. Unfortunately, some people still breed APBTs to fight or to be aggressive, but well-bred APBTs love all people.

Looks: APBTs are muscular dogs. They have big heads and strong jaws. Their ears are naturally semiprick or rose, but sometimes people crop them. They have very short coats that can be any color. Their tails are medium length.

Height: 18 to 22 inches

Weight: 35 to 60 pounds

Personality: APBTs are fun-loving dogs who are full of energy. They have a zest for life. They love just about everyone they meet. They adore playing with their favorite kids. Many APBTs don't get along with other dogs, and they may chase cats.

Activity Level: High

First Loves: Kids, playing

Best Families: APBTs get along with older kids and grown-ups who have had dogs before. Their families must have time to train them and give them lots of exercise. APBTs do best in houses with big yards.

Pluses: Easy to groom, great dogs to do sports with, great with kids, love to play.

Minuses: May fight with other dogs, need lots of exercise, stubborn, must always be purchased from a good breeder or shelter

Fun Fact: Petey, from *Our Gang* (the little Rascals, 1922–1928), was an American Pit Bull Terrier.

AMERICAN STAFFORDSHIRE TERRIER (STAFFIES)

Where They Are From: United States

History: American Staffordshire Terriers are related to the American Pit Bull Terrier and the English Staffordshire Terrier. They were bred from the bull and terrier crosses brought to the United States by English immigrants during the nineteenth century. They were used as general farm dogs. Like American Pit Bull Terriers, they were used in the cruel sport of pit fighting, which is now illegal.

Looks: American Staffordshire Terriers are muscular dogs. Their coats are short and can be any color but white. They have semiprick or rose ears. Sometimes the ears are cropped erect. The tail is short and tapered.

Height: 17 to 19 inches

Weight: 40 to 79 pounds

Personality: American Staffordshire Terriers are outgoing dogs who are full of fun. They are gentle and playful with kids. They are very brave. They adore almost every person they meet, but they often don't like other dogs. They may chase cats. As is true for other pit bull types, you need to get your dog or puppy from a good breeder or shelter.

Activity Level: High

First Loves: Kids, pulling, jumping, running

Best Families: American Staffordshire Terriers do well with older kids and adults who have had other dogs. Their families must give them lots of exercise and teach them to love everyone, including other dogs. Staffies do best in houses with big yards.

Pluses: Easy to groom, gentle, great for doggy sports, great with kids, love to play

Minuses: Can be aggressive with dogs, can be stubborn, may chase cats, must be well bred

Fun Fact: The most decorated war dog in U.S. history was Stubby, an American Staffordshire Terrier. Stubby was a stray whom soldiers snuck aboard a transport ship during World War I.

AMERICAN WATER SPANIEL

Where They Are From: United States

History: American Water Spaniels are true American dogs! They were bred in the United States to hunt birds from small boats and from the water. Despite their American pedigree, not many American Water Spaniels can be found in the United States.

Looks: American Water Spaniels are small to medium-size dogs with curly, dense coats. Their coats can be liver to brown in color with white markings on their chests and toes. They have drop ears, and their eyes are yellow or brown. Their tails are long and curved and act like rudders, helping them to balance and turn in the water.

Height: 15 to 18 inches

Weight: 25 to 45 pounds

Personality: American Water Spaniels are full of fun and energy. They love to play and to swim, and they like almost everyone. They can be a little greedy with food.

Activity Level: High

First Loves: Food, fun, water

Best Families: American Water Spaniels do well with older kids and adults who have had other dogs. Their families must understand that water spaniels need lots of training and exercise. They do best in the country or in a city or suburban neighborhood with lots of space.

Pluses: Easy to train, good dogs for sports, good with kids, good with other dogs, great swimmers, loving

Minuses: Greedy with food, need lots of exercise, need to be groomed

Fun Fact: The American Water Spaniel is the state dog of Wisconsin. (See the list of state dogs on page 66)

ANATOLIAN SHEPHERD DOG

Where They Are From: Turkey

History: Anatolian Shepherd Dogs' ancestors are ancient sighthounds (dogs that hunt by sight) and Mastiffs. They were bred to guard livestock against large predators like wolves. Some are still used for this today!

Looks: Anatolian Shepherd Dogs are large, strong dogs. They have big heads and drop ears. They have short rough coats that can be any color. They usually have a dark mask. The tail is long.

Height: 27.5 to 29 inches minimum

Weight: 88 to 143 pounds

Personality: Anatolian Shepherd Dogs love their friends and families, but they can be unfriendly with strangers. They are very protective. They are smart and stubborn, and they can be hard to train.

Activity Level: Moderate

First Loves: Their families

Best Families: Anatolian Shepherd Dogs like mature older kids and adults who have had dogs before. Their families must have time to train them and introduce them to lots of nice people.

Pluses: Excellent watchdogs, loving with their families, protective

Minuses: Can be overprotective, hard to train

Fun Fact: In Turkey, working Anatolian Shepherd Dogs are nomadic, meaning they move from place to place with the flock they're guarding.

APPENZELLER

Where They Are From:
Switzerland

History: There are four Swiss dogs who are believed to descend from Mastiffs. These dogs were brought to Switzerland by the Romans in the first century BC. The Appenzeller is one of the four. It was originally used to drive (move) cattle and as a guard.

Looks: Appenzellers are large dogs with big heads. They have small drop ears. Their long tails are curled over their backs. Their coats are short and tricolor. The base is either black or brown with both white and tan markings.

Height: 19 to 23 inches

Weight: 48 to 55 pounds

Personality: Appenzellers are happy, energetic dogs. They love playing and adore their families. However, they don't always trust new people. They love to learn new things.

Activity Level: High

First Loves: Running, playing, their families

Best Families: Appenzellers need active families with lots of time for them. They do best in the country.

Pluses: Affectionate, easy to train, good watchdogs, playful

Minuses: Bark a lot, may chase cars and other animals, need lots of exercise, shed, nervous with strangers

Fun Fact: To make stub-

(See the charts on pages 60–61 for term definitions.)

born cattle move, the Appenzeller lightly bites the animal on its hind foot or its nose!

AUSTRALIAN CATTLE DOG

Where They Are From: Australia

History: Australian Cattle Dogs were bred to be the ultimate ranch dogs. They herd cattle by nipping at their heels. Their ancestors include Australian Kelpies, Collies, and Dalmatians.

Looks: Australian Cattle Dogs are medium size and sturdy. They have prick ears and long bushy tails. Their coats are usually mottled, either blue (gray) or red. Sometimes they have tan, black, blue, or red markings.

Height: 17 to 20 inches

Weight: 33 to 55 pounds

Personality: Heelers, as Cattle Dogs are sometimes called, are very smart. They love to work. They tend to be one-person dogs. They are very loyal. They can be standoffish with people outside their families.

Activity Level: High

First Loves: Their person, herding, chasing things

Best Families: Australian Cattle Dogs do best with people who can spend almost every moment with hem. Kids who love hiking, running, and spending time in the country are perfect companions. These dogs do well in the

U.S. State Dogs

Only nine states have official dogs. Is your state among them? If not, maybe you can start a campaign to adopt a state dog.

- **Louisiana:** Louisiana Catahoula Leopard Dog
- **Maryland:** Chesapeake Bay Retriever
- **Massachusetts:** Boston Terrier
- **North Carolina:** Plott
- **Pennsylvania:** Great Dane
- **South Carolina:** Boykin Spaniel
- **Texas:** Blue Lacy
- **Virginia:** American Foxhound
- **Wisconsin:** American Water Spaniel

country or in a city or suburban house with a big yard.

Pluses: Easy to groom, easy to train, good watchdogs, good with other dogs, like kids, smart

Minuses: Chase smaller animals, need a lot of exercise, standoffish, tend to herd people and other animals

Fun Fact: Australian Cattle Dogs are supposedly the only breed to be part dingo. Dingoes are wild dogs

who live in the Australian Outback. Australian Cattle Dog breeders brought dingoes into the mix because dingoes are quiet and can work for a long time without a break.

AUSTRALIAN KELPIE

Where They Are From: Australia

History: Australian Kelpies were bred from English and Scottish Collies around 1870 to work as sheep herding dogs. In Australia, most Australian Kelpies are still working dogs. In the United States, some are kept as pets.

Looks: Australian Kelpies are medium size. They have very large prick ears and long brush tails. Their coats are short and either black, blue, red, or tan. Some have tan markings.

Height: 17 to 20 inches

Weight: 26 to 45 pounds

Personality: Australian Kelpies are very smart dogs who love to work but are mellow at home. Most Kelpies get

really close to only one family member. They are not much for cuddling with.

Activity Level: Moderate to high

First Loves: Herding, their person

Best Families: Kelpies do best with active families who like to get out into nature. They'd love to live on a ranch or farm but are also happy in a house with a big yard.

Pluses: Adapt to new situations, hardworking, loyal

Minuses: Don't bond with the whole family, must be trained, need a lot of exercise, not very affectionate

Fun Fact: In Australia, they say the country was built on the back of the Australian Kelpie. That's because Australian kelpies were so important to the sheep and wool industry, one of Australia's biggest industries.

AUSTRALIAN SHEPHERD (AUSSIE)

Where They Are From: United States

History: Yep, you read right: Australian Shepherds are from America! Their ancestors probably came from Spain, but American farmers bred them to be general farm dogs. Their fans say they are the dogs who helped tame the West. They were common farm dogs in the American West during the early part of the twentieth century.

Looks: Australian Shepherds are medium-size dogs. They have drop ears that fold forward when they are excited. Their tails are naturally bobbed or are docked. Their thick coats are blue merle, red merle, red, or black, with or without white or tan markings. The most common color is blue merle. They have very distinctive eyes. They can be brown, blue, amber, or any combination of these colors with flecks or marbling.

Height: 18 to 23 inches

Weight: 35 to 75 pounds

Personality: Australian Shepherds are full of pep. They are superenergetic dogs. They love to work and play. They adore their families. They like kids and other dogs. They like to chase things and will herd anything that moves.

Activity Level: High

First Loves: Herding, playing, their people

Best Families: Australian Shepherds love older energetic kids. Their families should have lots of time for training and exercise. Their houses should have big yards.

Pluses: Friendly, good watchdogs, good with kids and other dogs, good working dogs, great dogs for sports

Minuses: Need lots of exercise, need to be groomed, need to be trained, will herd and chase animals and kids

Fun Fact: In the early days of the American West, Australian Shepherds were popular performing dogs. Many were rodeo dogs, performing tricks during breaks at rodeos.

AUSTRALIAN TERRIER

Where They Are From: Australia

History: Australian Terriers are one of the smallest working terriers. They were bred to help control rodents and snakes but have always been house watchdogs and companions as well.

(See the charts on pages 60–61 for term definitions.)

Looks: Australian Terriers are small, wiry dogs. They have small erect ears and long blue-and-tan coats. Their tails are docked to half their length and held high.

Height: 10 to 11 inches

Weight: 14 pounds

Personality: Australian Terriers are full of life. They are small but spunky. They fight first and ask questions later. They love their friends and families but don't always get along with other dogs.

Activity Level: High

First Loves: Chasing things, running around in circles, their families

Best Families: Australian Terriers love to meet mature older kids. They don't mind where their families live.

Pluses: Full of fun, good dogs for sports, good watchdogs, good with kids and other animals

Minuses: Dig, need to be groomed, take a while to warm up to strangers

Fun Fact: Australian Terriers were once used to control rodents in Australia's gold mines.

BASENJI

Where They Are From: Zaire, Africa

History: Basenjis are ancient hunting dogs with a long history in Africa. Some say Basenjis were given as gifts to Egyptian pharaohs more than two thousand years ago!

Looks: Basenjis are wiry, medium-size dogs. They have wrinkled heads and erect ears. Their short coats are chestnut red, tricolor, brindle, or black. They have white on their feet, tails, and chests. Their tails are curled over their backs.

Height: 16 to 17 inches

Weight: 22 to 24 pounds

Personality: Basenjis are smart and alert. They know what is going on around them. Some people say they act more like cats than dogs. They don't even bark! They don't meow, though—they yodel! If they are upset, they may even scream. They love their families but don't always like strangers.

Activity Level: High

First Loves: Running, chasing things, playing with their families

Best Families: Basenjis like people who are energetic. They must understand that Basenjis need a lot of training and exercise.

Pluses: Affectionate with their families, don't need much grooming, good with most kids, good with other dogs

Minuses: Can be stubborn, chase cars and small animals, take a while to warm up to new people

Fun Fact: There are drawings of dogs that look like Basenjis on Egyptian tombs that date back as far as 4,000 BC.

BASSET HOUND

Where They Are From: France

History: Basset Hounds are a dwarf breed: in French, *basset* means "dwarf." They were originally kept by nobility and used to hunt small game in the sixteenth century. Basset Hounds became popular with commoners after the French Revolution.

Looks: Basset Hounds are long and heavy. They have short legs and large wrinkly heads with very long drop ears and droopy eyes. Their short coats are black, tan, and white. Their long tails are tapered.

Height: 14 inches

Weight: 50 to 65 pounds

Personality: Basset Hounds are friendly and gentle. Some people say they are clownlike. They are very easy to get along with, and they like almost everyone. They can be messy and loud—they slobber and like to howl! They can also be a bit stubborn. And like all good hounds, they love to sniff.

Activity Level: Moderate

First Loves: Their people, sniffing

Best Families: Basset Hounds get along well with kids who know how to laugh and don't mind a little slobber. They can live in the country or the city.

Pluses: Easy to groom, easygoing, friendly, good watchdogs, good with kids and other dogs

Minuses: Can be stubborn, loud, may wander, slobbery

Fun Fact: Bassets are one of the few dogs who can't swim. Their legs are too short and their bodies are too heavy.

BEAGLE

Where They Are From: Great Britain

History: Beagles were originally bred to hunt rabbit in packs in Great Britain. They first came to the United States in the nineteenth century. Now they are one of America's most popular pet dogs. The breed is at least 150 years old

Looks: Beagles are small dogs. They have big brown eyes and long drop ears. Their tails are medium length. They have short coats that are tan, black, and white. There are two sizes of Beagle.

Height: Up to 13 inches or 13 to 15 inches

Weight: 20 to 30 pounds

Personality: Beagles are friendly and bubbly. They get along with everyone—they love kids and other dogs. They are very playful, and they love to dig.

Activity Level: Moderate

First Loves: Their people, running and chasing, digging

Best Families: Beagles love kids with time to hang out. They don't mind living in the city or the country.

Pluses: Easy to groom, friendly, good watchdogs, good with kids and other dogs

Minuses: Bark, can be stubborn, dig, will wander

Fun Fact: The U.S. Department of Homeland Security (DHS) uses Beagles to search for illegal plants, fruit, and meat coming into the country. These detection Beagles are called The Beagle Brigade. The Beagle Brigade is made up mostly of Beagles rescued from shelters.

BEARDED COLLIE

Where They Are From: Great Britain

History: The Bearded Collie is one of Great Britain's oldest breeds. There probably were Bearded Collies in the sixteenth century! They are sheep herding dogs who are popular pets in Great Britain and the United States. They are related to the Border Collie and the Old English Sheepdog.

Looks: Bearded Collies are large dogs with medium-length wooly coats. They are black, blue, brown, or fawn, with white markings. They have drop ears and, as you would expect, heavy beards. Their tails are long and hairy.

Height: 20 to 22 inches
Weight: 40 to 60 pounds
Personality: Bearded Collies are happy and lovable, and they have a great sense of humor. They enjoy playing and get along with almost everybody. They like learning new things, and they love to herd. They may even try to herd kids and cats.
Activity Level: Moderate
First Loves: Herding, their people
Best Families: Bearded Collies do great with kids who like to get out and try new things as much as they do. They should have big yards to play in.
Pluses: Friendly, good watchdogs, good with kids and dogs, love their families
Minuses: Need to be groomed, will herd anything and everything
Fun Fact: Bearded Collies have many names, including the Highland Collie, the Mountain Scotch Collie, and the Old Welsh Grey Sheepdog. They were featured in 2006's *Shaggy Dog*, starring Tim Allen.

(See the charts on pages 60–61 for term definitions.)

BEAUCERON

Where They Are From: France
History: Beaucerons were first bred in the sixteenth century. They have been used as livestock guardians, herders, and pets. They are close relatives of Briards. Until the past few years, they were hard to find outside of France.
Looks: Beaucerons are large, strong dogs. They have long heads and ears that are drop or cropped. They have hook tails. Their short coats are black with rust markings or gray, black, and rust.
Height: 24 to 27.5 inches
Weight: Up to 110 pounds
Personality: Beaucerons are energetic, fun-loving dogs. They love to work, especially with their favorite person. They are smart and brave.
Activity Level: High
First Loves: Work, play, their families
Best Families: Beaucerons would love a family who is involved in dog sports. Even better, they like to have a real job. They are happiest if their families live in the country or the suburbs.
Pluses: Easy to groom, easy to train, fun loving, good watchdogs, smart
Minuses: Can be protective, need lots of exercise, need some kind of job
Fun Fact: Beaucerons' two colors have special names. The black with rust markings Beaucerons are called *bas rouges* (red stockings). The gray, black, and rust Beaucerons are called harlequins.

BEDLINGTON TERRIER

Where They Are From: Great Britain
History: Bedlington Terriers were first bred in the mid-nineteenth century in northern England. They were used by miners to get rid of rats and mice and also to hunt small game. They were also used for fighting.
Looks: Bedlington Terriers are medium size. They look like lambs. They have curly, wooly coats that are blue, sandy, liver, blue and tan, sandy and tan, or liver and tan. Their drop ears usually have tassels of fur at the end. They have arched backs and long thin tails.
Height: 15.5 to 16.5 inches
Weight: 17 to 23 pounds
Personality: Bedlington Terriers are plucky dogs—brave but also gentle. They like people but sometimes fight with

other dogs. They take a while to warm up to strangers. They can be sensitive and need a gentle touch in training.

Activity Level: Moderate

First Loves: People

Best Families: Bedlington Terriers love mature older kids who are used to dogs. Their families need to train them to be friendly with everyone. Bedlingtons are fine living in houses or apartments.

Pluses: Can live anywhere, fun loving, gentle, good watchdogs, good with kids

Minuses: Aggressive with other dogs, can be stubborn, need to be groomed, need training

Fun Fact: Bedlington Terriers are sometimes called gypsy dogs because they are said to have been popular among European gypsies, or Roma.

BELGIAN SHEPHERD DOG

Where They Are From: Belgium

History: There are four types of Belgian Shepherd Dog—Belgian Malinois, Belgian Tervuren (pictured here), Belgian Sheepdog, and Belgian Laekenois. In the United States, they are generally recognized as separate breeds, but they are essentially the same breed with different coats. They were first bred in the late nineteenth century and were used as herders and livestock guardians. Many still work today—in the military, as police dogs, as search and rescue dogs, and on ranches. The four types were bred in different villages, which is where their names come from.

Looks: Belgian Shepherd Dogs are all large, strong dogs with long muzzles (nose and mouth) and prick ears. Their tails are medium length and slightly curved. Each type has a different coat. Belgian Malinois have short, straight coats that are fawn to mahogany colored. Belgian Tervurens have long coats that are also fawn to mahogany colored. Belgian Shepherd Dogs have long black coats. Belgian Laekenois have wiry fawn to mahogany coats.

Height: 22 to 26 inches

Weight: 40 to 80 pounds

Personality: Belgian Shepherd Dogs are smart and love to work. They bond closely with one person, but they love their whole family. They are very protective and don't always like strangers.

Activity Level: High

First Loves: Their person, working, playing

Best Families: Belgian Shepherd Dogs do well with ma-

ture older kids with lots of time for them. Their families should have experience with dogs because Belgian Shepherd Dogs can be a handful. They need houses with big yards, preferably in the country.

Pluses: Easy to train, good watchdogs, great dogs for sports, great workers, love to learn, smart

Minuses: Can be overprotective, need lots of exercise, need to be groomed, need training, one-person dogs (don't bond with the whole family)

Fun Fact: In Europe, all four types are called *chien de berger Belge*, which is French for Belgian Shepherd Dog.

BERNESE MOUNTAIN DOG

Where They Are From: Switzerland

History: Bernese Mountain Dogs are one of four Swiss dog breeds. The other three are the Appenzeller, the Entlebucher, and the Greater Swiss Mountain Dog. They all come from crosses of local dogs and Roman Mastiffs. They were bred as an all-purpose farm dog. They also pulled carts.

Looks: Bernese Mountain Dogs are large and powerful. They have broad heads and drop ears. Their tails are long and bushy. The long thick coat is black with rust and white markings.

Height: 23 to 27.5 inches

Weight: 75 to 105 pounds

Personality: Bernese Mountain Dogs are sweet and easygoing. They love their families, and they get along great with kids and other dogs. They take a little while to warm up to new people.

Activity Level: Moderate

First Loves: Their families, pulling things

Best Families: Bernese Mountain Dogs love kids who like to play but don't mind just hanging out sometimes. They do best living in houses with yards.

Pluses: Friendly, gentle, good with kids, good with other dogs

Minuses: Need to be groomed, take a while to warm up to new people

Fun Fact: Bernese Mountain Dogs were named for their hometown—the canton, or state, of Bern in Switzerland.

BICHON FRISE

Where They Are From: France

History: The Bichon Frise's ancestors were first described by French sailors who found them in Tenerife in the Canary Islands during the fourteenth century. Sailors brought them to France, where they became popular pets for the nobles. In the nineteenth century, they were often used as performance dogs in circuses.

Looks: Bichons Frises are small and compact dogs. They look like powder puffs with a cottony white coat and round dark eyes. They have drop ears and long hairy tails that are curved over their backs.

Height: 9.5 to 11.5 inches

Weight: 10 to 14 pounds

Personality: Bichons Frises are happy-go-lucky dogs. They love everyone they meet, including kids and other dogs. They are very playful dogs.

Activity Level: Moderate

First Loves: Playing, their people

Best Families: Bichons Frises love older kids with time to adore them. They do fine living in apartments.

Pluses: Cheerful, easy to train, friendly, fun

Minuses: Hard to house-train, need to be groomed

Fun Fact: Bichons Frises are sometimes known as organ grinder dogs. In the nineteenth century, they performed tricks on sidewalks with organ grinders.

(See the charts on pages 60–61 for term definitions.)

BLACK AND TAN COONHOUND

Where They Are From: United States

History: Black and Tan Coonhounds were bred to hunt raccoon and opossums. They bay, or howl, to alert the hunter that they've chased an animal into a tree.

Looks: Black and Tan Coonhounds are large and muscular and have short, sleek black coats with tan markings. They have large heads and long drop ears. They have long sickle tails.

Height: 23 to 27 inches

Weight: 40 to 75 pounds

Personality: Black and Tan Coonhounds are typical hounds. They love everyone and enjoy being with kids and other dogs. They are very friendly and can be silly, but they are also stubborn and can be hard to train.

Activity Level: Moderate

First Loves: Hunting, kids

Best Families: Black and Tan Coonhounds love older kids who are patient. They do best living in houses with big fenced yards.

Pluses: Easy to groom, friendly, fun loving, good watchdogs, good with kids, good with other dogs

Minuses: Difficult to train, loud, steal food, stubborn, tend to wander

Fun Fact: The Black and Tan Coonhound is a fairly new breed but has a very old ancestor—the Talbot Hound. The Talbot Hound was popular in the eleventh century.

BLACK RUSSIAN TERRIER

Where They Are From: Russia

History: Black Russian Terriers were first bred by the Russian military in the early 1900s. They were bred from a cross between Rottweilers, Airedales, and Giant Schnauzers. They have worked as guards, herders, and even sled dogs.

Looks: Black Russian Terriers are large dogs with long heads. They have short drop ears. Their tails are naturally long but are often docked short. Their coats are short or medium length and can be wiry or straight. They are black or black and gray.

Height: 26 to 30 inches

Weight: No standard

Personality: Black Russian Terriers are fun-loving dogs

with a lot of energy. They adore their families, but they don't always like strangers.

Activity Level: High

First Loves: Their families, their home, working, playing

Best Families: Black Russian Terriers like mature older kids with a lot of time to train and exercise them and who are used to dogs. They don't mind where they live, but they need a lot of exercise.

Pluses: Affectionate with their families, full of energy, good watchdogs, hard workers, love to play

Minuses: Can be too protective, must be groomed, need lots of exercise, need to be trained

Fun Fact: Black Russian Terriers are also called Blackies.

BLOODHOUND

Where They Are From: Great Britain

History: The Bloodhound is a very old breed, dating to the twelfth century. Bloodhounds were once hunting dogs, but now they are kept as pets or as police dogs. They track down bad guys and victims.

Looks: Bloodhounds are very big dogs and have wrinkly skin all over their bodies. They have large heads with very long drop ears. Their eyes have heavy lids, and their jowls are big. Their feet are very large. Their tails are long and sickle shaped. They have short coats that are black and tan, liver and tan, or red.

Height: 23 to 27 inches

Weight: 80 to 110 pounds

Personality: Bloodhounds are big, energetic, goofy dogs with a zest for life.

They love everyone. They can be a little shy with new people. Sometimes they are stubborn.

Activity Level: High

First Loves: Sniffing, playing, eating

Best Families: Bloodhounds like families who are fun-loving, active, patient, and have lots of time for their dogs. They do best living in houses with big fenced yards.

Pluses: Amazing noses, friendly, good watchdogs, good with kids, good with other dogs, patient, playful

Minuses: Hard to train, loud, need lots of exercise, slobber a lot, stubborn, wander

Fun Fact: Early Bloodhounds were black or white. Black Bloodhounds were called Saint Huberts. White Bloodhounds were called Southern Hounds.

BORDER COLLIE

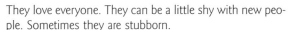

Where They Are From: Great Britain

History: Border Collies have herded sheep for more than two hundred years and are known for their "eye" when herding. *Eye* means they can tell the sheep what to do just by looking at them! Many say they are the world's best herders.

Looks: Border Collies are medium-size dogs with medium-length coats. Their coats are usually black with white around the neck and shoulders, although they can be any color. Their ears are erect or semiprick, and they have long furry tails.

Height: 18 to 22 inches

Weight: 30 to 50 pounds

Personality: Border Collies are superenergetic, superintense dogs who love to work and play. They are very intelligent and get along with most people. They may be shy with strangers, though. They herd anything, including kids and cats.

Activity Level: High

First Loves: Herding, playing, chasing, working

Best Families: Border Collies require families with as much energy as they have. They do best with people who will get involved in sports and other activities with them. They need to live in houses with big yards.

Pluses: Easy to train, fun and energetic, great sports or work dogs, smart

Minuses: Can be naughty, may chase cats, may herd kids, need tons of exercise

Fun Fact: In the 1995 movie *Babe*, a Border Collie named Fly adopts a wayward pig.

BORDER TERRIER

Where They Are From: Great Britain

History: Border Terriers are one of Great Britain's oldest terriers. They were bred to hunt with people on horses and flush foxes out of their dens.

Looks: Border Terriers are small but tough with round heads and black button noses. They have small drop ears, wiry coats, and bushy whiskers on their faces. Their tails are medium length and tapered. They may be red, grizzle and tan, blue and tan, or wheaten.

Height: 12 to 14 inches

Weight: 11.5 to 15.5 pounds

Personality: For terriers, they are easygoing and down-to-earth. They are gentle with kids and love to play. They will chase small animals and sometimes don't like other dogs.

Activity Level: High

First Loves: Playing, cuddles, chasing things

Best Families: Border Terriers do well with families who love cuddling but are also up for a hike or a long walk.

Pluses: Easier to keep than most terriers, up for almost anything, gentle, good with kids

Minuses: May chase small animals, may fight with other dogs, must be groomed, need a lot of exercise

Fun Fact: A Border Terrier was featured in the 2003 movie *Good Boy!* He played Hubble, an alien who comes to Earth.

(See the charts on pages 60–61 for term definitions.)

BORZOI

Where They Are From: Russia

History: There have been dogs that look like the Borzoi in Russia since the thirteenth century! They became an official breed in about 1650. They were popular with Russian nobility and were used to hunt wolves. The breed was almost wiped out after the Bolshevik Revolution in 1917.

Looks: Borzois are tall and elegant dogs with long legs and long heads. Their long silky coats can be any color.

Height: 26 to 32 inches

Weight: 55 to 105 pounds

Personality: Borzois are very independent, and they can be a little snappish. They adore their families but need to be introduced to kids as puppies, or they may become afraid of them. They will chase small animals.

Activity Level: Moderate

First Loves: Running, chasing, being adored

Best Families: Borzois do great with older kids or adults who give them lots of love and exercise. Their people must train them, or they can be naughty.

Pluses: Affectionate, good running partners, mellow

Minuses: Chase small animals, don't always get along with kids, need to be brushed a lot

Fun Fact: Because Borzois were once used to hunt wolves, they used to be called Russian Wolfhounds.

BOSTON TERRIER

Where They Are From: United States

History: Boston Terriers are small versions of the bull and terrier type dogs (including Bulldogs, American Pit Bull Terriers, and English Staffordshire Terriers). They were one of the first breeds created in the United States.

Looks: Boston Terriers are small and sturdy. They have square heads and short muzzles. Their eyes are big and round, and they have small prick ears, which may be natural or cropped. Their short coats are brindle, seal, or most commonly black with white markings.

Height: 15 to 17 inches

Weight: Dogs are split into three weight groups: less than 15 pounds, 15 to 20 pounds, and up to 25 pounds

Personality: Boston Terriers are gentle, fun-loving, and all-around good dogs. They are just as happy out for a romp in the woods as lying next to you on the couch. They are smart and get along with everyone.

Activity Level: Moderate

First Loves: People, playing, hanging out

Best Families: Boston Terriers need a family whose members are as affectionate with the terriers as they are with each other. Boston Terriers are flexible about where they live and what their families like to do.

Pluses: Easy to please, gentle, great dogs for families

Minuses: Can be a little stubborn, tend to have health problems

Fun Fact: Boston Terriers have been called a lot of different names, including the Little American Gentleman and Bullet Head!

BOUVIER DES FLANDRES

Where They Are From: Belgium

History: Bouvier des Flandres were first bred to be ranch dogs for herding and driving cattle. They have worked as police and military dogs, guide dogs, and search and rescue dogs.

Looks: Bouvier des Flandres are large and square-shaped dogs. They have big heads and small ears, which are naturally semi-erect or drop or are cropped erect. They have heavy, rough coats and mustaches, eyebrows, and beards. They are usually black but can also be salt-and-pepper, gray, brindle, or fawn.

Height: 23.5 to 27.5 inches

Weight: 65 to 100 pounds

Personality: Bouvier des Flandres are brave and protective dogs but very gentle and loyal. If they are raised with children, they do well with them.

Activity Level: High

First Loves: Their people, being outdoors

Best Families: Bouvier des Flandres do well with people who can give them love and attention but aren't pushovers.

Pluses: Devoted to family, good watchdogs, mellow

Minuses: Can be overprotective, must be brushed often, need to be trained or they can be bossy

Fun Fact: Bouviers are sometimes called Cow Dogs because they were originally used to herd cattle.

BOXER

Where They Are From: Germany

History: Boxers were originally herding dogs when they were bred way back in the sixteenth century. Since then, they have been fighting dogs, bull baiters, police dogs, military dogs, and pets to many, many families.

Looks: Boxers are medium size and muscular. They have wide heads, thick upper lips, and drop ears. Sometimes their ears are cropped so they stand erect. Their tails are

usually docked, meaning they are shortened. They have short coats that are fawn or brindle colored with black masks.

Height: 21 to 25 inches
Weight: 50 to 80 pounds
Personality: Boxers are fun-loving and all-around great family pets. They love to play and are very gentle with and loyal to their families. They love kids.
Activity Level: High
First Loves: Kids, playing
Best Families: Boxers do well with families who like to do lots of outdoor activities but also have time to train them.
Pluses: Easy to train, friendly, love kids
Minuses: Can be protective so they need to be trained, need a lot of attention
Fun Fact: Boxers were named for the way they fight. Like human boxers, they stand up on their hind feet and use their front paws to box.

BRIARD

Where They Are From: France
History: The Briard is a very old breed. Briards have been used for sheepherding and flock guarding since the Middle Ages. It's said that Thomas Jefferson brought the first Briards to America!
Looks: Briards are big, shaggy dogs. They have large heads and either natural drop or cropped erect ears. They are covered with long hair that is any color except white. Even their dark eyes are covered with hair.
Height: 22 to 27 inches
Weight: 70 to 90 pounds
Personality: Briards are protective, love to herd, and are loyal to their families. They are suspicious of strangers. They are very smart and need to be trained.
Activity Level: Moderate
First Loves: Herding, their families
Best Families: Briards love playful kids. They need families who will train them and give them lots of exercise.

(See the charts on pages 60–61 for term definitions.)

Pluses: Friendly, fun, loyal
Minuses: Can be protective, independent, need a lot of exercise, need a lot of grooming
Fun Fact: What do Briards have in common with cheese? Both Briards and Brie cheese are named for the French province of Brie!

BRITTANY

Where They Are From: France
History: Brittanys' ancestors are French spaniels and English setters. They were first bred for hunting in the mid-nineteenth century. They are still popular hunting dogs.
Looks: Brittanys are medium size and muscular with medium-length wavy coats that are orange and white or liver and white. Their noses are never black—they may be fawn, tan, brown, or pink. They have short drop ears and no tails.
Height: 17.5 to 20.5 inches
Weight: 30 to 40 pounds
Personality: Brittanys are full of spunk and love their friends and family. They can be a little wary with strangers. They are go, go, go dogs!
Activity Level: High

First Loves: Being on the go, their people, running, playing, hunting

Best Families: Brittanys do well with families who are full of energy, just as they are. They need lots of exercise to keep calm, so their families should be prepared for that.

Pluses: Always ready for a new adventure; love almost everyone, including kids and other animals

Minuses: Need lots and lots of exercise, need to be brushed a lot

Fun Fact: In France, they call the Brittany the *Epaneul Breton* (French Brittany). Breeders say the French Brittany is so different from the American Brittany they should be considered different breeds.

BRUSSELS GRIFFON

Where They Are From: Belgium

History: Brussels Griffons were first bred to be ratters on farms and in town. Some of their ancestors include Affenpinschers, Pugs, and English Toy Spaniels.

Looks: Brussels Griffons are small, solid dogs with large round heads and short noses. They may have smooth coats or rough coats with a fringe of hair around the face. They may be reddish brown, black with reddish brown markings, or black.

Height: 8 to 10 inches

Weight: 8 to 12 pounds

Personality: Brussels Griffons are spunky, sometimes overconfident little dogs. Every Brussels Griffon is an individual—some are friendly and outgoing, others can be shy.

Activity Level: Low

First Loves: Their person or people

Best Families: Every Brussels Griffon looks for something different in a best friend. Some love kids, others don't.

Pluses: Individuality, spunky, tons of personality

Minuses: Can be overconfident, not always friendly with strangers or kids

Fun Fact: In the 1997 hit movie *As Good as It Gets*, a Brussels Griffon named Jill played the canine character Verdell.

BULLDOG

Where They Are From: Great Britain

History: Bulldogs have changed a lot since they were first bred in the early nineteenth century. They were originally used to hold bulls for butchers, and then they were used as bull-baiting dogs. Bull baiting was a blood sport where a dog teased and attacked a tethered, or tied up, bull. Since bull baiting was made illegal in the mid-nineteenth century, Bulldogs have been popular companion dogs.

Looks: Bulldogs are short but powerful with heavy bodies. They have very large heads and big jowls. They have short coats that come in any color except black.

Height: No standard, but they tend to be around 12 to 16 inches

Weight: 40 to 50 pounds

Personality: Bulldogs are gentle dogs. They love people and most other animals and make poor watchdogs. They'd rather lick you than bark at you. They are very mellow.

Activity Level: Low

First Loves: Hanging out with their people, sleeping, eating

Best Families: Bulldogs' best families love to cuddle and are somewhat mellow.

Pluses: Patient with everyone, including pesky younger siblings; very friendly

Minuses: Don't like to play a lot; tend to drool, snore, snort, and fart a lot; very low key

Fun Fact: Some famous Bulldog owners include presidents Warren Harding and Calvin Coolidge, Ice-T, George Clooney, and Ozzy Osbourne.

BULLMASTIFF

Where They Are From: Great Britain

History: Bullmastiffs were bred in the mid-nineteenth century to help catch game poachers (illegal hunters) on large English estates. They were supposed to hold but not hurt the poachers. The breed was created by breeding Bulldogs and Mastiffs together.

Looks: Bullmastiffs are large, powerful dogs with big heads and wrinkly foreheads. They have short coats that are fawn, red, or brindle. They have dark masks and dark ears.

Height: 24 to 27 inches

Weight: 100 to 130 pounds

Personality: Bullmastiffs are gentle giants. They are brave but patient and get along with almost everyone. They are very mellow but will protect their people and their homes.

Activity Level: Low

First Loves: Their people, their home

Best Families: Bullmastiffs do well with people who love to cuddle but also have the time and experience to teach them how to control their strength.

Pluses: Brave, gentle, good watchdogs, loving

Minuses: Drool, need a lot of space, need to be taught to control their strength

Fun Fact: The Bullmastiff used to be called the Gamekeeper's Night Dog. A gamekeeper was a guard who kept poachers from hunting on private land.

(See the charts on pages 60–61 for term definitions.)

BULL TERRIER

Where They Are From: Great Britain

History: Bull Terriers were first bred in the mid-nineteenth century and were originally known as Bull and Terriers. They were used to bait bulls and in pit fights. They are now popular companion dogs.

Looks: Bull Terriers are medium size and muscular. They have egg-shaped heads, small eyes, and erect ears. Their short coats are white, red, fawn, or brindle. White dogs sometimes have dark markings on their heads. Dark dogs often have white markings.

Height: 21 to 22 inches

Weight: 45 to 65 pounds

Personality: Bull Terriers are lively and playful. They have a zest for life and are friendly and affectionate. They can be a handful. Many do not get along with other animals, especially other dogs.

Activity Level: High

First Loves: Their people, playing

Best Families: Bull Terriers love kids but their families must be able to train them and always keep them under control.

Pluses: Friendly and affectionate, fun, love people and kids

Minuses: Headstrong, need lots of attention, need to be kept busy, need training, often aggressive with other dogs and animals

Fun Fact: Probably because of their interesting looks, there have been more than a few Bull Terriers used as spokesmodels. A Bull Terrier puppy currently represents Target stores.

CAIRN TERRIER

Where They Are From: Great Britain/Scotland

History: Cairn Terriers are from the Isle of Skye and originally hunted otters, foxes, and rodents on the island's rocky cliffs. Some of their relatives include Dandie Dinmont Terriers and West Highland White Terriers.

Looks: Cairn Terriers are small but solid, with broad heads and shaggy coats. They have short tails that they carry upright. They may be any color other than white. Often their coats are darker on the ears, muzzles, and tail tips.

Height: 9.5 to 10 inches

Weight: 13 to 14 pounds

Personality: Cairn Terriers are outgoing and friendly. They are calmer than many terriers and get along with almost everyone, including kids and most animals. They can be a little bossy.

Activity Level: Moderate

First Loves: Playing, their people or person

Best Families: Cairn Terriers do best with people who will give them the love and attention they crave. Their families must be willing to train them.

Pluses: Get along with most people and animals, mellow compared to other terriers, outgoing

Minuses: Can be bossy and a little feisty so need training and socialization, must be groomed, require a lot of attention

Fun Fact: Toto in the movie *The Wizard of Oz* is a Cairn Terrier.

CANAAN DOG

Where They Are From: Israel

History: Canaan Dogs are ancient dogs. They have been kept by people in the area that is now Israel for more than four thousand years. They have been used as herders and guard dogs. Today, the Israeli military uses Canaan Dogs as mine detectors, messengers, and search and rescue dogs.

Looks: Canaan Dogs are medium-size dogs. They have small prick ears and dark eyes. Their tails are curled over their backs. They have thick, straight coats that are cream, red, brown, white, or black. Some have black masks or white markings.

Height: 19 to 24 inches

Weight: 35 to 55 pounds

Personality: Canaan Dogs are lively, alert dogs. They are always aware of what is going on around them. They love their families, but they don't like strangers. They are sensitive and don't like to be teased.

Activity Level: Moderate

First Loves: Their people, working, playing

Best Families: Canaan Dogs do well with kids who are older and mature and are used to dogs. Canaan Dogs don't mind whether they live in the city or the country.

Pluses: Affectionate with their families, good dogs for activities, good watchdogs, hard workers, independent, very intelligent

Minuses: Can be too protective, don't like to be teased, must be supervised with young kids and other animals, need training

Fun Fact: Canaan Dogs often lived with Bedouins, tribal people of the Arabian Desert. They herded camels, sheep, and goats and moved around following water and food sources. The dogs were flock and camp guardians.

CARDIGAN WELSH CORGI

Where They Are From: Wales

History: Cardigan Welsh Corgis are ancestors of ancient herding dogs brought to Wales by the Celts about three thousand years ago. They are heelers of the first order—using their tough mouths to nip at cattle's heels. Like their close relative the Pembroke Welsh Corgi, they have become popular companion dogs.

Looks: Cardigan Welsh Corgis are short but long and solid with bowed front legs. They have a foxy look to their faces and large erect ears. They have medium-length soft coats that may be brindle, sable, red, blue merle, or black, with or without tan and white markings. They have long brush tails.

Height: 10.5 to 12.5 inches

Weight: 25 to 38 pounds

Personality: Cardigan Welsh Corgis are very active dogs. They are smart, fearless, and full of vigor. They love to play and work and are loving with their families. They don't always like strangers.

Activity Level: Moderate

First Loves: Herding, their people, playing

Best Families: Cardigan Welsh Corgis do great with families who love to play and cuddle with them but who can be firm and let them know when they need to mellow out.

Pluses: Good watchdogs, loving, loyal, playful, smart

Minuses: Bark a lot, can be bossy, can be shy with strangers, may herd kids and cats, shed

Fun Fact: In Welsh, *cor* means "dwarf" and *cur* means "working dog." *Gi* means "dog." No one's quite sure whether the name *corgi* originally meant dwarf dog or working dog. Perhaps both!

CAVALIER KING CHARLES SPANIEL

Where They Are From: Great Britain

History: Cavalier King Charles Spaniels are related to the old spaniels seen in European paintings from the sixteenth century. These dogs had almost disappeared when in the 1920s, an American offered a reward for the best old-type spaniel. The contest spurred a revival, and they are now very popular dogs again.

Looks: Cavalier King Charles Spaniels are small with round heads and long feathered drop ears. They have long silky coats that are black and tan, red, white with chestnut markings, or black, white, and tan.

Height: 12 to 13 inches

Weight: 13 to 18 pounds

Personality: Cavalier King Charles Spaniels are loving and loyal to their people. They get along with most people and animals and are easygoing.

Activity Level: Low to moderate

First Loves: Their family, a comfortable couch, a good walk

Best Families: Cavaliers do best with people with lots of time for them. Their families should enjoy having a dog in their laps at all times.

Pluses: Easygoing and adaptable, loving and affectionate

Minuses: Need a lot of attention, need to be groomed

Fun Fact: Cavalier King Charles Spaniels are named after kings Charles I and Charles II of England, who both kept this type of dog as pets.

(See the charts on pages 60–61 for term definitions.)

CHESAPEAKE BAY RETRIEVER

Where They Are From: United States

History: Chesapeake Bay Retrievers are related to two Newfoundland-type dogs who were saved from a shipwreck in 1807. Named Sailor and Canton, the dogs were bred with other duck retrievers from the Chesapeake Bay.

Looks: Chesapeake Bay Retrievers are medium-size dogs with short coats and short drop ears. They may be brown, sedge, or dead grass in color, and their eyes are yellow or amber.

Height: 21 to 26 inches

Weight: 55 to 80 pounds

Personality: Cheerful and outgoing, Chesapeake Bay Retrievers love to work and to play. They love their families, especially the children. They don't always get along with strangers or other dogs and will even fight with other dogs.

Activity Level: Moderate to high

First Loves: Family, kids, water, working, playing

Best Families: Chesapeake Bay Retrievers love active kids who will teach them to get along with everyone.

Pluses: Good with kids, great dogs to do canine sports with, loyal to and loving with their families

Minuses: May fight with other dogs, not always good with strangers

Fun Fact: Chesapeake Bay Retrievers are made for swimming. The short coat is oily to protect it from the water, and the dogs have webbed feet to help them swim better.

CHIHUAHUA

Where They Are From: Mexico

History: It's not known whether Chihuahuas descend from an ancient breed kept by the Toltecs and the Aztecs called the Techichi, or if they were brought to Mexico by Chinese traders.

Looks: Chihuahuas are small, delicate dogs with round, apple-shaped heads and large erect ears. Their coats can be short or long and any color. The most common colors are red, sable, brindle, black and tan, fawn, and tricolor.

Height: 6 to 9 inches

Weight: 2 to 6 pounds

Personality: Chihuahuas are high-strung dogs who are playful and affectionate with their people. They can be nervous and don't always like kids or dogs of other breeds.

Activity Level: Low

First Loves: Their person, being pampered

Best Families: Chihuahuas do well with calm and mature older kids or adults who treat them like the royalty they are.

Pluses: Don't require much exercise or grooming, fit into apartment life, playful and affectionate with their families

Minuses: Can be nippy, delicate and can be injured easily, nervous

Fun Fact: The world's smallest dog is a Chihuahua named Danka. She is only 7.4 inches long and 5.4 inches tall. That's smaller than this book! One famous Chihuahua is the Taco Bell mascot, a doggy actor named Gidget. Gidget also played the mother of Bruiser in *Legally Blonde 2*.

CHINESE CRESTED

Where They Are From: China

History: No one is sure, but it is believed that Chinese Crested dogs were originally brought to China from Africa by traders. They were popular dogs with sailors, who used them as ratters on ships, and they were common in port cities.

Looks: Chinese Cresteds are small, delicate dogs with large erect ears. There are two varieties—hairless and powder puffs. The hairless Chinese Cresteds have gray and pink skin, with hair on the top of their heads, on their paws, and on the tip of their tails. Powder puffs have long hair all over their bodies. Their coats can be any color.

Height: 11 to 13 inches

Weight: 10 to 14 pounds

Personality: Chinese Cresteds are playful and curious and get along with almost everyone.

Activity Level: Moderate

First Loves: Their people, playing

Best Families: Chinese Cresteds do well with older kids who keep them warm, love them, and play with them.

Pluses: Easy to keep in an apartment, easygoing, friendly, like everyone, love to play, need minimal grooming

Minuses: Hairless dogs need daily skin care—washing and lotion, sensitive to cold (must wear clothes in cold weather), sensitive to sun (must wear sunscreen)

Fun Fact: Chinese Cresteds were once used as a sort of living hot water bottle! The warm body of a hairless dog was pressed against sore backs for pain relief.

CHINESE SHAR-PEI

Where They Are From: China

History: Chinese Shar-Peis are ancient dogs who may go back to the Han Dynasty in 200 BC! They were first used as all-purpose dogs, guards, hunters, fighters, and companions. They are now popular companions.

Looks: Chinese Shar-Peis are medium-size dogs with loose, wrinkly skin all over their bodies and with curled tails. Their oval-shaped muzzles look almost like hippopotamus', and they have small ears. They can have very short prickly hair or slightly longer coats. The coats can be any color. Their lips and tongues are bluish black.

Height: 18 to 20 inches

Weight: 45 to 60 pounds

Personality: Chinese Shar-Peis are warmhearted dogs who love their families but are not always good with

strangers—both human and animal. They are very smart and can be serious.

Activity Level: Moderate

First Loves: Their people, their homes

Best Families: Chinese Shar-Peis do well with mature older kids or adults who will teach them how to get along with both new and old friends.

Pluses: Good family dogs, good watchdogs, loving and friendly with their friends and families

Minuses: Need a lot of training, need to have their wrinkles cleaned because the folds get infected, not always friendly with strangers

Fun Fact: The name *shar-pei* means "sand-paper skin" in Chinese—referring to their short bristly coat.

CHOW CHOW

Where They Are From: China

History: Chow Chows may be so old that they go back to the Han Dynasty around 300 BC. They were originally hunting dogs and have also been used as herding dogs and guard dogs. Some of their ancestors include Tibetan Mastiffs and Samoyeds.

Looks: Chow Chows are medium-size dogs with large heads and very heavy coats that may be short or long. They may be cream, cinnamon, blue, black, or red in color. Their tails curl over their backs, and they have small erect ears. Their small eyes are deeply set, so it's hard for them to see objects that aren't right in front of them. They have bluish black tongues.

Height: 17 to 20 inches

Weight: 45 to 70 pounds

Personality: Chow Chows are smart dogs who are quiet and serious. They are very loyal to their families but don't always get along with strangers and often don't like other dogs.

Activity Level: Low to moderate

First Loves: Their people, their homes, their privacy

Best Families: Chow Chows do well with mature older kids or adults who make sure they get the training they need to get along with new people and animals.

Pluses: Adapt to city or country homes, good watchdogs, loyal

Minuses: Can be unfriendly if they are not trained, need to be groomed

Fun Fact: Cargo brought to England on Chinese ships was called chow chow. When Chow Chows were transported to England, sailors probably just called the dogs Chow Chow because they didn't know what else to call them!

CLUMBER SPANIEL

Where They Are From: Great Britain

History: Clumber Spaniels were originally bred by a French noble. Before the French Revolution began in 1789, he brought his dogs to the Clumber Park estate in England. They were used by nobles to hunt birds.

Looks: Clumber Spaniels are short, heavy dogs. They have large heads with long drop ears. Their silky coats are white with lemon or orange markings. Their large noses are light brown.

Height: 17 to 20 inches

Weight: 55 to 85 pounds

Personality: Clumber Spaniels are happy, mellow dogs. They love kids and other animals, and they are great family dogs. They don't always like strangers. They can be a bit stubborn.

Activity Level: Low

First Loves: Their families, kids

(See the charts on pages 60–61 for term definitions.)

Best Families: Clumber Spaniels love mellow kids who like to hang out. They don't mind whether they live in the city or the country.

Pluses: Don't need a lot of exercise, friendly, gentle, good watchdogs

Minuses: Can be unfriendly with new people, not much for doggy sports

Fun Fact: Clumber Spaniels probably resulted from breeding Basset Hounds with some type of spaniel.

COCKER SPANIEL

Where They Are From: United States

History: Cocker Spaniels are the smallest bird-hunting dogs. They were bred to hunt woodcocks (a shorebird), but now they are almost always kept as pets. They are closely related to the English Cocker Spaniel.

Looks: Cocker Spaniels are small with silky medium-length coats that can be black, ASCOB (any solid color other than black), or parti-colored. They have long drop ears and short docked tails.

Height: 14 to 15 inches

Weight: 18 to 25 pounds

Personality: Cocker Spaniels are lively, upbeat, and full of fun. They are smart and like to learn new things.

Activity Level: Moderate

First Loves: Their people, playing, children

Best Families: Cocker Spaniels do well with families who play and cuddle with them but also teach them manners.

Pluses: Always up for fun, good with kids, not too hyper

Minuses: Long ears tend to get cruddy, need to be groomed, overbreeding in the United States produced Cocker Spaniels with aggression problems (if buying a puppy, research breeders carefully before choosing one)

Fun Fact: In the United States, *Cocker Spaniel* refers to the American Cocker Spaniel. Outside of the United States, *Cocker Spaniel* refers to the English Cocker Spaniel.

COLLIE

Where They Are From: Scotland

History: Collies have worked as farm dogs for hundreds of years and have been herders, guards, and pets. They became popular in the nineteenth century. They were a favorite of Queen Victoria, who ruled Great Britain from 1837 to 1901.

Looks: Collies are large dogs. They have long, narrow heads with semiprick ears. They can have long hair (called rough coated) or short hair (called smooth coated). Their coats are black, tan, and white; blue merle; or sable and white.

Height: 22 to 26 inches

Weight: 55 to 80 pounds

Personality: Collies are bubbly, friendly dogs. They are very smart and love to learn new things. They like almost everyone. They are good with kids and make great family dogs. They can take a little while to warm up to new people. They tend to bark.

Activity Level: Moderate

First Loves: Their families, kids

Best Families: Collies love families who have time for them. They don't mind where they live, but they do like houses with yards.

Pluses: Easy to train, friendly, good dogs for canine activities, good watchdogs, great family dogs

Minuses: Bark a lot, can be a little unfriendly with strangers, shed a lot

Fun Fact: Their name comes from the word *colley*, which means "black sheep" in Scottish. Probably the best known Collie in U.S. history is Lassie. Lassie, a rough-coated Collie, was the main character of books, movies, and even TV series!

CURLY-COATED RETRIEVER

Where They Are From: Great Britain

History: Curly-Coated Retrievers were bred as hunting dogs. Their job was to retrieve waterfowl (ducks and geese) and birds such as quail and partridges. Some of their ancestors include Irish Water Spaniels, Newfoundlands, and Poodles.

Looks: Curly-Coated Retrievers are medium size with a curly coat that covers their entire bodies. The only place

the coat is straight is on their faces, fronts of their legs, and feet. They are black or liver colored and have medium-length drop ears.

Height: 23 to 27 inches

Weight: 65 to 85 pounds

Personality: Curly-Coated Retrievers are playful and outgoing and enjoy children and other animals. They take a while to warm up to strangers.

Activity Level: Moderate to high

First Loves: Their people, playing fetch, water

Best Families: Curly-Coated Retrievers are great with kids who love to run and swim as much as they do.

Pluses: Good watchdogs, live for their families, love to play

Minuses: Must be trained, need lots of attention, take a while to warm up to new people

Fun Fact: Their curly coats protect the retrievers from water, wind, cold, heat, branches, and anything else they may encounter in the field.

DACHSHUND

Where They Are From: Germany

History: Dachshunds may have been around since the sixteenth century. They were originally bred to hunt badgers and then bred to be smaller to hunt foxes and rabbits. Now they are popular pet dogs.

Looks: Dachshunds are often called wiener dogs because

(See the charts on pages 60–61 for term definitions.)

they are much longer than they are tall. They have very short legs and long drop ears. They can be smooth haired, wirehaired, or long-haired. The color can be red, cream, black, chocolate, blue, or fawn.

Height: 9 to 10 inches

Weight: 16 to 32 pounds

(There is also a miniature type who is 5 to 9 inches and 9 to 11 pounds.)

Personality: Dachshunds are smart, energetic, and friendly. They can get bored easily. They like almost everyone but can take a little while to warm up to strangers.

Activity Level: Moderate

First Loves: Their people, playing

Best Families: Dachshunds do well with families with the time and interest to walk them and give them lots of attention.

Pluses: Fit into an apartment or house, city or country; friendly, playful

Minuses: Can be stubborn, easily bored, hard to house-train, like to dig, long-haired dogs need grooming

Fun Fact: Dachshund mummies? It's believed that Dachshund-like dogs existed in ancient Egypt.

DALMATIAN

Where They Are From: Great Britain

History: Dalmatians' ancestors are believed to have come from Dalmatia, an Eastern European region along the Adriatic Sea. In Great Britain, Dalmatians were developed as coach dogs. Their job was to run alongside coaches and to guard the coach and passengers.

Looks: Dalmatians are large, strong dogs with short coats that are white with spots of black or liver. Their heads are pear shaped, and they have short drop ears.

Height: 19 to 24 inches

Weight: 45 to 65 pounds

Personality: Dalmatians are happy-go-lucky dogs who are always on the go. They love their friends and families but can take a while to warm up to new people. They live to work and to play.

Activity Level: High

First Loves: Running, chasing horses and cars, their people

Best Families: Dalmatians need families who will give

them lots of exercise and attention but make sure they don't get into trouble.

Pluses: Affectionate, enjoy sports, fun, good watchdogs, lively

Minuses: Can be unfriendly with strangers, chase cars and animals, need lots of exercise

Fun Fact: Dalmatians are born white and develop their spots as they grow. Dalmatians are associated with firefighters because fire engines were once drawn by horses. They guarded the fire engines as they guarded other coaches.

DANDIE DINMONT TERRIER

Where They Are From: Scotland

History: Dandie Dinmont Terriers were bred for hunting otters and badgers in the eighteenth century. They are usually kept as pet dogs now.

Looks: Dandie Dinmont Terriers are unusual-looking dogs. Sometimes they're described as having no straight lines. They are short with long backs, large round heads, and crooked front legs. Their coats are a combination of wooly and harsh hair and are pepper or mustard colored.

Height: 8 to 11 inches

Weight: 18 to 24 pounds

Personality: Dandie Dinmont Terriers are intelligent, gentle dogs with a happy outlook on life. They get along with kids, dogs, and other animals as long as they meet them early in life. They can be pushy.

Activity Level: Moderate

First Loves: Their people

Best Families: Dandie Dinmont Terriers do well with people who have time to play and cuddle with them, as well as teach them right from wrong.

Pluses: Brave, loving, low key

Minuses: Can be pushy, independent, need to be groomed, need to be introduced to kids and other animals when young in order to get along with them

Fun Fact: These terriers get their name from the book *Guy Mannering* by Sir Walter Scott, published in 1814. In the book, the character Dandie Dinmont keeps six of the terriers.

DOBERMAN PINSCHER

Where They Are From: Germany

History: Doberman Pinschers were bred by Louis Dobermann to be police, military, and guard dogs. Just some of their ancestors include Rottweilers, Manchester Terriers, Greyhounds, and German Pinschers.

Looks: Doberman Pinschers are large and muscular with long heads. They have short coats that are black, red, blue, or fawn with tan markings. They have drop ears and long tails. The ears are often cropped, and the tails are often docked.

Height: 24 to 28 inches

Weight: 55 to 90 pounds

Personality: Doberman Pinschers are smart, brave, and loyal. They love their families and get along with almost everyone they meet. They like kids and play well with other dogs.

Activity Level: Moderate

First Loves: Their people

Best Families: Doberman Pinschers need families who will play and snuggle with them but who will also train them.

Pluses: Easy to groom, fun, good watchdogs, loving, playful

Minuses: Can be overprotective, need exercise

Fun Fact: There is a life-size statue of a Doberman Pinscher on the island of Guam. It commemorates the twenty-five Dobermans who died there while serving with the marines during World War II. The statue is called *Always Faithful*.

ENGLISH COCKER SPANIEL

Where They Are From: Great Britain

History: English Cocker Spaniels were bred to hunt woodcocks, woodland game birds. Their ancestors include other field spaniels.

Looks: English Cocker Spaniels are medium-size dogs with long heads and very long drop ears. They have medium-length silky hair with feathering on their ears, tails, and legs. They may be white with red, blue, liver, or black markings or black, red, or liver with or without tan markings. Some dogs have ticking or are roan.

Height: 15 to 17 inches

Weight: 26 to 34 pounds

Personality: English Cocker Spaniels are smart and love to learn. They are full of energy and enjoy working and playing. They get along with most people and animals and adore their families.

Activity Level: Moderate

First Loves: Hunting, playing, working, family

Best Families: English Cocker Spaniels need families who include them in their activities.

Pluses: Fun loving, gentle, good watchdogs, love kids and other animals

Minuses: Ears tend to get dirty, need to be groomed

Fun Fact: English Cocker Spaniels were considered to be the same breed as Springer Spaniels until 1892. They were considered the same breed as American Cocker Spaniels until 1936.

ENGLISH FOXHOUND

Where They Are From: Great Britain

History: English Foxhounds were bred to hunt red foxes. Some of their ancestors include Bloodhounds and Greyhounds. They may have been around since the thirteenth century.

Looks: English Foxhounds are large dogs with long heads and drop ears. They have short coats that are black, tan, and white or piebald. They have long tails.

Height: 21 to 25 inches

Weight: 65 to 70 pounds

Personality: English Foxhounds are fun and playful and love to chase just about everything, including cats. They

(See the charts on pages 60–61 for term definitions.)

are typical hounds and like to bark (but not in a mean way) and will follow a scent trail. That means they will wander. They can also be a bit stubborn. They love children and other dogs.

Activity Level: High

First Loves: Chasing, sniffing, playing with kids and with other dogs

Best Families: English Foxhounds do best with people who can give them lots of playtime in the great outdoors but who are responsible enough to keep them from wandering or chasing critters. They probably should not have any cats or small animals in their homes.

Pluses: Easy groomers, gentle, great with kids and dogs, lots of energy for activities and sports

Minuses: Can be loud, can be stubborn, difficult to train, will chase small animals, will wander

Fun Fact: English Foxhounds tend to yodel when they speak rather than bark.

ENGLISH SETTER

Where They Are From: Great Britain

History: English Setters date back to the sixteenth century. They were first bred to find and point game. Pointing is when the dog stops and "points" in the direction of the bird. Now there are two types of English Setter: one for work and one for show. The show type is larger than the work type.

Looks: English Setters are large dogs with long heads and tails. They have long silky hair with feathering on their legs, chests, bellies, tails, and ears. They can be white and orange; white and black; white and lemon; white and liver; white, black, and tan; solid white; or blue, orange, liver, or lemon belton (meaning the color is ticked with white).

Height/Weight: There are two sizes of English setters.

Show English Setters are 50 to 70 pounds and 24 to 25 inches high. Working English Setters are usually bred about 25 percent smaller.

Personality: English Setters are sweet, friendly, and outgoing dogs. They love everyone and get along very well with children. They will bark but only as a greeting. They love to play.

Activity Level: High

First Loves: People, running, playing, being outside

Best Families: English Setters' best families are outdoorsy kids who love to play. They like to live in the country or at least in the suburbs with lots of open areas.

Pluses: Friendly and gentle, good watchdogs (they will bark but they won't bite), good with most people and other animals

Minuses: Can be difficult to train, must be groomed (their coats can get snarled), need a lot of exercise

Fun Fact: English Setters are known as the sweetest of all the setters.

ENGLISH SPRINGER SPANIEL

Where They Are From: Great Britain

History: English Springer Spaniels were originally bred as hunting dogs. Their specialty was to find, flush, and retrieve pheasants. (When hunting dogs "flush" birds, they spook the birds out of their hiding places so the hunter can see them.) They are closely related to the English Cocker Spaniel.

Looks: English Springer Spaniels are medium size and sturdy. They have long noses and long drop ears. Their medium-length coats are flat or wavy with feathering on the ears, legs, and chests. They can be liver and white; black and white; liver; blue roan; or liver or black and white with tan markings. They have freckles on their faces.

Height: 19 to 20 inches

Weight: 40 to 50 pounds

Personality: English Springer Spaniels are lively, alert, and eager to learn new things. They love playing and get along with kids and other animals. Sometimes they can be a little greedy with their toys and food.

Activity Level: High

First Loves: Playing, family, their stuff

Best Families: English Springer Spaniels like older kids who can keep up with their active lifestyle and teach them to share.

Pluses: Lively and playful, loving with almost everyone

Minuses: Can take a little while to warm up to new people; can be greedy or possessive with their toys, food, and people; need a lot of attention and exercise

Fun Fact: Millie, former First Lady Barbara Bush's English Springer Spaniel, "wrote" a book, *Millie's Book*, that was on the best-sellers list for twenty-nine weeks in 1992.

ENTLEBUCHER

Where They Are From: Switzerland

History: Entlebuchers are one of the four Swiss mountain dogs. They were probably originally bred from Roman Mastiffs and local Swiss dogs more than two thousand years ago. They were used to drive (move) cattle, to herd, and as guards.

Looks: Entlebuchers are medium-size dogs. They have small drop ears and bob tails. They have short coats that are tricolor, with a black base and white and rust markings.

Height: 16 to 20 inches

Weight: 55 to 65 pounds

Personality: They are happy, playful dogs. They are smart and love to learn new things. Most Entlebuchers are friendly with everyone they meet.

Activity Level: Moderate

First Loves: Playing, their people

Best Family: Entlebuchers do well with outdoorsy families. They prefer to live in the country or at least in a house with a big yard and plenty of parks nearby.

Pluses: Easy to groom, easy to train, friendly, good watchdogs

Minuses: Can be too much dog for some people, need training

Fun Fact: They are the smallest of the Swiss mountain dogs (although that doesn't mean they aren't just as energetic as the others!).

FLAT-COATED RETRIEVER

Where They Are From: Great Britain

History: Flat-Coated Retrievers were bred as hunters in the nineteenth century. A few of their ancestors are a now-extinct breed called St. Johns Newfoundlands, setters, and water spaniels.

Looks: Flat-Coated Retrievers look a lot like long-haired Labrador Retrievers. They are large with broad heads and drop ears. They have long straight tails. Their silky coats are black or liver with feathering on their bodies, ears, legs, and tails.

Height: 22 to 24.5 inches

Weight: 60 to 70 pounds

Personality: Flat-Coated Retrievers are outgoing and full of fun. They love to be busy, either working or playing. They get along with just about everyone, including dogs and kids. Sometimes they can be almost too friendly!

Activity Level: High

First Loves: Playing, family, work, swimming

Best Families: Flat-Coated Retrievers do very well with older kids who will keep up with their out-of-this-world energy!

Pluses: Enthusiastic, great dogs for activities or sports, very friendly

Minuses: Can get overexcited, may have too much energy for young kids or older people, need lots of exercise and attention, not good watchdogs

Fun Fact: Flat-Coated Retrievers mature more slowly than most dog breeds. They usually begin to act more like adults at around three to five years old.

FOX TERRIER (SMOOTH FOX TERRIER AND WIRE FOX TERRIER)

Where They Are From: Great Britain

History: Both the Smooth Fox Terrier and the Wire Fox Terrier were bred to flush foxes from their dens. Their ancestors include the Bull Terrier and the Beagle.

Looks: Fox Terriers are small, muscular dogs with narrow heads and semiprick ears. They have medium-length tails that are held erect. The Smooth Fox Terrier has a short coat, and the Wire Fox Terrier has a wiry coat. Both are

(See the charts on pages 60–61 for term definitions.)

mostly white with tan, black, or tan and black markings.

Height: 14 to 15.5 inches

Weight: 15 to 19 pounds

Personality: Fox Terriers are friendly, feisty little dogs who are brave and outgoing. They will chase smaller animals, and sometimes they'll fight with other dogs. They can be a little too active for young kids.

Activity Level: High

First Loves: Digging, playing, chasing

Best Families: Fox Terriers enjoy older kids who give them lots to do so they won't have to entertain themselves (a bored Fox Terrier can be naughty!).

Pluses: Adapt to city or country life, enjoy dog sports and activities, good watchdogs, like to play, loyal and loving, outgoing, smart

Minuses: Bark, can be possessive over their food and toys, chase small animals, dig, may fight with other dogs, need lots of exercise and attention, not easy to train

Fun Fact: The AKC recognizes the Smooth Fox Terrier and the Wire Fox Terrier as separate breeds, even though the only real difference between the two is their coats.

FRENCH BULLDOG

Where They Are From: France

History: When English lace workers moved to France for better jobs during the mid-nineteenth century, they brought their miniature Bulldogs with them. These dogs bred with local French dogs, and the result was the French Bulldog!

Looks: French Bulldogs are small but heavy dogs with big batlike ears. They have short faces and upturned noses and lots of loose skin and wrinkles around their heads and necks. Their short tails are straight or screw. They have short coats that are white, fawn, cream, brindle, or brindle and white.

Height: 10 to 12 inches
Weight: 18 to 28 pounds
Personality: French Bulldogs are sweet and easygoing. They like everyone but are especially attached to one person. They can be a little stubborn, but they are mostly happy to go with the flow.
Activity Level: Low
First Loves: Their person
Best Families: French Bulldogs need people with a lot of time to devote to them. They would rather be one person's dog than a family dog.
Pluses: Can live in an apartment, don't need much exercise, gentle, loving, loyal to one person
Minuses: Need to have their wrinkles cleaned, not good family dogs (only really bond with one person), not much for doggy sports, poor swimmers, sensitive to heat
Fun Fact: French Bulldogs have become popular movie actors. One starred in the 2003 Steve Martin film, *Bringing Down the House.*

GERMAN PINSCHER

Where They Are From: Germany
History: German Pinschers were first bred in the eighteenth century and used as guard dogs and ratters. They are ancestors of both the Doberman Pinscher and the

Miniature Pinscher.
Looks: German Pinschers are medium-size dogs with long heads and drop ears. Sometimes the ears are cropped erect. Their long tails are usually docked. They have short hair that is black and tan, black and rust, solid red, stag red, fawn, or blue.

Height: 17 to 20 inches
Weight: No standard
Personality: German Pinschers are busy dogs who are smart and brave. Sometimes they can be a little pushy, and they can be greedy with their toys, food, people, and homes. They must be taught as pups to share.
Activity Level: High
First Loves: Playing, their people, their stuff
Best Families: German Pinschers like older kids who like to play but who aren't pushovers. Their families should be willing to teach them to share and to be friendly with everyone.

Pluses: Affectionate with their families, easy to groom, good watchdogs, stay playful their whole lives
Minuses: Can be possessive, can be pushy, tend to jump up
Fun Fact: German Pinschers are related to the Standard Schnauzer. Originally, the Standard Schnauzer was called the Wire-Haired Pinscher and the German Pinscher was called the Smooth-Haired Pinscher.

GERMAN SHEPHERD DOG

Where They Are From: Germany
History: German Shepherd Dogs are a fairly new breed from the early twentieth century. They have been herding dogs, police dogs, military dogs, and guide dogs.
Looks: German Shepherd Dogs are large with large erect ears and long noses. They have long tails and medium-length thick coats that are usually black and tan or black.
Height: 22 to 26 inches
Weight: 60 to 130 pounds
Personality: German Shepherd Dogs are brave and confident. They get along well with almost everyone but may take a little while to warm up to new people. They like kids and other dogs. They are playful and fun but have a serious side, too. They are also very loyal.
Activity Level: High
First Loves: Their people, their home, investigating things
Best Families: German Shepherd Dogs do well with families who love to take long walks and enjoy being with their dogs all the time. They like living in houses with big yards.
Pluses: Always up for a new adventure, enjoy sports and activities, friendly and loving, good watchdogs
Minuses: Can be protective, need a lot of exercise and attention, shed a lot
Fun Fact: The first guide dogs in the United States were German Shepherd Dogs.

GERMAN SHORTHAIRED POINTER

Where They Are From: Germany

History: German Shorthaired Pointers were first bred in the nineteenth century to be all-around hunting dogs. They could point, trail, and retrieve birds on land and in water. Their ancestors include both pointers and hounds.

Looks: German Shorthaired Pointers are large and muscular with square heads and drop ears. They have big brown eyes and docked tails. Their coats are short and either liver or liver and white.

Height: 21 to 26 inches

Weight: 45 to 70 pounds

Personality: German Shorthaired Pointers have lots of energy, love kids, and live to play or work. They sometimes chase cats and other small animals.

Activity Level: High

First Loves: Playing, working, their people

Best Families: German Shorthaired Pointers need families who are very active and who will keep them very busy.

Pluses: Active, friendly, good for dog activities or sports

Minuses: Can be difficult to train, may chase cats or small animals, need lots of exercise or can be naughty, shed a lot

Fun Fact: A German Shorthaired Pointer named Carlee won 2005's Westminster Kennel Club Dog Show. This was only the second time a German Shorthaired Pointer took Best in Show since the country's biggest dog show began in 1907.

(See the charts on pages 60–61 for term definitions.)

GERMAN WIREHAIRED POINTER

Where They Are From: Germany

History: German Wirehaired Pointers were developed as pointing and retrieving dogs during the nineteenth century. Some of their ancestors are German Shorthaired Pointers and Pudelpointers.

Looks: German Wirehaired Pointers look a lot like German Shorthaired Pointers but with wiry hair all over their bodies. They have drop ears and docked tails. They are liver, liver and white, or liver and roan.

Height: 22 to 26 inches

Weight: 45 to 70 pounds

Personality: German Wirehaired Pointers are full of energy and love their families. They take time to warm up to strangers. They will chase small animals and sometimes fight with other dogs.

Activity Level: High

First Loves: Working, playing, water

Best Families: German Wirehaired Pointers do well with older kids who have had dogs before. Their families need to keep them busy and teach them not to chase other animals.

Pluses: Enjoy dog sports and activities, hard workers, loving and loyal to their friends and families

Minuses: Can be hard to train, can be unfriendly with new people, chase animals, may fight with dogs, need lots of attention and exercise

Fun Fact: German Wirehaired Pointers' wiry coats are completely water resistant.

GIANT SCHNAUZER

Where They Are From: Germany

History: Giant Schnauzers were bred to herd cattle. The breed was created by mixing standard schnauzers with Great Danes and sheepdogs.

Looks: Giant Schnauzers are large, powerful dogs with wiry coats that are black or salt-and-pepper. They have bushy eyebrows and long beards. Their ears are naturally button or are cropped erect, and they have short docked tails.

Height: 23.5 to 27.5 inches

Weight: 55 to 80 pounds

Personality: Giant Schnauzers are brave and serious

dogs. They can be friendly if they meet lots of nice people, kids, dogs, and cats as pups. They may get angry if teased or messed with.

Activity Level: Moderate

First Loves: Their people, their homes

Best Families: Giant Schnauzers do best with families who have had dogs before. Their families need to teach them to like everyone and give them lots of exercise and attention. They prefer living in the country or in houses with yards.

Pluses: Good watchdogs, loving, loyal

Minuses: Can have quick tempers, need grooming

Fun Fact: In Germany, Giant Schnauzers are still best known as police dogs.

GLEN OF IMAAL TERRIER

Where They Are From: Ireland

History: Glen of Imaal Terriers have been bred for hundreds of years in their hometown, Glen of Imaal. They were originally used to hunt vermin and small animals.

Looks: Glen of Imaal Terriers are big dogs with short legs. They have large heads and rose or semiprick ears. Their short front legs are bowed. Their docked tails are carried high. They have wiry coats that are blue, wheaten, or brindle.

Height: 12.5 to 14 inches

Weight: 35 pounds

Personality: Glen of Imaal Terriers are spunky and outgoing terriers. They love to work and play but are mellow at home. They like kids and cats but don't always like other dogs. They are smart and like to learn but can be a little stubborn.

Activity Level: Low to moderate

First Loves: Their people

Best Families: Glen of Imaal Terriers prefer families who like to play but who also enjoy good couch buddies.

Pluses: Friendly, good watchdogs (they have a loud, deep bark), good with kids

Minuses: Dig, need to be groomed, poor swimmers, will fight with other dogs

Fun Fact: Glen of Imaal Terriers were once used to power wheels that turned spits over fires—meat was cooked on the spits.

GOLDEN RETRIEVER

Where They Are From: Great Britain

History: Golden Retrievers were bred by British nobility in the nineteenth century. They were both hunters and companions.

Looks: Golden Retrievers are large dogs with broad heads and drop ears. They have long tails. They have medium-length wavy coats that are gold with lots of feathering on their bodies, ears, chests, and tails.

Height: 21.5 to 24 inches

Weight: 55 to 75 pounds

Personality: Golden Retrievers are gentle, affectionate, and all-around perfect family dogs. They love people and other animals. They are full of fun.

Activity Level: Moderate to high

First Loves: People, kids, playing fetch

Best Families: Golden Retrievers love big families—the more kids and dogs, the better. They like their families to be active and live in the country or at least have big yards and plenty of nearby parks.

Pluses: Friendly, great family dogs, like sports and activities

Minuses: Need to be brushed, not good watchdogs

Fun Fact: Golden Retrievers are still popular working dogs. Here are just a few of the roles they excel in: search and rescue dogs, therapy dogs, guide dogs, hearing dogs, assistance dogs, and drug detection dogs.

GORDON SETTER

Where They Are From: Scotland

History: Gordon Setters were bred by the Duke of Gordon in the 1820s as hunting dogs. There have been dogs similar to them in the British Isles since the seventeenth century.

Looks: Gordon Setters are large dogs with long heads and drop ears. Their long tails are held straight out. They have medium-length wavy coats that are black with tan markings. There is feathering on the ears, bodies, tails, and legs.

Height: 23 to 27 inches

Weight: 45 to 80 pounds

Personality: Gordon Setters are smart, energetic, and hard-working dogs. They are loving and loyal to their families. Sometimes they don't get along with other dogs. They should meet lots of nice kids as puppies so they learn to like kids.

Activity Level: High

First Loves: Running, playing, working, their families

Best Families: Gordon Setters do well with older kids who can give them lots of exercise and who will teach them to like dogs and little kids. They like living in the country or in a house with a big yard.

Pluses: Fun, good watchdogs, great running dogs, like sports and activities, loyal

Minuses: Don't always get along with other dogs, need lots of exercise and attention, need to brushed, need to meet kids when they are young or they can be afraid of them

Fun Fact: Gordon Setters are the only bird hunting dogs from Scotland.

GREAT DANE

Where They Are From: Germany

History: The Great Dane is the national dog of Germany. Its ancestors were first bred in the sixteenth century and were used to hunt boar. Now, Great Danes are popular pet dogs.

Looks: Great Danes are tall, muscular dogs. Their large heads are shaped like rectangles, and they have drop ears.

(See the charts on pages 60–61 for term definitions.)

Sometimes their ears are cropped erect. They have long tapered tails. Their short coats are black and white, black, blue, fawn, brindle, or harlequin.

Height: 28 to 32 inches minimum

Weight: 100 to 130 pounds

Personality: Great Danes are good-natured and sweet. They love to play and enjoy most people and other animals. They are great family dogs.

Activity Level: Moderate

First Loves: Their people

Best Families: Great Danes like families who enjoy cuddling and will help them learn to control their strength.

Pluses: Easy to groom, friendly to almost everyone, good watchdogs, good with people and other animals

Minuses: May not know their own strength, tend to live short lives

Fun Fact: The world's tallest dog is a Great Dane named Gibson. He is 42.6 inches tall—about as high as a standard-size donkey or a small pony. When he stands on his hind legs, he is more than 7 feet tall! Scooby-Doo is a Great Dane.

GREATER SWISS MOUNTAIN DOG

Where They Are From: Switzerland

History: Greater Swiss Mountain Dogs are one of the four Swiss breeds (the others are the Bernese Mountain Dog, Appenzeller, and the Entlebucher) created when invading Romans crossed their Mastiffs with local Swiss dogs. The Greater Swiss Mountain Dogs were used by farmers and merchants as guards and draft dogs (to pull things). They were often called the "butcher's dog" because they were often kept by butchers as general help dogs.

Looks: Greater Swiss Mountain Dogs are large dogs with

short glossy coats. They have large, strong heads and drop ears. Their long tails are tapered. They are black with white and rust-colored markings.

Height: 23.5 to 28.5 inches

Weight: 85 to 140 pounds

Personality: Greater Swiss Mountain Dogs are brave, outgoing dogs who are also gentle and patient. They are loyal and loving with their friends and families. They are protective of their homes and people. They enjoy learning new things and like to keep busy.

Activity Level: Moderate

First Loves: Pulling, their people, their homes

Best Families: Greater Swiss Mountain Dogs do well with families who keep them busy and have time to train them. They prefer to live in houses with big yards.

Pluses: Don't need a lot of grooming, easy to train, good watchdogs, good with kids, like to be involved in activities, patient

Minuses: Can be overprotective, need a lot of exercise and attention, sometimes quarrel with other dogs

Fun Fact: The invention of the automobile almost made Greater Swiss Mountain Dogs extinct! After the car was invented, there wasn't much need for a dog to pull carts, so people stopped breeding Greater Swiss Mountain Dogs. The breed was saved by people who just wanted to keep them as pets.

GREAT PYRENEES

Where They Are From: France

History: Great Pyrenees are flock guardians from the Pyrenees Mountains. Their job is to protect grazing sheep and other livestock from wolves and bears. They have also been pet dogs in France as far back as the seventeenth century.

Looks: Great Pyrenees are large dogs with heavy coats. They have large heads with small drop ears. Their long furry tails are held low. The coats are white or white with badger, gray, or tan markings.

Height: 25 to 32 inches

Weight: 90 to 125 pounds

Personality: Great Pyrenees are patient and gentle with a playful personality. They are loyal to their friends and families. Sometimes it takes them a while to warm up to new people and dogs. They tend to be night owls, sleeping during the day and patrolling their homes at night. They are protective of their homes and people.

Activity Level: Moderate

First Loves: Their families, their homes

Best Families: Great Pyrenees need families who help them be comfortable meeting new people and can give them a lot of attention. They prefer to live in the country or in houses with big yards.

Pluses: Friendly, good watchdogs, good with kids, love to play

Minuses: Can be territorial, need a lot of exercise and attention, need to be groomed a lot, suspicious of new people

Fun Fact: Great Pyrenees dogs contributed to many great breeds of dogs. The Landseer Newfoundland (black-and-white Newfoundland) is a cross between Newfoundlands and Great Pyrenees. When the Saint Bernard almost disappeared because so many had died in avalanches while doing their rescue work, Great Pyrenees were introduced into the breed.

GREYHOUND

Where They Are From: Great Britain

History: Greyhounds are ancient sighthounds (dogs who hunt by sight). The breed may be more than two thousand years old. Art from Ancient Egypt and Greece shows dogs who look like modern Greyhounds. They were popular hunting dogs in Europe and began to be used for dog racing in the eighteenth century. Now, most pet Greyhounds are retired racing dogs.

Looks: Greyhounds are tall, slender dogs with long legs. They have narrow heads, small folded ears, and long curved tails. Their coats are short and of any color.

Height: 27 to 30 inches
Weight: 60 to 70 pounds
Personality: Greyhounds are gentle and patient and very loving. They like almost everyone they meet, including kids and other dogs, but they will often chase small animals. Even though they love to run, they are usually happiest lounging on comfy couches.
Activity Level: Low to moderate
First Loves: Running, lounging around, their people
Best Families: Greyhounds do best with people who are happy just hanging out at home with this cuddle bunny. They want friends who are patient with them as they learn to be good pets.
Pluses: Content to hang out with the family, don't need much exercise, easy to please, gentle, like almost everyone, playful
Minuses: Almost all pet Greyhounds are retired racers so they need basic training to learn how to get along in "normal" society, can be a little shy with new people, chase small animals
Fun Fact: For more than five hundred years, only English nobility were allowed to own Greyhounds.

HARRIER

Where They Are From: Great Britain
History: They are a very old breed, at least several hundred years old. They were originally used to hunt rabbits and often still are.

(See the charts on pages 60–61 for term definitions.)

Looks: Harriers are medium-size dogs. They have drop ears and brown or yellow eyes. Their medium-length tails are curved. They have short coats that are black, tan, and white or red and white.
Height: 19 to 21 inches
Weight: 45 to 55 pounds
Personality: Harriers are smart and lively dogs. They love almost everyone they meet. They are very attached to their families and adore kids and other dogs. They can be stubborn and will run away if given the opportunity.
Activity Level: Moderate to high
First Loves: Their families, kids, playing, hunting
Best Families: Harriers love families who are full of fun, just as they are. They need people who are responsible so they can't run away.
Pluses: Affectionate, friendly, fun loving, good dogs for sports, good workers, smart
Minuses: Hard to train, stubborn, try to run away
Fun Fact: Although Harriers are usually pets in the United States, in their homeland they are still used mostly as hunting dogs.

HAVANESE

Where They Are From: Cuba
History: Havanese were first bred in the eighteenth century. They were once called Havanese Bichons. In Cuba, they were originally kept only by wealthy families but later became popular pets.
Looks: Havanese are small dogs with long silky hair. The hair on the heads covers the eyes in some dogs, so it is sometimes held back with a ribbon. They have drop ears and long tails that they carry over their backs—both their ears and tails blend in with the rest of their hair. They can be any color.
Height: 9.5 to 11.5 inches
Weight: 10 to 14 pounds
Personality: Havanese are gentle and sweet—full of love for everyone they meet. They like to learn new things and are quite smart.

Activity Level: Low

First Loves: Their people

Best Families: Havanese enjoy kids who are able to be gentle and give them the love and attention they deserve. They don't mind living in the city or the suburbs.

Pluses: Don't need a lot of exercise, easy to train, friendly with everyone, gentle with kids and other animals, not the typical yappy small dogs

Minuses: Need to be groomed, not big on doggy sports

Fun Fact: Cuban refugees brought the Havanese to the United States after the 1959 revolution in Cuba.

IBIZAN HOUND

Where They Are From: Spain

History: Ibizan Hounds are among the most ancient dogs. Their ancestors were used as hunting dogs in ancient Egypt. There are drawings of Ibizan Hound–type dogs on the walls of Egyptian tombs. They have been used as hunting dogs in Spain since the eighth or ninth century.

Looks: Ibizan Hounds are tall, slender, strong dogs. They have long heads and large erect ears. Their noses and lips are pinkish. Their long tails are sickle or ringed. Their coats can be smooth or wirehaired. They may be red or white, or a combination of the two.

Height: 22.5 to 27.5 inches

Weight: 42 to 50 pounds

Personality: Ibizan Hounds are smart, lively dogs. They get along with most people and like to play with other dogs. They may take a while to warm up to strangers. Some people say they have a catlike personality. Like cats, they like to keep themselves very clean. They may chase small animals.

Activity Level: Moderate to high

First Loves: Playing with other dogs, their people

Best Families: Ibizan Hounds do best with older, gentle kids. They should have a lot of time to spend with them. They prefer families who live in the country or in houses with big fenced yards.

Pluses: Easy to groom, easy to train, friendly, good dogs for sports and activities, good watchdogs

Minuses: May chase small animals, need a lot of attention and exercise

Fun Fact: Drawings of dogs who looked like Ibizan Hounds were found on King Tut's tomb. Inside the burial chamber was a statue of Anubis—the watchdog of the dead.

IRISH SETTER

Where They Are From: Ireland

History: Irish Setters were first bred in the eighteenth century to hunt birds. They are related to several other bird-hunting dogs such as Gordon Setters and English Setters.

Looks: Irish Setters are tall, thin dogs. They have long heads and long drop ears. Their tails are long. They have long silky red coats with feathering on the legs, bodies, tails, and ears. Some are red and white. Red and white setters are sometimes considered a different breed, called the Red and White Setter.

Height: 25 to 27 inches

Weight: 60 to 70 pounds

Personality: Irish Setters are superenergetic, fun loving, and friendly dogs. They love nothing more than to run and play. They hate to come when called because they can't stand for the fun to end. They adore kids and get along with other dogs. They can be hard to train.

Activity Level: High

First Loves: Running, playing, family, kids, almost everything

Best Families: Irish Setters adore kids who like to run and play as much as they do. Nonstop kids make great friends for Irish Setters. They should live in houses with very big yards and a lot of park access.

Pluses: Friendly, good dogs for sports, good watchdogs, good with kids and other dogs, loving

Minuses: Can be hard to train, need to be groomed, need tons of exercise and attention, tend to run away

Fun Fact: The national bus service in Ireland, Bus Éireann, uses an Irish Setter as its company logo.

IRISH TERRIER

Where They Are From: Ireland

History: Irish Terriers are one of the oldest terriers. They have been used as ratters and to hunt large and small animals. During World War I, the British army used them as military dogs.

Looks: Irish Terriers are strong, medium-size dogs. They have button ears and long heads, and they have bushy beards and eyebrows. Their tails are docked and carried high. Their wiry coats are red or wheaten.

Height: 18 inches

Weight: 25 to 27 pounds

Personality: Irish Terriers are brave and spunky dogs. They love to work and play. They are loyal, but they can be overprotective and a little greedy with their toys and food. They aren't always good with other animals.

Activity Level: Moderate

First Loves: Playing, working, their families, toys, food

Best Families: Irish Terriers do best with mature older kids or adults. They need families who have had dogs before and can manage their crafty ways.

Pluses: Fun and playful, good watchdogs, good workers, like kids, loyal

Minuses: Can be overprotective, chase cats and other small animals, hard to train, may fight with other dogs, some are greedy with toys and food

Fun Fact: Irish Terriers' nickname is daredevil because they are so brave and adventurous.

IRISH WATER SPANIEL

Where They Are From: Ireland

History: Irish Water Spaniels are probably descendants of ancient water spaniels. They were bred in the mid-nineteenth century to retrieve birds from freezing cold water.

Looks: Irish Water Spaniels are medium-size dogs. They have long drop ears and long thin tails. They have curly brown coats. The only places the coats aren't curly are on the tails, faces, and throats.

Height: 21 to 24 inches

(See the charts on pages 60–61 for term definitions.)

Weight: 45 to 65 pounds

Personality: Irish Water Spaniels are smart, lively, and brave dogs. They don't like to be messed with. They adore their families but take a while to warm up to new people.

Activity Level: High

First Loves: Playing fetch, swimming, their people

Best Families: Irish Water Spaniels like mature older kids who love to do outdoorsy things. Their families should be used to dogs and have time to train them and socialize them. They prefer living in the country or in houses with big yards.

Pluses: Good watchdogs, great dogs for sports, love to play

Minuses: Can be aggressive, don't always like other dogs or strangers, need to be groomed

Fun Fact: Irish Water Spaniels are sometimes called Rattails or Rattail Spaniels because their long thin tails don't have the curls that cover the rest of their bodies.

IRISH WOLFHOUND

Where They Are From: Ireland

History: Irish Wolfhounds are one of the oldest breeds in the world. The first record of these dogs is around 300 BC. Irish Wolfhounds were bred to hunt wolves, deer, and boars. When overhunting wiped out the wolf population in the late eighteenth century, Irish Wolfhounds mostly disappeared. Since the middle of the nineteenth century, Irish Wolfhounds have been bred as pets instead of as hunting dogs.

Looks: Irish Wolfhounds are very tall, powerful dogs. They look like larger, hairier Greyhounds. They have dark eyes and noses and small folded ears. They have long curved tails. Their wiry coats are gray, brindle, red, black, white, or fawn.

Height: 30 to 32 inches

Weight: 105 to 120 pounds

Personality: Irish Wolfhounds are patient, gentle, and loving dogs. They adore children and get along with most people and other animals. They can be a bit stubborn, however.

Activity Level: Moderate

First Loves: Children, their people, running

Best Families: Irish Wolfhounds do well with gentle, fun-loving kids who are patient enough to train them. They much prefer families who live in the country or at least have houses with very large yards.

Pluses: Friendly, good with kids, playful

Minuses: Must be brushed at least a few times a week, need a fenced yard, Need a lot of attention, not good watchdogs

Fun Fact: The first record of Irish Wolfhounds is from ancient Rome. Seven Irish Wolfhounds were given to Roman consul Quintus Aurelius as a gift in 391. They are the tallest of all dog breeds.

ITALIAN GREYHOUND

Where They Are From: Italy

History: Like the Greyhound, the Italian Greyhound is a very old breed. These dogs have been bred as pet dogs at least since the Middle Ages. They became popular among European royalty in the sixteenth and seventeenth centuries.

Looks: Italian Greyhounds are small, slender, and graceful dogs. They look like small Greyhounds. They have folded ears and long curved tails. Their short coats are usually blue, red, seal, fawn, or white.

Height: 13 to 15 inches

Weight: 7 to 15 pounds

Personality: Italian Greyhounds are quiet, nervous dogs. They are smart and like to learn new things, but they can be stubborn. They adore their families but can be a little shy with strangers.

Activity Level: Low

First Loves: Their people, being adored

Best Families: Italian Greyhounds enjoy mature older kids or adults who have time to pay a lot of attention to them. They are happy in the city or the suburbs.

Pluses: Adapt to apartment life, don't need a lot of exercise, easy to groom, good watchdogs, very affectionate with their person

Minuses: Can be shy, get cold easily—need a winter blanket in cold climates, need a lot of attention

Fun Fact: Italian Greyhounds are the smallest sighthounds (dogs that hunt by sight).

JACK (PARSON) RUSSELL TERRIER

Where They Are From: Great Britain

History: Jack Russell Terriers were first bred by Parson John Russell during the early nineteenth century. They were bred to hunt foxes alongside people hunting on horseback. Recently, they were renamed Parson Russell Terriers by the American Kennel Club (AKC). Other groups still call them Jack Russell Terriers.

Looks: Jack Russell Terriers are small, muscular dogs. They have button ears and short erect tails. Their coats can be smooth or wiry. They are mostly white with tan, black, and brown (or all three!) markings.

Height: 10 to 15 inches (AKC: 12 to 14 inches)

Weight: No standard (AKC: 13 to 17 pounds)

Personality: Jack Russell Terriers are spunky, lively little dogs with lots of attitude. They are smart and always on the go. They are loyal to their people. They usually get along with kids and other dogs, but they will chase smaller animals. They have minds of their own.

Activity Level: High

First Loves: Running, digging, chasing, their people

Best Families: Jack Russell Terriers do best with older kids who have had terriers before and have lots of time to train and exercise them. It's best if they live in the country or a suburb with lots of parks.

Pluses: Always up for fun, easy to groom (wirehaired may need professional grooming), friendly to most people, good watchdogs, great dogs to do canine sports with, loyal

Minuses: Can be aggressive with other dogs, can be possessive, chase (sometimes kill) small animals, need tons of exercise, not good city dogs

Fun Fact: Skip, from the movie *My Dog Skip*, which was released in 2000, was a Jack Russell Terrier. Skip was actually played by two dogs, father and son team Moose and Enzo. Moose and Enzo also played Eddie on *Frasier*, a television show that aired from 1993 to 2004.

JAPANESE CHIN

Where They Are From: Japan

History: Japanese Chins were first seen in Japan around AD 700. They were kept by royalty. They were also popular with shoguns, military generals who ruled Japan from around AD 1000 to the mid-nineteenth century.

Looks: Japanese Chins are small dogs with large round heads. They have short muzzles and drop ears. Their plumed tails are carried over their backs. They have long straight coats. There is a ruff at the neck and their legs and tails are feathered. They are black and white or red and white.

Height: 8 to 11 inches

Weight: 4 to 11 pounds

Personality: Japanese Chins are smart, gentle, mellow dogs. They like kids and other dogs, and they enjoy meeting new people. They are very clean, like cats. They even clean themselves with their paws!

Activity Level: Low

First Loves: Sleeping, their people

Best Families: Japanese Chins love mellow kids who like to hang out. They don't care if they live in the city or the country, but their families must like having a dog in their laps!

Pluses: Friendly, good with kids and other dogs, loving, mellow

(See the charts on pages 60–61 for term definitions.)

Minuses: Need to be groomed, not much for canine sports

Fun Fact: Japanese Chins' ancestors were originally from China. Paintings of Japanese Chins are seen on ancient Chinese pottery. They were brought to Japan as a gift from a Chinese Emperor.

KEESHOND

Where They Are From: Holland (in the Netherlands)

History: Keeshonden were first bred in Holland in the sixteenth century. They were used as guards on riverboats and farms.

Looks: Keeshonden are medium-size dogs with long heavy coats, which are especially thick around the neck. They have small prick ears. Their bushy tails curl over their backs. They have dark lines around their eyes that make them look like they are wearing glasses.

Height: 17 to 18 inches

Weight: 30 to 45 pounds

Personality: Keeshonden are gentle, outgoing dogs. They love everyone, including other dogs and kids. They are smart and like to learn new things.

Activity Level: Moderate

First Loves: Their families, people

Best Families: Keeshonden like kids who like to play and cuddle as much as they do. They don't mind where they live.

Pluses: Easy to train, friendly, good watchdogs, good with kids and dogs, loving

Minuses: Need to be groomed, shed

Fun Fact: You've probably noticed that the plural of *keeshond* is *keeshonden*, not *keeshonds*. So if you have two, you say, "I have two Keeshonden." This is how they say it Holland!

KERRY BLUE TERRIER

Where They Are From: Ireland

History: Kerry Blue Terriers were first bred in Ireland's County Kerry. At least since the late nineteenth century, they were used to hunt small game and birds. They have also been herders, police dogs, and military dogs during World War I.

Looks: Kerry Blue Terriers are medium-size, strong dogs. They have button ears and thick beards. Their medium-

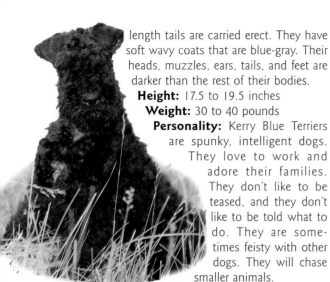

length tails are carried erect. They have soft wavy coats that are blue-gray. Their heads, muzzles, ears, tails, and feet are darker than the rest of their bodies.

Height: 17.5 to 19.5 inches

Weight: 30 to 40 pounds

Personality: Kerry Blue Terriers are spunky, intelligent dogs. They love to work and adore their families. They don't like to be teased, and they don't like to be told what to do. They are sometimes feisty with other dogs. They will chase smaller animals.

Activity Level: High

First Loves: Working, chasing, their people

Best Families: Kerry Blue Terriers do well with mature older kids or adults who have had terriers before. Their families must have time to train them and exercise them. They must be patient but firm with them.

Pluses: Adapt well, always ready to go, good watchdogs, good with well-behaved children, great dogs for canine sports, great running partners, love to work, loyal

Minuses: Can be aggressive with dogs, can be pushy and stubborn, can react to misbehaving small children, chase smaller animals, hard to train, need constant training and socialization, need grooming

Fun Fact: Irish patriot Michael Collins was a leader in the fight for Irish independence from England during the early part of the twentieth century. Collins was a huge fan of the Kerry Blue Terrier and even tried to get the Kerry Blue Terrier named as Ireland's national dog. His Kerry Blue Terrier was named Convict 224.

KOMONDOR

Where They Are From: Hungary

History: Komondors are probably descendants of dogs who were brought to Hungary more than one thousand years ago. In Hungary, they worked as livestock guardians. Many still work, but others are pets.

Looks: Komondors are large dogs with long white cords all over their bodies. The cords, which are made up of twisted hair like dreadlocks, cover their faces and touch the ground. Just their dark noses and pink tongues peek out. They have drop ears and long curved tails.

Height: 25.5 to 30 inches

Weight: 80 to 120 pounds

Personality: Komondors are mellow, brave dogs. They adore their families but don't like strangers. They can be possessive and pushy. They need training and socializing to be good family pets.

Activity Level: Moderate

First Loves: Their families

Best Families: Komondors do best with kids who are at least sixteen years old and mature. Their families should have had experience with dogs like them. They prefer to live in the country.

Pluses: Calm, good watchdogs, loving, loyal

Minuses: Aren't always good with kids, can be possessive, can be pushy, hard to train

Fun Fact: Komondors were bred to watch over large herds by themselves. They don't need a shepherd to tell them what to do.

KUVASZ

Where They Are From: Hungary

History: Kuvaszok are an old breed. (We use the Hungarian plural for Kuvasz instead of saying Kuvaszs!) They probably originally came to Hungary from Tibet in the thirteenth century. They have been hunters, livestock guardians, and pets. They were popular with Hungarian royalty. They were kept as guards by King Matthias I, a Hungarian king during the fifteenth century.

Looks: Kuvaszok are large, strong dogs with thick white coats, which are especially heavy at the necks and tails. They have small drop ears, black noses, and slanted dark eyes. Their long tails are set low.

Height: 26 to 30 inches

Weight: 70 to 115 pounds

Personality: Kuvaszok love their families more than anything. They will do whatever is needed to protect the children and animals in their families. They don't like strangers. They sometimes get confused when children wrestle or play roughly.

Activity Level: High

First Loves: Their families

Best Families: Kuvaszok like people who have had dogs like them before. Their families must be able to train them and socialize them. It's very important they learn to like meeting new people. It's best if their families live in the country.

Pluses: Devoted to their families, good watchdogs, good with kids and other animals in their families, loyal

Minuses: Can be aggressive, don't like strangers, don't understand when kids play roughly, shed, strong doggy odor

Fun Fact: The name *kuvasz* means "armed guard of nobility" in Turkish. The name was given to the breed when Ottoman Turks took over Hungary in the fourteenth century.

LABRADOR RETRIEVER (LAB)

Where They Are From: Canada

History: Labrador Retrievers were bred as hunting dogs in the nineteenth century. They are from the island of Newfoundland, off Canada. They have had a lot of jobs, but their number one job now is pet dog. They are the most popular pet dogs in the United States.

Looks: Labrador Retrievers are large dogs. They have drop ears and long otter tails. Their coats are short and can be black, chocolate, or yellow. Usually their noses are black, but some chocolate Labs have a brown nose and some yellow Labs have a pink nose.

(See the charts on pages 60–61 for term definitions.)

Height: 21.5 to 24.5 inches

Weight: 55 to 80 pounds

Personality: Labrador Retrievers love to have fun. They like almost everyone they meet, especially kids. They get along with other animals, including dogs. They like to learn new things. Some people say they are the perfect family dog.

Activity Level: High

First Loves: Swimming, fetch, their people

Best Families: Labrador Retrievers love big families and a lot of time to play and cuddle. They don't mind where they live but like to have yards to play in.

Pluses: Easy to groom, easy to train, friendly, fun loving, good watchdogs, great dogs for canine activities, hard workers, love to learn new things, smart

Minuses: Need a lot of attention and exercise

Fun Fact: The original Labs were called St. John's Water Dogs. They were a mix of small water dogs and Newfoundlands.

LHASA APSO

Where They Are From: Tibet

History: Lhasa Apsos are a very old breed. They have probably been around for more than one thousand years. They were used as watchdogs in Tibetan monasteries and temples for hundreds of years.

Looks: Lhasa Apsos are small and sturdy. They have drop ears. Their medium-length tails are curved over their backs. They have long heavy coats all over their bodies. The hair is parted down the middle from the head to the tail. They have long hair over their eyes and whiskers and beards.

Height: 10 to 11 inches

Weight: 14 to 15 pounds

Personality: Lhasa Apsos are mellow, smart dogs, who enjoy learning new things. They are loving with their families but may not get along with kids. They don't always like strangers.

Activity Level: Low

First Loves: Their families, relaxing

Best Families: Lhasa Apsos like mature older kids. They must be introduced to lots of kids, animals, and strangers so they know not to be afraid of them. They don't mind if they live in apartments.

Pluses: Easy to train, good apartment dogs, good watchdogs, loving, mellow, smart

Minuses: Can be unfriendly with kids, strangers, and other animals; need grooming

Fun Fact: The first Lhasa Apsos arrived in the United States in 1933. They were gifts from the Dalai Lama—the spiritual leader of Tibet—to an American naturalist.

LÖWCHEN

Where They Are From: Belgium

History: Löwchens have been around for four hundred years or more, and they have always been kept as pets. But no one knows whether they were originally from the Mediterranean or from Germany.

Looks: Löwchens are small dogs with long wavy coats, which are usually cut in a lion clip. This means that the coat is left natural in front but shaved in the back. They have drop ears and medium-length tails that curl over their backs. They have lots of hair on their faces. They can be any color.

Height: 12 to 14 inches

Weight: No standard

Personality: Löwchens are smart, spunky dogs. They love people and get along with almost everyone. They like to learn new things. They don't always get along with other dogs.

Activity Level: Low

First Loves: Their people

Best Families: Löwchens like mature kids who have time for them. They don't mind where they live.

Pluses: Can live anywhere, don't need much exercise, friendly, fun loving, like almost everyone, smart

Minuses: Don't always get along with other dogs, need to be groomed

Fun Fact: The Löwchen's name means "little lion dog." It was named after its lion haircut.

MALTESE

Where They Are From: Malta

History: The Maltese is a very old breed. It is one of the bichons, an old group of small long-haired dogs who originated in the Mediterranean. Maltese have been kept as pets by ancient Egyptians, Greeks, and Romans. In the sixteenth century, they became popular in England.

Looks: Maltese are small dogs with long silky white coats that part in the middle from their heads to their tails. People usually tie the long hair on their heads into a topknot. They have dark eyes and black noses. They have drop ears and long plumed tails that curve over their backs.

Height: 5 to 8 inches

Weight: 4 to 7 pounds

Personality: Maltese are playful, self-confident dogs. They adore their families. Sometimes they can be nippy with strangers. They get along with gentle kids. They can be a little nervous.

Activity Level: Low

First Loves: Their families

Best Families: Maltese love mature older kids. Families who like to read and hang out at home are great. It's fine if they live in apartments.

Pluses: Affectionate, don't need much exercise, friendly, good apartment dogs, good watchdogs, smart

Minuses: Can be nippy with strangers and rowdy kids, need to be groomed, will sometimes fight with other dogs

Fun Fact: Maltese were so beloved by the ancient Greeks that they erected tombs whenever a favorite Maltese died.

MANCHESTER TERRIER

Where They Are From: Great Britain

History: Manchester Terriers were first bred in Great Britain in the late nineteenth century. They are probably a mix of an old terrier called the Black and Tan Terrier and the Whippet. They were used as ratters.

Looks: Manchester Terriers look like small Doberman Pinschers. Their ears are erect or button, and their medium-length tails are tapered. Their short black coats have tan markings on the legs and chests, under the tails, on the muzzles, inside the ears, and above the eyebrows. There is both a standard and a toy Manchester Terrier.

Height: 15 to 16 inches (standard); 10 to 12 inches (toy)

Weight: 12 to 22 pounds (standard); under 12 pounds (toy)

Personality: Manchester Terriers are mellower than the average terrier. They are loyal and loving with their families but don't always like strangers. They like most other dogs but will chase smaller animals. Sometimes they can be protective over their food and toys. They tend to like most kids.

Activity Level: Moderate

First Loves: Their families

Best Families: Manchester Terriers do well with mature kids who will play and cuddle with them. They don't mind living in the city or the country.

Pluses: Affectionate, easy to groom, good watchdogs, good with most dogs, good with most kids, loyal, mellower than most terriers

Minuses: Bark, can be greedy with food or toys, can be nippy, chase small animals, dig

Fun Fact: Although Manchester Terriers look like tiny Doberman Pinschers, the two breeds are not related.

MASTIFF

Where They Are From: Great Britain

History: Mastiffs may have been bred in Great Britain two thousand years ago. Their ancestors were Roman war dogs. They were used as guarding dogs, fighting dogs, and pet dogs.

Looks: Mastiffs are very large dogs with huge, wrinkly heads and heavy jowls. They have small drop ears and long tapered tails. Their short coats are fawn, apricot, or brindle. They have dark masks and dark ears.

Height: 27.5 to 30 inches

Weight: 175 to 190 pounds

Personality: Mastiffs are gentle, patient, calm, and loving dogs. They get along with almost everyone, especially kids, and they like most other animals. They can be a little stubborn.

(See the charts on pages 60–61 for term definitions.)

Activity Level: Low

First Loves: Their people, sleeping

Best Families: Mastiffs love gentle, fun-loving kids. They don't mind where they live as long as they have room to get comfy.

Pluses: Easy to groom, friendly, good watchdogs, good with kids and other animals

Minuses: Big dogs have big needs (everything is more expensive), can be stubborn, drool a lot

Fun Fact: The term *mastiff* applies to the breed Mastiff, or English Mastiff. It is also used to describe dogs who descended from the ancient Molosser, such as the Dogue de Bordeaux and the Tibetan Mastiff. English Mastiffs also descended from the Molosser, so they are Mastiffs twice over!

MINIATURE PINSCHER

Where They Are From: Germany

History: Although Miniature Pinschers look like tiny Dobermans, the two breeds aren't related. They were first bred as ratters. They are probably related to Italian Greyhounds and Dachshunds.

Looks: Miniature Pinschers are small, wiry dogs. They have long heads and their ears are drop or cropped erect. Their tails are docked. They have short coats that are red, stag red, chocolate with rust markings, or black with rust markings.

Height: 10 to 12 inches

Weight: 8 to 10 pounds

Personality: Miniature Pinschers are little spitfires. They are bold and have no fear. They are very smart. They don't usually like strangers and will sometimes fight with other dogs. They don't like to be messed with.

Activity Level: Moderate to high
First Loves: Playing, their people
Best Families: Miniature Pinschers do best with mature older kids who have had dogs before. Their families must have time to train them and give them exercise.
Pluses: Easy to groom, good dogs for canine sports, good watchdogs, like to learn new things, playful, smart
Minuses: Can be nippy with strangers and kids, may fight with other dogs, need a lot of exercise, stubborn
Fun Fact: The Miniature Pinscher's nicknames include Min-Pin and King of Toys.

MINIATURE SCHNAUZER

Where They Are From: Germany
History: Miniature Schnauzers are the small version of the Standard Schnauzer. They were created in the nineteenth century by breeding Standard Schnauzers with other breeds, maybe Affenpinschers and Poodles. They were used as ratters on farms.

Looks: Miniature Schnauzers have wiry coats that are salt-and-pepper, black and silver, or black. They have bushy eyebrows, beards, and whiskers. They have small folded or cropped erect ears. Their tails are docked and held erect.
Height: 12 to 14 inches
Weight: 14 to 18 pounds
Personality: Miniature Schnauzers do not have the typical terrier personality. They are good-natured and become attached to their families. They love to learn new things and want nothing more than to please their people. They may chase small animals, and they like to bark.
Activity Level: Moderate
First Loves: Their people
Best Families: Miniature Schnauzers need loving families who enjoy playing but are also happy to just hang out. Miniature Schnauzers don't mind living in the city or the country.
Pluses: Close to families, easy to train, friendly, good dogs for activities and sports, good watchdogs, loyal
Minuses: Bark, chase small animals, need to be groomed
Fun Fact: *Schnauzer* means "nose" in German.

NEAPOLITAN MASTIFF

Where They Are From: Italy
History: Neapolitan Mastiffs' ancestors were ancient Roman fighting dogs. In Italy, Neapolitan Mastiffs have been herders, guards, drafting dogs, hunters, and pets.
Looks: Neapolitan Mastiffs are very large dogs with huge, wrinkly heads and loose, wrinkly skin all over their bodies. They have heavy jowls and small drop ears, which sometimes are cropped erect. They have thick tails that are usually docked. Their short coats are gray, black, mahogany, tawny, stag, or brindle. They may have white markings.
Height: 23.5 to 29.5 inches
Weight: 110 to 180 pounds
Personality: Neapolitan Mastiffs are gentle, easygoing dogs. They are brave and loyal. They love their families and like kids and other animals. They can be a little stubborn.
Activity Level: Low
First Loves: Their families

Best Families: Neapolitan Mastiffs like mature older kids who have had dogs before. They don't mind where they live as long as they have enough room. Their families shouldn't mind dealing with dog drool.
Pluses: Don't need much exercise, friendly, good watchdogs, like kids and other animals, low grooming needs
Minuses: big dogs have big needs (everything is more expensive), drool a lot, need wrinkles around face cleaned every day, sensitive to heat
Fun Fact: In the United States, the Neapolitan Mastiff is known just as the Neo. In Italy, it is known as Mastino Napoletano. In the *Harry Potter* series, Hagrid's dog, Fang, is a Neapolitan Mastiff.

NEWFOUNDLAND

Where They Are From: Canada
History: Newfoundlands were first bred on the island of Newfoundland in the nineteenth century. They were used on fishing boats to pull fishing nets and boat lines. They were also used to save drowning people. On farms, they were used to pull carts.

Looks: Newfoundlands are very large dogs with big heads and droopy lips. They have drop ears and long tails that are held low. Their long thick coats are black, gray, or brown. Black-and-white Newfoundlands are called Landseers.

Height: 26 to 28 inches

Weight: 100 to 150 pounds

Personality: Newfoundlands are fun, gentle, and playful dogs. They are loyal and adore their families. They love kids and get along with most other animals. They are fabulous swimmers.

Activity Level: Moderate

First Loves: Kids, water, swimming, their families

Best Families: Kids who love to swim make great families. Newfoundlands like living close to a lake or a beach. Their families shouldn't mind drool.

Pluses: Gentle, get along with other animals, good watchdogs, like to learn new things, love kids, love swimming

Minuses: Big dogs have big needs (everything is more expensive), drool a lot, messy, need to be groomed

Fun Fact: Sir Edwin Landseer, a famous nineteenth-century painter, loved black-and-white Newfoundlands. He painted them so often they became known as Landseer Newfoundlands.

NORFOLK TERRIER AND NORWICH TERRIER

Where They Are From: Great Britain

History: The Norfolk Terrier and the Norwich Terrier were considered the same breed until 1964. They were

(See the charts on pages 60–61 for term definitions.)

first bred in the nineteenth century to hunt rats and foxes. Their doggy ancestors include Yorkshire, Irish, and Cairn terriers.

Norfolk Terrier

Looks: The Norfolk Terrier and the Norwich Terrier are both small dogs with wiry coats. They have round heads with bushy eyebrows and whiskers. They are red, wheaten, or black and tan. Sometimes they have dark markings. Norfolk Terriers have drop ears, and Norwich Terriers have erect ears. Norfolk Terriers have foxier looking faces. Their tails are docked and held up.

Height: 9 to 10 inches

Weight: 11 to 12 pounds

Personality: The Norfolk Terrier and the Norwich Terrier are outgoing, spunky little dogs. They love to play and adore their people. They are hard workers. They may chase small animals.

Activity Level: Moderate

First Loves: Their families

Best Families: Norfolk Terriers and Norwich Terriers like kids who love a good time. They can live in the city or the country.

Pluses: Can live anywhere, easygoing, friendly, good watchdogs

Norwich Terrier

Minuses: Bark, can be stubborn, chase small animals, dig, need to be groomed

Fun Fact: They were popular pets at Cambridge University during the early twentieth century. Students called them the Cantab for short, after the Latin name for Cambridge, which is *Cantabrigiensis.*

NORWEGIAN ELKHOUND

Where They Are From: Norway

History: The Norwegian Elkhound is a very old breed. Norwegian Vikings used Norwegian elkhounds to hunt moose and bears. They were also used for guarding, for herding, and as sled dogs.

Looks: Norwegian Elkhounds are foxy-looking, medium-size dogs. They have small prick ears. Their thick coats are gray, silver, and black. Their bushy tails curl over their backs.

Height: 19.5 to 20.5 inches

Weight: 45 to 55 pounds

Personality: Norwegian Elkhounds are loving and loyal dogs. They adore their families and get along with most kids. They are brave and alert. They are smart and love to learn. They can be a bit noisy, and they need a lot of attention.

Activity Level: Moderate
First Loves: Their families
Best Families: Older kids who love to have fun make good friends for Norwegian Elkhounds. It's best if they live in the country or in houses with big yards.
Pluses: Easy to train, friendly, fun loving, good watchdogs, loyal
Minuses: Bark, need a lot of attention, shed a lot
Fun Fact: The skeletons of Norwegian Elkhounds have been found with Viking artifacts such as weapons and human remains.

NOVA SCOTIA DUCK TOLLING RETRIEVER

Where They Are From: Canada
History: Nova Scotia Duck Tolling Retrievers were bred in Nova Scotia in the early nineteenth century as hunting dogs. Their ancestors were probably a mix of collies, spaniels, retrievers, and setters.
Looks: Nova Scotia Duck Tolling Retrievers are medium-size dogs with medium-length drop ears and medium-

length soft coats that are red with white markings. Their muzzles are shorter than most retrievers'. They have long tails.
Height: 18 to 21 inches
Weight: 37 to 51 pounds
Personality: Nova Scotia Tolling Retrievers are smart, fun-loving dogs. They like almost everyone and enjoy playing with kids and other dogs. They like to learn new things.
Activity Level: High
First Loves: Playing, their people
Best Families: Nova Scotia Duck Tolling Retrievers do best with families with lots of time to play with them.

They should live in houses with big yards.
Pluses: Easygoing, friendly, good dogs for canine activities, good watchdogs, love to play, smart
Minuses: Need a lot of attention and exercise, need to be groomed
Fun Fact: Nova Scotia Duck Tolling Retrievers' job is to lure ducks to the hunter. They use their tails to get the ducks' attention. When the ducks come closer to see what this strange fluffy red thing is, the hunter shoots the ducks.

OLD ENGLISH SHEEPDOG

Where They Are From: Great Britain
History: Old English Sheepdogs were first bred in the late nineteenth century. They worked as drovers, moving herds of cattle and sheep from one grazing area to another. They were also herders and livestock guardians.
Looks: Old English Sheepdogs are large dogs. They have long, thick gray-and-white coats that cover their eyes. They have drop ears and bobtails.
Height: 21 inches and up
Weight: 60 to 100 pounds
Personality: Old English Sheepdogs are friendly, goofy dogs. They love just about everyone they meet and get along with kids and dogs. They are smart and like to learn, but they can be stubborn.

Activity Level: Moderate

First Loves: Their families, playing, kids

Best Families: Old English Sheepdogs love kids who are as full of fun as they are. They need people who have time to train and exercise them. They like to live in houses with big yards.

Pluses: Affectionate, friendly, good with kids and other animals, like canine sports, like to learn

Minuses: Can be stubborn, need a lot of exercise, shed a lot

Fun Fact: In the 1989 Disney movie *The Little Mermaid*, Prince Eric's dog, Max, is an Old English Sheepdog.

OTTERHOUND

Where They Are From: Great Britain

History: Otterhounds are a very old breed originally used to hunt otters. Since otter hunting was made illegal, they have been mostly pet dogs.

Looks: Otterhounds are big, strong dogs with large, narrow heads and long drop ears. Their tails are long and tapered. They have heavy, rough coats and beards and mustaches. They can be any color, but the most common colors are gray, white, sandy, blue and white, and black and tan.

Height: 23 to 27 inches

Weight: 80 to 115 pounds

Personality: Otterhounds are friendly, outgoing dogs with lots of energy. They love other dogs and kids. They don't like to be told what to do. They tend to be noisy, and they especially love to bay along with other dogs. They will sometimes chase smaller animals. They are prone to running away.

Activity Level: High

First Loves: Swimming, their people, other dogs, barking or baying

Best Families: Otterhounds love older kids who live in the country. Their families must have lots of time to train and exercise them.

Pluses: Always up for fun, friendly, good watchdogs, great swimmers, like kids and other dogs

(See the charts on pages 60–61 for term definitions.)

Minuses: Can be overwhelming, hard to train, loud, must be groomed, need lots of exercise

Fun Fact: Otterhounds are perfectly made to swim in cold water. They have a special oily coat, and their large feet are webbed.

PAPILLON

Where They Are From: France

History: Papillons have always been pet dogs. They were especially popular with noblewomen such as Marie Antoinette. Papillons were probably bred from larger spaniels—they used to be called the Dwarf Spaniel.

Looks: Papillons are small, delicate dogs with long silky coats. They are white with patches of any other color, usually black, red, and/or tan. They are known for their large erect ears, which are covered with silky hair and look like the wings of a butterfly. They have long plumed tails that are curved over their backs.

Height: 8 to 11 inches

Weight: 3 to 9 pounds

Personality: Papillons are smart, friendly, gentle dogs. They love almost everyone they meet, including kids and other dogs. They like to learn new things.

Activity Level: Low

First Loves: Their person

Best Families: Papillons like gentle kids who love to cuddle. They don't mind if they live in apartments.

Pluses: Affectionate, can live in an apartment, don't need a lot of exercise, easy to train, friendly, smart

Minuses: Need to be groomed, not great for canine sports

Fun Fact: The word *papillon* means "butterfly" in French. Papillons were named for their ears, which look like butterflies. Papillons without the butterfly ears are called Phalenes.

PEKINGESE

Where They Are From: China

History: Pekingese are one of the small dogs bred to look like the Buddhist lion dog (Fo Dog). They have been bred in China since the Tang Dynasty in the eighth century. In China, they were known by three names: Lion Dog (because of their coats), Sun Dog (because of their color), and Sleeve Dog (because they are small enough to be carried inside the sleeve of a robe).

Looks: Pekingese are short, sturdy dogs with short, wrinkly muzzles. Their drop ears are heart shaped. Their tails are curled over their backs. They have long straight coats and thick manes like a lion's. They can be any color, but they are usually red, white, fawn, black, or black and tan. They usually have dark masks.

Height: 8 to 9 inches

Weight: 8 to 14 pounds

Personality: Pekingese are dignified dogs. They tend to be independent and stubborn. They are gentle with their families, but they don't always like new people, kids, and other dogs.

Activity Level: Low

First Loves: Being treated like royalty

Best Families: Pekingese like mature older kids who can teach them to be friendly to everyone. They don't mind if they live in apartments.

Pluses: Don't need much exercise, good apartment dogs, loyal, smart

Minuses: Can be stubborn; can be stuck up; can be unfriendly with young kids, strangers, and other dogs; don't like to be trained

Fun Fact: Pekingese were so prized in eighth-century China that stealing one was punishable by death.

PEMBROKE WELSH CORGI

Where They Are From: Wales

History: Pembroke Welsh Corgis were bred as all-purpose farm dogs in Pembrokeshire, Wales. They were used to herd cattle and even geese! They are closely related to Cardigan Welsh Corgis. One way to tell the two apart is that Cardigans have tails, and Pembrokes don't.

Looks: Pembroke Welsh Corgis are long dogs with very short legs. They have a foxy look with big erect ears. They have no tails. Their coats are red, sable, fawn, or black and tan. They may have white markings.

Height: 10 to 12 inches

Weight: 25 to 30 pounds

Personality: Pembroke Welsh Corgis are lively, smart, and fun. They love to learn new things. They get along with most people and other dogs. They will sometimes try to herd children. They can be stubborn, and they are sometimes bossy.

Activity Level: Moderate

First Loves: Their families

Best Families: Pembroke Welsh Corgis love older kids who have enough time for them. They don't mind where they live.

Pluses: Easy to train, enjoy doggy sports, friendly, good family dogs, good watchdogs

Minuses: Bark a lot, can be bossy, shed, sometimes herd kids

Fun Fact: The Pembroke Welsh Corgi's ancestors were brought to Wales by Flemish weavers.

PERUVIAN INCA ORCHID

Where They Are From: Peru

History: Peruvian Inca Orchids are a very old breed. The dogs may have first come to Peru with sailors from Africa or Asia. Some Peruvian Inca Orchids are hairless, whereas others have hair. The two types originally had two different jobs. The dogs with hair were used as hunting dogs, and the dogs without hair were used as bed warmers on chilly nights!

Looks: Peruvian Inca Orchids are medium-size dogs. They have large prick or rose ears and long tapered tails.

The Peruvian Inca Orchids with hair are called powder puffs. The coat can be any length and any color. The hairless dogs have a little fuzz of hair on tops of their heads, on their feet, and on the tips of their tails.

Personality: Pervuian Inca Orchids are friendly but quiet dogs. They are smart and enjoy learning new things. They like to keep very clean.

Activity Level: Moderate

First Loves: Their people

Best Families: They do best with grown-ups and older kids who will give them lots of attention but aren't too rowdy. They can live just about anywhere, but they are especially good apartment dogs.

Pluses: Adapt to new situations, clean, easy to train, friendly

Minuses: Need skin care, need training, sensitive to the cold, sensitive to the sun

Fun Fact: Legend has it that Peruvian Inca Orchids were given their name by Spanish explorers who first saw the dogs relaxing among the orchid flowers in Peru.

PETIT BASSET GRIFFON VENDÉEN

Where They Are From: France

History: Petit Basset Griffon Vendéen were first bred about four hundred years ago to hunt rabbits. They are one of four Griffon Vendéen breeds, which are all from the French district of La Vendée.

Looks: Petit Basset Griffon Vendéen are medium-size, strong dogs. They have long heads with long drop ears. Their long tails are shaped like sabers. They have rough coats and bushy eyebrows, mustaches, and beards. They are white with markings that can be black, tricolor, grizzle, lemon, or orange.

Height: 13 to 15 inches

Weight: 25 to 40 pounds

Personality: Petit Basset Griffon Vendéen are happy, outgoing dogs, and they're smart and like to learn things. They tend to get easily excited. They love kids and other dogs. They can be a little greedy with their things. They like to bark.

Activity Level: High

First Loves: Playing, kids, other dogs

Best Families: Petit Basset Griffon Vendéen like older kids who can keep them busy. They like living in the country.

Pluses: Easy to train, friendly, fun loving, good for canine sports, good watchdogs

Minuses: Bark a lot, can be possessive with food and toys, can be pushy

Fun Fact: Because their name is so long, their friends usually call them PBGVs for short.

PHARAOH HOUND

Where They Are From: Malta

History: The Pharaoh Hound is the national breed of Malta. Its likeness is even on a Maltese silver coin. In Malta, Pharaoh Hounds were used to hunt rabbit. Dogs who look like Pharaoh Hounds are common in ancient Egyptian art. Until recently, they were believed to be direct descendants of these dogs. New research shows that it's more likely modern Pharaoh Hounds were bred to look like ancient Egyptian dogs, rather than being directly related.

Looks: Pharaoh Hounds are large, slender dogs with narrow heads and large erect ears. They have long whip tails. Their noses, lips, and the rims of their eyes are pinkish in color. Their short coats are tan or chestnut with a white mark on the chests and the tips of the tails.

(See the charts on pages 60–61 for term definitions.)

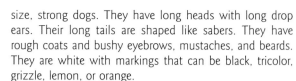

Height: 21 to 25 inches
Weight: No standard
Personality: Pharaoh Hounds are bubbly, happy dogs. They are smart and like to learn new things. They adore their families but are sometimes a little shy with new people. They will chase small animals.
Activity Level: Moderate to high
First Loves: Playing, their families
Best Families: Pharaoh Hounds do well with mature older kids who have time to exercise them at least once a day. They prefer living in houses with big fenced yards.
Pluses: Clean (sometimes people say they are like cats), easy to groom, easy to train, fun loving, patient
Minuses: Can be a little shy, need secure fenced yards and to be kept on a leash, like to chase things
Fun Fact: Pharaoh Hounds' pinkish noses blush when they get excited.

PLOTT

Where They Are From: United States
History: Plotts were bred by a German immigrant family named Plott, who brought their hounds to the United States in 1750. The Plott family bred their dogs to hunt bears and wild boars in the Smoky Mountains of North Carolina.

Looks: Plotts are large, strong dogs. They have large heads and drop ears. They have long tapered tails. Their short coats are blue, gray brindle, black, brown, tan, red, or yellow.
Height: 21 to 25 inches
Weight: 40 to 60 pounds
Personality: Plotts are smart, outgoing dogs who love to learn. They are very attached to their families, and they like kids and other dogs. They tend to be loud and a bit intense.
Activity Level: High
First Loves: Hunting, their families
Best Families: Plott Hounds like older kids with lots of energy who will keep them busy. They like to live in the country.
Pluses: Easy to train, friendly with kids and dogs, good watchdogs, lots of energy, loyal, smart

Minuses: Can be loud, drool, need lots of attention and exercise
Fun Fact: They were originally called Plott's Hound, meaning they belonged to the family that bred them.

POINTER

Where They Are From: Great Britain
History: Pointers were probably originally from Spain. During the seventeenth century in Great Britain, they were used by hunters to point game. That means when they found game, they froze and "pointed" in the direction of the animal to show the hunter where it was.
Looks: Pointers are large, strong dogs with strong heads and medium-size drop ears. They have medium-length tails that are carried high. Their short coats are black, orange, liver, or lemon (or all four!), usually with white as well.
Height: 23 to 28 inches
Weight: 45 to 75 pounds
Personality: Pointers are smart, brave, energetic dogs. They love to work and play. They are gentle and get along with kids and other dogs. They may chase smaller animals. They can be stubborn.
Activity Level: High
First Loves: Playing, working
Best Families: Pointers love older kids who like to do outdoorsy stuff as much as they do. Their families should have time to give them lots of exercise. It is best for them to live in the country or in houses with very big yards.
Pluses: Always up for a good time, easy to groom, fun, gentle, get along with kids and other dogs, great dogs for sports
Minuses: Don't do well in the city, need loads of exercise and attention, not good watchdogs
Fun Fact: The reason Pointers point for so long is because seventeenth-century hunters used flintlock guns. The flintlock gun had to be loaded with gunpowder and a bullet for each shot, which took some time. The hunting dog had to be able to "stay on point" until the hunter was ready to fire.

POLISH LOWLAND SHEEPDOG

Where They Are From: Poland

History: Polish Lowland Sheepdogs worked as sheepherders for hundreds of years. They are closely related to the Puli. A few Polish Lowland Sheepdogs were brought to Scotland in the sixteenth century. Some people say that these dogs are the Bearded Collie's ancestors.

Looks: Polish Lowland Sheepdogs are medium-size dogs with large round heads and drop ears. They have short tails. Their coats are long and thick and can be any color.

Height: 16 to 20 inches

Weight: 30 to 50 pounds

Personality: Polish Lowland Sheepdogs are smart, cheerful dogs who love to learn things. They adore their people and like kids and most other animals. They don't always like strangers, and they don't like to be told what to do.

Activity Level: Moderate to high

First Loves: Their families, herding

Best Families: Polish Lowland Sheepdogs love older kids who have had dogs before. Their families must have time to exercise them. They prefer living in houses with yards.

Pluses: Easy to train, enjoy doggy sports, gentle, good watchdogs, good with kids and other animals, loving, loyal

Minuses: Can be stubborn, can be unfriendly with strangers, need to be groomed

Fun Fact: In Poland, Polish Lowland Sheepdogs are called Polski Owczarek Nizinny, or PONs.

(See the charts on pages 60–61 for term definitions.)

POMERANIAN

Where They Are From: Germany

History: Pomeranians are probably from Pomerania in eastern Germany. They were originally larger sled dogs, but they have been their current size since the nineteenth century. They were a favorite dog of Queen Victoria, the queen of England from 1837 to 1901.

Looks: Pomeranians are small dogs with a foxy look. Their ears are small and erect, and their tails curl over their backs. They have thick coats that are especially thick around the neck. They can be any color, but they are usually red, orange, cream sable, black, or both black and tan.

Height: 8 to 11 inches

Weight: 3 to 7 pounds

Personality: Pomeranians are brave, outgoing dogs. They are smart and love to learn new things. They can be pushy and even a little mean if they aren't trained. They sometimes guard their toys and food.

Activity Level: Moderate

First Loves: Their people, their stuff

Best Families: Mature older kids who can teach them to be friendly to everyone are great companions. Pomeranians don't mind if they live in apartments.

Pluses: Brave, can live in an apartment, don't need a lot of exercise, good watchdogs, outgoing, smart

Minuses: Can be pushy, may guard food and toys, need to be trained and socialized or can be unfriendly

Fun Fact: Queen Victoria's Pomeranian, Turi, was at her bedside when she died.

POODLE (MINIATURE AND TOY)

Where They Are From: France

History: The Miniature and Toy Poodles were bred from the Standard Poodle in the eighteenth century. For the most part, they have always been pet dogs. Some worked as truffle hunters and circus performers.

Looks: The Miniature and Toy Poodles look like small versions of the Standard Poodle. Their drop ears are long and wide, and they have docked tails. Their curly coats are white, black, gray, blue, cream, silver, or apricot. The coat is either clipped or is left to form cords—kind of like dreadlocks—which happens when the fur gets long and twists together.

Height: Up to 10 inches (toy); 11 to 15 inches (miniature)

Weight: 5 to 7 pounds (toy); 14 to 16 pounds (miniature)

Personality: Miniature and Toy Poodles are smart and bubbly dogs. They love to play and enjoy learning tricks. They always want to please their people, and they thrive on human companionship. They can be a little nervous, especially with strangers and with young kids.

Activity Level: Moderate

First Loves: People

Best Families: Miniature and Toy Poodles like to share their homes with older, gentle kids who have lots of time for them.

Pluses: Adjust well to apartment life, good watchdogs, like to learn new things, low shedders, playful, smart

Minuses: Bark a lot, can be sensitive, hate to be left alone, need to be groomed

Fun Fact: Poodles were popular with French royalty during the eighteenth century. Poodles and other low-shedding dogs are often thought to be better for people with allergies. It may be because they produce less dander (dead skin cells), or it may just be because they go to the groomer more often!

POODLE (STANDARD)

Where They Are From: France

History: Despite their fancy looks, Standard Poodles were originally bred as hunting dogs. They were used to retrieve game from the water. Now, they are popular pet and show dogs. They have also been performing dogs.

Looks: Standard Poodles are medium to large dogs. They have long heads and long drop ears. Their tails are docked and held up. Their bodies are covered with curly hair. They are white, silver, gray, cream, café au lait, apricot, brown, blue, or black.

Height: Over 15 inches

Weight: 45 to 70 pounds

Personality: Standard Poodles are smart, playful, gentle dogs. They love to learn new things, and they always want to please their people. They like kids and other dogs, but sometimes they take a while to warm up to strangers.

Activity Level: High

First Loves: Their people

Best Families: Standard Poodles enjoy kids who love to play and will give them lots of cuddles. They like living in the country or in houses with big yards.

Pluses: Affectionate, friendly with kids and other animals, fun-loving, good for people with allergies (see Fun Fact on Miniature and Toy Poodle), good watchdogs, loyal

Minuses: Bark a lot, need lots of exercise and attention, need to be groomed

Fun Fact: The froufrou haircut some Poodles wear actually had a purpose—to make them faster in the water. The pom-poms at their knees and hips were to keep their joints warm when working in very cold water.

PORTUGUESE WATER DOG

Where They Are From: Portugal

History: Portuguese Water Dogs worked for Portuguese fisherman for hundreds of years, probably since the Middle Ages. They were used on boats to tow lines and fishing nets, to carry messages from boat to boat and from boat to shore, and to retrieve broken nets.

Looks: Portuguese Water Dogs are medium-size dogs with medium-size drop ears. They are covered with soft curly or wavy coats. Their tails are medium length. The coats are kept one length all over their bodies or with the hindquarters and faces shaved.

Height: 17 to 23 inches

Weight: 35 to 60 pounds

Personality: Portuguese water dogs are smart, brave, and full of spunk. They love their families and like kids and other dogs. They are playful and fun-loving. They are often quite loud.

Activity Level: High

First Loves: Water, playing, their families

Best Families: Portuguese Water Dogs love families with active kids who will take them swimming often. They need lots of exercise, so they like houses with large yards.

Pluses: Active, always ready to go, friendly, fun, good watchdogs, good with kids and other dogs, great dogs for canine activities

Minuses: Bark a lot, chew, need lots of exercise and attention

Fun Fact: You've probably heard of dogs herding goats, cattle, and sheep, but did you know that Portuguese Water Dogs herd fish? Really! They help fishermen by herding fish into nets.

(See the charts on pages 60–61 for term definitions.)

PUG

Where They Are From: China

History: Pugs may have been around for two thousand years. They have always been pet dogs. They were especially popular with Chinese royalty. In the sixteenth century, they became popular pet dogs in Holland after a Pug saved the life of the crown prince.

Looks: Pugs are small, stocky dogs. They have large round heads with lots of wrinkles and small rose or button ears. They have short muzzles and underbites. Their eyes are large and round, and their tails are tightly curled. They have short coats that are fawn, silver, apricot, or black. They have black masks and black ears.

Height: 10 to 11 inches

Weight: 14 to 18 pounds

Personality: Pugs are happy, sweet, playful dogs. They are smart and love learning. More than anything, they want to please their people. They love everyone, especially kids.

Activity Level: Low

First Loves: Their people

Best Families: Pugs love lively kids who enjoy spending lots of time with them. They don't mind if they live in apartments.

Pluses: Easy to groom, easy to train, friendly with everyone, gentle, loving, smart

Minuses: Can be sensitive to heat, need to have their head wrinkles cleaned, not much for doggy sports, shed, snore

Fun Fact: The Dutch call Pugs *mopshund*, which means "joke dog."

PULI

Where They Are From: Hungary

History: Pulik have worked as sheepherding dogs for more than a thousand years. They are probably related to Tibetan Terriers. They are very similar to another Hungarian breed, the Pumi.

Looks: Pulik are medium-size, strong dogs. They have wide heads and V-shaped drop ears. They have medium-length tails and long thick coats that are usually corded. The cords, which look like dreadlocks, reach all the way to the floor. They can be black, gray, or white.

Height: 15 to 18 inches
Weight: 30 pounds
Personality: Pulik are happy, smart, and energetic dogs. They adore their families, but they don't like strangers and don't always get along with young kids. They will usually herd other animals. They tend to be noisy.
Activity Level: High
First Loves: Playing, family
Best Families: Pulik like mature older kids who have had dogs before. Their families must have time to train and exercise them. It's best if they live in the country or in houses with very big yards.
Pluses: Fun loving, good watchdogs, like canine sports, loyal
Minuses: Bark a lot, can be unfriendly with young kids, don't like strangers, must be trained, need a lot of exercise, need to be groomed
Fun Fact: The plural of *Puli* is *Pulik*. So you don't have two Pulis, you have two Pulik!

PUMI

Where They Are From: Hungary
History: The Pumi's ancestors were Hungarian Pulik crossed with western European dogs brought to Hungary more 300 years ago. The Pumi was considered the same breed as the Puli until the early twentieth century. That's when breeders started breeding the original Puli again. Like the Puli, the Pumi is a herding dog. It is also used to hunt.
Looks: Pumis are medium-size dogs with long heads. They have semiprick ears and long tails that are curved over their backs. They have curly coats that form tufts. (Their coats don't form cords like the Pulik's.) They are gray, black, fawn, or white. Some have white markings.
Height: 13.5 to 17.5 inches
Weight: 18 to 30 pounds
Personality: They act a lot like terriers: very active and brave. They love their families but are a little shy with strangers. They don't like to be teased.
Activity Level: High
First Loves: Family, playing
Best Families: They enjoy mature older kids with lots of time for them. Their families should be able to train them and introduce them to lots of nice people. They prefer to live in the country or houses with big yards.
Pluses: Fun loving, hard working, loving, loyal
Minuses: Don't like to be teased, must be trained, need lots of exercise, very noisy
Fun Fact: Although they are herding dogs, Pumis are probably at least part terrier. They will even chase small animals into their dens.

RAT TERRIER (STANDARD AND MINIATURE)

Where They Are From: United States
History: Standard and Miniature Rat Terriers were common farm dogs during the early twentieth century. They were used as ratters. Later they were bred with faster dogs, such as Whippets, for hunting. They were developed by breeding terriers brought over by English immigrants. Some of their ancestors are the Manchester Terrier and the Smooth Fox Terrier.

Looks: Standard and Miniature Rat Terriers are small, strong dogs. They have large ears that are button, semi-prick, or prick. They have short coats that are solid white or white and black, tan, chocolate, blue, lemon, or apricot. There is a Miniature Rat Terrier and a Standard Rat Terrier.

Height: 13 to 18 inches (Standard); under 13 inches (Miniature)

Weight: 10 to 25 pounds

Personality: Standard and Miniature Rat Terriers are happy, hard working, and friendly. They like almost everyone. They are quite smart and can be a little noisy. They adapt to new situations well.

Activity Level: Moderate

First Loves: Their people

Best Families: Standard and Miniature Rat Terriers like kids who are as busy and as fun-loving as they are. Their families should have a lot of time for them.

Pluses: Can live in the city or the country, easy to groom, friendly, good watchdogs, like everyone, like to learn new things

Minuses: May chase small animals, need a lot of attention, need protection from the sun

Fun Fact: The Rat Terrier was a favorite dog of our twenty-sixth president, Theodore Roosevelt. There is even a short-legged Rat Terrier breed named after him.

RHODESIAN RIDGEBACK

Where They Are From: South Africa

History: White European settlers in the area that is now South Africa bred their dogs with the native ridgeback dogs kept by members of the Khoikhoi tribe. The resulting Rhodesian Ridgebacks were used for hunting African lions and as all-purpose farm dogs.

Looks: Rhodesian Ridgebacks are large, strong dogs. Their coats are short and wheaten colored. They have broad heads with lots of wrinkles on their foreheads. Their ears are drop, and they have long tails. They are best known for the ridge of hair along their spines.

(See the charts on pages 60–61 for term definitions.)

Height: 24 to 27 inches

Weight: 70 to 85 pounds

Personality: Rhodesian Ridgebacks are smart, brave, and playful dogs but also a bit stubborn. They are loyal to their friends and families, but they can be a little unfriendly with strangers. They must be trained. They will chase small animals and will sometimes wander off.

Activity Level: Moderate

First Loves: Their families

Best Families: Rhodesian Ridgebacks do best with mature older kids who have had dogs before. Their families must have time to train them.

Pluses: Fun, good watchdogs, smart

Minuses: Can be stubborn, hard to train, may chase small animals, unfriendly with strangers

Fun Fact: The Rhodesian's ridge is caused by two whorls of hair that grow in the opposite direction of the rest of the coat.

ROTTWEILER

Where They Are From: Germany

History: Rottweilers are probably related to ancient Roman cattle dogs. They were used as all-purpose working dogs in the German town of Rottweil. They have been cattle drovers, military and police dogs, guards, and pets.

Looks: Rottweilers are large, strong dogs with large heads and small drop ears. Their tails are docked. Their short coats are black with rust markings.

Height: 22 to 27 inches

Weight: 75 to 130 pounds

Personality: Rottweilers are calm, brave dogs. They are loyal and adore their families. Rottweilers get along with most kids and other animals. They take a while to warm up to strangers, though. They are protective, so they need to be trained and socialized from puppyhood.

Activity Level: Moderate

First Loves: Their families

Best Families: Rottweilers love mature older kids who have had dogs before. Their families must be able to train and socialize them. They prefer to live in houses with big fenced yards.

Pluses: Calm, easy to groom, easygoing, good dogs for doggy activities, good watchdogs, like to learn new things, loyal

Minuses: Can be overprotective, can be stubborn, need lots of attention, need to be trained and socialized, take a while to warm up to strangers

Fun Fact: Rottweilers may have first been brought to Rottweil by Roman armies. The Romans used dogs like them to drive their cattle.

SAINT BERNARD

Where They Are From: Switzerland

History: Saint Bernards are descendants of Roman Mastiffs. They were bred by Swiss monks at the hospice of the Great St. Bernard Pass in the Swiss Alps in the seventeenth century. There, they were used as guides and to rescue lost travelers. They have also been guardians and pet dogs, and they have even been used at times to pull wagons.

Looks: Saint Bernards are very large dogs. Their heads are large and they have medium-size drop ears. They have long furry tails. Their coats can be short or long, and they can be red, brown, or brindle, with large white markings.

Height: 25.5 to 30 inches

Weight: 120 to 180 pounds

Personality: Saint Bernards are gentle giants. They are very affectionate dogs. Fun and playful, they love children and get along with almost everyone. They like to meet new people.

Activity Level: Moderate

First Loves: Fun, kids, adults

Best Families: Saint Bernards love older kids who love to have fun. It's best for them to live in houses that have big yards.

Pluses: Affectionate, easygoing, friendly with almost everyone, fun

Minuses: Big dogs have big needs (everything is more expensive), can be messy, don't always know their own strength, drool, need to be groomed, need to be trained

Fun Fact: It's said that the Saint Bernards at the hospice have saved more than two thousand lives.

SALUKI

Where They Are From: Middle East

History: Many believe that Salukis are the oldest breed of dog still alive. Their ancestors hunted gazelle in Mesopotamia, the area that is now Iraq and Syria. In the Middle East, they are still used as hunting dogs, but they are pet dogs in the United States.

Looks: Salukis are tall, slender dogs with narrow heads and long drop ears. They have long curved tails. They can have short coats or long silky coats. They can be any color.

Height: 23 to 28 inches

Weight: 45 pounds

Personality: Salukis are quiet, gentle dogs. They are smart but independent, so they can be hard to train. Some people say they are more like cats than dogs. Some are shy, and they don't like to be left alone. They like to chase small animals.

Activity Level: Moderate

First Loves: Running, their people

Best Families: Salukis do well with mature older kids who can keep up with them. They hate to be left alone. Their families should also have fenced yards.

Pluses: Gentle, loyal, will play hard outside but like to be couch potatoes inside

Minuses: Chase small animals, hate to be left alone, long-haired dogs need to be groomed

Fun Fact: Salukis are a very old breed. There was a skeleton of a dog that looked like a Saluki found in Syria. It is believed to be from 2500 BC!

SAMOYED

Where They Are From:
Siberia

History: Samoyeds are a very old breed. They were first kept by the Samoyed people, a nomadic tribe—people who move from place to place—in Siberia. The Samoyed people used the dogs as hunters, sled dogs, and reindeer herders.

Looks: Samoyeds are medium-size dogs with very thick white coats. They have bushy tails that curl over their backs. They have prick ears. The corners of their mouths turn up, making them look like they are smiling.

Height: 19 to 23.5 inches

Weight: 35 to 65 pounds

Personality: Samoyeds are friendly, lovable dogs. They are smart but can be stubborn. They like to do things their way. They adore their families and hate to be left alone. They can be noisy.

Activity Level: High

First Loves: Family, playing in the snow

Best Families: Samoyeds love older kids with lots of energy and time for them. They are happiest living in a cold climate with lots of snow. They do well in the country but can also live in houses in a city or in a suburban neighborhood as long as there are big yards.

Pluses: Friendly with almost everyone, gentle, good watchdogs, great family dogs, love canine sports

Minuses: Bark a lot, can be stubborn, hard to train, hate to be left alone, shed a lot

(See the charts on pages 60–61 for term definitions.)

Fun Fact: The first Samoyeds in Europe were brought by polar explorers. In 1911, Roald Amundsen was the first explorer to reach the South Pole. His lead sled dog was a Samoyed named Etah. (Technically, Etah reached the South Pole first!)

SCHIPPERKE

Where They Are From: Belgium

History: Schipperkes were originally large sheepdogs, but they have been bred to be smaller since the seventeenth century. They worked as guards and ratters in shops and on canal boats. Their name means "little boatman" in Flemish.

Looks: Schipperkes are small to medium-size dogs with heavy black coats. They have erect ears and narrow fox-like faces. Their tails are docked.

Height: 9 to 13 inches

Weight: 7 to 18 pounds

Personality: Schipperkes are busy, fun-loving balls of energy. They are brave and curious and always want to know exactly what is going on. They can be a little pushy and greedy with their stuff. They get along with most animals but take a while to warm up to human strangers.

Activity Level: Moderate to high

First Loves: Their people, boating

Best Families: Schipperkes do well with active older kids who have lots of time for them. They don't mind where they live as long as their families have time to walk and train them.

Pluses: Energetic, fun, good watchdogs, loving

Minuses: Can be hard to house-train, can be pushy and greedy with their stuff, don't like to be messed with, take a while to warm up to new people

Fun Fact: Schipperkes were originally called spits or spitske.

SCOTTISH DEERHOUND

Where They Are From: Scotland

History: Scottish Deerhounds have been used to hunt deer since the sixteenth century. Until the mid-nineteenth century, only Scottish nobles were allowed to keep them.

Looks: Scottish Deerhounds are very tall, strong dogs. They have long, narrow heads with small semiprick ears.

Their long tails taper. They have shaggy, wiry coats and beards and mustaches. They are usually dark blue-gray but can be yellow, fawn, red, or brindle.

Height: 28 to 32 inches
Weight: 75 to 110 pounds
Personality: Scottish Deerhounds are friendly, easygoing dogs. They love everyone, especially kids. They are brave and smart. They like to learn new things. They sometimes chase small animals and can be a little stubborn.
Activity Level: Moderate
First Loves: Their families, kids
Best Families: Scottish Deerhounds enjoy kids who have enough time to play with them. They should live in houses with yards.
Pluses: Easygoing, friendly, good dogs for canine activities, good watchdogs
Minuses: May chase small animals, need to be groomed
Fun Fact: Scottish Deerhounds became less popular among hunters in the eighteenth century. This was when hunters began to use guns to hunt deer so there was less need for the dogs.

SCOTTISH TERRIER

Where They Are From: Scotland
History: Scottish Terriers were bred in the Scottish Highlands in the nineteenth century. They were originally used to hunt foxes and badgers.
Looks: Scottish Terriers are small, sturdy dogs. They have long bodies and short legs. Their ears are small and erect, and they have carrot tails. They have wiry coats, long beards, and bushy eyebrows. They can be black, sandy, wheaten, or brindle.

Height: 10 inches
Weight: 18 to 22 pounds
Personality: Scottish Terriers are outgoing and spunky with a lot of attitude. They love their people but can be a little pushy and stubborn. They don't always like other dogs or cats and will chase smaller animals. Some are sensitive and may snap if they are irritated.
Activity Level: Moderate

First Loves: Their people, playing
Best Families: Scottish Terriers do well with mature older kids who aren't wishy-washy. Their families should have time to train and exercise them.
Pluses: Can adapt to living in the city or the country, fun loving, good watchdogs, loads of personality
Minuses: Can be aggressive with other animals, can be snappy, hard to train, sensitive
Fun Fact: Fala, a Scottish Terrier, may be the most famous dog in world history. She was President Franklin D. Roosevelt's constant companion.

SEALYHAM TERRIER

Where They Are From: Wales
History: Sealyham Terriers were bred in the nineteenth century on a Sealyham estate in the town of Haverfordwest in Pembrokeshire, Wales. They were used to hunt foxes, badgers, and otters. Now they are popular show dogs and pets.
Looks: Sealyham Terriers are small dogs with long bodies and short legs. They have rectangular-shaped heads with heavy beards and whiskers. Their ears fold down. Their tails are docked short and held up. They have wiry coats that are white. Some have lemon, tan, or badger markings.

Height: 10.5 inches
Weight: 20 to 24 pounds
Personality: Sealyham Terriers are spunky dogs with an excellent sense of humor. They love their families but don't always like strangers. They don't like to be teased or messed with. They will chase small animals and can be stubborn.

Activity Level: Moderate
First Loves: Their people, playing
Best Families: Sealyham Terriers like mature older kids who have had terriers before. Their families must be able to train and exercise them. They don't mind living in the country or the city.
Pluses: Fun loving, good for people with allergies (low shedders), good watchdogs, loving, loyal
Minuses: Chase small animals, hard to train, need to be groomed, sensitive, stubborn
Fun Fact: Director Alfred Hitchcock loved Sealyham Terriers. In his famous movie *The Birds*, Hitchcock walks out of a pet store with his own Sealyhams, Geoffrey and Stanley.

SHETLAND SHEEPDOG

Where They Are From: Scotland
History: Shetland Sheepdogs were first bred as herding dogs in the Shetland Islands. These are the islands between Scotland and Norway in the North Sea. Shetland Sheepdogs look like small Collies, but Collies are only one of their ancestors. They are also related to the Spitz dogs first brought to the islands by Vikings.
Looks: Shetland Sheepdogs have long noses and semi-prick ears. They have long furry tails. Their long thick coats are especially heavy around their necks and back legs. They can be black, sable, or blue merle. They may have white

(See the charts on pages 60–61 for term definitions.)

and tan markings. Their eyes can be brown or blue or one of each color.
Height: 13 to 16 inches
Weight: 20 to 25 pounds
Personality: Shetland Sheepdogs are cheerful, lively dogs. They love their families. They can be a little shy with strangers. They like kids but don't like a lot of noise. They are smart and love to learn new things. They can be nervous and bark a lot.
Activity Level: High
First Loves: Their families, doggy sports
Best Families: Shetland Sheepdogs like mature older kids who like outdoorsy activities. They prefer to live in houses in the suburbs or the country.
Pluses: Easy to train, gentle, good watchdogs, great dogs for sports, lovable, loyal, smart
Minuses: Bark a lot, can be nervous, shed a lot, sometimes shy with new people
Fun Fact: Shetland Sheepdogs are just one of the compact animals bred in the Shetland Islands. There are also tiny Shetland ponies and Shetland sheep—all small versions of larger animals!

SHIBA INU

Where They Are From: Japan
History: Shiba Inus are the oldest of the Japanese breeds. They have been used to hunt birds, small game, and boars for almost two thousand years. They are the most popular pet dog in Japan. In 1937, they were made a national monument of Japan and are considered a national treasure.
Looks: Shiba Inus are medium-size dogs with a foxy look. They have thick, straight coats. They have prick ears, and their bushy tails curl over their backs. They are red, red with black tips, or black with tan markings.
Height: 13.5 to 16.5 inches
Weight: 15 to 25 pounds
Personality: Shiba Inus are smart, lively, curious dogs. They are very bold and can be greedy with their things. They are very confident, even arrogant, and they can be a little unfriendly. They hardly ever bark. Some people say they are catlike.

Activity Level: Moderate

First Loves: Their families, doggy sports

Best Families: Shiba Inus love mature older kids who can handle them. They don't mind where they live as long as they get lots of exercise.

Pluses: Clean, curious, enjoy canine sports, fun loving, good watchdogs, quiet, smart

Minuses: Can be greedy with their things, can be pushy, don't like to be teased, shed

Fun Fact: Shiba Inus don't really bark. Instead, they make a sound that sounds like a mix between a yelp and a howl.

SHIH TZU

Where They Are From: China

History: Shih Tzus are one of the small Asian dogs bred to look like the Buddhist Fo Dog (the tame lion Buddha kept as a pet). They are at least one thousand years old. They were bred in the Forbidden City in Beijing and kept only by Chinese royalty.

Looks: Shih Tzus are small dogs. They have very long coats that touch the ground. The long hair on their heads is usually tied into a topknot and often tied with a ribbon. They can be any color. They have long drop ears, and their tails curl over their backs.

Height: 8 to 11 inches

Weight: 9 to 16 pounds

Personality: Shih Tzus are happy, sweet dogs. They love everyone, including kids and other dogs. They love to sit on laps. They are smart and always ready to go.

Activity Level: Low

First Loves: Their people, warm laps

Best Families: Shih Tzus like kids who don't mind a dog on their laps all the time. They don't mind if they live in apartments.

Pluses: Friendly with everyone, good apartment dogs, loving, playful

Minuses: Need to be groomed, not much for canine sports

Fun Fact: One Shih Tzu nickname was Chrysanthemum-faced Dog because their hair sprouts around their faces like the petals of a chrysanthemum flower.

SIBERIAN HUSKY

Where They Are From: Siberia

History: Siberian Huskies may be more than three thousand years old. They were bred by the Chukchi Indians, a nomadic (traveling) tribe in Siberia, and they were used as sled dogs. In the early twentieth century, they became popular dogs for sled-dog racing.

Looks: Siberian Huskies are medium-size, strong dogs. Their tails are long and bushy. They have prick ears. Their thick coats can be any color but are usually a mix of gray and white or brown and white. Their eyes may be brown or blue, one of each, or a mix of both!

Height: 20 to 23.5 inches

Weight: 35 to 60 pounds

Personality: Siberian Huskies are bubbly dogs who love everyone. They are outgoing and get along with kids and dogs. They may chase small animals. They are known for running away.

Activity Level: High

First Loves: People, running, playing

Best Families: Siberian Huskies like older kids who are responsible. They need families who will give them lots of exercise and who will make sure they don't run away. They like living in the country or in houses with big fenced yards.

Pluses: Energetic, friendly, great family dogs, great running or hiking companions, great with kids, love everyone

Minuses: Can get into trouble if left alone, don't bond to one person, need lots of attention and exercise, run away, shed

Fun Fact: During World War II, Siberian Huskies worked as search and rescue dogs for the U.S. Army.

SILKY TERRIER

Where They Are From: Australia

History: Silky Terriers were first bred in the nineteenth century and have always been pet dogs. They were bred from Australian Terriers and Yorkshire Terriers.

Looks: Silky Terriers are small, delicate dogs with long straight coats that are parted down the middle, from head to tail. They have small erect ears and docked tails. They are blue and tan.

Height: 9 to 10 inches

Weight: 8 to 10 pounds

Personality: Silky Terriers are smart, outgoing, and always on the go. They love their people and want to be with them all the time. They can be a little nippy. They may chase other animals and can be greedy with their toys and food.

Activity Level: Moderate

First Loves: Their people

Best Families: Silky Terriers like mature older kids who have lots of time for them. It's fine with them if they live in apartments.

Pluses: Adapt to city life well, affectionate, fun loving, good watchdogs, love their people, loyal

Minuses: Bark, can be greedy with toys and food, can be nippy, may chase other animals, need to be groomed

Fun Fact: These terriers were originally called the Sydney Silky Terrier, then the Australian Silky Terrier, and now they are simply called the Silky Terrier.

SKYE TERRIER

Where They Are From: Scotland

History: Skye Terriers are from the Isle of Skye, an island off the coast of Scotland. They were originally bred in the sixteenth century to hunt small game. Later they became favorite pets of English royalty.

Looks: Skye Terriers are small but strong dogs with long bodies and short legs. They have long thick coats that cover their foreheads and eyes. They have prick or drop ears that are covered with hair. Their tails are long and feathered. Their coat color is a blend of black, blue, gray, silver, fawn, and cream.

Height: 9 to 10 inches

Weight: 23 to 28 pounds

Personality: Skye Terriers are brave, serious dogs. They are hard workers but like to relax at home. They adore their families but don't always like new people. Skye Terriers can be stubborn, and they don't like to be teased. They will chase small animals and sometimes fight with other dogs.

(See the charts on pages 60–61 for term definitions.)

Activity Level: Low

First Loves: Their families, working, relaxing

Best Families: Skye Terriers get along with mature older kids who have had terriers before. Their families must be prepared to train and socialize them. They don't mind living in the country or the city.

Pluses: Adapt to city or country, good watchdogs, love their people, very loyal

Minuses: Can be aggressive with other dogs, chase small animals, don't like to be teased, stubborn

Fun Fact: Skye Terriers' loyalty is legendary. The most famous story of a Skye Terrier's loyalty is that of Greyfriars Bobby. When Bobby's best friend John Gray died in 1852, the dog wouldn't leave his grave, in Greyfriars Kirkyard. Greyfriars Bobby stayed at Gray's grave every day for the next fourteen years. He left only for his supper.

SOFT COATED WHEATEN TERRIER

Where They Are From: Ireland

History: Soft Coated Wheaten Terriers may be related to Irish dogs from thousands of years ago, and they are probably related to Irish Terriers and Kerry Blue Terriers. They were originally used as all-around farm dogs as well as pets.

Looks: Soft Coated Wheaten Terriers are medium-size dogs with long heads. They have small ears that fold forward. Their tails are docked and held up. Their soft, wavy coats are wheaten colored, and they have fur covering their eyes and beards.

Height: 9 to 10 inches

Weight: 23 to 28 pounds

Personality: Soft Coated Wheaten Terriers are easygoing and love to play. They adore their families and hate to be left alone. They usually get along with kids and other animals, but they can be stubborn.

Activity Level: High

First Loves: Family, friends

Best Families: Mature older kids who have time to train and exercise them make great friends. Soft Coated

Wheaten Terriers prefer to live in houses with yards.

Pluses: Easygoing, fun, good dogs for sports, good for people with allergies (low shedders), good watchdogs, like almost everyone, loving, loyal

Minuses: Can be stubborn, may chase small animals, need lots of attention, need lots of exercise, need to be groomed

Fun Fact: They are known for the Wheaten welcome. This is when a friendly Wheaten greets you by jumping up and giving you a big doggy kiss.

STAFFORDSHIRE BULL TERRIER

Where They Are From: Great Britain

History: Staffordshire Bull Terriers were first bred in the early nineteenth century. They were created by breeding old-fashioned Bulldogs and terriers together. They were first used for dog fighting and ratting. When dog fighting was made illegal, they became popular pet dogs.

Looks: Staffordshire Bull Terriers are very muscular, medium-size dogs. They have big heads with lots of wrinkles and rose or semiprick ears. Their tails are medium length and held down. Their coats are short and can be brindle, white, black, blue, red, or fawn. Some have white markings.

Height: 14 to 16 inches

Weight: 24 to 38 pounds

Personality: Staffordshire Bull Terriers are happy, outgoing dogs who love almost everyone they meet, especially kids. They are very brave. They don't get angry easily, but they often don't like other dogs and will fight with them. They will chase smaller animals.

Activity Level: High

First Loves: Kids, playing, pulling

Best Families: Staffordshire Bull Terriers like all kids but do best with mature older kids. They need families who will train and socialize them because they don't always know their own strength. They don't mind where they live as long as they get lots of walks and love.

Pluses: Easy to groom, good dogs for sports, good with most people, like to learn new things, love kids, love to play, very affectionate

Minuses: May chase smaller animals, need lots of attention, need lots of exercise, often fight with other dogs

Fun Fact: In Great Britain, Staffordshire Bull Terriers are known as nanny dogs because they love children so much.

STANDARD SCHNAUZER

Where They Are From: Germany

History: Standard Schnauzers are the original Schnauzers, and the ancestors of both the Giant Schnauzers and the Miniature Schnauzers. Standard Schnauzers were first bred in the fifteenth century. They worked as general farm dogs, where they were ratters, guards, and pets. They were often used to guard farmers' carts when the farmers went to market.

Looks: Standard Schnauzers are medium-size dogs. Their heads are rectangular, and they have eyebrows, mustaches, and beards. They have button ears and docked tails that are carried up. Their wiry coats are salt-and-pepper or black.

Height: 17 to 20 inches

Weight: 30 to 50 pounds

Personality: Standard Schnauzers are smart, spunky, brave dogs. They like other dogs but won't back down from a fight. They love to play. They are very attached to their people but will bark at strangers. They can be a little naughty when they're bored.

Activity Level: High

First Loves: Their families, playing

Best Families: Standard Schnauzers love older kids with lots of time to play with them. They don't mind living in the city if they get enough exercise.

Pluses: Brave, good watchdogs, good with kids and other animals, great dogs for sports, lively, loyal

Minuses: Bark a lot, can be naughty, need a lot of exercise, need to be groomed, sometimes unfriendly with strangers

Fun Fact: During World War I, Standard Schnauzers worked as messenger dogs and Red Cross dogs.

SUSSEX SPANIEL

Where They Are From: Great Britain

History: Sussex Spaniels have been bred since the eighteenth century. They were first used as hunting dogs on large estates in Sussex, England. They almost disappeared after World War II, but a breeder worked very hard to bring the breed back. They are still used as hunting dogs, but they are also popular show dogs and pets.

Looks: Sussex Spaniels are long, sturdy dogs with short legs. They have long drop ears and a serious look. Their tails are docked. Their medium-length, golden liver coats

are either straight or wavy. They have feathering on their ears, legs, chests, and tails.

Height: 13 to 15 inches

Weight: 35 to 45 pounds

Personality: Sussex Spaniels are cheerful, outgoing dogs. They like kids and most other animals. They are full of love for their families and friends.

Activity Level: Moderate

First Loves: Their people

Best Families: Sussex Spaniels love families who will give them lots of love. They don't mind where they live as long as they get plenty of walks.

Pluses: Friendly with almost everyone, fun loving, good watchdogs

Minuses: Bark or howl a lot, can be a little stubborn, need to be groomed

Fun Fact: Sussex Spaniels were originally used by hunters who were on foot rather than on horses. The dogs were bred to move slowly so the hunters could keep up with them!

SWEDISH VALLHUND

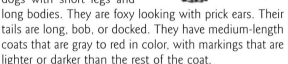

Where They Are From: Sweden

History: Swedish Vallhunds are a very old herding breed. The Vikings used them as all-purpose farm dogs. They are probably related to Corgis.

Looks: Swedish Vallhunds are small, strong dogs with short legs and long bodies. They are foxy looking with prick ears. Their tails are long, bob, or docked. They have medium-length coats that are gray to red in color, with markings that are lighter or darker than the rest of the coat.

Height: 12 to 14 inches

Weight: 25 to 35 pounds

Personality: Swedish Vallhunds are gutsy, curious dogs with sweet personalities. They are smart and love to learn new things. They love their families and like kids and other dogs.

Activity Level: Moderate

First Loves: Their people, playing

Best Families: Swedish Vallhunds love families with lots of energy. They don't mind where they live as long as their families can spend lots of time with them.

Pluses: Easy to train, friendly, good dogs for sports, good watchdogs, sweet

(See the charts on pages 60–61 for term definitions.)

Minuses: Bark, shed

Fun Fact: In Swedish, *vallhund* means "herding dog." However, Swedes don't call these dogs Swedish Vallhunds. Instead, they are called Västgötaspets, after the region they are from.

TIBETAN MASTIFF

Where They Are From: Tibet

History: It is believed that Tibetan Mastiffs are the original mastiff dogs. They were bred to be guards in Tibetan villages.

Looks: Tibetan Mastiffs are very large, strong dogs. They have big wrinkly heads and droopy lips. They have drop ears. Their long bushy tails curl over their backs. Their long thick coats can be black; brown; gold; black and tan; gray and blue; or blue, gray, and tan. They have tan markings.

Height: 24 to 30 inches

Weight: 75 to 160 pounds

Personality: Tibetan Mastiffs are smart and quite independent. They act a bit like cats. They love their people, but they can be stubborn. They are protective so they need to be trained and socialized. They are loyal and loving with their friends, but they take a while to warm up to strangers. They usually like kids and other animals.

Activity Level: Moderate

First Loves: Their families, their homes

Best Families: Tibetan Mastiffs like friends who are older and mature and have had dogs before. Their families must be patient and able to train them. It's best if they live in houses with very big yards.

Pluses: Good with kids and other animals, great watchdogs, loyal, patient

Minuses: Can be overprotective, need a lot of attention, need grooming, need to be trained and socialized

Fun Fact: Traditionally, Tibetan Mastiffs were kept tied to stakes in camps of nomadic (traveling) people during the day. In villages, they were kept tied to the gates of homes and monasteries. At night, they were let loose so they could guard the camps and villages.

TIBETAN SPANIEL

Where They Are From: Tibet

History: The Tibetan Spaniel was bred by Tibetan monks to look like the Buddhist Fo Dog. The Fo Dog was a tame lion said to be kept as a pet by Buddha. Tibetan Spaniels worked as guards inside Tibetan monasteries, where they barked at intruders from the top of the monastery walls.

Looks: Tibetan Spaniels are small dogs with small heads. They have drop ears. Their feathered tails curl over their backs. They have thick silky coats. There is extra hair around their necks, ears, and tails. They are fawn, cream, white, red, black, or black and tan.

Height: 9 to 11 inches

Weight: 9 to 15 pounds

Personality: Some people say Tibetan Spaniels act more like cats than dogs. They are gentle and loving with people and animals they know. They take a while to warm up to strangers. They can be a bit noisy.

Activity Level: Low to moderate

First Loves: Their people

Best Families: Tibetan Spaniels love families who have time to walk and play with them. They don't mind living in the country or the city.

Pluses: Friendly, good apartment dogs, good watchdogs, good with kids and other animals

Minuses: Can be unfriendly with strangers, need to be groomed

Fun Fact: Tibetan Spaniels aren't spaniels at all. They are most closely related to Pekingese and Japanese Chins.

TIBETAN TERRIER

Where They Are From: Tibet

History: Tibetan Terriers are a very old breed, going back maybe two thousand years. They were kept by monasteries in the Lost Valley of Tibet as guards and herders. But more important than their jobs was that they were symbols of luck. Although *terrier* is part of their name, they are not actually terriers. They are thought to be related to Lhasa Apsos.

Looks: Tibetan Terriers are medium-size dogs with long heavy coats that can be any color. Their coats are especially heavy on their heads, where the hair covers their eyes. They have large flat feet that help them walk in the snow (like snowshoes!). They have drop ears and medium-length tails.

Height: 14 to 17 inches

Weight: 18 to 30 pounds

Personality: Tibetan Terriers are smart, playful, outgoing dogs. They are unfriendly with strangers at first, but once they are introduced, they love almost everyone. They are friendly with kids and with other dogs. They can be loud.

Activity Level: Low to moderate

(See the charts on pages 60–61 for term definitions.)

First Loves: Family

Best Families: Tibetan Terriers like older kids who will give them lots of love and attention. They can get along in any lifestyle, so they don't mind living in the city or the country. Their families can be jogging partners or TV buddies.

Pluses: Adapt to new situations well, easy to train, friendly, good watchdogs

Minuses: Bark a lot, need to be groomed, unfriendly with strangers at first

Fun Fact: Traditionally, Tibetan Terriers were never bought or sold. They were only given as gifts.

VIZSLA

Where They Are From: Hungary

History: Dogs who looked like Vizslas have been found in Europe for close to a thousand years. They have been used as pointers and retrievers since the nineteenth century. They are also popular pets.

Looks: Vizslas are medium-size, muscular dogs. Their short coats are golden rust. They have drop ears, and their tails are docked short.

Height: 21 to 24 inches

Weight: 50 to 65 pounds

Personality: Vizslas are lively, sweet dogs. They love their people and like to meet new people. They get along with kids and other dogs. They don't like to be teased.

Activity Level: High

First Loves: Their people, playing

Best Families: Vizslas like older kids who can give them lots of exercise and attention. They like living in the country or in houses with big yards.

Pluses: Easy to groom, friendly, full of fun, gentle, good dogs for canine sports

Minuses: Can be naughty if they don't get enough exercise, need lots of attention (and exercise), sensitive

Fun Fact: Stone etchings from more than one thousand years ago show dogs that look like Vizslas.

WEIMARANER
Where They Are From: Germany

History: Weimaraners were bred to hunt large game in the nineteenth century. They were popular with German nobility. Later, they were used to hunt birds.

Looks: Weimaraners are large, muscular dogs. They have long drop ears, and their tails are docked. Their short coats are gray. They have light-colored eyes and gray noses.

Height: 23 to 27 inches

Weight: 55 to 85 pounds

Personality: Weimaraners are smart, fun, lively dogs. They love kids and get along with other dogs. Sometimes they will chase cats. They can be pushy and stubborn.

Activity Level: High

First Loves: Playing, their people

Best Families: Weimaraners like families with older kids who can give them at least one long walk a day. They love living in the country or near a big park.

Pluses: Always ready to play, easy to groom, friendly, good dogs for canine sports

Minuses: Can be naughty if they don't get enough exercise, can be pushy, can be stubborn, need lots of attention

Fun Fact: Weimaraners are sometimes called gray ghosts because of their color.

WELSH SPRINGER SPANIEL
Where They Are From: Wales

History: Welsh Springer Spaniels have been used as hunting dogs in Wales since the Middle Ages. Their ancestors are hunting dogs that were used in Britain as long ago as 250 BC! Welsh Springer Spaniels were very popular hunting dogs in the 1700s.

Looks: Welsh Springer Spaniels are medium-size dogs with medium-length silky coats. Their long ears are drop. Their tails are long but can be docked. There is feathering on their ears, bodies, and legs. They are red and white with red spots on their muzzles that look like freckles.

Height: 17 to 19 inches

Weight: 35 to 50 pounds

Personality: Welsh Springer Spaniels are spunky, sweet, and outgoing dogs. They especially enjoy children and other animals. They love to learn new things and always want to please their people.

Activity Level: High

First Loves: Their people, other dogs

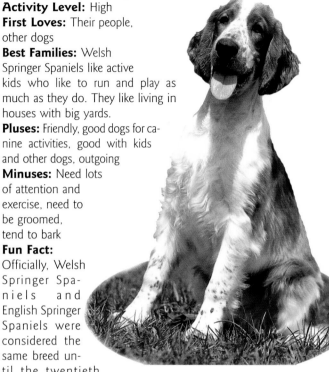

Best Families: Welsh Springer Spaniels like active kids who like to run and play as much as they do. They like living in houses with big yards.

Pluses: Friendly, good dogs for canine activities, good with kids and other dogs, outgoing

Minuses: Need lots of attention and exercise, need to be groomed, tend to bark

Fun Fact: Officially, Welsh Springer Spaniels and English Springer Spaniels were considered the same breed until the twentieth century. However, in Wales, Welsh Springer Spaniels have been a distinct breed for a couple of hundred years. They are smaller than English Springer Spaniels and much less common.

WELSH TERRIER
Where They Are From: Wales

History: Welsh Terriers were bred at least three hundred years ago. They originally were used to hunt otters, foxes, and badgers. Welsh Terriers first came to the United States in the late nineteenth century.

Looks: Welsh Terriers are medium-size dogs with long heads. Their small ears fold forward. Their tails are docked and carried up. They have short wiry coats that are tan with black markings. They have heavy beards and bushy eyebrows.

Height: 15 inches

Weight: 19 to 22 pounds

Personality: Welsh Terriers are hard workers but are also happy to relax at home. They adore their families.

They are smart and like to learn new things. They are full of energy and can play all day long. They may chase smaller animals and can sometimes be a little aggressive with other dogs.

Activity Level: High

First Loves: Playing, their people

Best Families: Welsh Terriers like families who like to play as much as they do. They can live almost anywhere, but they need a lot of exercise.

Pluses: Always ready to do something, friendly, fun, good watchdogs, great dogs for sports

Minuses: Can be possessive over their food and toys, may be aggressive with dogs, may chase small animals, need lots of exercise, need to be groomed

Fun Fact: Welsh Terriers are still used as hunting dogs in Wales, but almost all are pet dogs in the United States.

WEST HIGHLAND WHITE TERRIER

Where They Are From: Scotland

History: West Highland White Terriers were first bred on two Scottish estates: the Poltalloch estate owned by Colonel Edward Malcolm and the Roseneath estate that was owned by the Duke of Argyll. It is said that Colonel Malcolm bred them to be white so they would be more visible after one of his dogs was killed by a hunter. They were used to hunt foxes, badgers, and vermin. Later, they became popular pet dogs.

Looks: West Highland White Terriers are small, solid dogs. They have round heads, small erect ears, and carrot tails. Their thick coats are medium in length and white. They have dark eyes and black noses.

(See the charts on pages 60–61 for term definitions.)

Height: 10 to 11 inches

Weight: 15 to 20 pounds

Personality: West Highland White Terriers are smart, confident dogs. They like to meet new people and love to play. They are full of energy. They can be a little stand-offish, but they love their families. They do not like to be teased. They can be possessive over their toys and their food.

Activity Level: High

First Loves: Playing, their people

Best Families: West Highland White Terriers like mature older kids who love to play. Their families should have time to train them. They don't mind living in the city or the country.

Pluses: Adjust to city life, always on the go, don't shed much, friendly with most people, fun loving, great dogs for sports

Minuses: Can be possessive over their food and toys, must be trained, need lots of exercise, need to be groomed, sensitive (don't like to be teased)

Fun Fact: Several nineteenth-century paintings by Sir Edwin Landseer show West Highland White Terriers. One shows a West Highland White Terrier peeking out of a doghouse. Another shows a young boy feeding a group of dogs, including a couple of West Highland White Terriers.

WHIPPET

Where They Are From:
Great Britain

History: Whippets were first bred in the nineteenth century as racing dogs. They were probably bred from a mix of Greyhounds, Italian Greyhounds, and terriers. They also hunted small animals and rats. Today, they are mostly pet dogs.

Looks: Whippets are medium-size, slender dogs. They look like small Greyhounds. They have long thin heads and long thin tails. They have rose ears. Their short coats can be any color, but they are usually brindle and white or fawn and white.

Height: 18 to 22 inches

Weight: 20 to 28 pounds

Personality: Whippets are easygoing dogs who can live almost anywhere. They are smart and love to learn new things. They are gentle and like kids and other dogs, but they will chase smaller animals.

Activity Level: Moderate

First Loves: Their people, running

Best Families: Whippets like families who take them for long walks and let them sleep on their beds. They don't care where they live—apartment or castle, they are happy.

Pluses: Can live anywhere, easy to groom, easy to train, friendly, good with kids and other dogs

Minuses:
Chase small animals, don't like loud sounds, need to be kept on a leash, need to wear coats in the cold

Fun Fact: Whippets can run up to 35 miles per hour!

YORKSHIRE TERRIER

Where They Are From: Great Britain

History: Yorkshire Terriers were originally bred during the nineteenth century. They worked as ratters in cotton mills and coal mines in Yorkshire, England. They were kept as pets by miners and weavers. Later, they became popular pets in the United States.

Looks: Yorkshire Terriers are small, delicate dogs. They have prick ears, and their tails are docked to medium length. They have long silky hair that reaches to the ground and is parted in the middle from head to tail. They are born black and tan, but later their coats become blue and tan. The long hair on their heads is tied in topknots—usually with a bow.

Height: 7 to 9 inches

Weight: 3 to 7 pounds

Personality: Yorkshire Terriers are spunky, brave, and smart. Sometimes they act bossy. They are usually playful and loving but can be pushy and nippy if they aren't trained.

Activity Level: Moderate

First Loves: Their people

Best Families: Yorkies like mature older kids who have time to train them and give them lots of attention. They make great apartment dogs.

Pluses: Brave, fun, good watchdogs

Minuses: Can be nippy, can be possessive, need to be groomed, some are yappy

Fun Fact: The world's shortest dog is a Yorkshire Terrier. Whitney is just 3 inches tall at her shoulder.

Chapter 6

Dogs and Responsibility

Being a responsible dog owner means many things. It means making sure you give your dog what she needs. It also means taking the time to find the right dog and being prepared for your dog before bringing her home. A good dog owner considers the pros and cons of having a dog and is ready for all the ups and downs.

Doggy Needs

Dogs have many needs. They need to be kept safe and healthy. They need a warm, safe place to sleep. They need nutritious food, clean water, exercise, and training. And, of course, they need lots of playtime and love. All dogs should have a securely fenced backyard. If they don't, they need lots of outside time—but be sure to keep them on a leash so they don't run away or get hurt in traffic. Regular veterinary appointments and vaccinations are also important.

Before getting a dog, you should make sure your family can meet these needs. You should also have a plan for your dog if you can't care for her. Are there other family members or friends who can care for your dog if your family can't?

The most important thing you will do for your dog is to show her that you love her.

A dog can live many years, so having a dog is a lifetime responsibility. The key to having a happy, healthy dog is being a responsible, well-prepared owner.

Bringing a new puppy into your family's life is a huge decision for all of you.

Be Prepared

Taking care of a dog is a big responsibility. Are you sure it's something you are ready for? A responsible dog owner considers a lot of different things before getting a dog. A few of the questions you need to ask yourself are, why do you want a dog? What are you going to do to keep her safe and happy? How much time each day are you willing to spend with her? Are you willing to give up other things in your life to have a dog? What kind of dog do you want? If your dog doesn't turn out to be exactly what you expected, what will you do?

You should also consider how a new dog will fit into your family. Do you have other

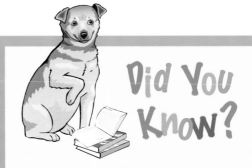

Did You Know?

Dogs need to live with their families, not in the backyard. Dogs are social animals, and when they are kept apart from their families, they are lonely. Dogs who don't live in the house with their families can get depressed or even aggressive. Backyard dogs tend to dig, bark, and even bite more than house dogs do. Your dog is part of the family; bring her inside with you.

Pro & Con

A Weimaraner gets a treat.

The wonderful, positive, pretty great, absolutely stupendous things about having a dog

- Someone to play with
- Good bed buddy
- Protects you
- Great cuddler
- Keeps you active
- Always loyal

The very bad, not-so-good, pretty awful, horribly terrible things about having a dog

- Lots of responsibility
- Must walk her every day
- Have to clean up after her
- Have to scoop poop
- Sheds hair
- Costs money

pets? Is anyone in your family allergic to dogs? Do you have a younger sibling who is afraid of dogs? Do your parents work long hours? Is your family on a limited income? Do you live in a house or an apartment? Do you have a fenced yard? Do you live in the city or the country? What is your day like? Are you involved in sports, Girl or Boy Scouts, music, or other activities? If you are busy, it may be difficult to give your dog all the attention, exercise, and care she needs.

A Family Decision

How do the other members of your family feel about getting a dog? Are they enthusiastic? Find out if anyone in your family has strong feelings against getting a dog. Do your parents want a new dog? If they are concerned about adding a new canine family member, there are several things you can do to help convince them.

A mother and child read together. Do research as a family. Read dog books, and talk to people with dogs.

Sit down with your family and write a list of pros and cons. Think of all the good reasons to get a dog as well as the bad ones. Be honest. Some things to think about on the pro side are that dogs are good companions, some dogs will bark when there is an intruder, and dogs get their owners active because they need to be walked and played with. Some things on the con side are that dogs take up a lot of time; dogs need to be walked, fed, played with, and trained every day; dogs cost money for vet bills, food, grooming, and other things; and

Good dog owners make sure their dogs see a vet on a regular basis.

dogs who aren't trained can destroy furniture or bite.

After you've finished your lists, look them over seriously. Do you still want a dog? If your family is skeptical about getting a new dog, these are just some of the questions they may ask you. It will be helpful for you to be ready with answers to these questions.

Despite your best efforts, your family may not agree to get a dog. Don't worry. You'll have the opportunity to have many dogs in your life. In the meantime, you can visit friends' dogs and go places where you'll have a chance to play with dogs. You can also volunteer with dogs at an animal shelter or a veterinary office.

Do Your Homework

You and your family may want to do some research about dog ownership before making a decision about getting a dog. There are a lot of sources to help you. Books give you information about breeds and day-to-day care. The best sources, though, are people with dogs and people who work with dogs. You can watch dog shows on TV and visit local dog shows to see breeds in action.

At a dog show, you can talk with owners and find out what makes their breed special and what things to worry about. Remember that all of these dogs have had a lot of training and socialization, and every dog is an individual. Your dog won't be just like any of the ones you meet. Bring a list of questions to ask owners. First, ask if this is a good time to talk, or get their business cards and arrange a time for your family to call and discuss their breed. Get both the pros and the cons of the breed, and ask questions specific to your family. If you know your mom will go nuts if a dog sheds long hairs all over her furniture, ask about the grooming needs of the breed.

Veterinarians, veterinary technicians, groomers, and trainers all see a wide variety of dogs and dog breeds. They can give you a lot of advice on the different types of dogs, their needs, and the responsibilities that come with them. They can also help your family understand the amount of time you need to spend with your dog every day, the costs of owning a particular breed of dog, and the kinds of

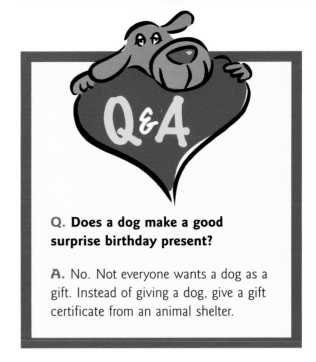

Q. Does a dog make a good surprise birthday present?

A. No. Not everyone wants a dog as a gift. Instead of giving a dog, give a gift certificate from an animal shelter.

things that can go wrong. Veterinarians have information on possible health problems of each breed. Groomers can tell you what kind of grooming a breed requires. A trainer can help you understand the need for training and

List of Responsibilities

Here are some sample jobs and the family members who may do them. What are the dog jobs in your house? Who is willing to do which job? Come up with a list of jobs, and talk to your family about who is taking responsibility for each.

Job to Do	Responsible Family Member
Dog walk a.m.	Mom
Dog walk p.m.	Lucas
Poop scooping	Dad
Feeding a.m.	Grandma
Feeding p.m.	Lucas
Water bowl patrol	Dad
Training	Whole family

socialization. A trainer can also discuss the particular needs of different breeds of dogs and the training needs of adult dogs versus puppies. Call a local veterinarian and grooming shop, and ask if you can interview the staff. Most professionals will be happy to talk to you. They know that when your family does find your treasured pet, you'll repay their helpfulness with years of business!

Shelters and breed rescues are also really good sources of information, and they will be up front with you about an animal's needs. These Good Samaritans don't want to see another dog abandoned, so they'll give you the real scoop on owning a dog.

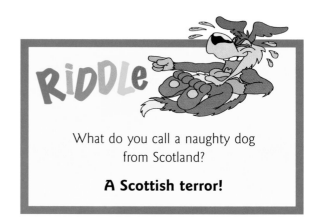

RiDDLe

What do you call a naughty dog from Scotland?

A Scottish terror!

You'll also want to talk to people with pet dogs. A good place to do this is your local dog park. Here, you'll find all types of breeds of dogs and lots of mixes. Ask each owner if you can pet his dog, and strike up a conversation about his specific dog. What kind of dog is she (or what mixes are in her)? What is the dog's personality like? What are the biggest pros and cons about his dog? Talk to him about the responsibility of owning a dog and how it's changed his life. You will find that most people with dogs have to make changes to keep their dogs happy and healthy. Owning a dog is a lot of work. It's best to find out just how much work it is *before* bringing a dog home.

You can make this process easier by splitting up the work among family members. Each person can make one or two phone calls or visits and then keep track of the information they receive.

Who will feed the dog each day? This is an important responsibility.

Make sure everyone in the family understands the rules. It's easy for younger siblings to forget things such as keeping the door closed so the dog doesn't run away.

List of Rules

Every family has special doggy rules. Your family may not want the dog on the furniture, or you may have a pool with a gate, so your rules may include no dogs on the furniture and always close the pool gate. With your family, put together a list of doggy rules that are important to all of you. Put it on the refrigerator so everyone can see it. Here are some sample rules you and your family can follow:

✓ Keep all outside doors closed.
✓ Do not feed dogs food from your plates.
✓ Always close the fence gates.
✓ No dogs on the couch.

The Big Decision

Once your family has gathered information about lots of different types of dogs, it's time to make some decisions. You may find after doing all this research that you're not so sure you want a dog any more. Maybe you've realized that it's going to be hard to go on daily walks with a dog and still play on the baseball team. That's OK! That's exactly why you did this. If it seems like too much work today, you can revisit the idea next year. It's better to face these realities now than be mad at your dog when you have to face them later.

On the other hand, all this research may have made you more certain than ever that you want a dog. Great! Doing this research is the first step toward responsible dog ownership. As long as everyone else in the family is on board, it's time to find your dog!

Divide and Conquer

Before bringing your dog home, decide which family member will be responsible for what. You should also decide on some house rules. Here are some of the responsibilities that come with owning a dog:

• Cleaning up accidents
• Cleaning up the yard

Some chores, such as taking a walk, are more fun than others!

- Feeding the dog
- Grooming the dog
- Playing with the dog
- Taking the dog to the veterinarian
- Training the dog
- Walking the dog

There are also things to decide.

- Where will the dog's crate be kept?

- Who will feed the dog, and what will she be fed?
- Will the dog be kept inside or outside during the day while you're gone? (All dogs need to be inside at night and spend at least part of the daytime hours inside with the family. Dogs are very social animals, much like humans. They need to

spend time with their loved ones to be healthy. Dogs who don't spend time with their families can become depressed or even aggressive.)

- Will the dog sleep with one of the family members?

Ask each family member to take on one or more of these responsibilities. Some of the jobs, such as taking the dog to the veterinarian and buying food, will be things an adult in the family will have to do. But that doesn't mean kids can't help out. That way, everyone will take part in the chores, and it will leave you all more time to have fun with your new buddy!

You should also make rules before bringing your dog home. If one person lets the dog on the couch and another person yells at the dog for being on the couch, you will end up with a confused and unhappy dog. Agree on doggy rules, and post this list of rules in a place where everyone in the family can see them. The kitchen is a good common area.

Fun & Games

Doggy Must-Haves Game

To be a responsible dog owner, you must give your dog proper care. Find some of the most important things you need to give your dog in this doggy word game!

socializationtlc! foodwatersheltervetevinarycaretrainingexercise

Responsibility Contracts

Some families like to create a responsibility contract for each member of the family to sign. In your responsibility contract, you promise to care for your new dog. Some ways of caring for your dog include providing clean water and food each day, protection from traffic and predators, a walk every morning and evening, playtime, and lots of TLC. Once everyone signs the contract, keep a copy next to the doggy house rules to remind everyone of his or her new dog care duties.

If you work hard and take excellent care of your dog, she will give you many wonderful years of love and companionship.

Responsibility Contract

Here is a sample responsibility contract. All the items in the contract are important. Are there any responsibilities you would add? Make your own responsibility contract, and ask each member of the family to sign it before bringing your new dog home.

I agree to take responsibility for my new dog.
I will care for her throughout her entire life.
I will feed her, walk her, and
    make sure she is safe.
I will treat her with love
    and respect.

I promise to give my
    dog food that is good
    for her and make sure she eats every day.
I promise to keep my dog's water bowl full of clean water.
I promise to give my dog shelter from the sun and the rain.
I promise to give my dog a warm, safe place to sleep inside my house.
I promise to keep my dog safe from things that could hurt her.
I promise to train my dog so she behaves well.
I promise to teach my dog that people and other animals are friends.
I promise to take my dog to the vet and make sure she gets her shots.
I promise to groom my dog—bathe and brush her and keep her teeth clean.
I promise to spend time with my dog every day.
I promise to give my dog the exercise she needs.
I promise to pick up after my dog.
I promise to give my dog a collar and ID so I can find her if she gets lost.
I promise not to let my dog run loose.
I promise to love my dog for her entire life.

Your signature here

Chapter 7

Choosing Your Dog

Bringing a new dog into your family is a little like bringing home a new baby. It involves many changes, new responsibilities, and a lot of fun! But before you get to bring your new friend home, you have some work to do. You must choose the type and age of dog you want, decide whether to adopt from a shelter or buy from a breeder, and find just the right dog for your lifestyle.

How to Choose a Dog

Do you want a big dog, a little dog, a fuzzy dog, a hairless dog? Does your family want an eight-week-old puppy or an instant adult

You may see many dogs and puppies before you find the perfect one for your family. This pup is ready to go home!

Here are some of the many types of dogs to choose from: big, small, skinny, fat, short, tall, hairy, and hairless.

companion? How about your dog's personality? Do you want a dog who loves everyone, or would you rather have a dog who has eyes only for you? There are a lot of things to think about when deciding what type of dog you want to get.

Luckily, there are lots of sources to help you. You can search the Internet, talk to dog breeders and animal shelters, read books like this one, watch shows on TV, and talk to local veterinarians and groomers. Talk to your friends, and visit places where dogs go, like dog parks and beaches. There you will see many types of dogs and be able to talk with their owners about the pros and cons of certain types of dogs. Don't be afraid to ask questions. Most people love to brag about their dogs!

Before you do anything else, sit down with the rest of your family and talk about what kind of dog all of you want. You may find that you, your parents, and your siblings have very different ideas about the new dog in your lives. Ask each family member to write down what kind of dog he or she wants, and then discuss as many of the positive and negative things about the dogs you come up with. Be specific as to age, breed, size, and coat type.

Breed

Each breed has its own special needs. What makes a perfect dog for one family is a nightmare for another. Border Collies, for example, are superfun dogs with lots of energy. They are great dogs to play with and like doing doggy sports. However, they require a lot of exercise and attention or else they can be out of control. Sometimes families with a lot of commitments are overwhelmed by these dogs. A Chihuahua may be a good choice for a family who likes to spend time at home reading or watching TV. But if you want a dog who is going to run next to you while you skateboard, the Chihuahua isn't for you!

Age

Age can be important when choosing a dog. A lot of people want a brand-new pup and refuse

A puppy will need your family's undivided attention.

Q. What are the most popular breeds in America?

A. According to the American Kennel Club (AKC), the ten most popular breeds are the Labrador Retriever, Golden Retriever, Yorkshire Terrier, German Shepherd Dog, Beagle, Dachshund, Boxer, Poodle, Shih Tzu, and Miniature Schnauzer. But remember that these are just the purebred dogs registered with the AKC. The mutt, or mixed breed, is America's most popular dog!

to even consider an older dog. But older dogs can make great pets because they often require less work than a youngster. What do the members of your family think? Does everyone feel strongly that your new dog come to you as a tiny ball of fur? Would some of you prefer an adult dog?

Adopting a puppy has both its good and its bad sides. Puppies are a clean slate. You have the chance to train them the way you want. Puppies are also a lot of fun. They are cute and full of energy. A puppy who receives lots of training, socialization, exercise, and love will usually grow up to be a healthy adult.

Don't expect kids to find the right dog on their own. Help them research breeds: take them to a dog show, visit the library, talk to vets and groomers. Encourage them to talk to other dog owners about their dogs. Finding a dog is a good lesson in responsibility for kids. The whole family should help choose a new dog or puppy, but the adults should have the final say. Adopting a dog is a lifelong proposition—consider your choices carefully. If you're shuttling kids back and forth between school, soccer games, and ballet, don't add

Two kids spend time with their Golden.

a high-energy dog to your responsibilities. Instead, look for a mellow older dog who can slide right into your existing schedule.

Puppies are also a lot of work. They need to be house-trained and crate-trained and taught not to chew, nip, and jump. During his first few weeks at your home, your puppy will need special attention. He will probably need to go potty during the night. He also may whine and bark late at night because he is lonely for his mom and littermates.

Puppies shouldn't be left alone all day. Someone in the family will need to take a long lunch or stay home to let your puppy out and give him a little playtime during the day. As the puppy grows, he will need even more attention from you. He'll probably become very energetic and will need lots of exercise and training.

Unless you buy your puppy from a good breeder, where you will get to meet your pup's mom and maybe even his dad, you probably won't know what your pup will look or act like as an adult. A shelter pup may grow up to be a tiny Chihuahua mix or a supersize Mastiff mix.

Adopting an adult dog also has its good and its bad sides. On the good side, an adult dog is full grown, with his adult looks and personality. This means you will probably be able to tell if he is unhealthy or is aggressive. Adult dogs make almost instant companions. They can join you in games and hikes almost immediately. Some adult dogs have received some training. They may be house-trained and even know some commands and tricks. They can start training classes soon after coming into your home. Adult dogs also require less hands-on work than a puppy because they are not as energetic as youngsters. Another great thing about adopting an adult dog is that so many of them need homes and not as many people want to adopt them as want to adopt puppies. When you adopt an adult dog from the shelter, you are really saving a life.

There are down sides to adopting an adult dog, though. Because most adult dogs are adopted through shelters or breed rescues, you probably won't know anything about your dog's background. An adult dog may come to you with some problems. He may have been raised in a home where people were mean to him or did not train or socialize him. Sometimes adult dogs must first lose their bad habits before learning new, good habits. And some young adult dogs may be right in the middle of their most challenging age—they look like adult dogs but still act like crazy puppies!

Size

Some people prefer big dogs, some prefer small dogs. Some people have a lifestyle that makes it difficult to have either a large dog or a small dog. Most people seem to find that a medium-size dog fits best into their home.

If you are adopting a puppy from a shelter, you won't have

Very big dogs such as this Great Dane may be too strong for little kids.

much control over his size. You may think you are adopting a Doberman mix, who will grow into a large dog, only to find yourself with a Miniature Pinscher. Or you may be looking for a petite terrier and find yourself with a Great Dane. Talk to the workers at the animal shelter for help determining the adult size of the puppy you are looking at.

A big dog may sound like fun, but remember that big dogs have big needs. If you live in a small house or an apartment, a big dog may bump into things and be constantly underfoot. Neither of you will be comfortable. Everything you buy for a big dog is more expensive, from toys and bedding to veterinary care and grooming. Big dogs cost a lot of money. Just consider the amount of food they eat each day!

Because big dogs eat a lot, they also poop a lot. Someone has to clean up that poop. If it's you, you may think twice about your ability to keep up with that chore!

Very big dogs also have some special medical problems. Because they are so heavy, their bodies do double the work of those of smaller dogs. All this strain on their bodies can lead to hip, elbow, and knee problems. Big dogs often don't live as long as smaller dogs.

A lot of people like the looks of small dogs. Many people assume they are easier to take care of because they are so small. This is not true. All dogs need to be fed, exercised, trained, and loved. Although much of a small dog's care may be less expensive than a giant dog's, small dogs can have their own special problems. For instance, many small dogs

Some toy dogs such as this Pekingese can get an attitude if they're not trained.

have dental problems and other health concerns. They are also more vulnerable than other dogs. A small dog can break a leg jumping off a couch. He can easily be injured by rowdy play. Sometimes small dogs can be very naughty because their families don't train them as they would a larger dog. It's important to remember that all dogs must be trained—even if they weigh only four pounds!

Many families find the ideal dog to be right in between the giant dogs and the tiny dogs. Medium-size dogs like Labs, Golden Retrievers, Australian Cattle Dogs, and Collies fit into most homes. They are in the middle of the range when it comes to the costs of their needs as well.

Coat

It may sound silly to choose a dog based on his coat, but grooming needs are serious business. Some dogs need daily grooming. If they don't receive it, they will turn into balls of tangled fur. Some dogs need professional grooming, and that can get quite expensive.

Coat type is also an important issue for people with allergies.

A dog who sheds heavily is going to be the worst choice for someone with allergies. Even dogs who don't need to go to professional groomers need basic grooming. They still need to be bathed monthly and brushed at least weekly. Even hairless dogs need grooming! Their sensitive skin needs to be washed and kept moist with lotion. They also need to be protected from the sun with clothing and sunscreen.

Sometimes people give up their dogs because of allergies or because they can't keep up with the grooming needs. Look at the grooming needs of different breeds before choosing your dog.

Personality

Every dog has his own personality. He may be energetic or mellow, friendly with everyone or shy. Dogs of a certain breed often have similar personalities. For example, Golden Retrievers tend to be very outgoing. Chihuahuas are often somewhat nervous.

It's a good idea for you to know what kind of doggy personality you want. Does your family have lots of dogs and kids coming in and out

If your family wants to participate in a doggy sport, such as sledding, you'll need to find a dog who is suited to the sport, such as this Siberian Husky.

Questions to Ask a Shelter or Rescue Organization

Here is a list of important questions and their answers. Bring these questions with you when you go to a shelter or rescue group.

Q. Was the dog a stray? Did the owners bring him in? Did they tell the shelter anything about him?
A. You want to find out as much as you can about your new dog's background.

Q. Is the dog spayed or neutered?
A. All pet dogs should be spayed or neutered.

Q. Has the dog been trained?
A. A dog with some training is good for a busy family.

Q. How old is the dog?
A. Older dogs can be great family dogs. However, they may not have as much energy as younger dogs have.

Q. Is the dog a good match for my family?
A. Tell the shelter what your family is like.

Q. Does the dog have any current illnesses or injuries?
A. A good rescue organization will have its own vet, but you should also take the dog to see your family vet right away.

Q. Is the dog friendly with people and other animals?
A. A family dog should be friendly with everyone.

Q. Is the dog energetic? Is he mellow?
A. A really hyper dog can be hard to take care of. A mellow dog may want to snooze when you want to play.

A Mastiff seeks a new home.

Q. Can you return the dog if the new home doesn't work out?
A. The shelter should let you bring the dog back if he doesn't fit into your home.

of your house? If that's the case, you probably don't want a Rottweiler or a Chinese Shar-Pei. Sometimes these dogs can get confused about who is a friend and who isn't. Your family may do better with a Labrador Retriever or a Boxer.

Remember that even dogs of the same breed can be very different. Irish Setters are known for being friendly and playful, but there are serious Irish Setters. Mastiffs are known for being gentle and mellow, but there are playful

Mastiffs. A mixed breed may take after one breed more than another, but it's hard to know what kind of personality a mutt puppy will grow up to have.

Finding Your Perfect Dog

Finally, you've decided on the type of dog you want. Now you need to find him! The best sources for a dog or a puppy are reputable animal shelters, breed rescues, and good breeders. Your search may take you through many different breeders or through a host of local pet rescues and animal shelters. Sometimes it takes a long time to find just the right dog you are looking for.

The Adoption Option

If you've decided to adopt an adult dog, you probably won't get him from a breeder. Instead, you will adopt your dog through an animal shelter, through a private rescue, or through one of the working dog training agencies that place retired dogs with private families. These can all be excellent places to find your new canine companion.

An animal shelter or rescue is a great place to find the dog of your dreams.

There are many wonderful dogs and puppies in animal shelters. Most people don't give up a dog because he is bad. Dogs are usually given up because of family issues—a divorce, a death or a birth in the family, or a move—or because the family pets don't get along. Sometimes people give up animals who just don't fit well into their lifestyles—the dogs require too much exercise or attention. Many shelter dogs are well trained. If they are older than a year or two, they are probably past most of their puppy antics. However, some shelter pets do have some problems. A neglectful family may have kept a dog outside all the time. A neglected dog

At your local animal shelter, there are many adult dogs, such as this Beagle, who need homes.

tion about the dogs in its care. Some may have even done some training with the dogs. Other shelters don't have the staff for these types of services. If you don't have a lot of experience with dogs, you may not feel comfortable adopting from this type of shelter. Instead, seek out another, more friendly shelter, or look into adopting through a breed rescue. Don't feel that you have to adopt the first dog you see when you visit a shelter. Take as much time as you need to find your pet.

Some people who want a specific type of dog would rather adopt the dog than buy one from a breeder. Breed rescues are a good source for dogs if you are looking for a particular breed. Rescue groups may also provide more training and often know more about the dogs they place for adoption. If you have never had a dog before, it's a good idea to work with an organization that can give you a lot of support.

Most breed clubs have rescue groups affiliated with them, but there are many other private nonprofit breed rescues. There are also rescue groups for certain types of dogs, including small, large, Mastiff or bully types, deaf, disabled, or mixed-breed dogs. It usually costs more to adopt a dog from a rescue group than from an animal shelter.

You can also adopt a dog from a working dog organization. Dogs do all kinds of different work, including doing search and rescue, assisting people with disabilities, acting, and working with the police or

may not be house-trained or even know basic commands.

Adopting a dog from a shelter doesn't mean you can't adopt a purebred. In fact, 25 percent of the dogs found in U.S. shelters are purebred. And it's not just adult dogs you will find in shelters. You can usually find puppies as well.

Not all shelters are equal. Many shelters are helpful, with adoption counselors who will help you find the right dog. A good shelter often has a lot of informa-

Look your pup over from head to paw. Does he seem to have any health problems?

True / False

It's important to visit your pup at the breeder's home before buying him.

TRUE.

If you don't visit your pup's home, you won't meet his mom and littermates. You can tell a lot about a puppy from meeting his family. It's great to meet a puppy's dad, too, but most dads don't live in the same home as the mom and pups do.

military. Not all dogs who are bred or raised to do this work end up succeeding at it. When a dog isn't able to do the job he was trained for, he may be placed in a different job or adopted out to a private family. Working dog organizations call these career-change dogs. Retired dogs are also put up for adoption. Working dogs usually retire when they no longer enjoy the work or when they can't physically do the work. This may be because of age or an injury or illness.

All these dogs need new homes, and this is where you can come in. Because these dogs are well trained and socialized, there's usually a long waiting list. With patience, however, you may just find yourself with an ex–guide dog or even a movie star for a pet!

A good breeder wants to make sure the pups go to the best possible homes.

Breeders

If you decide to buy a puppy rather than adopt one from a shelter, buy him from a good breeder. Not everyone who sells puppies is a good breeder. Good breeders have certain qualities. They care about their dogs and want them to go to the best homes possible. They care about the breed and work to make the breed better. They are active in training their dogs, and they probably even participate in dog activities. They may show their dogs or participate in doggy sports. Good breeders don't breed their dogs because they want to get rich. Instead, they breed dogs because they want to produce the best dogs possible. To do this, they make sure that the dogs they breed are healthy, both mentally and physically.

Your entire family should visit the breeder and spend time with all the pups.

They never breed a dog who is aggressive or has a health problem.

You won't find a good breeder just by looking in your local paper. Instead, get recommendations from dog professionals and dog owners. Once you find a breeder, ask questions about the dogs, and visit the breeder in person. Breeders who breed more than two breeds of dogs, breed the same dog more than once a year, or have many different litters at one time may not be good breeders.

It's best when puppies are raised inside a home. But whether the dogs live in the house or in a kennel, they should be clean, healthy, and friendly. They should have lots of room to exercise, and the yard, home, and kennel should be clean. Puppies need lots of socialization, so ask the breeder how much attention they receive.

A good breeder will introduce you to the mom and any other adult dogs in the home. If the mom is shy, unfriendly, or aggressive, the pups may also have these traits. Never buy a puppy from a breeder if you can't meet the mom or the other littermates.

A good breeder provides you with an adoption contract and something called a health clearance. An adoption contract promises that you can return the puppy if he has health or behavioral problems. A health clearance provides proof that neither the puppy's mom nor dad has health problems.

Puppies should have received their first shots and deworming. If they are pet-quality puppies, rather than show-quality puppies, they may also be spayed or neutered. Puppies who will be show dogs aren't spayed or neutered.

Questions to Ask a Breeder

Here is a list of important questions and their answers. Bring this list with you when you meet a breeder.

Q. When can the puppies go to their new homes?
A. Pups should be at least eight weeks before leaving their moms.

Q. Have the puppies received their first shots?
A. The answer should be yes—the breeder should do this.

Q. Do the puppies have any health problems?
A. Don't choose a sick puppy.

Q. Are there any common health problems in the breed?
A. All breeds have possible health problems. Any breeder who says there are none is lying.

Q. Do you require spaying or neutering?
A. Puppies who are sold as pets should be spayed or neutered.

Q. Does the breeder breed a female dog more than once a year?
A. The answer should be no—this is bad for the dog. (Male dogs can be bred more than once a year.)

An Australian Cattle Dog rests with her pups.

Q. Does the breeder breed more than two breeds?
A. Good breeders usually breed only one or two breeds of dogs.

Q. Does the breeder show her dogs or do other doggy sports or activities?
A. Doing activities shows that the breeder is interested in the dogs.

Q. Can I return the puppy if there is a problem?
A. Good breeders always want their puppies back if new homes don't work out.

Finally, you've found your pup! It's time to prepare for a lifetime together!

Pick the Puppy for You

Once you've found a good shelter or breeder, you need to choose your dog. Don't just pick the first dog you see. Spend some time with several dogs and puppies. Ask the shelter worker or breeder about their personalities. Is the dog you like pushy or laid back?

Does he like to play and be petted, or is he shy? Does he get along with other dogs?

Every dog has a distinct personality. Even puppies within the same litter are very different. For example, there is usually one puppy in a litter that acts like the leader. This puppy is often the biggest boy puppy. He is always first to eat and bosses around his siblings. A dominant puppy is perfect for someone looking for a search and rescue dog. However, he may be too much for a family looking for a pet. There is often a runt, as well. This puppy is usually smaller and shyer than the other pups, and he may need some special attention to become confident as he grows.

You will also want to make sure the dog you pick is healthy. You can tell a lot about a dog by looking at his coat, eyes, and ears. A healthy dog has a full, shiny coat. His eyes are shiny and clear without any discharge. His ears are pink without a lot of wax or dark buildup. His breath, coat, and ears should not stink. He should not appear overly fat or thin. Dogs at shelters sometimes have illnesses, or they may have fleas. The shelter workers should be honest about any health problems. If you adopt a sick dog, bring him to your vet right away.

Never buy a sick puppy from a breeder. Instead, contact your local animal control officers, and let them know about the puppy.

Chapter 8

Preparing for Your Pup

Before bringing your new dog home, you need to get ready. Just as you need to baby proof your house for a toddler, you need to puppy proof your house to make it safe for a puppy. (This applies to grown-up dogs, too. They sometimes act a lot like puppies!) You also need to buy supplies such as food, bowls, and a bed.

Puppy Proofing Your House

The whole family should help puppy proof (or dog proof) your home. First, clear everything off the floor. If you tend to throw games, books, and shoes on the floor, break that habit. Otherwise, there's a good chance your favorite toy will be ripped to shreds. This applies to any room where your new dog will be—den, living room, and bedrooms.

Act like a dog! Get a dog's-eye view of your house. Get on your hands and knees, and go through your house room by room. Look for things that will attract a playful puppy. Are there

Before bringing your new dog home, go to the store and buy the basic supplies.

Adult Alert!

What is bad for dogs is often bad for kids, as well. Children should not handle poisons, insecticides, or toxic substances such as paint thinner and antifreeze. Help your children prepare the home for their new four-footed friend by clearing your home of all toxins. Move things like household cleaners and alcohol to high shelves. Encourage your child to keep his or her room and living spaces tidy so a new puppy won't chew up shoes and kid toys.

tassels hanging off curtains, bedspreads, or rugs? Move these until you're sure your pup is safe in the house. Move remote controls and portable phones from low tables. Anything that you hold a lot will attract puppy teeth; they like to chew on things that smell like their people! Don't leave wallets, eyeglasses, or brushes where your pup can get them.

Keep toys and games on shelves or in a toy box. Kid toys and dog toys are a lot alike, so teach your dog which is which. There are good reasons dogs shouldn't play with kid toys. Your toys are dangerous for dogs. They have parts that a dog can chew off and choke on.

Totally Toxic

These are some of the toxins that may be around your house or the places you go. Keep all toxins away from your dog (and yourself, for that matter)!

- Blue-green algae (found in pools of water)
- Christmas tree water
- Cocoa bean mulch (used for potting plants and in gardens)
- Fertilizer
- Fly bait
- Household cleaners
- Human medicines
- Paint
- Paint remover
- Poisonous plants
- Rat poison
- Rubbing alcohol
- Slug bait
- Weed killer

Oleander is a poisonous plant.

Buy a big basket for dog toys, and teach your dog that her toys go here. Make sure your pup has toys she likes so she won't steal yours!

Think you're done puppy proofing? Now do it again! This time, look for things that can hurt your puppy. A puppy's curious chewing can get her into lots of trouble. Some plants are bad for dogs if they eat them. Wires can shock a dog if she chews them. Kitchen garbage can have rotting food, chicken bones, or aluminum foil. All of these items can hurt a dog. Bathroom garbage may have dental floss or old medicine. Put anything dangerous for your dog up high, and cover wastebaskets with tight-fitting lids.

Puppy Proofing Outside

There are also dangers outside of the house. If you don't have a fence, get one. If you do have a fence, make sure it is escape proof. Check for any loose boards or spaces between the fence and ground. Look for other areas that would allow a pup to escape. Point out any weak spots in the fence to your parents or another adult who can fix them before your new dog comes home.

True / False

Poinsettias are dangerous for dogs.

FALSE.

Poinsettias get a bad rap. They can irritate your pup's mouth and paws, but that's about it. Supposedly, more than a century ago, a child died after eating a poinsettia. The death was actually unrelated to eating the poinsettia, but that didn't stop the rumors!

Go through the yard. Ask an adult to check for any hazards (many things that are bad for dogs are bad for kids, too!). These include pesticides, poisons, or poisonous plants. If you don't know if a plant is bad for your dog, take one of its leaves to a local nursery. Ask what the plant is and if it is toxic, or poisonous. Toxic plants can make people or animals sick if they are eaten.

Your mom or dad may have special plants they don't want the dog to hurt. Replant them in a safe area where your dog can't go. Some people fence off an area of the yard for the dog.

Keep your dog out of the vegetable garden. Puppy paws are hard on baby plants. Some

Make sure there are no gaps or holes in your fence. Pups can squeeze through almost anything!

Anti-Antifreeze!

Antifreeze is the stuff people put in their cars to keep the engine from freezing during the winter. Antifreeze is a big help when it's really cold out. Unfortunately, antifreeze is a big problem for animals, and it is a problem for little kids, too.

Antifreeze is a green, thick liquid that is toxic. Even a little bit can hurt a dog, a cat, or a baby. It smells sweet, and to make things worse, antifreeze tastes good! Many animals are killed every year from drinking antifreeze.

There are ways you can keep your dog safe from antifreeze. Never let your dog sniff or lick puddles of liquid. Keep your dog away from parking lots and out of the garage. Don't let your dog go near cars that are dripping fluid.

Ask the grownups in your family to help you keep other animals safe by using nontoxic antifreeze. It is made with propylene glycol instead of ethylene glycol. Propylene glycol is safer for everyone.

dogs like to dig up the soft dirt in gardens. They may turn the vegetable garden into a litter box. Dog pee can kill plants, and dog poop is bad for us. We sure don't want it on things we eat!

Keep your dog out of the garage. When antifreeze drips out of cars, it leaves a sweet-tasting puddle that attracts curious dogs. Antifreeze is extremely toxic. The garage is also where dangerous items such as rodent poison, pesticides, and paint thinner are kept. All of these things can kill a dog with just a few licks or nibbles. Have an adult move all

Outside there are many things to catch a puppy's eyes: sprinklers, gardening tools, and plants.

toxic items to a high shelf in the garage. Never use any poison in an area where your dog might go.

Shop 'til You Drop

Now for the fun part of getting ready for your new dog—it's shopping time! Try to do your shopping at least a few days before you bring your pet home. It will make it easier if you have everything ready when your new pup comes home. Some must-haves for a new dog or puppy are toys, a crate, food and water bowls, food, a brush and a comb, ID tags, and a toothbrush. You may also want a

If you already have a dog and are adopting a new one, bring her with you when you go shopping for new dog supplies. Be sure to buy her a special treat.

bed, a doggy seat belt, puppy pee pads, and a variety of cleaning supplies.

Not all toys are safe for dogs. Buy toys made especially for dogs. Plush or lamb's wool toys are good for puppies who want a warm and comforting toy. Rope toys, rawhides, and nylon bones are good for chewing. Kongs and other toys that you can fill with treats are great for keeping a dog busy. Buy your pup a selection of toys. Always take toys away if they start to fall apart. And be sure to buy the right size toy for your dog. Dogs can choke on toys that are too small.

Buy your dog a crate to help her feel safe and comfortable. Having a crate also makes house-training a cinch. The crate should be large enough to allow your dog to stand up and turn around when she's in it. If she's a puppy, you may need a small crate now and a bigger crate when she gets older. Your puppy needs a crate her size so that she will feel safe—a larger crate may not do that. She also needs a small crate so she can't get away from the mess if

A young girl is checking out the toys and treats. Help your family pick out the supplies your new dog needs.

she pees or poops in the crate. This will help you when house-training her.

Put the crate in an area that isn't too loud or too far away from the family action. A corner of the kitchen or family room usually works. Place a cozy blanket in the bottom of the crate so your dog can get nice and comfy. Give her a soft lamb's wool toy to snuggle when she is in her crate.

When buying food bowls, stick to ones that are metal or ceramic. They are easier to clean than plastic bowls, and some dogs are allergic to plastic. Ask the breeder or shelter what kind of food they are feeding the dog. Buy this food for her first few days. If you want to switch foods, start with her current food, and then gradually replace it with the new food.

Basic grooming tools such as a brush, a comb, toothpaste, and a toothbrush are also good to have when your new dog comes home so you can start getting her used to them right away. If she's coming from a shelter, you may want to give her a good bath and brushing right away.

Name Your Dog

What's in a name? Sometimes a lot. Have you ever met a dog named Cujo or Killer? Did you feel a little scared? Most of us would! That's because names like these make people nervous. Some people think that it is cute or funny to give dogs scary names, but sometimes people act afraid of dogs with mean-sounding names like Killer.

How about a dog named Daisy or Buster? Do you get a good feeling when you meet dogs with names like these? Are you more likely to pet these dogs or feel comfortable around them? Friendly names make people less nervous. People like dogs with friendly names. That's why animal shelters and dog rescues often change the names of the dogs in their care. It's a lot easier to find a home for a Daisy than for a Cujo.

Some names also make it easier to talk with your dog. Dogs respond best to two syllable names. A name with a *y*-sounding ending is especially good. Names like Sandy, Desi, Shorty, and Lucy are all good dog names. If your dog's name has only one syllable like Mud, call her Muddy. Names with more than two syllables can be confusing. Can you imagine saying, "Come Mr. McGillicutty!" Now that would be a hard name for a dog to come to!

Try to find a name that works for your dog. Rusty is a good name for a red dog. Happy is good for a friendly dog. Don't name your dog after a popular athlete or star. That basketball player

may be traded to another team by the time your dog is two, or the actor may do a movie you hate. If you're going to name your dog after someone, name the pup after someone timeless like Mickey or Minnie (Mouse).

If you can't come up with a name for your dog, don't worry. Once you know your dog's personality, it will be easy to find the perfect name for her.

FUN & GAMES

The Shopping List Shuffle

Unscramble the letters to find some important items for your doggy shopping list.

1. tcear
2. oodf nda rewta owlb
3. dofo
4. soyt
5. eahsl
6. lalcor
7. stag di
8. ushrb
9. mboc

Answers:
1. crate 2. food and water bowls 3. food 4. toys 5. leash 6. collar 7. ID tags 8. brush 9. comb

Make sure to name your new companion something lovable!

Most Popular Dog Names

Male:

1. Max
2. Jake
3. Buddy
4. Bailey
5. Sam
6. Rocky
7. Buster
8. Casey
9. Cody
10. Duke

Female:

1. Maggie
2. Molly
3. Lady
4. Sadie
5. Lucy
6. Daisy
7. Ginger
8. Abby
9. Sasha
10. Sandy

Source: http://www.geocities.com (©2003–2006 dognames@yahoo.com)

Chapter 9

Welcome Home, Pooch!

You are antsy with excitement; today is the big day! You and your family are picking up your new dog. Make sure to wear your seat belt and to bring your dog's seat belt or crate. You want to keep your new dog safe.

Bring a cushy toy to comfort your new pup if he gets scared.

Leaving his mom and his brothers and sisters is hard. A rescue dog may be attached to the shelter workers or his foster family, so he may be scared, too.

Spend some time with your new dog before jumping in the car. He doesn't know you're his family yet. Let him sniff you and

Welcome home! Finally, the big day has arrived.

Q&A

Q. What do you do if your dog hates your new puppy?

A. This is a hard one! If your dog is used to getting all the attention, it can be hard for him to give that up. Sometimes the two dogs need time to figure out who is boss. Every house with more than one dog has a top dog. Sometimes it takes a while for two dogs to work this out. If you have more than two dogs, it can take even longer. You can help your dogs get along by making sure they both get a lot of love and attention. Take them on walks together and apart. That way no one

A dog meets the new puppy.

feels left out. If they are fighting over food, feed them away from one another.

lick your hand before petting him. Put a leash on him, and lead him around the yard or the shelter grounds. Take him out to go potty. Then let the dog meet the rest of the family one by one. Don't rush the dog. Let him come and greet each one of you on his own. Before leaving, an adult should get the new dog settled into the car, either cozily snuggled in his crate or strapped into a doggy seat belt.

This pup is secure in a crate. Make sure to keep your new dog safe on his way home.

Do you have any last-minute questions? Ask the shelter staff or breeder if there are toys your new puppy likes, and games he enjoys, or if he has a favorite snack. Ask what shots he's received and what kind of food he eats. Bring pen and paper with you so you can take notes. If you're buying from a breeder, make sure she gives you your puppy's health clearances and papers.

Your First Week "To Do" List

- Help your puppy explore his new world
- Take your puppy to the vet
- Get your puppy his shots (the breeder or shelter should have given at least the first set)
- Schedule spay or neuter surgery
- Shop for puppy stuff you weren't able to get ahead of time
- Sign up for training class
- Start crate-training
- Start house-training

Your Dog's New Home

You're finally home! Your new pet is probably pretty excited, and so are you. Don't let your puppy out of the car until you have a leash on him. He doesn't know where he is and barely knows who you are. Keep a tight hold of him until he's in the house or a safe, fenced area.

Your puppy will probably want to sniff and explore a little. He probably will need to go potty. Once he has checked out the front yard, bring him inside the house. Keep him on a leash while he explores his new house. He'll probably want to check out everything. He'll be very curious about this new turn of events!

Introduce your puppy to the rest of his new family. Let him meet one person at a time. It can be pretty scary to have

a bunch of new people towering over you. Ask everyone to take a seat and let the pup go to them on his own.

Once everyone has been introduced, offer your new dog some water, and take him into the backyard. If you have a secure fence, let him off his leash while he looks around. If he goes potty, tell him what a good dog he is.

Once all the sniffing and exploring is done, take a break! You all deserve it. Put the dog into his crate so he can rest.

Pets in the Family

Bringing a new dog home can be harder if you have other pets. An older dog may not take kindly to this new addition to the family. Cats who aren't used to dogs may become very afraid of a new dog or puppy.

Introduce your old dog to the new dog before bringing him home. Talk to the shelter staff or the breeder about this. Most will insist that the dogs meet before the new dog goes home. Make sure you can return the new dog if the dogs don't get along. Remember that your loyalty lies with your old dog. He is number one, even if he's the one causing the problems! Never adopt or buy a dog if you can't bring him back.

Introduce your new dog into the family slowly. Instead of going straight home after picking up your new dog, ask someone to bring your old dog to a local park. With both dogs on leashes held by adults, walk around the park with about twenty feet between the dogs. If the dogs seem OK, slowly move closer together. Finally, let them sniff and greet one another. If you have more than one dog, have the newcomer meet the nicest dog first. Then let him meet the other dogs.

After meeting at the park, bring the dogs home. Let the new dog explore the house while the other dog is in the yard. Let the dogs play together in the yard before moving back indoors. If your old dog is greedy with his food, food bowls, toys, or other things, put them away.

It may be easier to introduce two adult dogs at a park instead of at home.

With luck, your cat and dog will become fast friends.

If you have a cat, make sure your new dog is friendly with cats. Puppies who are raised with cats usually do fine with them. An older dog may not get along with cats. Talk to the breeder or shelter staff about this.

Keep your cat in a bedroom when you first bring your new dog home. Let her out of the bedroom only when the dog is outside. Over the next few days, an adult can open the door to the bedroom and let the dog peek in. Make sure your dog is kept on a leash when doing this. Give your dog treats for being calm around the cat. If he tries to chase the cat, say "no" and close the door. As the dog and cat get more comfortable, you can let them be around each other more as long as there is also an adult around. Use a baby gate as a barrier, or keep the dog on a leash. It can take a month or more for a new dog and a cat to get used to each other.

For the first few weeks, don't leave the animals alone together. Even if they seem to get along, an adult dog can seriously hurt a young puppy. Two adults can hurt each other if they fight. A dog can accidentally hurt a cat, and some feisty cats can hurt puppies! Wait until

RIDDLE

What is a dog's favorite kind of pizza?

Pup-eroni and cheese!

Snoopy

Snoopy must be the world's most famous dog. He's a Beagle, he's Charlie Brown's best friend, and he's also a World War I ace pilot, a mystery writer, and an explorer. Snoopy first debuted in the *Peanuts* comic strip drawn by Charles M. Schultz on October 2, 1950. Snoopy and the rest of the *Peanuts* gang quickly became beloved throughout the world. Snoopy was and still is everywhere. There are Snoopy TV shows, Snoopy books, and lots of stuffed Snoopy dolls.

Charles M. Schultz drew the *Peanuts* cartoon for almost 50 years. Sadly, in 2000, Schultz died from colon cancer. But Snoopy still lives on!

the animals are completely used to each other before leaving them alone. Never leave your dog alone with smaller animals such as birds, rabbits, or hamsters. Your dog can hurt them without even meaning to.

The First Day

You're home, and your pup has met the family and looked around his new home. It's time for a nice snooze in his crate. Once your pet has had a nap, bring him outside. Tell him he is good if he goes potty. Let him look around more. He'll probably want to explore his new digs for a few hours. Let him do this. This will help him get comfortable.

Dinner is your first chance for your family to start training your new dog. If he knows how to sit, an adult can ask him to sit before giving him food. Instead of putting his bowl down right away, have a grown-up feed him about half his food from the grown-up's hand, one kernel at a time. This will help teach him that food comes from people. He will learn to look to people for food and comfort. He can eat the second half of his meal out of the bowl.

After your dog finishes eating, wait ten or fifteen minutes, and then take him back outside. He'll probably have to go potty again. Praise him when he goes. Once he's eaten a good meal and gone potty, he will probably have a lot of energy. If he's a puppy or a young dog, he may start running in circles and generally acting very silly. Now is a good time to show him some of his new toys. Balls, Frisbees, or other toys to chase are good. Spend about a half hour playing outside. Let him get nice and tired. It will help him sleep during his first night.

End the evening by letting your new pet sit beside you while you watch TV, play a video game, or hang out with the family. Follow your house rules. If you have a no-pets-on-furniture rule, don't let the dog up "just this once." Dogs don't understand "just this once." If he's not allowed on the couch, hang out with him on the floor. After relaxing for a few hours, it's bedtime. Time for another potty break!

You may want your new dog to sleep in a bedroom with a family member.

Start crate-training your new dog as soon as you bring him home.

Your pup's first meal is the perfect time to start training.

This will make him feel cozy. Plus, you can hear him if he needs you. Nestle him into his crate with a soft toy. If he is very young, give him a hot water bottle filled with warm water and covered with a flannel cloth or a towel and a ticking clock. The warmth and sound will help him feel comfy.

The first night in a new home can be scary. Your puppy will be confused and lonely. Where are his littermates and mom? Maybe your dog has been in a foster home where he's become attached to the family and other pets. Even leaving a shelter can be frightening.

Your dog may whine and cry for a few minutes. That's OK. He needs time to adjust. If your new dog is a puppy, chances are he won't sleep through the first night. A puppy's bladder isn't big enough. When he wakes up (he'll probably start to bark and whine), take him directly outside and let him go potty. This is a good job for an older kid or a grown-up—younger kids need their sleep! Don't let him play. Once he's gone potty, take him back to his crate, and put him to bed with a nice cuddle. He will probably wake up once or twice a night for the first few weeks he's home. Puppies also wake up early in the morning. Even if you usually like to sleep late, your puppy will have other plans!

The First Weeks

The first couple of weeks after you bring a new dog home is a busy time. There is so much to do and learn! Your puppy is learning how to use his legs. He's trying not to pee in the house. Older dogs are also learning how to behave in their new homes. A new puppy will spend a lot of time exploring the world. He will learn how to get what he wants when he wants it. He'll sleep a lot. He'll also spend a lot of time playing and running around.

Many older dogs go through

Give your new dog or puppy safe toys such as these to chew on.

what trainers call a honeymoon period. That means that they are on their best behavior at first. Sometimes adult dogs act quiet and shy when first adopted. Later, they come out of their shells. They may be more energetic than they seemed. They may have issues you didn't know about. They may not like other dogs or may be jealous of toys or food. All new dogs should start a training class shortly after arriving in their new homes. A good trainer will help you work through the post-honeymoon period. No matter what, get help from a trainer if your new dog ever growls, snaps, bites, or bares (shows) his teeth.

Make a vet appointment for your new pet. The vet will look for any health problems. She will give your pup shots and maybe deworm him. Most puppies are born with worms, so lots of vets deworm all puppies. The vet will check for fleas and will probably start your dog on monthly flea control. The vet may also start your dog on monthly heartworm control.

Your vet will let you know when you need to spay or neuter your dog. Puppies can be altered as young

It's important that your dog see a veterinarian to make sure he is healthy.

as eight weeks, but some vets prefer to wait until around five months. Make sure to get your female dog spayed before her first heat. This happens when she is about six months old.

See if someone in your family can stay home during your dog's first week. This will help him get a good start. It will help him learn the rules and speed up house-training. Puppies shouldn't be alone all day. If school is close, can you go home at lunch? Maybe an adult can. This way your puppy can get a potty break and a chance to stretch his legs. If no one in the family can do this, you may find a neighbor who is willing. There are also dog walkers who can come to your home.

Chapter 10

Sit, Stay, Good Dog!

Your dog doesn't need to be a genius to learn how to be a good dog.

Training a dog is a lifelong project. It is something that everyone in your family must be part of. It doesn't start and stop with teaching her to sit and stay. Training means teaching your dog not to go potty in the house. It means teaching your dog how to be nice to people and other animals. If you want to do canine sports or activities, you also need to train your dog for those. Different members of your family can be responsible for different parts of your dog's training. Adults and older kids should be the main trainers, but younger kids can be great helpers. Never try to train your dog without an adult around.

Some people think that training a dog is too much work or that dogs don't like it. The truth is that dogs who are well trained are less work and more fun. A trained dog can go to lots of places with you, such as the park and friends' houses. If a dog is trained, she can have more freedom. She will come to you when you ask her to. A trained dog also gets along with other dogs and people. Dogs who aren't trained may feel afraid or unsure in new situations. They get into trouble a lot, but they aren't sure why you are mad. Untrained dogs are often tense and anxious, but a trained dog is relaxed and friendly.

First Things First: Crate-Training and House-Training

Teaching your dog not to potty in the house is called house-training. House-training is something the whole family can help with. Crate-training is teaching your dog to sleep and relax in a crate. Dog crates are boxes made of wire or plastic with a door that opens in the front. Although a crate may look uncomfortable to you or me, dogs like them. Crate-training and house-training go together like milk and cookies.

Crate-Training

Wild dogs live in cozy dens, often dug in the ground. They like to feel enclosed, with something pressed against their backs when they sleep. It makes them feel safe. Puppies feel unsafe when left by themselves out in the open. They miss the feeling of their mom and littermates pressing against them while they sleep. Have you ever noticed that your dog likes to sleep under your bed or under a table or desk? The crate is a lot like that except that you control when your dog goes in and out of it.

A pup explores her new crate. Crate-training your dog will make house-training much easier.

Support your child's interest in dog training by signing up for a training class. A class will help your child learn safe, positive ways to train your dog. Help handle the dog in class, or take notes from the sidelines. This way, you can help your child with dog training homework. Some classes may require that the lead trainer be over a certain age. In this case, let your younger child watch from the sidelines, and then ask him or her to help you when training at home.

A young pup gets a lesson.

Puppies are a lot like babies; they get overtired and overwhelmed. The crate is a nice safe place to go to when life gets tough. A crate is a good place for any dog to sleep and relax in at night and when you can't watch her. After a couple of days of crate-training, your puppy will probably go into the crate on her own. Don't leave your dog in the crate for more than a few hours at a time during the day.

Your dog's crate must be just big enough for her to lie down, stand up, and turn around in. If you adopt a puppy, you'll probably end up buying two crates. Or you can buy a crate with panels that can be used to make the crate bigger or smaller. You want to make sure that the crate isn't too big for

your dog. If it is, she may poop in one corner and sleep in the other!

Teach your dog to love her crate as soon as she comes into your home. Put a cozy blanket in the crate so your pup has something to snuggle up to. Give her a soft toy without any filling to snuggle with. A hard rubber toy is good for chewing on. Don't give her rawhides, plush toys with filling, or bones while she is in her crate. She can rip these up and choke on them. She should play with these toys only when you are with her.

Introduce your pup to the crate slowly. Let her sniff around the outside and then the inside if she wants to. Do NOT close the door. This can make her afraid of the crate. Put treats outside the crate and at the door of the crate. Let her find them on her own and

Some dog-training techniques can be dangerous. Individual dogs may react strongly to being physically moved or restrained. Always supervise your child when he or she is working with a dog.

A young child makes a great training assistant. She can hold the training treats, call the dog when teaching *come*, or act as a distraction when teaching the dog to concentrate. As children mature, they can participate in training more actively by helping to reinforce basic commands, such as *sit* or *down*. Many older children enjoy training tricks, such as *spin* and *shake*. Try to schedule some family training time each day. It's a great education for everyone!

ROLL OVER

eat them. Then put treats inside the crate. Let your dog follow the path of treats into the crate. Be sure to place some at the very back and in the blanket so she has to get all the way in to find them. Let her find treats in her crate three or four times.

Once your dog is going in and out of the crate on her own, shut the door quietly. Don't slam it because this will scare her. Feed her a few treats through the door, and then open the door. Do this three or four times. Then let her stay in the crate for a few minutes at a time. Stay with her and give her treats every once in a while. Increase the amount of time she stays in the crate. If she starts scratching at the door, whining, or barking, wait until she is quiet and calm. Then let her out. Don't let her out right away when she whines and barks. It will make it harder for her to learn to relax in the crate if she thinks barking will make you let her out.

After your dog is comfortable in the crate with you nearby, leave her alone in the crate. The first time, leave the room for only a minute. Then leave the room for two minutes, three minutes, and so on. Once you can leave for ten minutes at a time, your dog is crate-trained! When you come back you'll probably find her fast asleep or happily chewing on a toy. Some dogs are crate-trained in an hour. For other dogs it takes days or weeks of training before they are comfortable in the crate. Older dogs usually take more time than pups. That doesn't mean they won't ever bark or whine to get out of their crate. They will, especially when they wake up after a nap. Just wait until your dog calms down, and then let her out of the crate.

If you have had a puppy before and thought house-training was a big drag, you'll be surprised by how easy it is when you use a crate. In fact, house-training your dog is a lot easier than potty training your little sister or brother. And no one will have to change any diapers!

House-Training

There is only one real rule to house-training: never let your puppy go potty inside. OK, that's easier said than done, right? Isn't that the whole point of house-training—to teach your puppy not to go potty in the house?

The trick to this is to never let your puppy out of your sight. Unless she is in her crate, she should be with someone at all times. That means your puppy should not wander around the house or be left in a room alone. When she isn't sleeping, playing, cuddling, eating, or chewing a toy in front of you, she should be in her crate. To remind yourself of this, keep your dog close by attaching her leash to your belt.

The trick to house-training is to never let your dog pee in the house. Make sure she is never alone inside the house, and give her lots of opportunities to pee outside.

Q. Is it possible to train deaf dogs?

A. Yes. Deaf dogs can be trained with sign language! American Sign Language, or ASL, is the language that deaf people use to talk to one another. You can teach your dog to understand basic ASL signs for commands such as *sit* and *down*.

This deaf dog has learned ASL.

That way you know the puppy is always nearby. (Younger kids shouldn't do this because an excited pup could pull them over!)

Why won't a puppy just go potty in her crate? Dogs are very clean despite what some people say about them. They hate to sleep or relax in the same area where they go potty. They will do almost anything to avoid it. If your puppy does pee or poop in her crate, she has probably been in there for too long or is sick.

Give your pup lots of chances to go potty outside. She needs to go potty at least every two hours. She also needs to go potty after playing, napping, and eating. Every time you take your pup out of her crate, take her outside. Take her outside after playing a game and after meals.

Learn the signs that your dog is getting ready to go potty. She will circle, sniff, and scratch at the floor when she is looking for a good spot. If you see her doing this, take her outside right away. If your puppy begins to squat or lift a leg in the house, say "no" and take your pup outside. Never yell at a dog for going potty in the house or rub her nose in the accident. This won't teach her anything except to be afraid of you.

Once your pup is outside, say "go potty." When she does, tell her what a good girl she is. Do not play with your puppy until she goes potty. Potty breaks should be all business.

If you and the rest of your family follow these instructions to a tee, your puppy may never have an accident in the house. It's easier to prevent a habit than to break one. This is especially true with house-training!

Collars and Leashes

There are a lot of different kinds of training equipment people will say you need. There are special training collars and leashes that are short and long, leather and nylon. There are head halters that go around a dog's nose and harnesses that go around a dog's chest.

All this special equipment has special uses. Each must be used properly, or it can hurt the dog. When you are training your dog, the best

Did You Know?

There are many kinds of leashes and collars. Some are used for training, others for day-to-day walking. There are head halters and harnesses. There are short and long leashes. There are traffic leashes and training tabs. Phew! What's a kid to do? For your pup's first leash and collar, buy a standard flat nylon or leather collar and a six-foot leather or nylon leash. Ask the teacher in your puppy kindergarten if you should buy anything else.

thing to use is what is called a flat collar. This is just a basic leather or nylon collar with a buckle. It should be loose enough around your dog's neck that you can put two fingers under

There are many types of collars. This is a harness, which goes around the dog's chest instead of around her neck.

Clicker Training

Many commands are easier to teach if you use a clicker. Clicker training was invented by a dolphin trainer to teach dolphins tricks. You can buy clickers at pet supply stores.

Clickers replace your spoken "good dog" reward with a quick clicking sound. By the time you tell your dog what a good girl she is, she may be doing something bad. The click tells her she is good at the exact moment she is being good. For example, by the time you say "good sit," your dog may be standing up. But you can click at the moment she is sitting.

To teach your dog that the click means "good girl," you need a pocketful of treats and a clicker. Click and give your dog a treat. Do this about thirty times. By the time you're

A girl teachers shake using a clicker.

done, your dog knows the click is a good thing! Then whenever she follows a command, you just click instead of using your voice to prompt her.

the collar. The leash you use for training should be nylon or leather with a small loop at one end and a clip at the other. You hold the loop in one hand, and the clip attaches the leash to the dog's collar. It should be a standard length, which is six feet long.

If you think you need special training equipment for your dog, talk to a trainer first. There may be better alternatives.

How to Teach Commands

Dogs need to know basic commands to be well behaved. A dog who knows her basic commands is a lot nicer to live with. The basic commands are *come*, *sit*, *down*, *leave it*, and *stay*.

Your dog should also learn how to walk nicely on a leash. Some people also teach their dogs more difficult commands such as long *stay* and *heel*.

Start teaching your dog her basic commands as soon as you bring her home, whether she's an eight-week-old pup or a five-year-old adult. A dog who knows her commands knows who's the boss (you and your family), and that keeps her and the rest of your family safe. A dog who knows her commands will come when you call her instead of running into a busy street. She'll also understand to stop jumping up on people, something that can knock down older people or young kids.

Pay Attention

Sometimes it's hard for puppies and young dogs to pay attention when they are being trained! They get fidgety and bored. They'd rather go run and play. So you must teach your dog how to pay attention to you.

1. Show your dog you have a treat in your hand.

2. Then say "look at me" (or you can say "attention" or "heads up"). At first, your dog will look at your hand. Wait until she looks at your face. You may need to bring the treat up to your face the first couple of times.

3. When your dog looks at you, say "good look at me" and give her a treat. Do this three or four times every day. Pretty soon, your dog will look at you when you ask her to. If she's not really interested in treats, teach her to look at you with a squeaky toy. If she gets distracted or walks away, show her the treat or toy again. If your dog is really distracted, you may need a partner to hold her on a leash while you show her the treats.

Sit

It's time to teach your dog the king of commands, *sit*! This is one of the commands you will use the most. Luckily, it's also one of the easiest to teach.

1. Stand in front of your dog with a treat in your hand.

2. Show your dog the treat in your hand, and hold it near her nose. Slowly move your hand in a straight line above her

STEP 1: From a sit, show your dog a treat and tell her "down."

STEP 2: Bring the treat toward you to the ground.

STEP 3: Once your dog is lying down, give her the treat.

This boy is teaching his dog to stay. Once your dog learns to stay, it is easy to keep her away from the dinner table and keep her from running off.

nose. She will raise her nose to follow the treat. As her nose goes up, her bottom will go down.

3. Once her nose is in the air and her bottom is firmly on the ground, say "good sit" and give her the treat. It's important that her front feet stay on the floor. If she jumps up to follow the treat, have a friend hold her front feet down.

4. Repeat the exercise, but say "sit" as you raise the treat. Once the bottom is down, say "good sit" and give her the treat.

5. Practice this at least ten times a day. Pretty soon, your pup will be sitting pretty!

Down

After learning to sit, it's time to teach the *down* command. Use *down* when you want your dog to lie down. It can help her calm down and relax. It's a good command to use while you're eating dinner or when friends are over. You may need a partner to help you with this one.

1. Stand directly in front of your dog, and say "sit."

2. Once she is sitting, hold a treat in front of her nose. Slowly move the treat toward you to the ground. This will be a diagonal line from her nose to your feet. She will try to follow the treat, but she

won't be able to reach it. To reach it, she must lie down.

3. Once she is lying down, say "good down" and give her the treat. Some dogs will simply stand up to try to get the treat. If your dog does this, ask a helper to gently hold her bottom down on the ground.

4. Once your dog is following the treat into the down position, add a command. This time, say "down" as you lower the treat. Say "good down" once your dog is lying down.

5. Practice this ten times a day until your dog is lying down at the drop of a hat.

Stay

The *stay* command is important because it helps you keep control over your dog and helps your dog stay safe. *Stay* asks your dog to stay in one place without moving. Teaching *stay* isn't as easy as teaching *sit* or *down*. It's a skill that you'll probably have to work on during your dog's entire life.

1. Ask your dog to sit or lie down.

2. Stand directly in front of her, and say "stay." Put your hand out with the palm facing her as if you were telling someone to stop. Give her a treat. Do this several times.

3. Say "stay," show her the palm of your hand, and wait five seconds before giving her a treat. If she stays for the five seconds, say "good stay" and give her the treat. If she moves, put her back in position and start again. You may need a

STEP 1: From about six feet away, show your dog a treat, and tell her to "come."

STEP 2: Call your dog's name as she comes toward you. Pull her forward with her leash if she gets distracted.

STEP 3: When she reaches you, give her the treat.

helper to do this. Do this five to ten times a day for three or four days.

4. After your dog stays for five seconds, have her stay for ten seconds, and so on. Once she stays for twenty seconds, take a step back and start over. Keep doing this until your dog stays even when you are across the room. Make it harder by adding distractions such as having a friend jump up and down, clap, or walk in front of your dog. You will probably need to do each step five to ten times for three or four days.

Come

Teaching your dog to come is the most important command you will ever teach her. You use the *come* command when you want your dog to run to you right away. Your dog must know to come right to you when you call her. If your dog doesn't know this, she could run away or be hit by a car. Teaching *come* is about avoiding bad habits.

We don't mean to, but we teach dogs NOT to come all the time. Doing things like chasing your dog, not making her come when you call her, or calling her name only when it's time to stop the fun will just teach your dog that she doesn't have to come when you call her.

To avoid teaching your dog NOT to come, follow these rules:

1. Never chase your dog. Chasing your dog teaches her to run away from you.
2. If you ask your dog to come, make sure she does. That means keeping her on a leash so she won't run away until you know she will always come when you call her.
3. Always give your dog praise or a treat when she comes. Never punish her

Take your dog to school! These pups are in puppy kindergarten—a great start to your dog's education.

Many pups, such as this one, will try to bite at the leash when you first take them for a walk.

This owner keeps treats by her side while she trains the dog to walk nicely on a leash.

when she comes, even if it took a very long time for her to get to you!

4. Ask your dog to come for good reasons. Don't just ask her to come when you are leaving the park. Call her and give her a quick butt rub or a treat.

To teach your dog TO come, follow these rules:

1. Teach your dog to come in your own yard first. When teaching the *come* command, always keep your dog on a leash. If she won't come to you, you can pull her to you by her leash.

2. Show your pup that you have a handful of really good treats. Run away from her saying "come Daisy" (or whatever her name is).

3. When she catches up to you, turn around and face her. Give her a treat and

say "good come." Do this at least ten times so your pup understands that she gets good treats every time she runs after you.

4. Ask a friend to hold your dog in place by her leash. Stand ten feet away from them. Show your dog that you have some good treats in your hand. Tell your dog to come, and clap your hands or slap your legs to get her excited about running toward you.

5. When she gets to you, say "good come." Give her a treat and a good cuddle. Repeat this at least ten times.

6. Next, ask some friends and their dogs to walk around in your yard. Stand about ten feet from your dog. Show her you have treats. Tell your dog to come, and clap your hands.

An owner trains her dog to leave an attractive stick. *Leave it* is a useful command whether you are playing a game (even in the snow!) or keeping your dog from eating your steak!

7. When she comes, tell her she's a good girl and give her a treat. If she doesn't come, pull her toward you by her leash. Give her a treat when she gets to you. Keep doing this until she comes to you.

8. Once your dog comes to you in your own yard, teach her to come to you in other places. Practice in a local park. Start from the very beginning, and go through each step at least ten times. Practice each step ten to twenty times for three or four days before moving to the next step.

9. Train your dog to come for the rest of her life. That means practicing the *come* command every day. Teach her that coming to you is a positive thing. When you are out doing fun things, call her to you and then give her a treat. Don't just call her when it's time for the fun to end, or she won't want to come.

Leave It

Learning the *leave it* command will keep your dog from running after your cat, stop her from eating food off the floor, and keep her away from dangers on your walks.

Here is how to teach your dog to leave it:

1. Show your dog that you have a piece of food in your hand. Don't let her take it. If she's very pushy, you may want a helper to hold her on leash as you do this first step.

2. Say "leave it," but keep showing her the food. If she doesn't take it for a few seconds, say "good leave it" and give her

the food. Have her wait for up to ten seconds between saying "leave it" and giving her the treat. Do this ten to twenty times a day for three or four days.

3. Then put the food on the floor. Say "leave it." Do not let your dog take the treat. Wait two seconds, and say "take it." Now let her eat the treat. Increase the amount of time she has to wait. Do this ten to twenty times each day for three or four days.

Once your dog understands the *leave it* command, you can teach her to leave other things besides food. When she starts to chase the cat, pull her away by her leash, and say "leave it." If she stops chasing, say "good leave it" and give her a treat. On walks, tell her "leave it" if she starts to sniff something you don't want her to. Pull her away, and say "good leave it." Then give her a treat.

Walk on a Leash

Do you walk your dog? Has the neighborhood comedian ever asked, "Hey, are you walking your dog, or is your dog walking you?" Don't you hate this? Wouldn't it be more fun to walk your dog if she wasn't pulling you down the sidewalk?!

Dogs who walk nicely on a leash get more walks and enjoy their walks more. If your dog pulls on the leash, you probably won't walk her as much. Pulling on the leash isn't much fun for your dog, either. It can even hurt her!

Try to teach your dog to walk nicely on a leash right from the start. Give your new pup a leash and a collar so she gets used to them right away. When together at home, attach her leash to your belt. That way, she can get used to having the leash on, and you can keep a close eye on her.

Once that you have the right equipment, it's time to get walking. Walking the dog in daylight with a buddy or an adult is a great job for an older kid. Younger kids can help out by carrying the plastic bags and keeping the dog walker company.

For your dog's first walk, arm yourself with lots of treats. Don't expect to go very far. Start walking. If your dog pulls, stop. Turn around and walk in the other direction. When your pup catches up to you, give her a treat. Do this every time she pulls.

Start walking again. Hold your bag of treats at your hip in your left hand if your dog is on your left, and in your right hand if your dog is on your right. Be sure your dog sees the bag. She will probably look up at your hip as you walk. Give her a treat every once in a

Canine Good Citizen

If you think your dog is an especially good citizen, a test will prove it! The Canine Good Citizen (CGC) test is done by a representative of the American Kennel Club. Any dog can take the test, purebred or mix, as long as he is at least one year old. The CGC tests cover whether your dog is friendly and whether he listens to you.

Test 1: Accepting Strangers
Test 2: Sitting Politely for Petting
Test 3: Appearance and Grooming
Test 4: Walking on a Loose Leash
Test 5: Walking through a Crowd
Test 6: Sit, Down, and Stay
Test 7: Coming When Called

Test 8: Reacting to Another Dog
Test 9: Reaction to Distraction
Test 10: Supervised Separation

If your dog passes each test, he's officially a good citizen!

If you want your dog to take the Canine Good Citizen test, visit the AKC Web site for more information: www.akc.org/events/cgc.

while. If she starts to walk ahead of you, stop. Give her a treat from your treat bag, and say "good dog!" when she walks back to you. Repeat this several times.

Keep training your dog every day until she always walks nicely on her leash. Always bring treats on your walks. Be ready to stop whenever she starts pulling. If you make it only halfway down the block the first couple of times, don't worry. It's normal. Keep training, and never let your dog get into the habit of pulling. That way, she will be a good leash walker from the start.

As with all training, it's easier to train a dog to walk nicely than to train a dog to stop walking badly! But it can be done. If your newly adopted dog is already pulling at the leash, here's a good trick:

1. Start walking with a treat bag at your hip. If your dog pulls, stop. Wait until she stops pulling, give her a treat, and then start walking again.

2. If you wait and she does not stop pulling, turn around and begin to walk in the other direction. Give her a treat when she follows you.

3. Do this each time she pulls until she stops pulling. This will probably take one to two walks every day for at least two or three weeks.

4. Once she stops pulling, you can start training her to walk nicely.

Naughty Things Dogs Do: Digging, Barking, and the Rest

There are so many things dogs do that make us mad. They bark, dig, bite, chew, and jump up. But dogs are only doing what comes naturally. It's totally normal for a dog to steal food. Dogs are scavengers. They survive by eating the leftovers from other animals. No wonder they like to eat garbage!

We expect dogs to do all kinds of things that don't make much sense to them. We ask them not to dig up our gardens when they're just trying to check out the good stuff buried there. We ask them not to bark at people when they're trying to protect us and their house. We ask them not to eat food off our tables when they're just trying to keep their bellies full. All in all, they're pretty nice about it. Sometimes it doesn't happen as easily as we'd like. Here are just some of the dog behaviors humans don't like.

Digging

Some dogs are just born to dig. The terriers were bred for hundreds of years to dig after animals in underground burrows. For them, digging is almost like breathing. Sometimes dogs dig because they are bored. Don't leave your dog

Some dogs simply love to dig. You may just have to give them their own digging spot.

alone outside for long periods, and make sure she gets lots of exercise. This may end your digging problems.

You can cut down on digging even if your dog is a natural digger. Does your dog like digging in your dad's prized flower beds? Fill in the holes with her own poop. Cover the poop with soil. Sounds gross? Dogs think so too! Dogs hate to touch their own poop. The first time they dig up this surprise, it may put them off digging for good! But use only your dog's own poop to do this. As much as dogs hate their poop, they often like other dogs' and cats' poop. Finding cat poop may seem like a great treat!

If your dog is a true digger, she'll probably just find somewhere else to dig. The best solution for a die-hard digger is to give her a digging spot of her own. A sandbox works well. Fill the sandbox with soft soil. In the soil, bury lots of your dog's favorite things such as toys, bones, or whatever she really loves. Show her the sandbox. Dig in it yourself to show that this is a prime digging spot. When she digs there, tell her what a good girl she is.

Barking

Dogs usually bark for a reason. They want to come in the house, they want to go outside, or they want some food. When dogs bark for no reason, it usually means they are bored. A dog who is left outside all day or night will bark just to keep herself busy. If she doesn't get enough exercise, she will bark because she is anxious. It's easy to solve this kind of barking—bring your pup inside, and give her lots of exercise. Puzzle toys such as Kongs can help fill her days.

Sometimes dogs bark because they see things they want to get to. If your neighbor has a dog, the two dogs may bark at each other through the fence. To stop this, put something in between the dogs. Hang a bamboo screen from the fence. Once they can't see each other, they won't bark as much.

Jumping Up

Jumping up is another habit that is easier to prevent than to cure! When a puppy jumps up, people think it's cute. Everyone laughs and gives her kisses. She learns that jumping up is a good thing to do. When your puppy grows to be 50, 100, or 150 pounds and is still jumping up, no one will think it's cute.

To keep your dog from jumping up, get down to her level. Ask your visitors to squat down to greet your pup. Ignore your puppy if she jumps on you. Give her lots of praise and love when she stays on all four paws. If everyone does this, she'll quickly learn not to jump up. It's easy to teach your puppy not to jump, but it's a lot harder to teach visitors to not let her jump!

Older adopted dogs often are already jumpers. The best way to cure them of this habit is to ignore it. But that doesn't mean let them do it. When your older dog jumps on you, walk away. Don't pet her or give her any love. Once she calms down, squat down to her level, and give her treats and affection. She'll quickly learn that jumping gets her nowhere.

Chewing

You can't really teach dogs not to chew. Chewing is just what they do. You can teach a dog to chew on the right things, though.

When your dog first comes home, she has no idea what she can or cannot chew. She'll just chew whatever looks good and is easiest to get to. Puppies are especially bad chewers. They often like to chew things that smell like their people and like food. Shoes, wallets, remote

A puppy nips during playtime. Nipping is a bad habit that can become dangerous as a dog gets older.

controls, and glasses are often victims of puppy teeth!

To teach your pup what to chew and what not to chew, give her lots of her own safe dog toys. Don't let her chew on anything else. If you don't want something to be chewed, don't

A dog munches on her owner's shoe. Dogs often chew the things that smell like their people, even their shoes!

leave it out. If you leave your shoes out and she chews them, you only have yourself to blame. Pretty soon, your dog will start to figure out what are her toys and what are your toys.

Never give your dog old socks or shoes to chew on. This will teach her that these things are OK to chew. She can't tell the difference between a holey sock and a new one!

Nipping

Puppies like to nip. They use their teeth and mouths to explore the world. But those tiny needlelike teeth hurt.

Littermates and doggy moms teach puppies not to nip by yelping when a nip is too hard. You can do this too. When your pup nips you, say "ow!" Most pups will be surprised enough to stop nipping for at least a moment or two.

This dog is trying to steal food. Prevent this by not leaving food out where your dog can reach it.

Do this every time your pup nips, and soon she'll replace those nips with licks.

Some pups, though, get more excited when you yelp. If your puppy is like this, just stop playing with her. Let her calm down, and then start playing again. Stop the game whenever she nips. If she nips three times in a row, take her to her crate, and give her time to calm down. Do not scold her. This will only make her more excited. Sooner or later, she'll figure out that nipping means the fun ends. And no pup wants the fun to end!

Other Naughty Habits

There are many other naughty doggy habits. They include begging and getting on the furniture. We hate to sound like a broken record, but you can keep bad habits from starting if you don't let your pup do them in the first place. Beggars learn that begging gets them food. If you never give your dog food off your plate, your dog won't beg from you. Your dog should get all her food from her bowl, and all treats should be earned. Always make your dog do a trick or something else before you give her a treat.

A lot of people let puppies on furniture. When they grow into big, hairy, slobbery dogs, these people don't want them on the furniture anymore. Imagine that! If you don't want your adult dog on the couch, don't let your puppy on the couch. It's as simple as that. If your dog is never allowed on the couch, she probably won't get on the couch. It's when you change the rules that the trouble starts!

A dog's education is never done. You must train your dog every day for her entire life.

Chapter 11

Your Dog, the Social Butterfly

Teaching your dog to be comfortable in new situations is called socializing. It sounds as if your dog is being invited to a party, but socialization isn't about drinking soda and eating pizza! Dogs aren't born being comfortable in every situation. They need to learn what is and what isn't scary. When dogs aren't socialized with other dogs, people, household noises, and other things, they can become afraid of them. Dogs who are scared of everything have a hard time getting along. They can even become aggressive.

Here are some basic rules for socializing your dog:

1. Never coddle your pup when he is afraid. We humans like to be comforted when we are scared. But when you coddle your dog, he thinks you are agreeing with him. When you hug and kiss him when he's scared of something new, you are saying "yes, this is very scary!" Instead of comforting your pup when he is scared, teach him not to be afraid. Use a happy, jolly voice, and act very excited about whatever it is that scares your

A Poodle is making friends. Be sure your dog meets lots of kids. Dogs who don't spend a lot of time with kids can sometimes be scared of them.

pup. If he is afraid of firecrackers, clap your hands and say in your happiest voice, "Wow! Firecrackers! I just love firecrackers!"

Q. **Why are dogs so afraid of thunderstorms?**

A. The doggy fear of thunderstorms probably comes from several things.

1. Sometimes a dog becomes scared of thunder after being left outside during a storm. Always bring your dog inside during a storm.

2. Most dogs are afraid of loud sounds—and thunder can be really loud! Dogs who are afraid of thunderstorms are often afraid of fireworks, too. Dogs have better hearing than we do. The thunder probably sounds louder to them. They can also hear it before we do.

3. There is static electricity in the air during a thunderstorm. Dogs are very sensitive to this. Getting a static electricity shock may make them more fearful.

4. They smell it. The smell of the air changes before a thunderstorm. Dogs have an amazing sense of smell and can probably tell a storm is coming before you can. If they are afraid of thunder, they may act scared hours before the storm starts!

5. The air pressure changes. Dogs' ears may be more sensitive to air pressure changes. The changes in air pressure may even give them earaches! They may start to think that a storm always means they'll get earaches.

2. Never tease your pup with something he is afraid of. It may seem funny to make your pup run away from the vacuum cleaner, but your pup is really scared. His fear will only get worse as he gets older. Your family won't be happy if the dog growls and barks every time someone tries to vacuum the floor!

3. Never push your fearful dog into a new situation. The more you push, the more afraid he'll become. Instead, coax him with treats and happy talk. If he's afraid of a new person, let the person offer your dog a treat.

4. Make socialization part of your daily routine. If you don't keep it up, your

dog can develop new fears. Take your dog to new places whenever you can. Introduce him to lots of nice people.

5. Use toys, food, happy talk, and whatever else works. Don't be afraid of spoiling your new friend. When he first comes into your home, he needs your help to feel safe.

Your Puppy's Social Schedule

Puppies change a lot during their first few months of life. They go from tiny helpless creatures to rambunctious adventurers in just a few short weeks. As they grow, they go through phases that can make them more fearful or more curious.

It's a lot like a human child's first five years of life. Maybe you've watched a little brother or sister go through these kinds of changes. As a tiny baby, she was held by your mom and dad all the time. She couldn't do much on her own. She may have cried whenever anyone else tried to hold her. As she got older, she wanted to explore everything, and she got into all kinds of trouble! Later, she may have had a couple of months where things suddenly scared her a lot. This is all normal for a baby.

Like babies, puppies are growing and changing. When tiny pups are exposed to new situations in a good way, they feel safe and secure. If they see new situations in a bad way, they feel unsafe and scared.

Socializing in the Home

Puppies need to learn that the things in your home are not scary. That's why it's important that a breeder raise the

Being a puppy can be scary. Make sure all his new experiences are positive.

puppies in a home. Puppies should learn right away that strange household things aren't scary.

Here are some good ways to teach your pup to feel safe at home:

1. Take out the vacuum cleaner. Don't turn it on. Give your pup a few treats while he sniffs it. Then turn on the vacuum cleaner, and give him more treats. Act as if a running vacuum is the most fun thing ever!

2. Play with pots and pans. Remember how your kid brother liked to take out pots and pans and bang them together? Well, now you get to do that! In a

Puppy Socialization Timeline

Newborn: At birth, a puppy needs the warmth and comfort of his mom and litter-mates. He can wait a while to meet all the friendly humans in his life.

Two weeks: The puppy's eyes are now open, and he's starting to explore, so it's time for him to meet people. Gentle, quiet people can hold and pet him now, but he should still spend most of his time with his mom and his littermates.

One month: The puppy can begin to meet people out-side of his family. Gentle kids and other visitors may play quietly with him. The breeder will take him outdoors for some fresh air and the chance to run around in soft grass. The breeder will have him walk on both carpet and linoleum so he gets used to both indoor surfaces.

Two months: It's time for the puppy to go to his forever home! It's a big adjustment. Don't expect your new pup to be perfectly comfortable right away. It may take a couple of weeks before he is totally used to his new home and his new family. For the next cou-ple of months, he can meet new people and friendly dogs who have had their shots. You can take him places like the local park, but keep him away from large groups of dogs.

Don't let him sniff poop because poop can have a lot of diseases in it! And remember that bad experiences at this age can scar a puppy for life. If a man in a hat is mean to him, he may grow up disliking all men in hats. Keep his experiences upbeat and happy.

Three to four months: Your pup now has had all his shots. He's ready to meet all the great people and dogs out there! With an adult, take him to parks, and take him down-town. Make sure everyone he meets is friendly. He may still be frightened of new things. This is a good time to enroll in a puppy kin-dergarten class.

Six months: Your pup is close to full grown. He's full of curiosity. He loves long walks and fun games. He's confident and will enjoy trips around your neighborhood. Remember that he's still growing. Keep his mind and body active, but don't overdo it.

One year: Your pup is officially an adult. Take off the kid gloves, and let him live life to the fullest. Take him to the beach, to the park, downtown, on buses, in cars, to your friends' houses. (Always make sure an adult knows where you and your canine buddy are off to!) The more positive experiences he has, the happier he will be. Keep exposing him to new, fun experiences throughout his life.

A well-behaved dog goes nose to nose with a goldfish. Does your family have fish, guinea pigs, or rabbits? Get your puppy used to them when he is small so he will not be aggressive with them when he is older.

fun voice, say, "let's play" to your puppy. If he acts scared, stop banging, and let him come and sniff the pots. Give him treats while you softly bang a pan. Get louder if he seems OK with it. If he acts excited, let him play while you bang.

3. Some dogs are afraid of stairs and slippery flooring such as linoleum. Use treats to get a puppy to climb up and down stairs. Put a treat on each stair, and let him figure out how to get to each treat. Put a line of treats across a linoleum floor, and let your puppy follow the trail. Never push him.

4. Turn on the dishwasher, the washing machine, and the clothes dryer. Run a hair dryer or a fan. Use a jolly voice, and give your pup lots of treats.

5. Ask a friend to ring the door bell. When you open the door, have your friend give your pup a treat.

Socializing Outside Your Home

Socializing your puppy outside the home can be a little trickier than socializing him inside the home. The big world can seem scary to a little puppy, and things outside the home are harder for you to control. Start slowly. Make your pup's first outings short, and give him lots of breaks. Avoid scary situations. Always bring an adult with you when you take your pup out into public, and always have your dog on a leash. Here are some good opportunities for socializing your new dog.

With an adult, take your pup on a walk around the block. Bring a bag filled with tasty treats. Let him sniff and

A dog meets children in a stroller. Sometimes dogs get afraid of strollers, wheelchairs, and bicycles if they are not used to them. Expose your dog to lots of things with wheels.

explore to his heart's content. Every so often, give him a treat. If anything seems to scare him, a passing car or a dog behind a fence, give him an extra treat.

Take your puppy to a local park. Let him explore and play, and give him lots of treats. Give him an extra big treat and lots of praise when he bravely meets a friendly new person.

Take your puppy to an outdoor market or a shopping area. These places are noisy, and there are lots of people, so they can be scary for puppies. To make sure your pup doesn't get scared, give him lots of good treats, and give him extra treats whenever he is especially brave. Let strangers give him treats. If he starts acting scared, give him a whole bunch of treats and lots of happy talk.

Socializing with People

You must socialize your puppy with lots of friendly people. Just because your dog likes you doesn't mean he'll like everyone. Sometimes dogs are afraid of people who look a certain way. If a man with a beard scared a puppy once, the pup may think all bearded men are scary. If a puppy has never seen a person with a hat, he may be scared when he meets one.

Make the Social Scene!

Here are some things a puppy should learn are not scary:

Adult dogs
Alarm clocks
Babies and toddlers
Babies crying
Baby strollers
Boys
Cars
Cats, rabbits, and other
   pets
Delivery people
Dishwashers
Dog parks
Dog-friendly stores
Dogs (of all shapes, sizes
   and colors)
Dogs off leash
Dogs on leash
Door bells
Downtown streets
Firecrackers
Girls
Groups of dogs
Groups of kids
Horses, sheep, and other
   farm animals
Linoleum floors
Loud music
Mail carriers
Men
Men with beards and
   moustaches
Motorcycles
Outdoor shopping areas
People jumping

Even an umbrella can be scary to a pup!

People of all ages, shapes,
   and sizes
People running
People singing
People talking loudly
People using a cane, walker,
   crutches, or a wheelchair
People wearing boots
People wearing hats
People wearing sunglasses
Playgrounds
Puppies
Riding in cars

Riding on boats
Riding on busses
Skateboards, bicycles, and
   scooters
Stairs
Telephones
Thunder
Trucks (any kind), tractors
Umbrellas
Visiting people and dogs
Visitors (any kind)
Washers and dryers
Women

Q&A

Baring teeth is a classic sign of aggression.

Q. What are some signs of aggressive behavior in dogs?

A. Dogs have many ways of showing they may bite. Here are some of them:

- Baring teeth
- Biting
- Growling
- Lunging
- Nipping
- Positioning ears forward
- Raising hackles (the hairs on the back of the dog's shoulders and neck)
- Wagging tail slowly and stiffly

Introduce your pup to as many people as you can. Ask your family members to invite friends over—men; women; children; babies; people of different races, heights, and weights; men with beards; people with long and short hair; people in wheelchairs and using walkers or canes; people in baseball caps and with huge parkas; boys with big tennis shoes; and women with high heels.

When you are out walking your puppy with an adult, ask friendly strangers if your puppy can meet them.

Carry treats with you every time you take your puppy out. Give him treats whenever he meets someone new.

Because some dogs get scared when people come to their house, invite lots of friends over when your puppy is little. Ask an adult to help you with a welcome home puppy party. Invite people who you know will be very nice and gentle with him.

Socializing with Animals

It seems funny that a dog would be afraid of other dogs, but many are! Some puppies are taken away from their moms and littermates too early. They don't

Friendly adults greet a puppy. Make sure your pup meets only friendly adult dogs. Some puppies develop fears of other dogs if they are treated roughly by dogs as puppies.

learn how to get along with other dogs. Other puppies just don't meet enough other dogs. Some dogs need extra help learning that other dogs are friends. All dogs should have lots of good doggy experiences right away.

Never adopt or buy a dog who is less than eight weeks old. Puppies need to spend at least eight weeks with their moms and litter-mates. They learn a lot of important things from their families. They learn how to get along with other dogs, how to understand what other dogs are telling them, how to play without getting into a fight, and how to show respect to older dogs.

Once your eight-week-old or older puppy is in your home, keep up his doggy education. Have him meet friendly neighborhood dogs. Some people say puppies shouldn't be around other dogs until they get all

Sometimes dogs can be shy of other animals, such as horses. This Great Dane goes nose-to-nose with a very alert Shetland pony!

their shots. This isn't true! Just don't let your puppy around dogs you don't know. Do let your puppy around dogs you know are healthy and who have all their shots. Ask an adult to talk to the dog's family to make sure they have done this. Make sure your pup meets gentle dogs who will treat him well. Don't let him meet bossy or rough dogs. That can make him afraid of other dogs.

Your dog should also meet other animals. Cats, horses, pigs, mice, rabbits, and ferrets are some of the animals your dog may meet in his life. Teach him they are not scary. Let him know that they are not to be chased or teased. Even if your dog seems to adore smaller pets, don't leave him alone with them. Dogs can accidentally injure small animals when they are trying to play.

Food for Thought

To dogs, food is a big deal! Their food is pretty much what they live for. Dogs love to eat, but more important, food keeps your dog's engine running. However, food can also be a problem for some dogs. A lot of dogs eat way too much food and end up weighing too much.

Choosing food for your dog can be confusing. What's the best kind of food? What's in the kibble you buy her? You take vitamins with breakfast every morning—does she need them too? You may have heard that there are gross ingredients in dog food. Is this true?

These are just some of the questions you may have about food and feeding your dog.

History of Dog Food

What is dog food? Up until the mid 1900s, dogs ate pretty much what we did. We just gave dogs leftovers from our dinner. So what happened? Why do most modern dogs eat crunchy kernels of food from big bags?

The fact that our dogs eat commercial dog food is really about marketing. In 1860, the first dog biscuit was invented in England. The

A Corgi checks out the grocery list. If your dog had her pick, she'd probably choose to eat steak and potato chips for every meal. It's up to her humans to make sure she eats a healthy diet.

biscuit was quickly followed by dry dog food, but it didn't catch on then. Canned dog meat was first introduced in the United States after

World War I, around 1918. That trend didn't catch on either. Most dogs continued to eat table scraps.

It wasn't until the 1960s that dry dog food started to get popular. The food got better, but more important, the commercials got better! The advertising of commercial dog food went into full swing. By the 1970s, most dogs ate commercial dog food.

Now, in the 2000s, the tide is turning again! Some people have decided what is good for them is good for their dogs. They think their dogs' food is healthier if they make it themselves. They also believe that their dogs like it more. Dog food makers argue that commercial dog food has all the ingredients a dog needs in a day so it is better for dogs.

So, what's the truth? Well, a little of both. What you feed your dog depends a lot on her individual needs. Veterinarians say that most dogs do just fine on commercial dog food. A good commercial dog food has all the protein and vitamins your dog needs. But dry dog food has some ingredients some people don't want to feed their dogs. For example, dry dog foods have preservatives, which are chemicals that keep dog food fresh. Dog food also loses a lot of vitamins while it's being made. To make up for this, vitamins are sprayed onto the dry food before it is put in bags. Some people believe that the sprayed-on vitamins just aren't enough for dogs, and they worry that some of the preservatives used can be unhealthy.

This pup is ready for dinner! This is most dogs' favorite time of day!

People who feed their dogs homemade diets don't just scrape their leftover dinner into a bowl. Some of the food we eat is bad for dogs, and our food may not give dogs the key nutrients they need. A good homemade diet includes whole foods such as meat, vegetables, eggs, and grains as well as supplements such as vitamins and nutritional yeast. Dogs shouldn't eat TV dinners, pasta mixes, white bread, or sweets. Then, again, we probably shouldn't either!

Dog Kibble

What's in dog food? Is it really full of scary ingredients? Despite rumors you may have heard, there isn't anything too weird in dog food. If you wanted to eat dog food, you could. You probably wouldn't like the taste much, though. Dog food is specially made to appeal to dogs' taste buds—

not yours! It also has ingredients in it that aren't very appealing to most of us—stuff like chicken feet and ground-up bones.

There are lots of differences in dog foods. Some dog foods are cheap. You can buy them at your local grocery store. Other dog foods are expensive. You can buy them only at pet supply stores or health food stores. Some dog foods are

A Pug rests among the biscuits. Dog biscuits were actually the first commercial dog food and are still pretty popular today!

Q. I'm confused. Is my dog an omnivore or a carnivore?

A. You probably know what a carnivore is. Carnivores are animals that eat mainly animal protein: meat. The lion is a carnivore, and so was the Tyrannosaurus Rex. Spiders are also carnivores. The house cat is an obligate carnivore. That means cats need meat to survive. Cats can't live on vegetarian, or meatless, diets. An herbivore is an animal that eats only plants. Elephants are herbivores. So are kangaroos and rabbits.

People are omnivores—we can eat animals and plants (although some people choose to only eat plants). Other omnivores are bears, chickens, and wasps. (Wasps eat insects and nectar from flowers, but they'll also eat meat and soda pop, which you may know from your last barbecue!). Bears eat salmon, but they also eat bark from trees and adore blueberries and huckleberries. Omnivores can survive without eating any meat.

So is the dog an omnivore or a carnivore? Well, that's where it gets a little confusing. Some people say dogs are carnivores. Others swear they are omnivores. Dogs definitely have teeth like carnivores. They are made for ripping and swallowing prey. Wolves, dogs' closest relatives, are carnivores. Most dogs enjoy a meat-heavy diet.

However, dogs are definitely not obligate carnivores. They do not need meat to survive. Some dogs eat a vegetarian diet and do just fine. Even in the wild, dogs eat some fruits and vegetables. They don't pluck berries off bushes, but they do eat the stomach contents of the animals they kill or scavenge—herbivores such as rabbits or omnivores such as rodents.

for senior dogs or for puppies. Others are for dogs with allergies or for dogs who need to lose weight. There are organic dog foods, natural dog foods, even vegetarian dog foods! You also have a choice of dry foods and wet foods—even in-between foods. There are so many types of food to choose from, you may get confused.

Dry kibble is what most of us feed our dogs. Kibble is dry, hard kernels usually packaged in large bags. Wet food is basically the same stuff, but it is moist so it is sold

This pup is sampling a variety of foods. There are many types of dog food you can offer: dry or wet commercial food or a homemade diet.

in cans. Some dogs prefer one over the other. Kibble is better at keeping doggy teeth clean. Other than that, there isn't much difference between the two.

Basically, dog food is made up of a protein, such as chicken, fish, lamb, eggs, or beef; a grain, such as rice, corn, wheat, or barley; and supplements, such as vitamins and fatty acids. Depending on the quality of the food, the protein may be whole meats or poultry, meat or poultry by-products, or meat or poultry meal. Whole meat or poultry is just the flesh (basically, these are the parts that we usually eat).

Meat or poultry by-products are other parts of the animal, such as internal organs, blood, bones, and feet. Meat or poultry meal is the by-products ground up. If you look on the package of dog kibble, you'll find these ingredients listed in order of how much is in the food.

Try to buy a food that lists meat as its first ingredient. By-products sound pretty gross, but remember that in the wild a dog eats the whole animal. Have you ever seen scat (poop) from a coyote? It is full of hair and other things the coyote can't digest. Most vets say it's OK for a food to have some by-products, but they shouldn't be the first ingredient.

Danger! Some Human Food Is Not for Dogs!

Not all people foods are good for dogs. Never feed the following foods to your pup:

Alcohol: Alcohol is really bad for dogs. Dogs absorb the alcohol quickly. They can have seizures, get kidney damage, or even die.

Chocolate: It's hard to imagine that something that tastes this good could be bad for anyone! Chocolate contains theobromine and caffeine. Both are poisonous for dogs. The darker the chocolate, the worse it is for your dog—baking chocolate is the worst. Dogs have even died from eating chocolate.

Coffee: Coffee contains caffeine. Don't let your dog drink coffee or eat coffee-bean candy.

Onions: Onions taste yummy, but they are very dangerous for dogs. Raw and cooked onions can cause hemolytic anemia (hee-muh-LIT-ic ah-NEE-mee-ya), the destruction of red blood cells. This is a serious condition—it can even cause death.

Garlic: This is a little confusing because garlic is often used in dog food. A little garlic is fine for your dog. A lot is not. Garlic in large amounts can cause hemolytic anemia.

Grapes and raisins: These sound like healthy snacks for your dog, but they're not! Experts aren't sure why, but grapes and raisins can cause kidney failure in some dogs. Sometimes dogs even die from eating grapes or raisins. Raisins are can be especially dangerous. If you've fed your dog grapes as snacks in the past, don't worry. Just avoid them in the future.

Macadamia nuts: Not that you'd want to give up these Hawaiian delicacies to anyone—not even your dog—but macadamia nuts are toxic for dogs. So don't give your dog a macadamia nut from your gift box—and definitely don't give her your chocolate-covered macadamia nuts!

Homemade Food

Why would someone want to feed a dog a homemade diet? For one, it may taste better to the dog. Some people believe that their dogs get bored with the same food day in and day out. Dog kibble just can't compare with chopped meat and fresh veggies. There's no question that dogs love homemade food, and they gobble it up with gusto!

Vets sometimes prescribe homemade diets for dogs with special health problems, such as food allergies. The dogs may have fewer symptoms when they eat food made especially for them. Dogs with cancer, autoimmune diseases,

Avocados are poisonous for dogs.

FALSE.

Rumors that avocados are unsafe for dogs to eat are untrue. The fruit of an avocado is perfectly safe. It makes a good occasional treat. The oily fruit is great for a dog's coat. The skin, pit, leaves, and branches of the avocado, however, can be toxic (for people, too!).

A pup eyes her owner's meal. Remember that feeding your dog a homemade diet doesn't mean just giving your dog anything you would eat.

skin problems, and even arthritis are sometimes prescribed a homemade diet as part of their treatment. Some pet owners believe that every dog does better on a homemade diet.

If your family wants to try a homemade diet, a grown-up should talk to your vet. He can help your family create a menu for your pup. He may have recipes your family can use or be able to suggest a canine cookbook for nutritional meals. An example of a doggy meal may be a breakfast of boiled eggs, oatmeal or brown rice, ground carrots, and brewer's yeast. A doggy breakfast should not include frozen waffles with syrup, pastries, or a glass of OJ!

Some people foods are actually poisonous for dogs to eat. Large amounts of onion and garlic are toxic for dogs. So are grapes, raisins, chocolate, caffeine, and alcohol. Your dog should never, ever eat these foods. If she accidentally eats them, have an adult take her to your vet right away.

Special Diets

Sometimes dogs have medical conditions and need special diets. When a dog gets older, she may have kidney problems. Your vet will recommend that she eat food with less protein. You can buy a low-protein commercial diet through your veterinarian, or you can make her low-protein food at home. Dogs with epilepsy, diabetes, or other illnesses may also need special diets. A grown-up should always talk to your vet before changing your dog's diet.

Puppies also need special diets. They need extra protein and vitamins to help them grow strong. That's why most vets recommend that puppies eat a puppy food. Some puppies need a special puppy food. Giant breed puppies such as Saint Bernards and Great Danes may grow too fast with a regular puppy food, so they must eat puppy food made for giant breeds.

Food Problems

Food helps dogs grow and makes them strong. Food keeps their system running all day long. It builds strong muscles and bones. A good diet keeps the skin healthy and the coat full and shiny. A dog who eats well has energy to burn. But food can also cause problems for dogs.

Many dogs have a hard time controlling themselves when it comes to food. And many owners have a hard time

This pup can't wait to get into her meal! Most vets recommend that puppies eat a special food made just for puppies.

Jack Sprat Could Eat No Fat, His Wife Could Eat No Lean

Is your pup like Jack Sprat or his wife? Take a look at your dog. Is she overweight or underweight? Here are a few signs to look for:

Is your dog full of energy?
Dogs who eat too much or don't eat enough are tired and less playful.

Can you feel your dog's ribs?
You should be able to feel your dog's ribs, but you shouldn't be able to see them. Dogs with ribs that stick out may be too skinny. If you can't feel your dog's ribs, she may be overweight.

What is the view from above?
Look down at your dog's back. Can you see her waist? If her waist goes in a lot, she may be too skinny. If she has no waist at all, she's probably overweight.

What's the view from the side?
Look at your dog from the side. Does her belly tuck up? A hanging belly may mean she is overweight. If it tucks up a lot, she may be too thin.

If your dog seems too heavy or too thin, ask an adult to take your dog to the vet.

controlling themselves when it comes to feeding their dogs! We like to give our dogs treats, and they like to eat them. But we're not always doing our dogs a favor when we slip them cookies. Dogs who eat too much can get fat, even obese. An obese dog can't run and play the way she should. She gets out of breath, feels tired, and has less energy. She may get sick. She may even die at a younger age than if she weren't overweight. Dogs

Is this pooch pooped? A tired-acting dog may not be getting the right amount or kind of food.

who weigh too much need to eat less food! Your family should talk to your vet about the right amount to feed your dog.

Small dogs tend to gain more weight than bigger dogs do. Sometimes small dogs compete with bigger dogs for snacks. A couple of dog biscuits a day won't make much difference for your eighty-pound Lab, but it can make your five-pound Yorkie very chunky! If you give

Healthy Snacks

So, what's a kid to do? You want to give your dog a tasty snack, but you don't want her to gain weight. Here are a few healthy snacks to try:

Baby carrots make excellent dog snacks.

- Apples and pears cut into bite-size pieces (don't feed your dog the core; the seeds can be toxic)
- Bananas cut into bite-size pieces
- Blueberries, raspberries, blackberries, and strawberries
- Carrots cut into bite-size pieces
- Chunks of boiled egg
- Cubes of low-fat cheese
- Melon cut into bite-size pieces

your dog snacks during the day, cut her meals by the same amount.

Your dog also needs exercise. She may be overweight because she is not doing enough to burn off her calories. If your dog is overweight, your vet can tell you how to get your pup fit. Sometimes overweight dogs need to start exercising slowly.

A dog who doesn't eat enough or who eats the wrong foods may become malnourished. That means her body doesn't get the nutrition it needs to run well. A malnourished dog is tired and doesn't have much energy. Her coat and skin are dry and don't look shiny the way a healthy dog's do. She may be very skinny but with a big tummy that is filled with air. You can see her ribs and her spine. If you see a dog who looks very skinny, she may be neglected. You can help her by asking a grown-up to call your local animal control.

A vet checks a dog's weight. Small dogs can gain weight very easily, even if they have only a few extra biscuits a day.

Chapter 13

Lovely Locks

Every dog must be groomed. That doesn't mean every dog needs to go to the Poodle Palace and have his hair clipped into pom-poms! It just means every dog needs to be brushed and bathed. His nails need to be cut, and his teeth need to be brushed. Most grooming can be done at home.

Grooming helps strengthen the bond between you and your dog. Grooming also makes your dog look better and smell nicer. And grooming is fun!

Puppy Pampering

For a lifetime of good grooming, get your pup used to it early. It will be much easier to groom your adult dog if you begin when he is a puppy. Later, if you take your dog to a groomer, the groomer will thank you for it!

Get your new pup used to being touched. Hold him in your lap. Stroke his ears, snout, body, and legs. Touch his paws and nails, and rub his tummy. Don't be rough. If anything seems to scare him, stop and give him a treat. If he pulls his paws away when you touch them, give him a treat while touching his paws

Bath time! A well-groomed dog is usually healthier and happier than an ungroomed dog.

A child gets help grooming her dog. An adult can help groom your dog so you learn how to do it correctly.

very gently. You'll find that pups respond very well to bribery!

Show your pup the grooming tools, and let him sniff them. Then gently brush and comb him. Be especially gentle around the tender areas—his ears, snout, paws, and under his tail. Get him used to having his toenails clipped: hold your pup in your lap while your mom or dad gently clips the very tips of his nails.

Give your pup a treat and lots of happy talk every time you do something new. Don't let his first grooming experiences be bad ones.

Different Coats for Different Folks

Different dogs have different kinds of coats. Some dogs have single coats. That means they have only the outside hair that we can see. Other dogs have double coats. That means they have the outside coat plus another coat underneath. The undercoat is usually very thick and fuzzy and helps keeps the dogs warm in cold climates. There are also long coats, short coats, curly coats, and straight coats! Each type of coat needs different types of grooming.

A wash-and-go coat is the easiest to take care of. Some dogs with

Shed Cycles

Dog hair grows in cycles. The hair grows to a certain point and then rests. Then new hair starts to grow and pushes out the old hair. The old hair falls out, or is shed, and new hair grows in. Some hair is shed hair by hair, and some hair is shed in clumps. A dog's shed cycle depends on the type of dog he is, the climate he lives in, and how healthy he is. Some dogs, called low shedders, have a slow shed cycle. Low shedders such as Poodles and Bichons Frises need to get haircuts because their hair keeps growing! Their hair doesn't keep growing forever the way ours does, but it grows long enough to get messy and matted.

A professional groomer works on a dog. Some dogs, such as this Soft Coated Wheaten Terrier, need special haircuts. It's usually easier to take them to a professional groomer.

These puppies seem to enjoy being brushed. It's a good idea to get your puppy used to being brushed when he's young.

wash-and-go coats are Labrador Retrievers and Boxers. Their coats are short or medium long. They need basic grooming. That means they need to be brushed every couple of days or once a week. They need to have a bath once a month. They need their teeth brushed every day. They need their nails clipped whenever they seem long. They don't need to have their coats cut or clipped.

All dogs shed. Dogs with undercoats usually lose their undercoats twice a year. During this time, some look a lot like unshorn sheep! Even dogs with very short single coats shed. During shedding time, dogs need to be brushed every day. Some people like to take their dogs to the groomer while they are shedding a lot. Dogs who are kept indoors may just shed a little all year long instead of shedding a lot twice a year.

Some dogs are said to have nonshedding coats, but this isn't quite true. It's just that

This Shih Tzu is fresh out of the bath! He has long silky hair that needs a lot of care.

some dogs have fur that sheds less than others. You can call these dogs low shedders. Their shed cycle is longer than that of other dogs. Because their hair doesn't stop growing when it gets two or three inches long, they need haircuts. Some dogs with low-shedding coats are the Poodle and the Bichon Frise.

If you have ever watched a dog show, you have probably seen dogs with very fancy hairstyles. Show Poodles are often shown in what is called a Continental clip. This haircut features big poufs of hair at the ankles, hips, and tail. Most pet Poodles wear a puppy cut. The coat is shaved all over to about one inch long. It looks nice and clean and is easy to take care of. Most low shedders are kept spiffy by a professional groomer. There are also low shedders whose coats form into cords. One breed with a corded coat is the Komondor.

Combs and Brushes

Depending on what kind of coat your dog has, you will need to use different types of brushes and combs. Here are some of the kinds used on dogs:

- **Curry brush:** This is a brush with rubber nubs. It is used on dogs with short coats.

- **Double-sided comb:** This comb has wide teeth on one side and narrow teeth on the other. The wide-toothed side is used on dogs with medium to long coats for general grooming. The narrow-toothed side is used to get out small tangles.

- **Flea comb:** This comb has very narrow teeth to catch fleas in.

- **Grooming rake:** This is a wide-toothed comb that you use to pull out the undercoat hairs. They are used on dogs with heavy double coats, such as Alaskan Malamutes and Samoyeds.

- **Mat splitter:** This is a knifelike tool used to break up mats in dogs with medium to long coats.

- **Pin brush:** The end of the bristles on this brush are rounded so the dog doesn't get slicker burn. It's usually for medium- to long-coated dogs.

This Greyhound's smooth coat needs only regular brushings with a curry brush.

- **Slicker brush:** This brush has wire or rubber bristles. It is used for general brushing on dogs with any coat type.

These dogs have long dreadlocks all over their bodies. They need to be groomed by a professional groomer.

Other dogs with special grooming needs are terriers. Some terriers have a strange coat that is rough and wiry. Terriers were bred to hunt small animals underground, so they needed tough coats to protect them against rough tunnel walls. To keep the coat wiry, groomers pull hair out by hand or with a special knife. If the terrier coat is cut with clippers, it loses its wiriness and grows back soft.

Some dogs such as Irish setters and Yorkshire Terriers have silky coats. Silky coats need

Single or Double?

Dogs have either a double coat or a single coat. A dog with a double coat has an undercoat that is downy and soft and an outer coat, sometimes called guard hairs, that is longer and coarser. A dog with a single coat has only the longer outer coat. Dogs from cool northern climates usually have double coats.

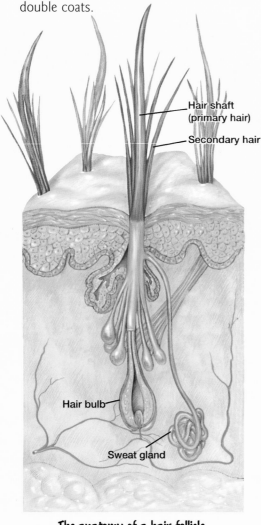

Hair shaft
(primary hair)

Secondary hair

Hair bulb

Sweat gland

The anatomy of a hair follicle

more brushing and combing than other dog coats. If they aren't brushed every day, they can get tangled. Some silky coats grow very long. Because it's hard for a dog to have such long hair, many pet owners cut their dogs' hair short all over. This short style is also called a puppy cut.

Northern dogs have heavy double coats that shed a lot. Some Northern dogs are Alaskan Huskies and Samoyeds. Brushing the coat every day cuts down on shedding. Northern breed dogs should never be clipped. Sometimes the outer coat won't grow back, and the dog is left with only the soft undercoat.

There are even dogs with no hair at all! Mexican Hairless Dogs, Chinese Cresteds, and Peruvian Inca Orchids are dogs who have hair only at the top of their heads, on their feet, and on the tips of their tails. Even these dogs need grooming! Their wispy hair needs to be combed. More important, their skin needs special care. Hairless dogs need weekly baths. Their skin can get dry, so they need moisturizing lotion every day. They also need to be protected from sunburn! If you have a hairless dog, be sure to slather him up with sunscreen whenever he goes outside. A sunscreen with zinc oxide works well. (Dogs with pink noses should also wear sunscreen when they're out during the day.)

Home Grooming

To keep your dog looking sharp at home, you must brush and comb his hair, bathe him, clean his ears and eyes, clip his nails, and brush his teeth. You also need the right tools for each grooming job. Grooming should always be done with a parent or another adult. Older kids can help brush, comb, and bathe their dogs. Younger kids can be excellent grooming helpers.

Adult Alert!

Always supervise your child's dog grooming activities. Dogs can be unpredictable, and younger children are not always aware of a dog's limitations. Grooming the dog together can be a great way to spend time with your child.

This Collie has all the grooming tools he needs. To properly groom your dog, you need brushes, combs, and clippers.

Q. Is it true that low-shedding dogs are good for people with allergies?

A. Some say that low-shedding dogs cause fewer allergies in humans. Allergies to dogs are usually caused by the dog's dander—the dog's dead skin cells—not the hair itself. Low shedders may shed less dander as well as less hair.

However, it may just be that low-shedding dogs are bathed and groomed more often than other dogs are. A dog who is frequently bathed usually triggers fewer allergies. Low-shedding dogs also tend toward the small side. Smaller dogs have less skin and therefore less dander. Smaller dogs cause fewer allergies than bigger dogs do. Puppies are also known to cause fewer allergies than adults do—probably because they are still small!

Bichons are low shedders.

The Equipment

The basic equipment you need to take care of your dog's grooming needs include:

- Brush
- Comb
- Cotton balls
- Dog shampoo
- Ear cleanser
- Flea comb
- Nail clippers
- Styptic powder
- Tooth brush
- Toothpaste made especially for dogs

Some people who groom their dogs at home use a special bathtub and a grooming table. Most people just use their own bathtubs and the bathroom counter, their laps, or even just the floor.

Depending on the type of coat your dog has, you may need a special kind of brush or comb. For example, dogs with smooth coats need to be brushed with a curry brush, a rubber brush that pulls out dead hairs and makes the coat shine. Dogs with thick double coats need a grooming rake, which is a comb with long metal teeth that pull out the dead undercoat.

Brushing and Combing

Brush your dog every day or at least every week. If you have a small dog, place him on your lap or on a counter or table. Brush larger dogs on the floor. Brush your dog in an area that's easy to clean such as outdoors or in the laundry room. If he's shedding, you can have a big mess after a good brushing! Brush in the direction his hair grows, the way you brush your own hair. Brush his entire coat thoroughly, from head to tail. Be careful not to brush too hard. This can cause slicker burn, which makes the skin red and irritated. Be gentle when brushing around his head and ears, under his tail, and his legs. If you find tangles, try to separate the hair with your fingers, and then brush it out. If your dog has longer hair that some-times tangles, go over him one more time with a comb.

RIDDLE

What is a dog's favorite outfit?
Her fur coat!

Bathing

Before you begin your dog's bath, make sure you have all your equipment. You will need cotton balls, dog-gy shampoo, doggy conditioner if your dog's fur tends to get tangled, a bowl for rinsing, and towels. Bathing your dog is definitely a two-person job, so make sure an adult is right there to help you.

Before beginning your dog's bath, put cotton balls in his ears. This will keep the water out. If your dog has medium or long hair, brush him before giving him a bath. Knots and tangles will get worse when wet.

Fill the tub or sink about halfway with lukewarm water. Make sure it is not too hot or too cold. Use a plastic bowl or

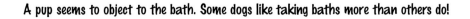

A pup seems to object to the bath. Some dogs like taking baths more than others do!

Doggy toothpaste
and human toothpaste are just the same.

FALSE.

Never give your dog human toothpaste. One reason is that your dog probably won't let you put human toothpaste into his mouth. Mint isn't a flavor most dogs like. Doggy toothpaste comes in all kinds of doggy-favorite flavors. But the most important reason is that doggy toothpaste is safe to eat. Dogs don't know how to rinse and spit. They swallow whatever is in their mouths. Human toothpaste isn't meant to be eaten. It will give your pup quite a bellyache and even make him throw up.

a shower attachment to get your dog's entire body wet. Start with his head. Cover his eyes, and push the water away from his face. Get your dog's coat soapy. Use a shampoo made especially for dogs because human shampoos dry out a dog's skin. Start with the head area and work backward to his tail and bottom. Be sure to clean behind his ears, his belly, below his tail, and his legs.

Use your bowl or shower attachment to rinse your dog with clean water. Make sure you get all the soap out. Leftover soap will make him itchy. After shampooing, you can use a doggy conditioner on his coat if you want. It will make his fur nice and soft. Rinse out the conditioner well.

Once your dog is squeaky-clean, lift him out of the sink or bathtub. If he is very large, you will need at least two people to do this. (Some people with large dogs decide it's easier to use a specially made grooming tub.) Cover him with a large towel before he has the chance to shake off the water. Remove the cotton balls, and rub him to get him dry. Don't let your dog outside before he's completely dry. He can catch a chill if he goes outside while he's still wet. And all your efforts will be for nothing if he decides to dry himself off in the dirt!

Teeth Brushing

Brush your dog's teeth every day. Dogs usually don't get cavities, but they do get all kinds of other nasty dental problems. These can lead to gum disease, lost teeth, and even diseases in other parts of their bodies, such as heart disease. Some dogs are sensitive about having their mouths touched so it's important an adult helps you brush your dog's teeth.

The hardest part about brushing a dog's teeth is getting him used to it. If you start brushing his teeth when he is a puppy, this won't be a problem. Even older dogs learn to enjoy it. Luckily, the makers of doggy toothpaste make it easy for dogs to like getting their teeth brushed. Dog-gy toothpaste comes in a lot of flavors that sound weird to us but taste heavenly to them. Some of the flavors are beef, peanut butter, even liver! And doggy toothpaste can be swallowed, unlike human toothpaste. Never use human toothpaste on your dog.

Ask an adult to help you the first time you brush your dog's teeth. If your dog doesn't like his mouth touched, don't try brushing his

A dog gets his teeth brushed. Be sure to brush your dog's teeth every day.

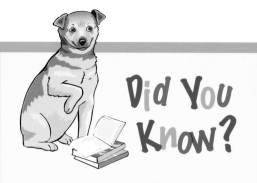

Did You Know?

Dogs rarely get cavities. That's because the bacteria in a dog's mouth usually don't create acids the way they do in a person's mouth. It is the acid that causes the cavities. Dogs also don't eat a lot of sugary snacks the way we do. Sugar also causes cavity-making acids. Don't slack off on toothbrushing just because dogs don't get cavities. Daily brushing cuts down on tartar, which prevents plaque buildup.

teeth! Instead, talk to your vet about other ways to have your dog's teeth cleaned.

Start by putting some doggy toothpaste on your finger, and let your dog lick it off. Yum—it tastes good to him! Use your finger to rub his teeth and gums. But if he doesn't like you doing this or if he seems to be in pain, stop! Have your vet clean his teeth.

Once your dog is used to you touching his teeth with just the toothpaste and your finger, move on to a finger brush or a doggy toothbrush. A finger brush is a rubber glove that goes on one finger and has a brush at the tip. Some people like to use this with smaller dogs. A doggy toothbrush is a lot like a human toothbrush, but it has a slightly different shape and a smaller brush.

Pick one area of the mouth to begin (don't forget where!), and brush gently. Don't brush so hard that you hurt your dog or make his mouth bleed. Brush in gentle circles all the way around the outside top teeth and then the inside top teeth. Do the same for the bottom teeth. You may want to add some toothpaste partway through to keep your dog happy. Once you're done, let your dog lick the toothbrush to get his tongue clean. You don't need to rinse his mouth with water. Just clean off the toothbrush and you're done.

Nail Trimming

Your mom, dad, or another adult should be in charge of cutting your dog's nails while you help. Some dogs don't like their paws touched. If your dog growls, snaps, or whines when you touch his paws, don't cut his nails yourself. Instead, have your vet or a groomer cut them.

Start cutting your dog's nails when he is a young puppy. He won't need it, but it will help him learn that nail cutting isn't scary. You can cut just the very tips off of the nails. Touch your puppy's feet and nails often so he knows you aren't trying to hurt him.

To cut your grown-up dog's nails, have him stand in front of you (or in your lap). Gently lift one front leg so you can see his nails. If your dog has clear nails, you'll see a dark area

Be careful not to cut the quick when you trim your dog's toenails.

This pooch is really being pampered! If your dog is patient enough, you may even give him a pedicure!

in the nail. This is the vein, called the quick. Clip your dog's nails up to right before the quick begins. If your dog has dark nails, you can't see the quick so you'll have to guess a little. When the nail grows out, it begins to curve downward past the quick. Clip right where it begins to curve down.

Sometimes accidents happen, and the quick gets clipped. It will bleed, which is scary. It may cause your dog to yelp and pull away. Stay calm and keep your dog calm. Talk to him in a soft voice. To stop the bleeding, put a little bit of styptic powder on the tip of the

nail. Quickly move on to the next nail. This way your dog learns that nail clipping isn't always painful (be sure to take less nail than you did on the last one!). When you finish clipping the nails on each foot, be sure to clip the dewclaw on each leg if he has them. Dewclaws are the nails on the inside of the leg right above the foot.

Give your dog lots of cuddles and treats while you cut his nails. If he is nervous, ask a friend or family member to hold him. This can make clipping his nails easier on both you and your dog.

Chapter 14

No Bites!

Biting is a form of aggression. Dogs bite for many reasons. Fear is one reason dogs may bite. Some dogs are scared of people, and some dogs are especially scared of kids. This may be because a kid did something bad to them, or it may be because they've just never been around kids before. The jerky movements of very little kids may scare a dog. And little kids may not know how to stroke a dog gently. A dog who hasn't spent much time with kids can be scared by them if they play and run around her.

Some dogs are aggressive for other reasons. They may be dominant dogs trying to boss people or other dogs around. They may be jealous dogs who are afraid a toy or food will be taken from them. Sometimes dogs are raised to be aggressive. Their owners may use them for fighting or for guarding. Occasionally, dogs who have aggressive moms or dads are born aggressive. Very rarely, dogs have a disease that makes them aggressive.

Even friendly dogs can bite in the right situation. Teasing or scaring a dog can make her bite. Old dogs may bite because they get a little grumpy or because they are in pain. A dog in pain or who is sick may bite if she is touched

This dog is biting as a form of protection. Some dogs are dominant and act aggressively by barking or growling when people come near them or their property, and they may resort to biting.

roughly. Sometimes a friendly dog will bite because she feels cornered or threatened.

It's very important to remember that all dogs are capable of biting at some time. That's why it is so important to always practice good dog etiquette.

Dog Etiquette

Dog etiquette is the art of getting along with a dog. Dogs have definite likes and dislikes. Some things that most dogs dislike include being in a crowd, being poked or prodded, and being teased. Some examples of teasing a dog are when someone pretends to throw a ball but doesn't and when someone pretends to hit a dog. There are also things that only some dogs dislike. They may include running kids, high voices, and even men with beards. Dogs will usually try to tell you when they dislike something. The problem is that we don't always understand what they are trying to say!

This is the wrong way to introduce yourself to a dog. When first meeting a dog, don't grab her around the head or try to hug her.

This is the right way to greet a dog. Let her come to you once she feels comfortable. Then you can see if she will let you touch her.

Despite media images of bloodthirsty pit bulls running mad in the streets, most bites are actually from family pets. The typical victim of a dog bite is a young child—bitten by a dog he or she knows. Dogs bite for a number of reasons: they are scared, protective, aggressive, ill, in pain, confused, or feel threatened.

Even gentle dogs may bite when they are treated roughly. Some dogs are afraid of children and will bite out of fear when a child approaches them. Other dogs bite children when they become overexcited by a child playing.

Always supervise interactions between your children and dogs, even your own pets. Never let your child play roughly with a dog, approach a dog he or she doesn't know, or pet an unknown dog who is leashed, in a car, or behind a fence.

Any dog can bite—even this playful Pug! Use proper dog etiquette with every dog you meet.

Be careful when meeting a new dog. You don't know what this particular dog likes or dislikes.

Good Dog Etiquette

There are some basic rules to follow when you are around a dog:

- Always ask if it's OK before petting a dog you don't know.
- Always stroke a dog gently.
- Don't get near a mother dog with puppies.
- Don't go up to a dog who is sick or injured. Tell an adult about it.
- Don't jump up and down or run around a dog you don't know.
- Don't play aggressive games like tug-of-war or wrestle with a dog.
- Don't run away from a dog; this may make her chase you.
- Don't sneak up on dogs who are sleeping or are resting. A startled dog may bite.
- Don't stare at, or even look directly into the eyes of, a dog you don't know and trust.
- Don't tease, poke, or hit a dog.

This little girl is letting the dog sniff her hand to get acquainted.

- Don't try to pet a dog who is behind a fence, tied up, or in a car.
- Don't try to take a stick or toy away from a dog.
- Let dogs come up to you. Don't run toward them.
- Move slowly around a dog you don't know. Sudden or jerky movements may scare her.
- Never go near a dog who is eating.
- Never pretend you're about to hit a dog.
- Never put your face up to a dog's face.
- Never trap a dog in a place it can't get out of.
- Always speak quietly to dogs.

Meeting a New Dog

You can't tell what a dog is like just by looking at her. The fuzziest, sweetest-looking dog in the world may bite. And a huge, mean-looking Rottweiler may be a snuggle bug. That's why it's really important never to pet a dog who isn't with her owner. A dog who is running loose may be scared, injured, or aggressive. If you see a dog running loose, tell a parent or another adult. If there isn't an adult around, call your local animal control. You can find this number at the front of most phone books. If there isn't an animal control office in your area, call the police.

Don't go near dogs who are tied up, behind a fence, or in a car. Sometimes dogs who are usually friendly will act aggressively when they are tied up or in a fenced area. A dog who is tied up may feel cornered. She may get scared because she can't get away. Dogs behind fences or in cars may feel protective of their houses or cars and may bite.

If you meet a person who is walking his dog, ask if you can pet his dog. Never, ever just walk up to a dog and pet her. Don't be offended if the person says no. There is usually a good reason. Some dogs get nervous being petted when they are on a leash. Or the person may be training his dog. The dog

Signs of a Biter

Because dogs can't talk, they must use body language. Body language means that they show what they are feeling by their expressions and the way they move their bodies.

• **Fearful body language:** Sometimes dogs bite out of fear. A frightened dog may look away from you. She may have her tail tucked between her legs. Her ears may be back, and she may even twist her body away from you.

• **Dominant body language:** Sometimes dominant dogs bite to defend their toys or food or to show their strength. A dominant dog may wag her tail stiffly or rise up on her front toes. Her ears may go forward, and her hackles may rise.

• **Baring teeth:** Dogs bare, or show, their teeth to give you a warning. Heed it!

• **Growling:** A growl sounds like a low rumble. A dog growls when she wants to be left alone.

• **Snapping:** A dog may bite at the air, or snap, as a warning for you to go away.

• **Raising hackles:** The hackles are the hairs on the neck and back that sometimes rise when a dog is trying to look tough. It is another warning sign.

True False

When a dog wags her tail, it means she is happy.
FALSE.

Sometimes dogs wag their tails when they are happy. Other times they wag their tails when they are curious. And sometimes they wag their tails when they are about to attack. A happy tail wag is usually loose and fast. For example, when a people-happy Lab bounds up to greet you, her tail will wag so hard and fast that it almost hits her sides! A dominant dog will sometimes wag her tail when she is interested in something or when she is about to attack. An aggressive tail wag is slow and stiff. The tail is usually held almost even with the dog's back, and it goes back and forth in short, slow wags.

This Golden Retriever is getting hugs and kisses from her family. Goldens are known for their gentleness and friendliness.

may even be working. People with guide dogs and service dogs sometimes won't let people pet their dogs while they are working so they aren't distracted from the job at hand.

If the owner says that you can pet his dog, put out the back of your hand to let the dog sniff you. Don't move quickly. Once the dog has sniffed you, pet her behind the ears or on the body. Never reach out to touch her face. Don't make quick movements; this can be scary to some dogs. Pet her in the same direction that her fur lies, and be very gentle. If the dog pulls away, growls, or bares (shows) her teeth, stop petting her right away.

Raising a Nonbiter

Why do dogs bite? Some dogs are born with mental or physical problems that make them more likely to bite. But most dogs who bite learn to be biters. Sometimes people train their dogs to bite on purpose. More often, people accidentally train their dogs to be aggressive or fearful.

Dogs who don't learn that all types of people are friendly are more likely to bite. This is because they become afraid easily. It is usually the most fearful dogs who bite. Confident dogs may threaten people and other animals, but they rarely actually bite. A frightened dog may bite to protect herself.

Dogs who are always held and who are allowed to be bossy about furniture, people, and toys may also bite. Good examples are the small, yappy dogs whose owners carry them everywhere. These dogs sometimes get an inflated view of themselves. They don't want anyone to touch their stuff, including their people! They may bite when they are being held or when they are playing with a toy. Even little dogs need to be trained and socialized.

Dogs can also become biters when they are chained or tied up all the time. In some cities, it is illegal to chain or tie up a dog for more than a short period of time. Dogs who are left in a fenced backyard all day long can sometimes become aggressive, too.

Treating a dog roughly, playing tug-of-war games with a dog, and hitting or teasing a dog

Gentle Touches

All kids should learn to give dogs gentle touches. Have you ever watched a younger relative play with a dog? Young children don't always understand how to treat a dog gently. Help teach your younger friends and relatives to be gentle with dogs. Show them how to stroke a dog gently along her fur instead of against it. Teach them that dogs like it when you scratch behind their ears but not when you touch their mouths and eyes. Show them how to scratch above their tails but not to pull on their tails.

are all things that can make her more likely to bite as well.

Sometimes it's not what you teach a dog but what you don't teach her. Dogs become afraid of things they don't understand. That's why it's very important to expose young dogs to lots of good experiences. A puppy who is introduced to people with beards and in wheelchairs, big dogs and little dogs, busy parks, and loud street sounds is not afraid of these things when she becomes an adult.

To raise a dog who doesn't bite, follow these rules:

A pup remains calm while being petted at mealtime. Many dogs become protective over their food. Teach your pup to happily allow humans near her while she is eating.

Q. Why is it a bad idea to stare at a dog?

A. A dog may think you are trying to challenge her when you stare at her. In the wild, dogs stare at other dogs to show them they are in charge. If you meet a strange dog on the street, don't look directly at her. Instead, look to the side of her, and back away slowly.

- Bring your dog into your home. Dogs raised in the home are friendlier and better behaved.
- Don't chain or tie up your dog. Dogs who spend a lot of time tied up often become biters.
- Don't play aggressive games with your dog. These include playing tug-of-war, wrestling, and fighting.
- Never encourage your dog to fight with other dogs.
- Never, ever tease a dog. Teasing can teach a dog to become aggressive.
- Socialize your dog with all types of people and animals. Expose your puppy to lots of positive experiences.

- Spay or neuter your dog. Altered dogs tend to bite less.
- Teach your dog not to nip. Usually mom and littermates teach a puppy to bite gently when playing, but some pups need extra help.
- Train your dog. A well-trained dog is less likely to bite.
- Treat your dog gently. Never hit her. Hitting a dog can make her fearful of all humans.
- Young kids should never be alone with dogs. Really little kids like toddlers and infants have a hard time understanding that they shouldn't pull ears and tails or hit dogs. Someone should always supervise toddlers when they are interacting with the dog.

When Dogs Bite

Sometimes dogs bite no matter how hard you try to stop it. There are around five million dog bites each year in the United States. Most of them happen to children, and boys are bitten more often than girls. Usually, the dog who bites isn't a stranger to the child. She may be the child's own dog or the dog of a friend or a relative. Sometimes dogs bite because they are in pain. If your dog suddenly bites or snaps when she is touched, see your vet! She

This shepherd has been trained to walk well on leash. Dogs who are trained and not allowed to run free are much less likely to bite.

may have an injury or an illness that is causing her to be sensitive.

If a threatening dog comes up to you, don't run! This can cause the chase instinct. This means when you run, they become excited and chase you. Some dogs will become so excited by chasing someone that they will bite.

Instead, back away from the dog very slowly. If the dog keeps coming toward you, stop moving and say "go home" in a low, stern voice. Do not yell or scream. Stand very still, like a tree. Do not look the dog in the eyes. The dog

Read Your Dog

Sometimes kids get bitten because they don't understand what their dog is saying to them. Look at the pictures and try to figure out what the dog is telling you.

A. Baring teeth

B. Growling

C. Barking

D. Yawning

E. Averting eyes

F. Bowing

G. Ears back

H. Head cocked

A. She is irritated—stay away!

B. This warning means don't get any closer, or she will bite you!

C. This dog is being aggressive and dominant. She is about to attack.

D. Dogs sometimes yawn when they are nervous. Give her some space.

E. This dog is submissive and a little timid. Submissive dogs sometimes bite out of fear.

F. This dog is friendly, inviting you to play!

G. This dog is afraid. Most bites are from fear biters. Leave her alone.

H. This dog is curious and interested. Let her come and investigate you.

will probably get bored of you and go away. When she does, continue backing up slowly until you are out of the dog's sight.

If the dog attacks you, curl into a ball with your hands covering your face, head, and neck. If you have a backpack or book bag, try to get it between you and the dog. Try to move as little as possible. Never, ever try to run from a dog who is attacking you. If a dog chases you when you're on your bike, stop. Get off your bike but keep it between you and the dog. Be very still. If the dog attacks you, keep moving the bike between you and the dog.

If a dog bites you, tell an adult right away. The dog must be checked to make sure she doesn't have any diseases that could hurt you, and you need to go the doctor. Even if the bite isn't bad, your doctor will want to clean it. You will also need a tetanus shot. Because dog mouths have a lot of germs, the doctor may want you to take antibiotics to prevent an infection.

Chapter 15

Healthy and Happy

We don't want to think about our dogs getting hurt or becoming sick, but it happens. Dogs need veterinary care throughout their lives. Most health problems are small—a skin rash or a tummy ache. Sometimes dogs get serious injuries or serious diseases, though. If something bad happens, it's important you know what to do.

There are steps you can take to keep your dog healthy. Know when to take your dog to the vet, how to prevent injuries and illnesses, and how to choose a good vet. Although it is probably a grown-up who pays the vet bills, the whole family should know how to keep your dog healthy and what to do in an emergency.

This little pup is feeling under the weather. Just as kids do, dogs sometimes get sick.

Adult Alert!

Although it's up to you to take financial responsibility for your pet's veterinary care, encourage your children to participate. Bring them to vet appointments, and let them ask questions. Include them when you make decisions about your pet's health care. Be open and honest about injuries and illnesses.

Keep Your Dog Healthy

The most important part of your dog's health care is to keep him from getting sick in the first place. How can you do that? In the same way the adults in your life keep you from getting sick. Make sure he eats right. Don't let him get too fat or too skinny. Keep him warm and dry. Make sure he doesn't get too hot or too cold. See the vet for regular checkups. Make sure he gets all his shots.

Your dog's health care starts from the moment you bring him home. One of the first things you do should do after adopting or buying your new dog is to make an appointment with your vet. It's great if you can go with your family on the first vet visit. The vet will give you a lot of information about keeping your dog healthy at this visit. The vet will examine your dog to make sure he isn't sick. The vet will also give him any necessary shots. Vaccination shots keep your puppy or dog from getting diseases such as parvovirus and

This puppy is being weighed by his vet. Your vet is your family's partner when it comes to keeping your dog healthy.

distemper. (You probably get yearly shots for diseases like polio, mumps, and measles.) Puppy shots are given in a series. A puppy needs

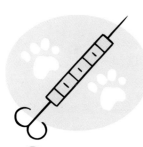

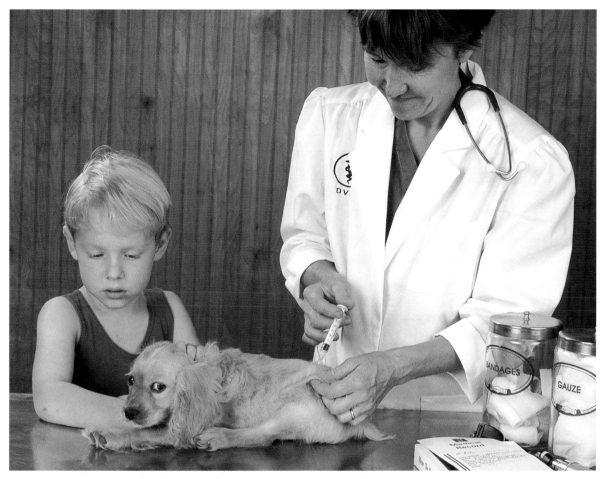

A young owner accompanies his dog to the vet. Your vet should be willing to answer your questions and talk to you and your family about your dog's health.

to see the vet three or four times in his first few months of life to get all his shots.

The vet will check to see if your dog has worms. Many puppies are born with worms or get them when they are very young. Worms live in the intestines and eat the food the puppy needs to grow healthy and strong. Sometimes you can tell when a puppy has worms because his body is skinny but his tummy feels swollen and tight. Sometimes you can even see worms in his poop or around his bottom! They look like little pieces of rice or like spaghetti noodles (ick).

Your vet will also give your dog a physical exam. She will listen to your dog's heart; look at his ears, throat, and nose; feel his bones;

Did You Know?

Dogs in smoking households have a 60 percent greater risk of getting lung cancer than other dogs do. Dogs with short noses, such as Pugs and Bulldogs, are especially prone to lung cancer. Dogs with long noses have a higher chance of getting nasal cancer when they live with smokers.

and test his joints. The vet will look to see whether the coat is shiny and full and whether your dog's skin is elastic. That means when the vet pulls it, the skin goes right back into place. When a dog is dehydrated (doesn't get enough water), his skin gets dry and does not go right back into place when it is pulled. A dull, thin coat may mean the dog is not getting enough to eat or has a problem digesting his food, meaning his body has trouble turning the food he eats into fuel (the extra becomes waste; in other words, poop). Other signs of poor digestion are sleepiness and diarrhea.

Your first vet visit is a good time to ask your veterinarian any questions you have. Don't be shy. Answering questions is part of a vet's job. Ask questions about health care but also about food, grooming, and training. If your new dog isn't spayed or neutered, ask your vet when you can make an appointment

to have this done. Some vets like to wait until a dog is five months old to do the operation. Others will do it when the dog is as young as eight weeks.

All About Veterinarians

A good veterinarian is your number one partner in raising your dog. A good vet helps keep your dog healthy and cares for him when he becomes sick. A good vet gives you lots of good advice along the way. A good vet is interested in all dogs and is good at talking to people about their dogs.

Some veterinarians do acupuncture and chiropractic work on dogs, as shown here.

Suggest that your family talks to a few veterinarians before choosing one. Maybe you can help come up with a list of important questions to ask a veterinarian. Some veterinarians specialize in certain types of health care that may be important to you. For example, some vets use massage, acupuncture, and herbs in addition to traditional medical care. If this is important to you and your family, look for a vet who is open to these alternative treatments.

Choose a vet who is good with your dog and your family. That means the vet is willing to answer questions and doesn't rush you through the exam. The vet should treat your dog gently and try to make him comfortable. If that means getting down on the ground to treat your dog, the vet will do it. A good vet always tells you what is being done and why. In a way, a good vet becomes part of your dog's family. The vet should care about what happens to him and act happy to see him.

The best way to find a good vet is through word of mouth. Talk to friends, neighbors, pet supply store workers, groomers, and other dog people. Ask them about their vets and what they like or don't like about them. Do you have a friend who takes great care of her dog? Ask her about her vet.

This vet is available after hours. What are your veterinarian's hours? If he is not available for emergencies, does he work with another local vet who is?

Once you have a couple of recommendations, make appointments to meet and talk with the vets (they should not charge you for this). Ask them for a tour of the veterinary hospital. Bring a list of questions to ask and a list of things to look out for at the hospital.

Here are some things to look for:
- A clinic that looks and smells clean
- A friendly receptionist and friendly animal caretakers
- A vet who is gentle with your dog and tries to make him comfortable
- A vet who is polite to you and your family
- A waiting room large enough for dogs to have some space
- Kennels that are clean with no poop in the cages

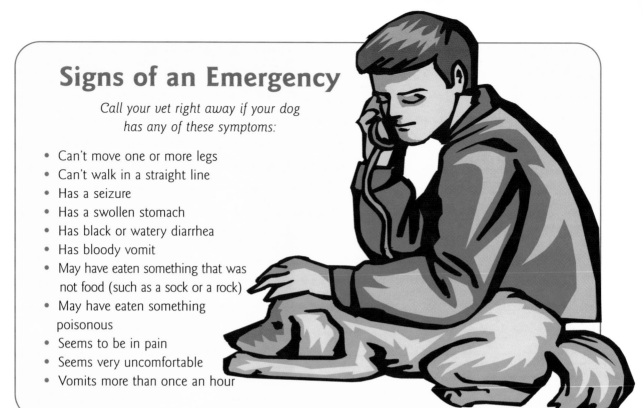

Signs of an Emergency

Call your vet right away if your dog has any of these symptoms:

- Can't move one or more legs
- Can't walk in a straight line
- Has a seizure
- Has a swollen stomach
- Has black or watery diarrhea
- Has bloody vomit
- May have eaten something that was not food (such as a sock or a rock)
- May have eaten something poisonous
- Seems to be in pain
- Seems very uncomfortable
- Vomits more than once an hour

Here are some questions you should ask the vets:

- Can I make a same-day appointment? (You should be able to see your vet right away if you need to.)
- Do you keep up with changes in veterinary medicine (for example, going to conferences and reading veterinary journals)?
- Do you prefer to treat dogs or cats or other types of animals?
- Do you provide emergency care? (If she doesn't, she should refer you to a local emergency vet she trusts.)
- How much do you charge for an office visit?

- How much do you charge for common procedures (for example, spaying and neutering)?
- When did you graduate from vet school? (Recent graduates may know more about new advances in veterinary medicine. Older graduates may have more experience working with animals.)

Spay and Neuter

Spaying and neutering are operations that make it so dogs cannot have puppies. Female dogs are spayed, and male dogs are neutered. This means their reproductive organs are removed. These operations are also called altering. Spaying or neutering

Four littermates snuggle together in a basket. Often, unwanted litters end up in shelters.

your dog is really important. It's something that all pet owners should do.

There are many good reasons to have your dog altered. The main reason is that there are far too many homeless dogs in the United States. About four million dogs are put to sleep (euthanized, or killed) each year simply because they have no homes. Most of these dogs are from accidental litters or from litters bred by people who do not care where the puppies go. Sometimes people want to make money by breeding puppies. They sell puppies to families who can't take care of them. Other people just never get around to spaying or neutering their dogs. They take the puppies to an animal shelter or give them to people who can't take care of them. ALL dog owners must help prevent unwanted litters.

Spaying and neutering are also good for the dog's health. Dogs who are spayed or neutered are less likely to get certain types of cancers. Altering makes dogs friendlier to people, less territorial, and less likely to run away. Male dogs who are not neutered may mark a lot, peeing on things that they consider theirs, including things such as couches and chairs. The younger a dog is when neutered, the less likely he will mark. Unneutered male dogs also often fight with other male dogs. Once they are altered, they tend to fight less. All in all, it's a really good idea to have your dog spayed or neutered as soon as possible.

Doggy Health Problems

Just like people, dogs get diseases. Puppies can get diseases such as parvovirus. Some diseases, such as cancer, can strike a dog at any age, although cancer is common in older dogs. In fact, half of the dogs who make it to age ten will get cancer. Dogs can also get injuries (especially those super rambunctious dogs!), by playing or by falling. Injuries can range from a torn toenail to a broken back. If your dog has any new symptoms, such as limping or not eating, he should see a vet.

This pup is ignoring his food. Not eating may be a sign that there is something wrong with your dog. If your dog doesn't eat for more than a day or two, an adult should call the vet.

Eyes

Eye problems can be minor or very serious. A dog can get something stuck in his eye, such as dust or even an eyelash. A condition that causes eyelashes to turn in or turn out can irritate the eye and make it tear. Some dogs get pink eye or dry eye. There are also serious eye diseases, such as glaucoma (glau-KO-muh) or progressive retinal atrophy (REH-tin-al A-truh-fee). Both of these can lead to blindness. Dogs can also be born blind. Usually, this is because of a hereditary disorder—a physical problem a dog gets from his mom or dad. It is sometimes also called a genetic disorder. A congenital disorder means it is a problem that the puppy was born with.

Here are some of the signs that may mean your dog has an eye problem:

- Tearing
- Discharge (thick, sticky liquid) coming out of an eye
- Squinting or blinking a lot
- Closing eyes in bright light

A vet examines a dog's eyes. There may be something wrong with your dog's eyes if they are very dry or weepy or if he blinks a lot.

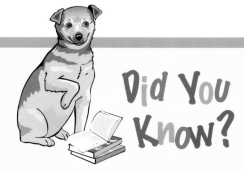

Did You Know?

Sometimes the nicest dogs will bite if they are hurt or scared. Before treating your injured dog, ask an adult to put a muzzle on him. Loop a belt or scarf around his mouth, and tie it behind his ears to keep his mouth shut. Make sure he can still breathe. Take off the muzzle once he is settled.

- A crusty buildup in an eye
- Filmy or cloudy eye
- Pawing at an eye

If your dog has any of these symptoms, he should see a veterinarian.

Ears

The most common problem with doggy ears are ear infections and ear mites. A dog can also get things, such as a burr, stuck in his ear. Some dogs are born deaf. This is usually caused by a hereditary disorder.

Ear infections can be caused by many things. Some breeds tend to get more ear infections than others do. Dogs with long drop ears get more infections. Long ears trap moisture, which can cause ear infections. Dogs with allergies, dogs with hairy ears, and dogs who swim a lot get more ear infections than other

This pup sits patiently while his ears are examined. Many dogs have problems with their ears, but fortunately they are usually minor.

dogs. Very serious infections can lead to deafness. Ear mites are the same as other types of mites except they live in a dog's ears. They are teeny-weeny bugs that look like white spiders.

Here are some of the signs that may mean your dog has an ear problem:

- Acting depressed or tired
- Dark brown, red, yellow, or black ear wax
- Hearing loss
- Holding the head to one side
- Pawing or scratching at an ear
- Shaking the head a lot
- Smelly ear
- Swollen or red ear

If your dog has any of these symptoms, he should see a vet.

Nose

The nose is a special part of a dog's body. Sniffing is how dogs talk to one another. The sense of smell also lets dogs taste their food. And some working dogs use their noses to make a living. They may use

Canine Emergencies

Although most dog diseases and injuries are not too serious, sometimes they are life threatening. If your dog has an emergency, it may be up to you and your family to save him. An adult should help you follow the steps below:

1. Take a deep breath and stay calm. Don't panic.
2. Have an adult treat his injuries. If he is bleeding, apply pressure. If he is choking, have an adult do the Heimlich maneuver. Do what you can to keep your dog safe on the way to the vet.
3. Have an adult call your vet and let the vet know you are coming. An adult should tell the vet what happened to your dog and what his symptoms are.
4. Get someone to drive you and your dog to the vet. In the case of an emergency, you may need to see an emergency vet. This is a vet who is open twenty-four hours a day. An adult should know who your local emergency vet is and where the clinic is before your dog has an emergency.

their noses to find illegal drugs or to find missing people.

It's important to help dogs keep their noses healthy. Sometimes a dog gets things caught in his nose, such as seeds. Doggy flu and colds make a dog's nose run and make the dog sneeze. A dog

A dog's nose is his best asset, so it's important that it's kept in working order.

can get allergies or an infection in his nose. A dog can also get a rash on the skin of his nose. Some nose problems are congenital, meaning it was a problem your dog was born with. One congenital problem in the nose is called stenotic nares (sten-AH-tik NAR-eez or NEH-reez). This means that the nostrils are collapsed.

Here are some of the signs that may mean your dog has a nose problem:

- Drippy nose
- Missing fur around the nose
- Pawing at the nose
- Red, irritated skin on the nose
- Sneezing
- Swollen nose

If your dog has any of these symptoms, he should see a veterinarian.

Mouth and Throat

The mouth and throat are where your dog eats his delicious treats. This is one place a dog wouldn't want problems.

A dog can cut or burn his mouth by chewing on something sharp or by chewing on an electrical cord. He can get things caught in his mouth or throat, which can make him choke or keep him from eating. A dog can also get tumors and cysts in his mouth. Tumors are lumps that may or may not be cancerous, and they usually do not hurt. Cysts are bumps filled with liquid, and cysts often hurt, especially if they get infected. If your dog eats something that is poisonous, his mouth and tongue may swell up. Sometimes the throat will swell up, too. This is an emergency.

Usually, mouth problems are related to the teeth. Dogs can break teeth by chewing on hard objects. They can get gum infections. They can also get so much tartar on their teeth that it makes it hard

A vet examines a dog's teeth. Your dog's vet will check to see whether your dog's teeth need to be cleaned or whether he has cracked or broken any teeth.

Q. Do dogs need to be careful in the sun the way people do?

A. Yes. Dogs can get sunburns. They can even get skin cancer from being in the sun too much. Dogs with light fur or no fur have the most problems with the sun. If you have a blonde or hairless dog, keep him out of the sun during the hottest time of the day. Hairless dogs should wear sunscreen whenever they go outside. Pink-nosed dogs can get bad sunburns on their noses. If your dog has a light nose, put a dab of sunscreen on it when you go out on sunny days.

for them to eat. Tartar is a hard yellow buildup of food and saliva on the teeth that can't be cleaned off with a toothbrush.

Here are some of the signs that may mean your dog has a mouth or throat problem:

- Acting as if he is in pain when eating
- Broken teeth
- Dark yellow or brown stains on the teeth
- Pawing at the mouth
- Refusing to eat
- Stinky breath
- Swollen mouth, tongue, or throat

If your dog has any of these symptoms, he should see a veterinarian.

Skin and Coat

A dog's skin and coat keep him warm and protected. Most dogs get a skin problem at some point in their lives. A common skin problem is allergies. A dog may be allergic to fleas, his food, or grass. Dogs with allergies have itchy skin that they scratch so much that they lose hair, make their skin dry, and even make themselves bleed. Sometimes allergies lead to hot spots. These are areas of skin that get very warm, smell bad, and have pus coming out. Dogs can also get lick granulomas (gran-yoo-LOW-muhs). These are open sores that a dog causes by licking one spot over and over. Lick granulomas are usually found on the paws or ankles. The dog may start licking an existing hot spot or may just lick a spot because he is bored or anxious and cause a hot spot.

Other common skin problems are cysts and abscesses. As mentioned before, cysts are pockets of fluid underneath the skin that can hurt if they get infected. Abscesses are usually caused by a bite or scratch that gets infected. They are pockets of pus, and they can be very painful.

Skin problems can cause dogs to lose patches of their coat. Dogs can also lose hair from other illnesses.

Here are some of the signs that may mean your dog has a skin and coat problem:

• Bumps and lumps

You can usually tell a dog has fleas because he will scratch a lot, as this dog is doing.

- Dark or red skin
- Discharge or pus from skin
- Dull or thin coat
- Loss of hair
- Patches of warm, red skin
- Scratching
- Skin that is thick or scaly

If your dog has any of these symptoms, he should see a veterinarian.

Paws

A dog uses his paws to get to all the exciting places he goes. He uses his feet to walk on hot concrete, on rough ground, and through cold snow and rain. All without shoes! It's no wonder paws get beat up.

Dogs can get cuts, burns, and puncture wounds on their feet. They can break nails and even break toes. They can also develop cysts between their toes. Dogs may get itchy skin on

Sometimes dogs cut their paws or get things trapped between their pads. Check their feet and between their pads as shown here.

their paws from allergies. They can also develop lick granulomas on their paws.

Here are some of the signs that may mean your dog has a paw problem:

- Broken nails
- Hot or swollen pads (the skin on the bottom of your dog's feet)
- Licking paws
- Lumps between the toes
- Limping

If your dog has any of these symptoms, he should see a veterinarian.

Heart

The heart pumps blood throughout a dog's body. When something goes wrong with the heart, the dog can become very sick. Sometimes a dog is born with a heart problem. Other times, a heart problem develops as a dog gets older. Some heart problems are benign, meaning they are not serious. Others are very serious and require medical attention.

The most common heart problem is heart murmurs. Heart murmurs occur when the heart valves don't close completely. With each beat, a little blood goes back into the heart. A heart murmur can be minor and won't affect a dog at all. It can also be very serious. It can even be fatal. Many puppies are born with slight heart murmurs. These slight murmurs usually do not affect the puppy, and they may even go away with time.

Congestive heart failure is a common disease in older dogs. In this condition, the heart is unable to pump enough blood to run the rest of your dog's body properly. Dogs with congestive

A veterinarian listens to a Pug's heart to make sure it is working properly.

heart failure will eventually die of the disease unless they die of another disease first. However, there are many treatments that can help them live longer and better with the disease.

Here are some of the signs that may mean your dog has a heart problem:

- A big, round tummy
- Acting tired or depressed
- Coughing
- Fainting
- Heavy breathing

If your dog has any of these symptoms, he should see a veterinarian.

Lungs and Breathing

The respiratory system is the system that helps us breathe. The nasal passages, the throat, and the lungs are all part of the respiratory system. When an animal breathes, the air goes into the nose, through the nasal passages, down the throat, and into the lungs.

Your dog can have problems at any point in this system. Some are minor, and others are very serious. Some dogs have a palate (the roof of the mouth) that is too long. This makes it hard for them to breathe. Other dogs have a nose that is too short—this is called brachycephalic (brah-kuh-suh-FAH-lik) syndrome. This also makes it hard for them to breathe, especially when they are hot. In small dogs, sometimes the trachea (TRAY-kee-uh) collapses. The trachea is made up of the tubes that bring air to and from the lungs. Dogs can also get infections, such as pneumonia, in their lungs.

Here are some of the signs that may mean your dog has a lung or breathing problem:

- Acting tired or depressed
- Breathing through the mouth
- Coughing
- Gagging
- Heavy breathing
- Sneezing
- Wheezing (you hear a whining noise when the dog breathes)

If your dog has any of these symptoms, he should see a veterinarian.

Digestive System

The digestive system is where all that tasty food is made into energy. The food a dog can't use ends up as waste, meaning poop and pee.

This little pup is ill. Dogs don't get humans' colds, but they can get something that is a lot like our flu.

If your dog eats something poisonous or rotten, it can affect his digestive system.

Your dog can get problems anywhere in the digestive system, including the esophagus (the tube that connects the throat to the stomach), the stomach, the small and large intestines (the tube that connects the stomach to the anus, where food is broken down into fuel and waste), the liver (this organ gets rid of toxins and creates bile), the pancreas (this organ controls the level of sugar in your blood), and the anus (the hole that poop comes out of).

Gas is one type of problem in the digestive system. Some dogs pass gas a lot, and sometimes passing gas means there is a problem. Gas can also build up in the stomach and cause bloat, which is a swelling of the intestines. Bloat can kill a dog.

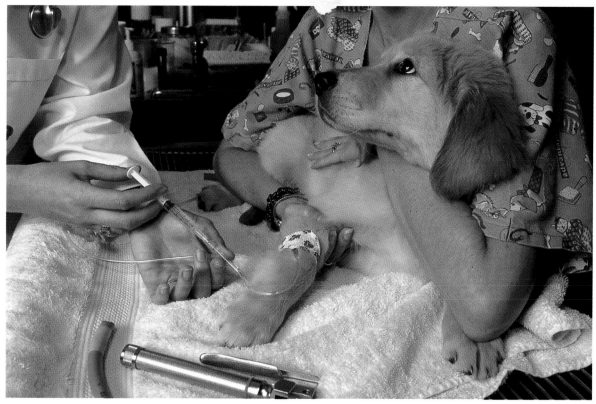

A vet is giving this puppy medicine from a syringe. If he becomes very ill, he may need IV fluids.

Sometimes dogs eat things that aren't food, such as socks, bones, even rocks. These things can get caught almost anywhere along the digestive track. Dogs can also eat food that has gone bad or that is poisonous for them.

Dogs can get ulcers in the stomach or intestines. An ulcer is basically a sore in the lining of the stomach or intestines. They can also get infections. Diabetes is a disease in which the pancreas doesn't produce enough insulin. That means the dog has too much sugar in his blood.

Some dogs become constipated, meaning they can-not go poop. They may not be drinking enough water, or they may have swallowed something, such as a sock or a rawhide, that is blocking them up.

Here are some of the signs that may mean your dog has a digestive problem:

- A hard, round tummy
  - Acting confused
  - Acting restless and uncomfortable
    - Acting tired
    - Blood in the poop or vomit
    - Burping more than usual
    - Constipation
    - Diarrhea
    - Drinking a lot of water

First Aid Kit

Ask an adult to help you put together this first aid kit. Ask your vet how much medicine you should give to your dog (it will depend on how much your dog weighs). Keep your first aid kit with your other doggy emergency supplies:

- 3 percent hydrogen peroxide
- Activated charcoal
- Antibacterial ointment
- Antibiotic ointment
- Benadryl
- Blunt-tipped scissors
- Cotton balls and swabs
- Ear-cleaning solution
- Gauze (roll and squares)
- Gauze tape
- Kaopectate
- Muzzle (long strip of cloth)
- Nail clippers
- Needle-nose pliers

- Oral syringe
- Pepto-Bismol
- Rectal thermometer
- Saline eyewash
- Styptic powder
- Tweezers

- Fainting
- Going poop in the house
- Licking lips a lot and drooling (the dog may be nauseous)
- Passing gas more than usual
- Scooting (when a dog rubs his bottom on the ground)
- Scratching or licking the bottom
- Seizures (brief periods when the dog shakes or twitches)
- Shaking
- Throwing up (especially if it is bloody or smells like poop)
- Urinating a lot

If your dog has any of these symptoms, he should see a veterinarian.

Nervous System

The nervous system includes the dog's brain, spinal cord, and nerves. The nerves send information to the brain, and the brain sends information back to the nerves. The spinal cord is the main road that connects the brain to the nerves.

A lot of problems can happen in a dog's nervous system. Tumors and epilepsy, a disease that causes seizures, can affect the brain. Problems can develop in the spine as well. A dog's spinal cord is protected by bones called vertebrae. Each vertebra has a little cushion between it and the next vertebra. The cushion is called an intervertebral disk. Sometimes a disk can slip or break open. This can hurt the dog's spinal cord and even cause paralysis.

For dogs, nervous system problems usually happen because of injuries. Dogs can be injured by cars, in fights with other dogs, or in falls. Dogs can get head injuries that affect the brain. They can also hurt their backs, which can affect the spinal cord. Some illnesses, such as distemper and rabies, affect a dog's nerves also.

Here are some of the signs that may mean your dog has a nervous system problem:

- Avoiding being touched
- Drooling
- Seizures
- Unable to move one or all of the legs
- Unable to move the head
- Unable to wake up
- Weakness

If your dog has any of these symptoms, he should see a veterinarian.

Bones, Joints, and Muscles

The musculoskeletal system is made up of the bones, muscles, ligaments, and tendons. The bones are connected by joints. Ligaments keep the joints together. Tendons attach the bones to the muscles. Muscles make you move.

A dog can be born with problems in his musculoskeletal system. Hip dysplasia (dis-PLAY-zsuh) and patellar luxation (puh-TELL-er lux-AY-shun) are hereditary problems. In hip dysplasia, the leg bone doesn't fit into the hip socket correctly. Patellar luxation means that the knee bone slips out of place.

Dogs can also get musculoskeletal problems when they are injured. They can break bones, pull muscles, and strain joints and ligaments. As dogs age, they often get arthritis. With arthritis, the ligaments have become worn down and the bones rub together without any cushion between them.

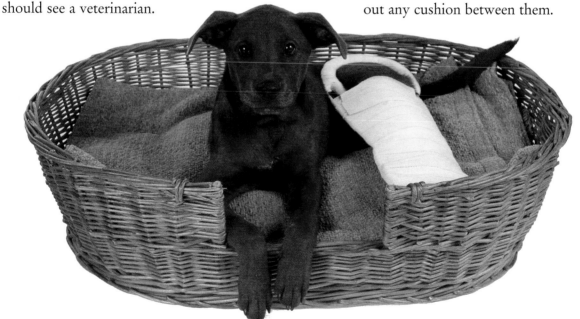

This little guy has a splint on his leg. An active pup can find plenty of ways to break or sprain a leg.

Here are some of the signs that may mean your dog has a bone, joint, ligament, or muscle problem:

- Avoiding having a leg touched
- Falling down
- Limping
- Stiffness when the dog first gets up
- Unable to walk on one or more legs
- Unable to walk up stairs or jump onto furniture
- Yelping when getting up

If your dog has any of these symptoms, he should see a veterinarian.

Diseases and Parasites

There are other diseases and conditions your dog can suffer from. Some are very serious, such as cancer. Others are more of a nuisance, such as fleas.

Cancer

Cancer is the most common disease in dogs. Cancer can affect a dog's mouth, skin, nose, ears, brain, lungs, stomach, intestines, liver, pancreas, heart, bones, and blood system. All cancers are serious. Some cancers are more aggressive than others, spreading more quickly and becoming more destructive. Dogs can't be cured of cancer, but they can be treated for cancer. Some treatments include surgery, radiation, and chemotherapy. With radiation, high-energy X-rays are used to kill cancer cells. With chemotherapy, the dog is given a drug that helps kill cancer cells. With surgery, the cancer is cut out. With treatment, many dogs live a long time after getting cancer.

Many older dogs such as this Golden Retriever, get cancer. Luckily, there are many treatment options that can help them live longer.

Here are some of the signs that may mean your dog has cancer:

- Acting depressed or tired
- Constipation
- Dark spots on the skin
- Diarrhea
- Drinking lots of water
- Going to the bathroom in the house
- New lumps or bumps
- Not wanting to eat
- Sores that won't heal
- Throwing up

If your dog has any of these symptoms, he should see a veterinarian.

Viruses

Some of the worst diseases dogs get are from viruses. A virus is a disease dogs catch from one another. Some viruses are passed through blood or saliva (spit). Others are passed through feces (poop). Distemper, parvovirus, rabies, and adenovirus are all viruses that can kill a dog.

Puppies are most affected by viruses. That's because their immune system isn't strong enough to fight off these bad germs. Vaccines can keep a puppy from getting some viruses. A vaccine is basically a small amount of a particular virus. It's injected into a puppy to make his body ready to fight the real virus.

Puppies usually receive three rounds of vaccines. The first one is given when the pup is about two months old. The last one is given when the pup is about four months old. Vac-cines aren't perfect. Sometimes puppies get sick from the vaccine, and sometimes the vaccine doesn't work well enough. However, far fewer dogs now die from viruses than they did when there were no vaccines.

There are many different types of viruses that can affect different parts of a dog's body. Here are just a few signs your dog has a virus:

- Acting very tired
- Coughing
- Diarrhea (especially bloody diarrhea)
- Not wanting to drink water
- Not wanting to eat
- Runny eyes
- Seizures
- Sneezing
- Throwing up

If your dog has any of these symptoms, he should see a veterinarian.

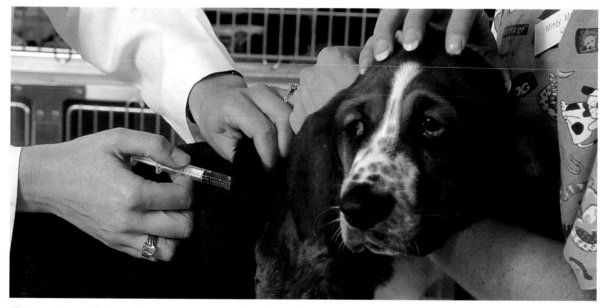

This pup doesn't look too happy about getting his shots. To keep your dog from getting viruses, his veterinarian will give him a series of vaccines.

Bugs

Ugh, bugs! Bugs love dogs. A doggy coat is a great place for a bug to hang out and feast. Unfortunately, dogs don't like bugs much—especially when bugs are making their skin itch. Dogs often pick up bugs from playing outside in the grass.

The most common bug found on dogs is the flea. This bug makes dogs miserable. When a flea bites a dog, it leaves saliva (spit) in the wound. The saliva makes the dog itch, so he scratches and licks the spot. Sometimes the itching is so bad that the dog licks away hair and scratches until he draws blood. Dogs with lots of flea bites can even become anemic. Being anemic means not having red blood cells, which will make your dog very tired. It will also affect his growth and can even kill him. Dogs with lots of flea bites become anemic because the flea has eaten so much of his blood!

Dogs also get bugs called mites. Mites can live in a dog's ears or on his skin. Mites eat dead skin. Sometimes the number of mites living on a dog gets out of control. This is called mange. Mange causes the dog to lose his hair and to get patches of red, scaly skin.

Ticks are bugs that are common in wooded areas. They jump on a dog and suck his blood. If a dog has many ticks, he can become anemic. Worse, ticks spread lots of diseases. Lyme disease is one serious disease that dogs (and people) can get from ticks.

Did You Know?

A dog's normal temperature is between 100.5 degrees Fahrenheit and 102.5 degrees Fahrenheit. A human has an average temperature of 98.6 degrees Fahrenheit.

Luckily, there are a lot of new treatments for keeping bugs off a dog's body. In fact, dogs have never had such a bug-free life. This is also nice for people because when dogs have bugs it usually means we have them, too.

Here are some of the signs that may mean your dog has bugs:

- Areas where the skin is thick
- Black or brown bugs in the fur
- Dark, almost black wax in the ears
- Hair loss
- Licking
- Red, scaly skin
- Scratching
- Smelly ears
- Stuff that looks like pepper in the fur, especially above the tail (this is flea blood)
- White bugs around the eyes

If your dog has any of these symptoms, he should see a veterinarian.

Fleas bites can cause big problems for pups.

Worms

What's worse than bugs? Worms, of course! Especially worms living inside the body. Many types of worms live in a dog's gut. Worms hang out inside a dog's intestines waiting for food to come to them. Sometimes they eat so much of the dog's food that he suffers from malnutrition (that means he doesn't get enough to eat). Some of these worms are hookworms, roundworms, whipworms, and tapeworms.

Your dog can also get heartworms. Heartworms live inside the heart and blood vessels. Heartworms can kill a dog. Luckily, dogs can take a special medicine to prevent heartworms.

Here are some of the signs that may mean your dog has worms:

- Acting tired or depressed
- Diarrhea
- Dull coat
- Long white worms that look like spaghetti in the poop or coming out of the bottom
- Potbelly in a skinny dog
- Stuff that looks like white rice around the dog's bottom, in his poop, or in his bedding
- Vomiting
- Weight loss

If your dog has any of these symptoms, he should see a veterinarian.

Genetic Diseases

As mentioned earlier, many doggy diseases and disorders are genetic. A genetic disorder is a hereditary physical problem such as flipped-under eyelids (called entropion) or deafness.

This is a healthy dog. He has a shiny coat, bright eyes, and plenty of energy.

The dog's mom or dad may have the disease or disorder, or one of them may just be a carrier. That means she or he didn't actually have the disease or disorder but was still able to pass it on to the puppies through his or her genes. Purebred dogs tend to have more genetic problems than mutts do.

Some genetic diseases include an eye disease called progressive retinal atrophy (see page 242) and a nervous system disease that causes seizures called epilepsy. Some genetic disorders include hip dysplasia and dwarfism. Genetic diseases and disorders can affect almost any part of the body and can have a huge range of symptoms.

Guide to Symptoms

When a dog is acting sick, it's difficult to know exactly what is wrong.
Is he drooling because he's hungry or because his tummy is upset?
If you're not sure if your dog is sick, call your veterinarian.

Common Symptoms	Possible Diagnosis	What to Do
Drooling	Dogs drool because they are scared, nervous, or hungry. They also drool after eating something toxic or because they have a tummy ache.	If your dog doesn't usually drool and isn't in a new or scary situation (like riding in a car), have an adult call your vet.
Vomiting	Dogs throw up for many reasons. Sometimes they vomit because they have eaten something funny or eaten too much. Sometimes they throw up from riding in the car or being nervous. Sometimes throwing up means that they are very sick.	If your puppy is under six months old and he vomits more than once, call your vet. If he is over six months old, give his tummy a break. Talk to your parents about not giving him food or water for eight hours. Then offer him water and something bland, like white rice or boiled chicken. Ask an adult to call the vet if the dog doesn't stop vomiting after twenty-four hours or if he vomits more than several times in one hour. Ask an adult to take your dog to the vet right away if the vomit is black, looks like coffee grounds, has blood in it, or smells like poop.
Coughing	Dogs may cough because they have a virus such as kennel cough or because there is something wrong with their throats. There is a new canine flu that can make a dog cough. Dogs may also cough if they have a problem with their lungs or their hearts.	It's hard to tell why a dog coughs, so ask an adult to take your dog to your vet right away.
Passing gas	Some dogs just fart a lot. Bulldogs, for example, are known for being particularly gassy. Sometimes passing gas means your dog has eaten something bad or is sick.	If your dog suddenly starts to pass gas more than usual, ask an adult to call the vet. A vet can also help you figure out ways to cut down on a gassy dog's fart production.
Drinking a lot of water	Dogs drink a lot of water when they are hot or after playing hard. They may also drink a lot of water when they have an illness such as diabetes.	If it is not hot and your dog drinks a lot of water for more than a few days in a row, ask an adult to call the vet.

Diarrhea	Dogs get diarrhea from stress, eating something icky, and from changing foods. They may also get diarrhea from serious illnesses.	If your dog has moderate diarrhea for a day or two, ask your parents to adjust his diet. Talk to them about not feeding your dog for twelve hours (give him water). Then feed him a bland diet of white rice and boiled chicken. If your dog has diarrhea for more than a couple of days, ask an adult to call the vet. If the diarrhea is black or bloody or happens at least once an hour, ask an adult to call your vet. If your dog seems to be very sick, ask an adult to take the dog to the vet right away.
Sneezing	Dogs sneeze when something in the air itches their noses. Your dog may also sneeze if something is stuck in his nose.	If your dog sneezes often for more than a day or two, call your vet.
Acting tired or depressed	Dogs get sad, too. When a dog is stressed out, he may act unhappy and sleep a lot. But acting depressed or tired can also mean he is sick.	A day or two of being especially tired is no reason for panic. If your dog seems depressed and sleepy for more than a couple of days, though, ask an adult to call the vet. If he has other symptoms such as vomiting or diarrhea, ask an adult to take him to the vet right away.
Scratching and licking	Dogs will scratch and lick when they feel itchy or when they are in pain.	If your dog scratches one particular spot a lot or won't stop licking himself, ask an adult to call your vet.
Not eating	Many dogs will go a day or two without eating. They may be being picky or they may not be hungry. Sometimes not eating means a dog is very sick.	If your dog goes more than two days without eating, ask an adult to call your vet. If he won't eat and is depressed, is vomiting, or has diarrhea, ask an adult to take your dog to the vet right away.
Something's stinky	If your dog has stinky breath, stinky ears, or stinky skin, he may have an infection.	It's probably not an emergency, but ask an adult to call your vet for an appointment.
Lumps and bumps	Lumps and bumps on a dog may just be fatty tumors, or they may be the first sign of cancer.	Don't take a chance—ask an adult to call your vet for an appointment right away.
Straining to pee or poop	Straining to poop may just be constipation from not drinking enough water. It can also mean your dog has a serious blockage. Straining to pee may mean he has a bladder or a kidney infection.	Ask an adult to call your vet to help you figure out whether this is an emergency.

Chapter 16

Doggy Dilemmas

Americans love dogs. We love them so much that there are almost 70 million pet dogs in this country. That is twice as many people as there are in the entire country of Canada! Many of us love our dogs so much that we treat them like furry babies. We cuddle them, love them, and spoil them.

But not all dogs are treated well. Some dogs are abused or neglected. Other people let their dogs have litters they can't take care of. Some of these puppies go to homes where they are not loved. Others end up in animal shelters.

Many laws affect dogs. Leash laws and poop scoop laws are meant to protect people from dog bites and disease. Some laws protect dogs. These include laws against abusing dogs. Luckily, there are people who help dogs who are abused or neglected. They work to find them homes where they will be loved for the rest of their lives.

Animal Abuse

Not everyone takes good care of their animals. Some people hurt their animals or take such poor care of their animals that they get sick or

This pair is having fun just hanging around together. But as much as we love dogs, we don't always do what is right for them.

Signs of Animal Abuse and Neglect

If you see a dog with these problems, tell a grown-up right away:

- A dog being hit, kicked, or punched
- A dog left in a car with the windows closed on a warm day
- A dog who is too thin
- A dog who seems to be in pain but is not being cared for
- A dog with injuries or illnesses that aren't being treated

- A person yelling, screaming, or threatening a dog
- Dog-collar injuries from a collar that is too small
- Empty water bowls, especially water bowls that are empty during hot weather or frozen over during cold weather
- Lack of shelter, such as a doghouse or porch

die. It's hard to understand why someone would want to hurt a dog.

Animal abuse means an animal, such as a dog, is intentionally hurt by a person. That may mean she is kicked or hit or even killed on purpose. Another kind of abuse is using a dog to fight another dog. Sometimes people hurt dogs to hurt another person. For example, an abuser may hurt his friend's dog because he is mad at her. Some kids may hurt dogs because they are curious about what will happen or because they want to show off for their friends. Sometimes people who abuse animals hurt people, too.

Neglecting an animal is a kind of abuse. In fact, it is the most common type of animal abuse. When a dog is neglected, she isn't being taken care of well enough. It may mean she doesn't have shelter to protect her from the rain or the sun, or she may not have

Leaving a dog tied up like this for many hours is a form of abuse called neglect.

enough food or water. In some cities and states, it is illegal to chain or tie up a dog for a long time. That is one kind of neglect. A sick or injured dog is neglected when no one is taking care of her. Sometimes people neglect dogs because they don't care about them. Some people neglect dogs because they don't understand what dogs need.

There are laws that make it a crime to hurt dogs and other animals. Animal cruelty laws are different from state to state. In some states, animal abuse is a felony offense, meaning that it is a very serious crime and deserves a serious punishment. In other states, animal abuse is a misdemeanor crime, meaning that it is not punished as severely.

If you ever think that an animal is being abused or neglected, there are things you can do. First, tell an adult. Tell your mom or dad, a teacher, or another adult you trust what you

This sign means "no dogs allowed."

have seen. Second, ask the adult to call your local animal control office. Have this person tell animal control as much information about what you have seen as they can. Don't talk directly to the person who is abusing an animal. People who abuse animals may also hurt people.

Dog Laws

Sometimes we need to protect people from dogs. Poop scoop laws are common in most parts of the United States. These laws require dog owners to clean up their dog's poop in public places. Some cities also have poop scoop laws that require dog owners to keep their own yards clean of dog poop. Dog poop can have parasites that can cause disease in people and in other dogs. When it rains, the poop runs into the rivers and oceans, making swimmers and fish sick. It also isn't very nice to step in dog poop, and it doesn't smell very good! All in all, the poop scoop laws do a good job of keeping the streets cleaner and safer for all of us.

In most cities, dogs must be on a leash in public when they are not in a special off-leash area. Leash laws protect both humans and dogs. Dogs who are allowed to roam are more likely to bite people and attack other dogs and animals. They are also more likely to be killed by traffic

Some cities and states have laws that make dog owners responsible if their dog bites a per-

Reasons Dogs Are Given Up

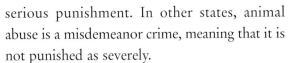

- Dogs are too expensive.
- There is no time for the dog.
- There is no place for the dog.
- The family is moving.
- The landlord doesn't allow pets.
- There are too many pets in the home.
- The dog is sick.
- The family has problems to deal with.
- The dog bites.
- The family can't find homes for puppies.

Source: National Council on Pet Population Study and Research

A responsible owner picks up after her dog. There are laws that say that we must pick up our dogs' poop.

son or another dog. Most places have a one-bite-free card. The first time a dog bites, as long as she doesn't cause a serious injury, the owner is given a warning. After that, the owner may receive fines or even be sent to jail! The dog also receives a punishment. If she continues to bite or causes a serious injury, she may be taken away from her owner, be quarantined, or even be killed. (See the section on Dog Bites on the following page.)

There are also laws that restrict the number of animals in one home. Most cities allow a person to own only three or four animals at once. Cities also make it illegal for a dog to bark constantly. Noise laws are common in areas where homes are very close to one another.

Report It!

If you witness animal abuse or neglect, report it! Have an adult call your local animal control or humane society. If your area does not have one of these organizations, an adult can call the local police department. You can also find the numbers for local humane organizations at http://www.aspca.org.

In the country, there are laws to keep dogs away from livestock. Sometimes dogs attack and kill livestock. A playful dog can cause sheep and goats to hurt themselves because they panic. In most rural areas, it is legal for farmers to shoot dogs who are on their property. It's very important to keep your dog on a leash or within a fence if you live in an area where there is livestock.

In both the city and the country, dogs must wear a license. A license is usually a metal tag that attaches to the dog's collar. Dog licenses are important because they can help you find your dog if she is lost. They also help your city or town keep track of how many dogs live there.

The Americans with Disabilities Act (ADA) is a series of laws created to protect the rights of people with disabilities, problems that make it difficult for them to function normally. They may have trouble seeing, hearing, or walking. The ADA makes sure disabled people have access to all public places. That means disabled people must be able to get themselves into restaurants, office buildings, and other public places. Public buildings must have wheelchair ramps and disabled parking and bathrooms. Guide dogs, hearing dogs, and assistance dogs must be allowed to go anywhere their handlers go. That includes restaurants, hotels, and movie theaters.

Dog Bites

Every year, almost five million people are bitten by dogs in the United States. Almost one million of these bites are serious enough to be treated by doctors. Most of the victims of dog bites are kids.

Dogs bite for a lot of reasons. They may not be trained, they may be sick or injured, they may have been treated roughly, they may be scared, or they may be protecting their territory, especially if a male dog has not been neutered. Rarely, a dog is born with a medical problem that makes her aggressive. There are ways you can help prevent dog bites. For some pointers, see chapter 14.

Are Some Dogs Mean?

Some people think that certain dog breeds are born mean. Some of the breeds they believe to be mean are pit bull types, such as American Staffordshire Terriers and American Pit Bull Terriers, Doberman Pinschers, Rottweilers, and American Bulldogs. In some countries, people are not allowed to own or breed these dogs. In the United States, some cities have made it against the law to own certain breeds.

It's true that dogs of the same breed share some characteristics. Breeds were developed for many jobs. Some breeds were developed for guarding, some for herding, some for hunting, and even some for fighting. If a dog isn't used for the job specific to her breed, she will still have some of the breed's traits. For example, Labrador Retrievers who don't hunt still like to swim and chase birds. American Pit Bull Terri-

Any dog is capable of biting.

True ☜ False

Only guide dogs are allowed in restaurants and hotels.

FALSE.

All assistance dogs are allowed in restaurants and hotels. The Americans with Disabilities Act (ADA) was passed in 1990. This law promises all people with disabilities access to all public places. That means hotels, restaurants, and other public places have to be accessible to people with disabilities and their tools. They have to have wheelchair ramps, have wider doorways, and be open to assistance dogs. Assistance dogs help people who are blind, deaf, and can't walk. They also help people with emotional and mental illnesses.

ers, who were originally bred for fighting, don't always like other dogs. To be friendly with other dogs, they must meet lots of nice dogs from the time they are very little. Guard dogs such as Chow Chows may be cautious and untrusting when meeting strangers. Chow Chow puppies need to meet lots of nice, friendly people as soon as possible. Herding and hunting dogs, including Border Collies and Pointers, sometimes chase small animals such as cats. They need to learn not to do this from when they are very young.

But dogs, like people, are individuals. One pit bull–type dog may not like other dogs, but another one may love other dogs. It depends a lot on what their parents were like. It also depends a lot on how they were raised. Even though pit bull types don't always like other dogs, they are well known for loving children. In England, they are called nanny dogs because

With excellent care and training, this American Pit Bull Terrier pup will grow into a friendly adult.

Q. Is the pit bull a breed?

A. No! There is no such breed as the pit bull. There are pit bull–type breeds. Some of these are the American Staffordshire Terrier, the Staffordshire Terrier, and the Bull Terrier. There is also the American Pit Bull Terrier. All of the pit bull–type dogs are bull and terrier dogs. That means they are from a cross between Bulldogs and terriers. Some of the pit bull types were used to fight other dogs or to fight bulls. This was called pit fighting. Pit fighting is now illegal.

This is a pit bull–type breed.

Some dogs have a reputation for being meaner than other dogs, but this isn't necessarily true.

they love kids so much. Similarly, a Doberman Pinscher who barks at strangers usually adores her favorite person. A Pointer may chase a neighbor's cat but peacefully share the couch with her own family's cat.

So why do some breeds have such bad reputations? Is it true that pit bulls and Dobermans are mean? Do pit bull types bite people more than other breeds do?

Although there are lots of news stories about pit bulls biting people, most pit bulls are friendly, loving dogs who adore their families. The fact is, we don't know which dog breeds bite the most. Only about one-fifth of all dog bites are seen at a doctor's office. Doctors' reports tell us the breeds of the dogs that bite. That means we do not know which breeds are responsible for about four-fifths of the dog bites in the United States each year. In addition, many people have a hard time saying which breed of dog bit them because so many dog breeds look similar to one another. Of the dog bites that were reported, German Shepherd Dogs and Chow Chows were the most frequent offenders.

Another reason pit bull–type dogs have a bad reputation is because they are very popular right now. In some areas of the United States, there are more pit bull types than there are any other dog breed. When Rottweilers were popular during the 1980s, there were more Rottweiler bites than there are now. When Doberman Pinschers were popular during the 1970s, there were more Doberman bites than there are now.

Being popular has another downside. Many people breed popular breeds to make a quick buck. They don't pay attention to breeding healthy dogs with gentle personalities. Some even breed their pit bull–type puppies specifically to act mean. Bad reputations attract bad owners. Some people want pit bull types because they have a reputation for fighting. Then they raise the dogs to be mean. People who fight dogs don't care about their dogs. Dog fighting is a serious form of animal abuse.

Studies show that the dogs who bite people are usually male, unneutered,

During the 1980s, this loving Rottweiler had the same kind of reputation pit bulls have now.

chained or tied up, untrained, and living in a house with kids and other dogs. It is rare for a dog who is spayed, female, trained, and raised as part of a family to cause a serious bite injury.

Blaming dog bites on a couple of breeds is a bad idea for many reasons. It groups together a lot of wonderful dogs with a few bad dogs.

A pup waits for a home. Unfortunately, there are simply too many dogs for the available homes.

It also takes the attention away from the real problems that cause dog bites. Dogs who are kept on chains, abused, and neglected are more likely to bite. Dogs who are trained, who are spayed or neutered, and who get a lot of love and attention from their families are less likely to bite. Dog bites from all breeds are much too common. To prevent dog bites, we need to work harder to train dogs and educate people—not just look for one breed to blame.

Dog Overpopulation

Dog overpopulation is a huge problem in this country. Overpopulation is caused when there are more dogs than there are homes to care for them. About four million dogs are put to sleep each year because they have no homes.

The only way to end the overpopulation problem is to spay or neuter your dog. If all of us do this, the overpopulation problem would end very quickly. The only people who shouldn't spay or neuter their dogs are responsible breeders. Who are responsible breeders? They are people who love a breed and work hard to keep the breed healthy. They are the breeders we talked about in chapter 6. Before breeding a dog, they have the dog checked by a veterinarian to make sure there are no problems he or she could pass on to puppies. When they sell puppies, they make sure the puppies are neutered or spayed. Responsible breeders also work closely with veterinarians and other pet professionals. They never breed a female dog more than once a year because that is unhealthy for her. They breed only one or two breeds of dog, and they raise their dogs in a home environment. Good breeders make sure their dogs are healthy. They refuse to sell a puppy to a bad home, and they will always take their puppies back if the new home doesn't work out.

If we all make a commitment to spaying and neutering our dogs and getting dogs only from responsible breeders, rescue groups, or animal shelters, we can end this horrible problem in no time at all.

Spay and Neuter Myths

Some people think that spaying or neutering will make their dog fat and lazy or that the dog will feel bad about it.

This couldn't be further from the truth! There are many more good reasons to spay and neuter than reasons not to. Here are just a few of the funny ideas that people have about spaying and neutering, and the real facts!

My dog will get fat. Some people think that female dogs get fat after they are spayed. This is not true. Like any dog (or person!), if they don't get enough exercise or they eat too much, they may gain a little weight. If your

A family checks out a shelter pup. Some ways your family can help with overpopulation are by spaying and neutering your dog and adopting your next dog from a shelter or rescue.

True / False

Puppies can be spayed or neutered before they go to their forever home.

TRUE.

Puppies can be spayed or neutered at eight weeks old! All pet dogs should be altered by six months old.

dog eats a good diet and gets daily exercise, there is no reason for her to gain any weight after being spayed.

My dog will get lazy. Dogs do not get lazy or lose energy after being spayed or neutered. If anything, they become more interested in playing. A pregnant dog and a dog in heat are much lazier than a dog who has been spayed or neutered.

My dog won't feel like a boy if he's neutered. Some men think that neutering a dog makes him less of a boy. They think the dog will feel this. But dogs don't think about things like this. Dogs don't know they have been neutered.

My dog's personality will change. There is no reason for a dog's personality to drastically change after being spayed or neutered. A male dog may become more friendly and interested in people because he isn't busy looking for a dog to mate with.

Spaying and neutering are dangerous operations. Neutering and spaying are done under general anesthetic. That means the dog is not aware of what's going on. Anytime a dog is under general anesthetic, there is a slight risk of injury or death. However, both spaying and neutering are simple operations. Most veterinarians have done this surgery hundreds or thousands of times. Giving birth and being pregnant and roaming and fighting are riskier than this surgery. Spaying and neutering also reduce the chance of getting some cancers.

Spay and Neuter Truths

Now here are some truths about altering your male or female dog.

Your male dog won't roam as much. Male dogs who aren't neutered will do almost anything to get to a female dog in heat. Neutered dogs are less likely to escape, and that's a very good thing. Dogs who roam can get hit by cars, attacked by other animals, or stolen.

Your dog will be more loving. Now that they aren't driven to find another dog to mate with, many male dogs become more loving and more interested in interacting with their people.

Your dog will be less likely to get cancer. Both female and male dogs have less risk of getting cancer in their

With luck, all of these puppies will go to good homes. But pet overpopulation is a big problem.

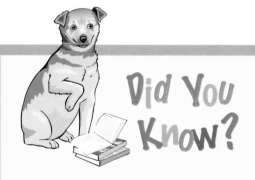

Did You Know?

In 1990, 7 to 8 million dogs and cats were euthanized because they had no home. Today, the number is half that. Now, 3½ to 4 million dogs and cats are euthanized each year. Experts say this is because spay and neuter laws work!

reproductive organs after they are spayed or neutered.

Your male dog will be less likely to bite. Unaltered males fight over females in heat and are more aggressive than neutered dogs.

Your dog's puppies won't be among the four million dogs euthanized each year. This is the best reason to spay or neuter your dog. Too many dogs are killed each year simply because they have no home. Even if you find good homes for your puppies, that means other puppies won't have homes. Be a part of fixing the problem.

Animal Welfare Organizations

American Society for the Prevention of Cruelty to Animals (ASPCA)

424 East 92nd Street
New York, NY 10128
212-876-7700
http://www.aspca.org

Humane Society of the United States (HSUS)

2100 L Street, NW
Washington, DC 20037
202-452-1100
http://www.hsus.org

American Humane Association (AHA)

63 Inverness Drive E
Englewood, CO 80112
800-227-4645 or 303-792-9900
http://www.americanhumane.org

Many organizations can help this dog find a home.

Dog Rescue and Animal Welfare

It's not all doom and gloom for American dogs. Many groups in the United States work to protect dogs. Some get stray dogs off the street and into good homes. Others rescue dogs from city shelters where they otherwise would be killed.

Some groups are advocates for dogs. These organizations work to pass laws to protect dogs. They also teach people about taking care of dogs. They may try to get people to spay and neuter their dogs, or they may work to end animal abuse. Some of these organizations are very large, such as the Humane Society of the United States (HSUS), which has thousands of members. Others are very small, with just ten members. You can talk to your family about getting involved in an animal welfare group if that's something that appeals to you. Some groups have programs that teach kids how to train shelter dogs. Some even have animal shelter day camps for kids! Talk to one of the big animal welfare organizations, such as the HSUS, the American Society for the Preven-

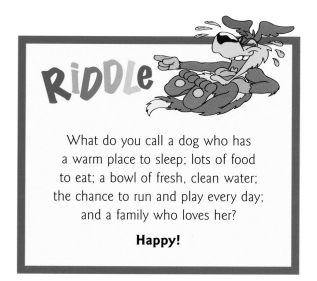

RIDDLE

What do you call a dog who has a warm place to sleep; lots of food to eat; a bowl of fresh, clean water; the chance to run and play every day; and a family who loves her?

Happy!

tion of Cruelty to Animals (ASPCA), or the Animal Humane Association (AHA). If you would rather work with a smaller group, ask one of the larger organizations to recommend a smaller group in your area. You can also talk to your local animal shelter to find out how they help dogs. Research the different types of work each group does to find the right one for you. You may be able to help train shelter dogs, pass out pamphlets, or represent an organization at your school.

Most shelters work very hard to find new homes for the animals in their care. Modern shelters try not to euthanize healthy animals. Some shelters are no-kill shelters. That means that they don't euthanize adoptable dogs—dogs who are healthy and friendly enough to be adopted. In the past ten years, shelters have been able to use the Internet to find homes for their animals.

Spay and neuter laws have cut down on shelter populations. There are about half as many dogs and cats euthanized now than there were ten years ago.

Animal shelters aren't the only organizations helping dogs find homes. There are also rescue groups. These are private organizations that take in unwanted dogs and find them homes. Often they focus on dogs of a certain breed. They may find homes for lots of dogs every year or for just a few.

If you feel sad after reading about all the bad things happening to dogs in the world, don't give up hope. There are many people doing great things to help dogs. You can too!

A Greyhound advertises for adoption.

Chapter 17

Doggy Sports

Dogs are natural athletes. Their bodies are specially made to run, jump, stretch, and swim. Some dogs were bred to work for a very long time without stopping to eat or rest. Others were bred for speed. A dog's talents and interests depend on the type of work the dog was originally bred to do. A dog's breed may decide what sports he likes best. Super-speedy Greyhounds love lure coursing, a sport in which the dog chases after a white plastic bag, which is pulled just out of reach. (The goal of the sport is to see how fast the dog will run compared with the other dogs on the course.) Quick, athletic Border Collies live to

Here are a few canine athletes. There are a number of sports you and your dog can play.

Adult Alert!

Help your child get involved in canine sports. It's great exercise and training for your dog, but it's also great exercise for your child.

Children who are active are less likely to become obese and to develop weight-related illnesses such as diabetes. An active child has more energy, is better able to focus in school, and spends less time watching TV.

Your child may need your help to participate in canine sports. Some classes will require an adult to attend, there may be expenses for class fees and equipment, and your child may need you to drive to practices and events. Think of your participation as an investment in your child's physical and mental health. Plus, you won't be stuck walking the dog!

herd. Even dogs who were bred to be doggy pets, like Chihuahuas and Pekingese, can enjoy doggy sports. They may not win, but they enjoy playing the game!

Kids are natural athletes, too. You and your dog are alike in that way. Both of you should get at least one hour of exercise each day! Does that sound like a lot? It doesn't have to be one hour of straight running. Maybe you take your dog for two half-hour walks each day. Or alternate days when you can play fetch or go for a run with your dog. On the

A boy and his dog play ball.

weekend, take a family hike with your dog. Try a couple of different sports with your dog to see what you both like. Exercising your dog is a fun chore! It sure beats scooping poop!

The Best Sports

There isn't one sport that is perfect for all dogs. It's important to pick the right sport for your dog. That doesn't mean choosing the sport he will win at; it means finding a sport he likes and is able to do.

Think about what your dog likes to do. Does he love to run?

Q. Are biking, in-line skating, and skateboard-ing good sports to do with a dog?

A. Some adults like to bike, in-line skate, or skateboard with their superactive pooches. Unfortunately, these aren't safe activities for kids. With a dog pulling you, it's easy to lose control. Your dog can get tangled in the leash and make you fall, or your dog can get free and run into traffic. Don't bike, in-line skate, or skateboard with your dog. Instead, get really good at these sports so you can do them with your dog when you get older.

Whether your dog wins the blue ribbon or comes in last, doggy sports are for fun more than glory.

Lure coursing, agility, Flyball, and Frisbee may suit him (see Organized Dog Sports.) Does he love to swim? Maybe he can get involved in hunting field trials or water rescue. If he likes to do things at his own pace, maybe an organized sport isn't the right thing at all. He may like running or hiking better. Some dogs are happiest spending the day at the beach, chasing birds and swimming.

Look at your dog. Does he have a solid body, or is he slight? Is he a giant dog or a miniature dog? If he is small-boned, sports such as carting (pulling carts) or sledding can be dangerous for him. He could get serious back injuries. If he is heavy, a sport with a lot of jumping such as agility or Flyball can be hard on his joints.

Some dogs just don't perform well under pressure. They get stage fright. They love to run and swim with you, but being part of group with everyone watching scares them. Your dog doesn't need to be part of an organized sport. Anytime you go outside and do something fun with your dog is a good thing!

Organized Dog Sports

Organized doggy sports have become popular in the doggy world. Some people take these sports very seriously. They travel all over the world to compete. Other people do them just for fun. The great thing about these sports is that they are made just for dogs. They cater to their needs and interests. The bad thing is that they can be expensive.

First, do some research about the sport you're interested in. Read books and magazines about doggy sports. Look up the sport on the Internet. Then, find a local club and watch a practice or a competition. Talk to people about the sport. Look for a beginning class to see if it's right for you. Go to a doggy sports camp. These are often organized by doggy sports organizations. Ask a teacher if she or he knows of a good sports camp. You can also find doggy sports camps through magazine and Internet advertisements. At a dog camp, you can try lots of different sports. It takes a while to find the right sport and the right club. You may have to try out a few.

This group is taking a break. Playing doggy sports is a great way to meet other kids with similar interests.

A Poodle participates in an agility trial. Agility is probably the most popular doggy sport right now.

Agility

Agility is basically an obstacle course. A dog runs the course while the handler runs alongside him and tells him which obstacle to go to next. Some of the obstacles include jumps (called hurdles in agility), a dog walk (two ramps connected to a long board), a tire jump, an A-frame (two ramps making an A-shape), and weave poles (the dog zigzags, or weaves, between the poles). The handler can't touch the dog, and the dog can't skip any of the obstacles. The goal is to finish as quickly as possible with as few mistakes as possible.

Agility is the most popular dog sport. You can even see agility competitions on ESPN! Agility was invented in the late 1970s. It was first seen at the annual Crufts Dog Show, in England. Since then, the sport has become popular all over Europe and North America. It's also popular in Australia and New Zealand, some Asian countries, and South Africa.

Agility isn't a team sport. It's just you and your dog. That means you can do agility just for fun. If your Basset Hound strolls over the course, that's just fine—as long as he is having fun! Herding dogs tend to be the best at agility. Border Collies, Australian Shepherds, and Australian Cattle Dogs all excel at the sport. But any dog can enjoy agility because it can be done at the dog's own pace. Tiny dogs can do agility and so can giant Mastiffs. Just make sure to keep hurdles low for the tiny dogs and so Mastiffs won't hurt their joints jumping. Because it's not a team sport, no one cares how fast or how slow your dog goes!

There are a lot of kids involved in agility. There are no age limits on competitions. Some agility teachers may ask you to bring your parents to class. Look for an agility class just for kids. You can also do agility through 4-H. Agility competitions are held by the AKC, the North American Dog Agility Council (NADAC), and the United States Dog Agility Association (USDAA). All three have opportunities for junior handlers.

A girl directs her dog through the course. Most agility clubs welcome junior handlers.

American Kennel Club (AKC)
260 Madison Avenue
New York, NY 10016
212-696-8200
http://www.akc.org

North American Dog Agility Council (NADAC)
11522 South Highway 3
Cataldo, ID 83810
http://www.nadac.com

United States Dog Agility Association (USDAA)
PO Box 850955
Richardson, TX 75085
972-487-2200
http://www.usdaa.com

Flyball

Flyball is a sport for dogs who love to run and fetch. It's a relay race in which a dog jumps over four hurdles, then hits a spring-loaded box with both paws. A tennis ball shoots out of the box, and the dog catches the ball in his mouth. He turns around, jumps back over the four hurdles, and crosses the start-finish line. Once he crosses the line, the next dog goes. There are four dogs on each team. The first team to cross the finish line with no mistakes wins. Mistakes are dropping or missing the ball and missing a hurdle.

The height of the hurdles is based on the shortest dog on each team. Teams try to find the perfect balance of larger

A Yorkie jumps a hurdle while playing Flyball.

and smaller dogs. Larger herding dogs like Border Collies do really well in Flyball. Small, quick Terriers—especially Jack (Parson) Russell Terriers—also do great.

Because this is a team sport, the other dogs and handlers depend on each other. Flyball can be really competitive! If you want to do Flyball but don't care so much about winning, look for a team that thinks the same way.

Flyball started in the late 1970s and was first seen by the general public on *The Tonight Show Starring Johnny Carson!* It is a popular sport in North America, Europe, Australia and New Zealand, South Africa, and Japan.

Most areas have Flyball clubs. Some clubs offer opportunities for junior handlers to train and compete. Flyball competitions are overseen by the North American Flyball Association (NAFA), which does have a junior handler division.

North American Flyball Association (NAFA)
1400 West Devon Avenue, 512
Chicago, IL 60660
800-318-6312
http://www.flyball.org

Canine Freestyle (Dancing with Dogs)

Dancing with dogs may sound a little goofy, but it's a real sport! And it's not as easy as it sounds. Canine freestyle actually combines a lot of different canine sports—agility, obedience, even herding. And it's all put to music. Have you ever seen equine dressage? Canine freestyle is a lot like dressage except you are next to your dog instead of on top of a horse.

The dog is off leash and performs a dance routine. The handler can tell him what to do and use hand motions, but she can't touch him. A

A group practices Flyball. Many dogs take to Flyball right away.

good freestyle dog can do lots of moves without help from a handler. He can come to the handler and run away from her. He can lie still or jump over the handler's arm. He can even stand on his hind legs! Very good freestyle dogs do all this in a rhythmic motion that is just like dancing.

Canine freestyle started in 1989. It is getting popular in North America and Europe. Canine freestyle competitions are overseen by the Canine Freestyle Federation and the World Canine Freestyle Organization (WCFO). Both offer junior handler opportunities. The Musical Dog Sport Association is a national organization that promotes the sport.

Canine Freestyle Federation
4207 Minton Drive
Fairfax, VA 22032
http://www.canine-freestyle.org

Musical Dog Sport Association
http://www.musicaldogsport.org

World Canine Freestyle Organization (WCFO)
PO Box 350122
Brooklyn, NY 11235-2525
http://www.worldcaninefreestyle.org

Canine Disc (Frisbee)

Do you love to play Frisbee with your dog? Did you know that you can compete against other kids and their Frisbee-focused hounds? It's called canine disc, and it's a superpopular sport for dogs and their people. Canine disc isn't just about throwing a Frisbee around in

If your dog loves to be at the center of attention, as this dog does, he may make a perfect canine freestyler.

your backyard, though. These dogs are true athletes. Herding and gun dogs who are good at running and jumping seem to do best.

In Frisbee competitions, dogs are scored on the number of Frisbees they catch, how quickly they catch them, and how hard it is to catch them. To make it more difficult, handlers throw Frisbees behind their backs and under their legs. They even throw more than one Frisbee at a time! Dogs are also judged on the longest catches and how many Frisbees they can catch in a timed period.

In the United States, disc dogs compete through the International Disc Dog Handlers' Association (IDDHA), US Disc Dog Nationals (USDDN), Unified Frisbee Dog Operations (UFO), Ashley Whippet Enterprises, or Skyhoundz. Although they don't offer junior handler divisions, kids are allowed to compete.

Ashley Whippet Enterprises
PO Box 9435
Anaheim, CA 92812
714-488-1042
http://www.ashleywhippet.com

International Disc Dog Handlers' Association (IDDHA)
1690 Julius Bridge Road
Ball Ground, GA 30107
770-735-6200
http://www.iddha.com

Skyhoundz
1015 Collier Road
NW, Ste C
Atlanta, GA 30318
404-350-9343
http://www.skyhoundz.com

Unified Frisbee Dog Operations (UFO)
http://www.ufoworldcup.org

US Disc Dog Nationals (USDDN)
635 N. DeQuincy Street
Indianapolis, IN 46201
317-281-3398
http://www.usddn.com

A dog grabs the Frisbee on the fly! Disc, or Frisbee, comes naturally to many dogs, although some dogs have more natural jumping ability than others do.

Conformation

Dog shows are called conformation events. People who show their dogs do conformation. The word *conformation* means to conform to, or meet, a standard. In conformation, dogs are judged on how closely they meet the breed standard. The breed standard is a written description of the perfect dog of that breed. Every breed has a standard. You've probably seen conformation dog shows on TV. It may look as if people are just walking dogs in a circle, but there is a lot more to a dog show than that.

It takes a lot of work before a dog gets into the show ring. Breeders spend a lot of time breeding very special dogs to each other, hoping for amazing puppies! Once such a puppy is born, he gets lots of training. He gets exercise so he is healthy and strong, and his coat is kept in perfect shape. A show dog must always act and look his best—from the tip of his pert nose to the end of his perfectly groomed tail. A great show dog is not only beautiful but also full of energy and personality. He has to have a special spark that makes him stand out from the others. A great show dog is like an actor or actress with star power.

Conformation is a very old sport. It began in the 1800s in England. There are very small dog shows held at the local level, and there are very large dog shows held at the international level. The two really big dog shows are the Westminster Kennel Club Dog Show, which takes place in New York City, and the Crufts Dog Show, which takes place in England. With more than ten thousand dogs competing, Crufts is the biggest dog show in the world. The dogs who compete at

A judge examines a dog at a dog show. If your dog is purebred and registered, you can compete in AKC dog shows.

these shows are the best of the best! For people who show these dogs, conformation is a big business. Top show dogs sell for lots of money. The best show dogs rarely live with their families. Instead, they live with handlers who groom, train, and show them. Some people compete in local dog shows just for fun, to show off their beauty pageant barkers.

In the United States, conformation competitions are overseen by the AKC, the United Kennel Club (UKC), the American Rare Breed Association (ARBA), and the Mixed Breed Dog Clubs of America (MBDCA). The AKC, the UKC, and the ARBA offer junior handler divisions.

American Kennel Club (AKC)
260 Madison Avenue
New York, NY 10016
212-696-8200
http://www.akc.org

Junior handlers show off their dogs. Conformation, or dog showing, is a sport even little kids can participate in.

American Rare Breed Association (ARBA)
9921 Frank Tippett Road
Cheltenham, MD 20623
301-868-5718
http://www.arba.org

Mixed Breed Dog Clubs of America (MBDCA)
13884 State Route 104
Lucasville, OH 45648-8586
740-259-3941
http://www.mbdca.org

United Kennel Club (UKC)
100 East Kilgore Road
Kalamazoo, MI 49002-5584
269-343-9020
http://www.ukcdogs.com

Sledding

You've probably seen sled dog teams in movies or on TV. You may even have heard of the world's largest annual dogsled race, the Iditarod (eye-DIT-ah-rawd). The Iditarod is an almost 1,200-mile dogsled race that takes place on snow-covered ground in Alaska each year. The course takes competitors ten to seventeen days to complete!

You don't have to compete in the Iditarod to be a musher, though. (A musher is what the person who drives the dog sled is called.) There are many people who mush for fun or who just compete in short local races. There are plenty of kids who mush, too. Many young mushers come from dogsledding families. If you live in

This team of dogs loves the snow. Kids who live in cold climates can try sledding as a sport.

a snowy area, try to find a local dogsled club. Someone there may be willing to show you the ropes. Look for a musher who is willing to help you out.

Dog sledding is an expensive sport. You need to have at least two dogs to pull your sled. Plus, there is the sled, towlines, and other equipment. Mushers use all-terrain vehicles (ATVs) to train their dogs when there is no snow. You can try dogsledding without buying anything, though. There are groups who host sledding tours. You can go for a couple of hours or even for a couple of days!

The dogs who enjoy sledding the most are usually the ones who were originally bred for it: Siberian Huskies, Alaskan Malamutes, Samoyeds, and Alaskan Huskies. Alaskan Huskies are mixed-breed dogs specially bred by mushers for racing. They are usually a mix of traditional sledding breeds and hounds and gun dogs. Alaskan Huskies are like snowflakes —no two dogs are the same!

If you catch the bug and decide to pursue dogsledding, maybe you'll end up racing in the Jr. Iditarod. It's not 1,200 miles, but it is a 160-mile race through the wilds of Alaska. It's open to fourteen- to seventeen-year olds. Mush!

The International Federation of Sleddog Sports (IFSS) and the International Sled Dog Racing Association (ISDRA) oversee both sled dog races and skijoring races. Both have junior handler divisions.

International Federation of Sleddog Sports (IFSS)
3381 Troy Brett Trail
Duluth, MN 55803
218-525-4012
http://www.sleddogsport.com

International Sled Dog Racing Association (ISDRA)
22702 Rebel Road
Merrifield, MN 56465
218-765-4297
http://www.isdra.org

Skijoring

Do you love to ski? Do you hate to leave your dog at home when you go skiing? Skijoring may be just the sport for you! Skijoring is basically cross-country skiing with a dog. The dog wears a harness attached to a towline. The towline is attached to a belt or harness that is worn around the person's waist. The dog helps pull some of the person's weight while the person skis behind the dog.

Skijoring is a Norwegian sport that has been around for hundreds of years. It has recently become popular in other parts of Europe and North America. Most skijorers participate in the sport for fun, but there are also skijoring races.

To do skijoring, you must be a very good skier and have good control of your dog. Older kids who are comfortable on skis can jump right into this sport. Work on your skiing and dog-handling skills until you are eleven or twelve. Then you'll be ready to start skijoring!

A dog gets a hug after a skijoring session. Skijoring and sledding are great wintertime sports.

Other Doggy Sports

There are plenty of other doggy sports. It seems as if there are new ones being invented every day! Some popular sports are drafting or weight pulling, field trials and hunt tests, lure coursing, earthdog trials, schutzhund, and herding. In carting, dogs compete by pulling carts. In weight pulling, dogs compete by trying to pull the heaviest object. In field trials and hunt tests, the dogs' hunting skills are tested by how well they find and retrieve fake prey. In field trials, dogs compete against one another, and in hunt tests, they compete against a set score. In lure coursing, sighthounds (dogs who hunt by sight) chase a fake rabbit. Whichever dog reaches the finish line first wins. In earth-dog trials, a terrier tracks the scent of an animal through tunnels in the ground. Each terrier is timed, and the dog who finds the scent animal in the shortest amount of time wins. In herding trials, dogs try to herd sheep, goats, even geese! The dogs are scored on how well they work their handlers, how quickly they are able to herd their flock, and how many mistakes they make. Schutzhund is a German sport, which is said to test how well working dogs do their jobs. Schutzhund dogs are trained in obedience, tracking, and protection and then tested in these areas. To pass the test, they must reach a set score in each area.

You can do any of these sports for fun. You can also compete against other dogs. Most doggy sports clubs have junior handler divisions. Junior handlers are usually kids under the age of seventeen. If there is not a junior handler division, you may still be allowed to compete against adult handlers. Even if you can't compete, you can probably join a club to practice with your dog.

Sports Just for Fun

People are inventing new canine sports all the time. Maybe you can invent your own sport. Is there an activity your dog loves that you can imagine as a sport? How about a race to see

A boy helps his dog practice scent discrimination—picking one scent out of the many on the dumbbells.

how many times your dog can "give you five" in one minute? Maybe your dog can race another dog across a pool. You and the other dog's person can stand at the end of the pool, calling your dogs. Whoever reaches the end first wins!

You don't have to compete to have fun with your dog. In fact, not all dogs like competing. Some dogs just like to be outdoors for the fun of it. Most dogs love the chance to run and swim. If you need to add a little competition, compete against yourself. Every day, add a little time or distance to your activity. It will be good for both of you! Following are some of the fun sports that you and your dog can do every day.

Basic Rules for Sports

Here are a few basic rules you should follow whenever you participate in sports with your dog:

Train your dog. A well-trained, well-socialized dog who is friendly with people and other dogs is going to enjoy sports much more than a shy, fearful, untrained dog.

Don't overdo it. Both you and your dog need to pace yourselves. You know that you shouldn't run a marathon without training. Your dog shouldn't either.

Keep calm. Sometimes it's hard to keep your cool when your dog acts up or doesn't behave while you're doing sports or training him. You may even feel like yelling or hitting. Instead, take a deep breath. Give your dog a two-minute time-out. Tie him up, and go about twenty yards away. Have a drink of water, and take a little break. When you release your dog from his time-out, you'll both feel better.

Don't push. It's easy to get overexcited and want to push your dog to do better. He can jump eight-inch hurdles? Why not try twelve- or even sixteen-inchers? Pushing your dog can lead to mistakes. A mistake can scare him or get him injured. If the hurdles are too high and he trips, he may not want to try again. If he falls off the A-frame, he could sprain or even break a leg!

There are many sports you can do with your dog without competing, including swimming.

Running

Do you and your family like to go running? So will your dog! Going for a run together can be fun and can help build the bond between you. It can also help build strong muscles and good exercise habits for your future. You and your dog were both made for running.

Running can be hard on growing bones and joints, though. Both of you need to be careful and to take it easy. Your dog shouldn't go on runs until he is at least one year old. If neither of you have run long distances before, talk to your doctor and your dog's vet before starting. They may have ideas for how to start slowly so you don't hurt yourselves.

You can also join a local running club just for kids. Ask if your dog can come along for the run. If there isn't a group in your area, start one. There are Web sites on running that are especially for kids where you can find good information—http://www.kidsrunning.com is just one good Web site you can visit.

Here are some rules for running:

Get fitted. Make sure you have a good pair of running shoes that fit you. These shoes should be used only for running. If you always wear these shoes when running, your dog will quickly learn what they mean. Next time you pull on your running shoes, he'll be at the door waiting for you to go!

Warm up. Always warm up before do-

Running is good exercise for this boy and his dog.

ing any exercise. It's especially important when you run. If you don't warm up, you can stretch or even tear muscles. You can also hurt your joints. It's good for dogs to warm up, too. Before starting, take a walk around the block. Stretch out your legs. Ask your dog to do a play bow (see page 290). That gives him a good all-over body stretch.

Start slowly. When you start running, both your body and your dog's body need time to adjust. Ask your mom or dad to show you a half-mile mark from your front door by resetting the odometer on the car

Dog Stretches

A nice stretch feels as good to a dog as it does to you. Plus, it helps warm up the muscles he'll use when doing sports. Here are a few good stretches your dog can do before playing:

Bow: The canine bow is a great back stretch. Teach your dog to bow on command (it's also a good trick!). The easiest way to teach a bow is to catch your dog in the act and then reward him. When playing, dogs often do what is called a play bow. It's basically a way of inviting someone to play. You've probably seen your dog do this to other dogs. To get your dog to do a play bow, jump around, clap your hands, and generally carry on. Your dog will start playing, too. Every once in a while, lean over and do your own version of a bow. At some point, your dog will probably bow at you. When he does this, say "good bow" and give him a treat. If you use a clicker, click and treat when he bows. Repeat until your dog will bow when you say "bow." Ask him to bow before going for a run or starting practice.

Jump up: OK, we usually tell our dogs not to do this. However, jumping up onto his hind legs with his front legs against you is a great all-over body stretch for your dog. Just be sure to teach him to jump up only when he's asked.

First, give good jumping up a name. It can be "hugs," "paws up," or "stretch"—whatever you prefer. Pick up your dog's front legs, say "good hugs" and give him a treat. Do this several times so he relates the word to the action. Do not pat your chest to get your dog to jump up. Use only your voice to ask him to jump.

You also need a word for bad jump ups. When your dog jumps up without being asked, say "no jump ups" and put his feet down on the ground. Never treat your dog or give him positive attention when he jumps up without a cue.

and stopping at half a mile. Or go to a local school or another place with a running track. School running tracks are usually four hundred meters, about a quarter of a mile. Two laps around the track equals about half a mile.

At first, walk the half mile there and half mile back (or four laps around the track) each day. This is a mile walk. After you have done this for a week or two, start running to the halfway mark (or run two laps). Then walk back (or walk two more laps). Stick with this half-mile run, half-mile walk for as long as you want. After a few weeks, you may want to move up to running the half mile back (or the extra two laps). Now you are running a full mile! Be sure to cool down—walk around the block a couple of times (or walk another lap). As you get older, increase the distance you run.

Keep cool. Don't run during the hottest times of the day. This can be dangerous for both you and your dog. Both of you can get heatstroke—a serious illness caused by getting too hot. Dogs have no protection for their paws. Hot cement can cause blisters, and melted tar and gum can get stuck to a dog's paws.

Make sure to drink enough water. If you get thirsty, you're not drinking enough. Give your dog water before and after your run. Drink some yourself, too! Don't let your dog gulp the water. That can give him a tummy ache.

Run with a buddy. Running with a buddy is fun and helps keep you safe. It also helps

Did You Know?

Dogs need fuel for fun! It's important you feed your dog a healthy diet. Ask your vet to recommend good dog food. Always feed your dog a diet that is complete and balanced—it will say this on the bag. Keep treats to a minimum. When training your dog with treats, be sure to adjust his meals for the extra calories. Never feed your dog right before or after exercise. It can lead to bloat, an often fatal condition in which the stomach twists.

Both you and your dog should drink water before and after your run.

you get going. A buddy will push you to do better. It's harder to skip a day when your running buddy is waiting for you. It's best if a grown-up will run with you.

Follow the light. Run during the daylight. Running at night can be dangerous because cars can't see you.

No headphones. A lot of adults listen to music while they run. This is not safe. When you have headphones on, you can't hear traffic. You can't hear if someone comes up behind you. Plus, it's hard to tell your dog what a good job he is doing if you are wearing headphones.

Cool down. Cooling down helps your bodies go back to normal. If you cool down, you won't be as sore the next day. Always end your run with a slow walk around the block.

Walking

Walking with your dog is one of the all-time great things about having a dog. All dogs enjoy a walk around the block. They like the chance to sniff things and say hi to other dogs and people. Young, active dogs may want a longer, brisker walk. If you use a wheelchair or have problems walking, ask a friend or adult to help you take a short walk with your dog. Don't worry about how fast you go—it's all about getting outside with your dog. Always walk your dog with a buddy or an adult.

Walking is good exercise, but it's also a time to get out of the house and have new experiences. Dogs can get exercise by playing ball in their own yards, but a walk opens up their world. They get to check out what's going on with the other neighborhood dogs.

Walking your dog around your neighborhood is easy, but try to branch out. Maybe your mom or dad can drive you somewhere where your dog can sniff and see new areas. Walk along a beach or a lake or a river to give your dog a new experience. Walking through the woods is a lot different from walking on sidewalks. And the smells and sounds are completely different. How about a walk through downtown or a shopping district with your family? Let your dog meet new people and other friendly dogs. Bring treats so kids you and your family meet can give them to your dog.

Walking your dog every day is good for both of you.

This will help teach him that people are his friends, and it will help teach other kids to be kind to dogs.

A lot of the rules for running are the same for walking. Walk with a buddy, don't walk after dark, don't walk your dog during the hottest part of the day, and skip the headphones. Headphones are unsafe, and you miss out on the great experience you and your dog are having. Bring water for you and your dog on your walk. Stop and offer your dog water occasionally.

True · False

There is a snakebite vaccine.

TRUE.

The vaccine reduces a dog's reaction to the snakebite. But dogs who are vaccinated still need to be treated for snakebites. At this time, few veterinary clinics stock the vaccine.

Avoid snakebites by avoiding snakes!

Hiking

Does your family like to hike? This is something you can definitely do with your dog. Dogs love to hike. It's great exercise and it gives them a chance to experience a whole bunch of new sights, smells, and sounds. Hiking with your dog exercises his mind and his body at the same time.

Hiking is not as hard on growing bones and joints as running is. It is harder than a regular walk, though. You go up and down hills. You may go through rough areas, where you can stumble. A hike can last for an hour or for a couple of days if you are camping. If you are going on a long hike, your dog may need booties to protect his paws. If he's not used to hiking, his paws may not be tough enough for a long hike.

Start out with short, easy hikes. Most trails have mile-long or even half-mile hikes. Add miles to your hike slowly. Don't overdo it.

Once your dog gets used to hiking, you may want to buy him a doggy backpack. Dog packs fit over a dog's back and allow him to carry some of the supplies (at least his own!). Only strong, healthy dogs without any spine or hip problems should carry packs. Talk to your vet before buying one.

When you return home from a hike, help an adult give your dog the once-over. Check through his fur for ticks, which can carry diseases. Remove any ticks you find by gently pulling them out with tweezers. Check for burrs and seeds caught in your dog's fur, ears, and nose. Check his paws to be sure there are no cuts or broken nails.

Not all parks allow dogs on their trails. Find out before showing up. It's no fun

A well-equipped group takes a hike. The next time your family goes for a hike, bring your dog!

to drive all the way to a good hiking spot just to find out you can't bring your dog!

Here are some rules for hiking with your dog companion:

Buddy up. Hiking is not something you should do alone. Always go hiking with at least one adult.

Drink, drink, drink. Keep hydrated when hiking. Bring enough water for everyone, and bring a travel bowl for your dog.

Food power. Keep your energy up with snacks. Bring gorp, or trail mix, for the people and high-protein liver snacks for your canine buddy to snack on.

Be prepared. Even if you are going only for a short summer hike, follow the Boy Scout motto: Be Prepared. Bring a warm layer of clothing, extra water and food, a compass, and a cell phone just in case you get lost or there is an emergency.

Tell them about it. Always tell someone where you are going and when you will be back. That way, someone will look for you if you get lost.

Stay on leash and stay on trail. Don't let your dog off leash. You'll probably want to let him explore the bushes and chase little creatures. Don't! For his sake and the sake of the wild animals and plants, keep your dog on leash. Your dog could trample and kill growing plants. He may tease or even hurt or kill small animals. An off-leash dog could get attacked by large animals like mountain lions and bears. He could also be bitten by a snake. He could fall off trail edges and cliffs, get caught in white water, or fall into unmarked wells. Anyway, there is a leash law in most parks. Keep your dog on a leash, and you won't end up spending the next ten years paying your family back for the hefty fine!

Skiing and Snowshoeing

Your dog doesn't need to pull you to have fun in the snow. Lots of cross-country skiers and snowshoers bring their dogs along. For your dog, it's just hiking in the snow. Of course, hiking in the snow is a lot harder than hiking on a regular trail. There are also other dangers.

Stick to well-maintained trails. Lots of cross-country resorts offer dog-friendly trails. Some resorts have special trails just for dogs.

Playing in the snow is lots of fun, but always make sure your dog is warm enough.

The resort may have a leash law, but some resorts allow dogs to be off leash as long as they are well mannered.

Don't let your dog get too cold. And don't let him eat snow. This can make his insides cold! But dogs do need water, even in very cold weather. Bring water in a thermos so it doesn't freeze. Check your dog's paws once every hour to make sure there is no snow or ice caught between his pads. If he has a short coat, get him a doggy jacket. Yep, that's right—there are jackets for dogs! A dog jacket is basically the same as a horse blanket. It's a square of fabric that is wrapped around a dog's middle, from neck to tail. It's kept in place with Velcro straps.

Swimming

If your dog is a Lab, you can bet he loves to swim. But almost any dog enjoys a quick dip now and again. Swimming is great exercise without putting a lot of stress on the body. Many vets suggest swimming for dogs with arthritis or other injuries.

Your dog can swim in a lake, an ocean, or a river. If you're lucky enough to have one, he can swim in a pool. He may like to chase a ball in the water, or he may prefer a little relaxed wading. It's a great way to keep cool in the summer, but most dogs aren't picky. Unless the water's frozen over, dogs will happily jump in, rain or shine.

Always bring an adult with you when you take your dog swimming. You could slip in, or your dog could get into trouble. Don't let your dog swim in areas you haven't been before. If there is a lifeguard, ask about water conditions.

Target Touch!

Teach your dog to touch his nose to a target by using a clicker and some treats. Show your dog the brightly colored lid from a plastic tub. He will probably want to investigate it by smelling it. When he gets close to it, click and give him a treat. Do this several times until he touches his nose to the lid every time you hold it up. Then say "touch" and click and treat when he does. Do this until he touches his nose to the target whenever you say "touch." Next, you can teach him to touch other things—your hand, an agility target, or a potted plant by your pool so he can find the stairs!

In the ocean, riptides are not always obvious. Rivers can seem calm but have hidden currents. A strong current can knock your dog off his feet. Not all beaches allow dogs. Find out if your beach allows dogs before you try to take your dog there.

If your dog gets into trouble, don't go in the water after him. Chances are you'll need to be saved, too! If he's caught in a riptide, run down the beach. Yell for him to follow you. The riptide should let up after about one hundred yards or so. Then he'll be able to swim to shore. If he's caught in a river current, follow him along the river bank, and call him to the side. Swimming at an angle toward the shore is the best way to get out of a strong current. Try to get help from other people.

Swimming in a pool has its own dangers. Sometimes dogs get confused or overtired. They forget how to get out of the pool. Make sure your dog knows how to get out of the pool on his own. To make sure he always gets out at the shallow-end's stairs, put a potted plant or something else next to the stairs. Teach him to touch the plant with his nose every time he gets out of the pool. (see Target Touch!) This will help him remember how to get out if he gets scared. For an extra ounce of safety, get your dog a doggy life preserver to help keep him afloat. Don't leave him alone in the water even if he is wearing a life preserver. Always use a life preserver when out on a boat.

Safety First

We've learned that no matter what sport you are doing with your dog, there are things you need to do to keep him safe. Here are the basic rules one more time:

Take it slowly. Dogs can be out of shape, too! If you and your dog hang out on the couch all week and then go all out at agility practice, one of you is going to get hurt! Do something with your dog every day. It can be a walk, a run, a hike, agility practice, or a good game of fetch.

Then, when it comes time to perform, your dog won't get pooped.

Warm up. Dogs are athletes. They need to warm up just as human athletes do. It doesn't have to be anything fancy. A walk around the block and some stretching before practice is fine.

Cool down. After you finish exercising, have your dog cool down. You could take a walk around the block and stretch out.

Keep cool. Avoid doggy sports in the heat of the day. Try to practice in the morning or evening. Let your dog rest in the shade in between drills. Give him lots of water. Make sure there is a big bucket of cool, clean water all the time. Fill a kiddy pool with cool water. Let your tuckered dog play in the water to cool off.

Keep warm. Just as you need to keep your dog cool when it's hot outside, you need to keep him warm when it's cold! Dogs with thick coats do fine. Dogs with thin coats need some extra warmth. Keep them warm with doggy jackets.

Sometimes dogs get "snowballs" when they play in the snow. These are balls of snow and ice that form in the hair between the pads of their paws. Check your dog's paws for snowballs every so often. Booties can protect his paws from snowballs. They are also good for paws when it's really icy out.

It sounds funny, but even in very cold weather, dogs need water. But don't let your dog eat the snow! Snow will lower his internal body temperature. That means his insides get frosty! Instead, bring water with you. Carry it in a thermos so it won't freeze.

On hot days, fill a plastic pool with water, and let your dog soak in it in between games of fetch.

Chapter 18

Doggy Games

Every dog likes to play. Not all doggy games require super athletes. There are plenty of games you can play in or around your home. Some games exercise a dog's body. Some games exercise her mind and help her learn. Some of these games should be played only when there is an adult around. And some games are better than others. Don't play games that encourage your dog to bite or run away from you. Whether your dog is 5 pounds, 50 pounds, or 150 pounds, there is a game for her!

Games to Learn By

Some games are just about fun, but other games teach a dog lessons while she's having fun.

Almost every dog loves a game of ball — even if the game is just to chew on it!

Tug

Lots of people play tug-of-war with their dogs. Tug-of-war is a game that almost every dog knows how to play. You may notice that your dog plays it with her doggy friends as well as with people. To play tug-of-war, the dog takes one end of a toy, and someone else (dog or human) takes the other end. Then the players pull back and forth. Whoever pulls the hardest wins. The problem with tug-of-war is that it can teach a dog that aggression is a good thing.

Instead, play tug. In tug, you control the game at all times. Tug teaches your dog that working with you is better than working against you. Tug-of-war teaches your dog that being tough and aggressive gets her the toy. Tug teaches her that releasing the toy when you ask works much better!

To begin, offer your dog one end of a tug toy. This can be a piece of rope or a specially made rubber tug toy. Say "take it" or "tug," whatever word you

This dog is playing tug with her kid. Don't let your dog win tug games. Instead, always end the game with the toy in your hand.

want your dog to learn. When your dog tugs on the rope, tug back. Every once in a while, ask your dog to drop it. When she drops the toy, tell her what a good dog she is. If she doesn't drop the toy, offer her another toy in exchange. Praise her when she drops the tug toy.

To begin tugging again, ask your dog to sit. Say your tug word, and offer her the tug toy. If you think your dog is getting too excited, ask her to drop the toy. Always end the game with the toy in your hand. Don't tug too hard, and never let go of the rope suddenly while your dog is tugging. This can hurt her.

Most dogs really love this game and will try to get people to play it with them. If your dog tries to push a toy into your hand, ignore her. The game should begin only with you. Ask your friends to ignore tug requests as well.

Tug teaches your dog to control her excitement and to understand that you are boss. But tug games can make dogs overexcited. Play tug only when there is an adult present.

Adult Alert!

Tug can get some dogs overexcited. An over-excited dog can bite by accident or on purpose. Never let your children play tug with dogs they don't know. Always supervise your dog and kids when they are playing tug. Stop the game if it ever becomes too rough. Help remind your kids that the point of the game is to teach your dog to contain her excitement, not to become excited!

Come to Me

Teaching your dog to come is very important. (You learned how to teach your dog to come in chapter 10.) It can also be fun. Once you've taught your dog to come, play this game to reinforce her new skill.

This trio is enjoying the play equipment. If you have an adult's permission, you can use your backyard play equipment to teach your dog to balance and climb.

Start with a treat bag full of goodies. Show your dog the treats. Then run from your dog to the other side of the room or yard. Stand tall and say "come" and your dog's name. When your dog comes, give her lots of praise and hugs and a treat. Then say "go play" and let her go. Go to another part of the yard or room and repeat.

This game teaches your dog that coming to you means good things. It can be played anywhere—at a park, at the beach, in your living room, and in your backyard. Keep it upbeat and always reward your dog for coming.

Come to Us

This game teaches your dog to come to other people besides you. Start this game in your backyard or another safely fenced area. You and a friend or family member should each have a bag of treats. Show the treats to your dog.

To begin, each person should go to one side of the room or yard. One person should call the dog. When the dog comes, give lots of

Don't Play These Games!

Here are some games that aren't good for your dog:

Never play tug-of-war with your dog.
Tug should not be a war. If you play a tug game, don't let the game end with your dog in control of the toy. Don't let your dog start a tug game, and don't let your dog win a tug game. If your dog starts to get overexcited when playing tug, stop immediately.

Never chase your dog.
Chasing your dog teaches her that running from you is a game. This can be dangerous for her and frustrating for you.

Don't let your dog chase animals like cats, rabbits, birds, or mice.
Chasing animals teaches a dog that it is OK to scare and hurt smaller animals. Don't let your dog bark at or tease wildlife or neighborhood animals.

Don't let your dog herd other kids.
It can seem funny when your dog rounds up your friends, but sometimes people get scared. They may run or scream, which can cause your dog to chase or even bite them.

Don't play rough games with your dog.
Some rough games are wrestling, play biting, and pretend fighting. Dogs play this way with one another, but they shouldn't play this way with you. Rough games teach them that it's OK to be rough with humans and can lead them to being pushy for food, toys, and your attention.

praise and a treat. Hold her collar and face her toward the other person. The other person should then call "come Daisy!" and show Daisy the treats. When Daisy runs to the person, give her a treat and praise. Repeat this game about 20 times. End the game before Daisy gets bored.

As Daisy gets better at this game, increase the distance between you and the other player. This allows Daisy a better workout and also reinforces the *come* command at a distance.

Backyard Obstacles

You don't need fancy equipment to start training your dog for sports. You can teach even a young pup to feel comfortable with obstacles. Set up a beginning agility course in your own backyard with everyday items you may find around your house.

Here are some ways to teach your dog about obstacles using household items:

Find her feet: Lay a ladder flat on the ground. Lead your dog over the ladder. This

A boy and his dog ride down a slide. Going down a slide can help get your dog ready for her future agility career.

helps her learn where her feet are so she can do more difficult obstacles.

Get balanced: Place a sheet of plywood on top of a brick, with the brick in the center of the plywood. It will be wobbly. Coax your dog onto the plywood with lots of treats. This helps her learn to balance.

Do the twist: Buy six cheap toilet plungers. Place them upright in a line with about one and one-half feet between each of them. Have your dog weave through the plungers.

Jack be nimble: If your dog is a year old or older, teach her to jump. Take a broom handle, and lay it down with each end placed on a brick. Lead your dog over the broom handle. Give her a treat when she walks over it. Slowly make the jump higher by adding a brick to each side. Don't do jumps if your dog is less one year old because jumping can be hard on growing bodies.

Games for the Body

Most dogs are happiest when they get lots of exercise. But they also get bored with the same old walk around the block. Here are some games to shake things up.

Fetch

If there is a number one favorite doggy game, it must be fetch. Almost every dog likes to play fetch. Some dogs love to run after a stick and bring it right back to your hand. Others just like to run after things. If you have to fetch it, you are getting more exercise than your dog is! Learning how to bring something back to you can help your dog move on to other games and sports. It will make playing fetch more fun for you and better exercise for your dog.

Get a toy that your dog is very interested in. It may be a ball, a stick, or a stuffed bunny. Make sure your dog is looking at you before you throw the toy. Say "go fetch" and throw it. After your dog picks up the toy, make sure she comes back to you by calling her name. Show

Fetch is probably the most popular doggy game.

her you have a treat. Make her bring the toy all the way to your hand before giving her the treat. Say "good fetch" and give her the treat. As your dog gets better at the game, give her a treat after every third or fourth throw.

Races

Some dogs like to race each other and people. You can race your dog in the water or on land. To begin, have a friend or family member stand at one side of the yard or at one end of a pool. You and your dog are at the other end of the yard or pool. Hold your dog's collar until you are both ready. Say "go race" and start running or swimming away from your dog and toward your friend. At the same time, your friend should call your dog. When your dog reaches your friend, give her treats and praise.

Marmaduke

Marmaduke must be the funny papers' biggest dog, if not one of the most popular. Marmaduke is a Great Dane who is known for causing havoc in his family's life. The Winslows try, and they try, but they just can't get that darn dog to obey! The comic strip *Marmaduke* has been read in newspapers since 1954. Marmaduke was created by cartoonist Brad Anderson, who still draws the cartoon today!

Marmaduke is definitely one of America's most loved dogs. Many of his fans think he

is a lot like a few dogs they know. How about you? Is there a Marmaduke in your life?

This dog is getting a lot of exercise chasing after bubbles! It can be a fun game to play!

Chase Me

Chase Me is a learning game that is also good for your dog's body. A lot of people play games where they chase their dogs. Don't do this! It can create bad habits. By chasing your dog, she learns that not coming to you is a game.

Instead of playing that dangerous game, teach your dog to chase you. This reinforces the *come* command by teaching her to always run after you. Most dogs will chase after someone instinctively. Call your dog's name, and run away from her. At first, let her catch you quickly, and reward her with a quick game of fetch or tug. Then run away again. As she learns the game, make it more difficult for her to reach you. Run behind a tree or up stairs. Always reward and praise your dog when she catches you.

Games for the Mind

Some games are less about the body and more about the mind. These can be good games for an older dog, for a dog who isn't very active, or just to make things interesting. They can also be good rainy-day games.

Hide and Seek

Hide and seek is a good game for a dog with a super sniffer. Show your dog a favorite toy, and let her smell it. Ask a friend to cover your dog's eyes. Very quietly, hide the toy under a cushion or behind the couch. Let your dog go, saying "find it." Tell her she is a good girl when she gets close. Then hide the toy in harder to find locations or even in other rooms.

Find the Biscuit

This is a memory game. Bring your dog into the room, and show her that you have a biscuit.

Put the biscuit in a corner or behind a piece of furniture. Make sure your dog sees where you put it. Take her out of the room for ten seconds. Bring her back into the room. Tell her "find it." Let her know when she gets close. To make it harder, keep her out of the room longer. See if she can find the biscuit after she's been out of the room for a minute or two.

Find Me

It's time to move on from toys and treats to the big find—you! Dogs will do anything to be with their people. This is the same game that search and rescue dogs play. If you find that your dog does well at this game, you may consider joining a search and rescue organization.

Show your dog that you have a favorite toy of hers. It should be something that gets her really excited. Ask a friend to hold your dog while you go behind a couch or another piece of furniture. Make sure your dog sees where you are going. Once you are behind the furniture, your friend can let your dog go. Your friend should say "find" and your name. If your dog doesn't run straight to you, call her

name. When she finds you, give her lots of praise, and let her play with her toy.

Let your dog see where you hide until she understands the game. Then, have your friend hold your dog while you hide. Don't let your dog see where you are hiding. Your hiding place should not be difficult to find. Once you are hidden, have your friend let your dog go and say "find" and your name. Let your dog look for you for a few minutes. If she is having trouble, call her. Let her play with her toy when she finds you. Slowly make the places you hide harder for her to find.

Next, hide behind a closed door. Your friend should hold your dog until you are hidden. Then he should let her go and say "find"

If your dog is ball crazy, like this Boxer, play Find Me while hiding with a ball.

and your name. When your dog finds the door you are behind, call her name. Open the door if she barks, whines, or scratches at the door. Let her play with her toy. Tell her what a great dog she is!

Now you can teach your dog to find other people. This time you hold your dog as your friend hides with the toy. Go through the same steps until your dog can find your friend behind a door.

The Nose Knows

Dogs know their people's scent. That's why it's easier to train your dog to find you than it is to train her to find someone else. Teach your dog to find something with your scent on it. You need rubber gloves or a friend to help with this game.

Start with six clean, empty pop cans. Do not touch them without gloves on. In obedience classes, they play this game using small metal dumbbells.

Take one can and show it to your dog. Hold the can in your bare hand for a minute or two. Toss the can. When your dog goes to the can, tell her "good girl" and give her a treat. Use the same hand you are breaking up treats with to pick up the can and throw it again. Once your dog is going to the can each time you throw it, throw a second can. This time wear a rubber glove to touch it or ask a friend to throw it. If your dog goes to the first can, give her a treat. If she goes to the second can, say "uh-oh!" Throw the cans again. Once your dog always goes to the can with your scent, add a third, fourth, fifth can, and so on.

Fun Stuff

You can have fun with your dog without playing games. You can take pictures of your dog, paw paint, or even give your dog a four-star massage!

Photo Star

Do you like taking pictures? If so, you will love to take pictures of your dog. Dogs are excellent models. Some even pose! You don't need a fancy camera to take good pictures of your dog. If you don't have a camera, ask if you can borrow an adult's camera, or buy a disposable

A Bloodhound mugs for the camera. Is your dog a photo star?

This dog is sitting still while her young owner snaps her picture. Say "cheese!"

camera. Some are very cheap. There are also Polaroid cameras that give you instant prints or make special sticker prints.

Before starting your dog's photo session, get ready. If you want her to put her best paw forward, you need to help her look her best. Give her a nice bath and brush out her coat, trim her nails, and clean the sleep from her eyes. You may want to put a fancy bow around her neck or even dress her up in a doggy costume.

Once your dog is ready, it's time to get your backdrop ready. Have you ever had a great picture that was ruined because of a bunch of clutter? Take pictures of your dog against a clean background. Look through the camera at what you'll see. Are there dirty socks, old toys, or piles of books in the frame? Get rid of them! You want your dog to stand out, not the pile of laundry behind her!

If possible, have the photo session outside. The light is better, and you won't have to use a flash. This way, you won't get the dreaded red eyes in your photo. Be sure not to face the sun when you are taking the picture.

Find a nice spot in your yard or at a local park. If it is spring, maybe there are flowers in

bloom. That can make a beautiful photograph. If possible, take your pictures where you can have your dog off leash.

To get the best picture, you will want a buddy to help you. Ask your dog to sit or lie down and tell her to stay. Your buddy should stand behind you (or you can have him take the picture while you stand behind him) and use a doggy toy or a treat to get your dog's attention. When your dog is looking toward you at full attention, take the picture!

Once you have some formal pictures, it's fun to get some unposed shots. Let your dog sniff around, throw her a ball, ask her to shake or do another trick, or just let her play. Try to take her picture when she is looking up toward the camera.

Paw Painting

You know how your parents display your artwork on the refrigerator? Now you can hang your dog's art. To paw paint, you just need a dog with a willing paw, some paint, and something to paint on. Just be sure to paw paint outside and to keep your dog on a leash! You don't want her to run off into the house with paint on her paws!

You will need nontoxic and washable paint, paper plates, a large piece of paper (you can also paint a smooth rock or a sanded piece of wood), a bucket with warm water, and towels. You can buy nontoxic paint and large art paper at most toy stores, craft stores, and art supply stores.

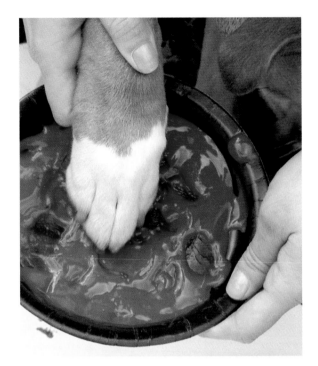

STEP 1: **Dip the dog's paw into nontoxic paint.**

STEP 2: **Gently press the dog's paw onto the paper.**

STEP 3: Everyone have fun! Paw painting can be a great activity for just you and your dog or for a group of kids and dogs. Maybe you can do paw (and hand) painting at your next doggy party.

Pour some paint onto a paper plate. If you want to use more than one color, use one plate for each color. Dip your dog's paw into the paint, then press her paw firmly on the paper. Dip her paw once for each print. To change colors, rinse her paw in your bucket of water and dry it. Dip her paw into the new color, and press the paw against the paper.

When you are done, clean her paw in the water, and dry it with a towel. Then use paint or a special colored pen to write your dog's name and the date under her paw print!

Paw Sculpture

Does your mom have a copy of your handprint from when you were little? It's funny to see how tiny you once were. You can do the same with your dog. You will need plaster of paris (you can buy this at a craft store), a mold, aluminum foil, a pencil, and a bucket of warm water. You may also want nontoxic paint.

1. To mix the plaster of paris, follow the instructions on the package.

2. Buy a mold (at a craft store) or make your own. To make a mold, just take long pieces (about two or three inches wide) of thin cardboard (old cereal boxes work). Staple them into the shape you want. You can make a round mold, a heart-shaped mold, whatever you want!

3. Place the mold in the middle of a sheet of aluminum foil.

4. Pour the mixed plaster of paris into the mold.

5. Press your dog's paw into the plaster for about twenty seconds.

6. Wash and dry her paw.

7. Use a pencil or a chopstick to engrave your dog's name and the date beneath her paw print.

8. Let the plaster dry overnight. When it's dry, take off the mold. Your masterpiece is complete!

9. If you want, paint the paw print with nontoxic paint.

Adult Alert!

Supervise your children when they give your dog a massage. Never let them massage a dog they don't know well or a dog who is sensitive. If your dog dislikes having her feet or tail touched, do not let your children massage her. Watch for any signs the dog is feeling uncomfortable. Signs can be overt (growling, baring teeth, whining, yelping, or snapping) or subtle (stiffening, moving away, or holding the ears back against her head).

Dog Massage

The next time it rains, give your dog a spa day. Most dogs like to be massaged as much as people do. But if your dog doesn't like being petted a lot, she probably won't like being massaged. Always make sure an adult helps you massage your dog. To begin, get comfortable. It's easier to massage your dog if you are both sitting on the floor. Have a pillow for yourself and a cozy blanket for your dog. Lay your dog on her side, and slowly pet her from head to tail. This will help her relax.

Next, gently rub the top of her head, her ears, and her cheeks. Work your way down to her neck. Use your fingers to press lightly against the muscles in her neck. Rub the muscles along her spine. Press lightly over her ribs. Stroke down her legs and paws. Most dogs really like to have the top of their tails rubbed. Spend a little extra time there. Gently stroke her tail from the top to the tip. Be careful not to pull on it.

It should take you about twenty minutes to work your way from head to tail. Doggy massage should be very slow and very gentle. You are just trying to make your dog feel good and relaxed.

It's hard for a dog to tell you what she likes or doesn't like. Pay attention to the signals she gives you. When your dog is enjoying the massage, she may lean into you, close her eyes, fall asleep, or groan a little. If she doesn't like it, she will move away, wince, cry, or even growl. Stop massaging your dog if she gives you these signs. AND NEVER MASSAGE A DOG WHO GROWLS. Do not massage your dog if she doesn't like being touched. Don't massage your dog if she is sick or hurt. Always ask an adult before massaging your dog.

Tricks

Do you want a dog who can wave, roll over, or bow? Dog tricks can be a lot of fun for both of you. It helps with training and helps make you and your dog better friends. Start off with some easy tricks such as shake and spin. Some people like to use a clicker when teaching tricks. In fact, clicker training was invented by a dolphin trainer to teach dolphins tricks! (See the box in chapter 10 on page 178 for more on clicker training.)

Shake

Shake is probably the easiest trick for a dog to learn. Ask your dog to sit. Stand in front of her and say "shake." Use your right hand to lift up her right paw. Say "good shake" and give her a treat. Release the paw. Repeat about ten times a day for three for four days until your dog automatically picks up her paw when you say "shake."

This dog has learned to balance a treat on her nose—and to wait to eat it!

Give Me Five!

Once your dog understands shake, teach her to give you five. Again, ask your dog to sit in front of you. Lift your right hand with the palm up. Make sure that your hand is not too high for your dog to reach. She will lift her right paw to shake. Instead of taking her paw, keep your palm up. When she touches your palm, say "good five" and give her a treat. Do this about ten times a day for three or four days or until she does it every time you ask her to.

You can also teach your dog to give a high five. This time, hold your hand with the palm facing your dog. When she touches your palm, say "good high five" and give her a treat.

Like most dogs, this pooch quickly learned how to spin.

Spin

Teaching your dog to spin seems hard, but in fact it's very easy. Begin with your dog in a sitting position. Stand directly in front of her with a treat in your hand. Place the treat in front of your dog's nose, and slowly move it in a circle behind her head. As you move your hand, her head will follow the treat. When she can no longer turn her head to follow the treat, she will stand up to move with your hand. When she is facing you again, give her the treat and say "good spin." Do this five to ten times. Once she always follows the treat to spin, say "spin" as you move the treat. Do it about ten times for two or three days. Most dogs pick up on this trick very quickly.

Wave

Teach your dog to wave hello or good-bye. Show your dog you have a treat in your hand. Put your hand out as if you are going to shake

your dog's paw. When she puts out her paw, do not take it. Instead, move your hand back and forth, saying "wave." When her paw follows your hand, give her the treat.

Play Dead

This is a classic dog trick. Get your parents to help you with this one! Don't try to teach this to a dog you don't

A pooch waves good-bye! Waving bye-bye is a great trick to teach your dog, but it may take some time.

know. If your dog doesn't like being touched, don't do this trick with her.

To teach your dog to play dead, she needs to be good at following the *down* command. From the down position, gently push your dog onto her side. (Most dogs lean to one side or the other when they are lying down. Gently push yours in the direction she is already leaning.) Stop if your dog won't let you push her or acts irritated.

Once your dog is on her side, make sure her head is on the floor. When she is lying still, give her a treat. Do this about five times. Next, say "play dead" when you push her onto her side. From the down position, say "play dead" and gently push her onto her side. Give her a treat. Do this several times a day for several days until she lies on her side every time you say "play dead."

Now teach your dog to play dead from standing up. Tell your dog "down." When she is down, say "play dead." Give her a treat when she is lying on her side. Do this four or five times in a row. Finally, say "play dead" when she is standing. (You may have to still tell her "down.") When she is on her side, give her a treat. Do this four or five times a day for two or three days until she will lie down on her side every time you say "play dead."

A boy teaches his dog to roll over. If your dog has learned to play dead, she may also learn how to roll over.

Roll Over

Get help from your parents or another adult for this trick. To keep things safe, have the adult do the pushing while you give the commands and hold the treats. If your dog is sensitive about being touched or poked, don't teach her this trick. Some dogs get scared or mad when they are pushed onto their backs.

Once your dog knows how to play dead, teach her the *roll over* command. When she is on her side, say "roll over" and gently push her onto her back. Give her a treat. Say "roll over" and push her to her other side. Give her a treat. Finally, push her back onto her front. Give her a treat and say "good roll over." Do this four or five times a day for six or seven days.

Bow

Dogs like to bow. They bow when they are playing, when they are stretching, and when they say hi. You can teach your dog to bow on command.

Always have treats with you when trying to teach this trick! Next time you catch your dog doing a bow, say "bow." Then give her a treat and say "good bow." Say "bow" and give your dog a treat every time you see her bow. Pretty soon, she'll bow whenever you tell her to! If you use a clicker, click every time you see her bow.

Give Me a Kiss

Most dogs don't need to learn how to give kisses. They love to kiss you all on their own.

But you can teach your dog to kiss on command. Do this trick only with your own dog. Never put your face up to your dog if she is nervous, sleeping, or has a toy or food. Always let your dog kiss you—never kiss your dog.

Wait for your dog to give you a kiss. When she does, say "good kiss" and give her a treat. Repeat this whenever your dog gives you a kiss. After a few days of doing this, you will notice when your dog likes to give kisses. When she

This play bow doubles as a warm-up. Once your dog knows how to do a play bow, you can ask her to do it as a stretch before you do sports.

looks as if she's coming for a lick, say "give me a kiss." If she does, give her a treat. Pretty soon, all you'll need to say is "give me a kiss" for a few well-deserved slurps.

If your dog isn't a natural kisser, you can still teach her to give you a kiss. Smear a little peanut butter on your cheek, and say "give me a kiss." When she licks it off, say "good kiss."

Good Toys

Is there such a thing as a bad toy? Actually, yes! Not all toys sold for dogs are good for them. Here are some of the pluses and minuses of the many toys in dogland.

Soft Toys

Most dogs love a soft, furry stuffed friend. It makes them feel safe and cozy and gives them something to play with. A lot of puppies sleep better with a snuggly toy. Some dogs even treat soft toys like baby dolls. They sleep with them,

A dog can never have too many tennis balls.

True / False

You can't teach an old dog new tricks.

FALSE.

Old dogs love to learn new things. Sometimes they learn better than young dogs do.

carry them around, even rest their heads on their snuggly toys.

If your dog likes to tear things up, though, don't give her soft toys. Instead of a snuggly baby doll, she sees a soft toy as something to rip, tear, and shred. She can choke on the ripped pieces of toy, the squeaker, or the stuffing inside. Pieces of the toy can get stuck in her intestines.

Buy only good-quality stuffed toys. What does that mean? Some stores sell cheap stuffed toys. Don't buy these for two reasons. One, the toys don't last. Two, they can be dangerous for your dog. Look at how a toy is made. Are there any loose seams? Seams should be very firm on dog toys. Ask the store clerk to suggest a toy that is very tough.

Buy only stuffed toys made for dogs. The toys made for kids are different and aren't as strong. They aren't safe for dogs to play with. And remove all tags before giving a soft toy to your dog. Many dogs will pull on tags, creating a hole.

The best soft toys for a dog are unstuffed lamb's-wool toys with no squeaker. A disk made of lamb's wool is another good toy.

Rope Toys

If your dog is too rough with soft toys, give her a rope toy. They are soft and cozy, but they also stand up to chewing and pulling. If you have more than one dog, a long rope toy makes a good tug toy. Throw away rope toys when they start to come apart.

These are some safe toys that will keep your dog busy when you can't play with her.

Tough Toys

Toy companies know that some dogs need tougher toys than others. The Kong is a popular tough dog toy. Hard rubber toys such as Kongs are good for dogs who like to chew things apart. Hard rubber toys are good for teeth and keep dogs busy for hours. They also last for a couple of years!

Puzzle Toys

Besides being tough, Kong toys and other puzzle toys are great for your dog's mind. These toys have a space inside the toy where you can put treats. Different toys provide different ways for a dog to get the treat. Make it even more fun for your dog by filling the hollow space in the toy with peanut butter. Freeze it to make the peanut butter even harder to get out.

This little pup has figured out how to get the treats out of a puzzle toy. A puzzle toy is a great way to keep a curious pup busy.

This family of people and dogs plays together. Don't just let your dog play by herself at the dog park— always play with her instead!

Action Toys

Action toys are made for dogs and people to play with together. These include balls, Frisbees, and floating toys. These toys aren't made for a dog to play with by herself. Always put action toys away when you are finished playing with them.

Waterproof floating toys are for water fun. Water-loving Labs love this kind of toy. When in the water, the toy bobs on the surface. Tennis balls are good, cheap floating toys that many dogs love. They float and fit easily into most dogs' mouths.

Dog Park

Does your dog like to visit the dog park? Kids and dog parks don't always go together. Some dog parks don't allow children under the age of twelve or even sixteen. There are some good

Start a Dog Park!

No dog park in your town? Start one! Here are a few tips to get you started:

Find help. You're not the only one who wants a dog park. Ask around to find adults who will help you.

Find a friend. A friend in government is a friend indeed! Find out if anyone in your local government—the mayor or someone on the city council—is a dog lover. Ask for his or her help.

Find a spot. Look around for a place to use as the dog park. It should be an open area that isn't being used for anything else. There should be parking close by.

Stay the course. Lots of people have good ideas. The difference between a person with a good idea and a person who gets something done is staying with it.

reasons for this. Some dogs are uncomfortable with kids. They are scared of them because they aren't used to them. Sometimes kids don't know how to act at a dog park. They don't know that you shouldn't run from a dog, for instance. This can be dangerous.

Before visiting a dog park, find out what the rules are. Always go with a parent or another adult. Dog parks can be a little scary. There are often a lot of dogs there. Some are better trained than others. Sometimes dogs fight. Sometimes people at dog parks get mad at each other, too! If you ever feel weird at the dog park, leave. If a dog or person at the park makes you uncomfortable, tell an adult.

Here are some basic dog park rules:

• Always go to the dog park with an adult. An adult can help you control your dog. An adult can also help you if a dog or person makes you uncomfortable.

Does your dog have a birthday coming up? How about throwing a dog party such as this one?

• Don't bring dogs who are in heat to a dog park. Male dogs may fight over her. Plus, you don't want your dog to get pregnant!

• Don't bring treats to a dog park. Save your training treats for later. Dogs can get into fights over treats. Your dog may act more protective if she knows you have treats.

• Don't jump up and down, wave your hands, or do other silly stuff. This can make some dogs act aggressive. If you and your dog like to play like this, do it at home.

• Don't keep the leash on your dog in a dog park. Leashed dogs often feel scared of other dogs. Sometimes they get in fights with other dogs because they are scared. If you're holding the leash, you could get caught up in the fight.

• Don't scream, yell, or use a high-pitched voice in a dog park. Some dogs get overly excited when they hear loud or high noises.

• Keep moving. Dogs tend to be more protective of you if you stay in one location. And anyway, aren't you there to have fun with your dog?

• Never run in a dog park. Some dogs see a person running and think they should chase them or even bite them. Herding dogs may try to herd you if you run. Other dogs just get overexcited. Let the dogs do the running at the dog park.

• Pick up after your dog. No one wants to step in dog poop!

Dog Parties

A party for dogs! What will they think of next? Throwing a party for your dog can be lots of fun. It's a good way to get your dog's friends and your dog-loving friends all together. You and your family can throw a party for your dog's birthday, for Halloween, or just for fun. Maybe you can ask your parents for a dog party for *your* next birthday!

For a good dog party, you need friendly dogs, yummy food for dogs and people, and fabulous games. Here are some tips for throwing a dog party:

Make up your guest list. Invite only dogs who get along with one another. Don't invite dogs you don't know well or dogs who haven't met one another. Don't invite dogs who get jealous or are shy. You can have fun with these dogs on another day, but they don't make good party guests.

Pick a place. If the party is at your house, invite four or five dogs and their people. If the party is at a park, you can invite more dogs. Your local dog park or dog beach may let you have a party there. (You'll have to serve the cake outside the park, though!)

Treats or feasts? Do you want a full spread or just cake and treats for your guests? If it's a birthday party, get cakes for people and special cakes for dogs. You'll also want tasty treats and maybe even goody bags for doggy guests to take home.

Give each dog a piece of cake on a plate. Make sure there is a lot of room between each dog. If there are any food thieves, ask their people to put them on a leash while food is being served. You don't want any fights over doggy cake!

Go for a theme. Try a spider-shaped cake for a Halloween party or snowflake-shaped dog cookies for a winter holiday party. Buy doggy cakes and cookies at a dog bakery, or make your own. Make sure you have bowls with fresh, clean water. Have juice or water for your people guests.

Follow dog party etiquette. There should be at least one person per dog. All dogs must be under their person's control at all times. Every dog must have a leash in case she needs a time-out. Don't allow food stealing, fighting, or any other bad doggy behavior.

Send party invitations. Be sure to include the time, the date, the location, and the rules. If you want every dog to come with a trick or in costume, be sure to write this on the invitations.

Have some organized games for your party. Party games should be about fun, not about winning. You

This dog is ready for a pirate-themed party!

can play people party games or teach dogs new activities. Ask an adult to hire an agility trainer to set up a beginning agility course. Or a grown-up can hire a cowboy to bring sheep to your party and allow the dogs to herd them! The sky is the limit if you want to go all out for your doggy party!

Here are a few games that give both dogs and people a chance to be silly:

Bobbing for hot dogs. You've heard of bobbing for apples, right? Well this is the canine version. Fill a plastic tub or wading pool with water. Cut up chunks of hot dogs, and put them in the water. Give each dog thirty seconds to gobble up as many hot dogs as she can. The dog who eats the most wins!

Tricks on command. In your invitations, ask each dog to come to the party with a trick.

No-Cook Cake

Ok, this cake sounds pretty horrible. But your dog and her friends will love it!

4 cans wet dog food
2 cups dry dog food
4 cups soft peanut butter
1 box medium-size treats or
    dog biscuits

Mix the wet food together. Pour it onto a large plate. Shape it into a circle. Pour the dry food over the wet food. Spoon soft peanut butter over the dry food. Use a spatula to make the peanut butter an even layer. Stick treats or dog biscuits into the peanut butter.

Chill the cake in the refrigerator for about three hours or until it's hard. Cut into slices.

Each dog gets ten seconds to do her trick while the rest of the party watches. After all the dogs have done their tricks, ask the human guests to vote for the best one.

Best costume. Ask that the dogs come dressed in costumes. When all the guests have arrived, have a costume contest. The human guests are the judges. After the costume judging, take off the costumes. Some dogs get crabby when they are wearing costumes, and some costumes can be dangerous when dogs play.

Chapter 19

Fun Away from Home

Next time you and your family go on a trip, why not bring your dog? It can be fun to travel with your dog. And your dog will surely love to travel with you. Most dogs enjoy sniffing out new places.

Lots of tourist spots are dog friendly. There are hotels that welcome dogs. Some restaurants with outdoor tables allow dogs, too. There are even some vacations made just for dogs. Doggy camp, anyone? Yes, you heard right. You know about horse camp, sailing camp, science camp, and space camp, but there are also camps for dogs and their people!

Hounds on Vacation

Bringing your dog on vacation can be a blast. It can also be a lot of work. When you travel with your dog, you can't just stop anywhere.

A trip to the lake is an ideal doggy vacation.

You always have to think about him first. Would your family enjoy planning a holiday around the dog?

Here are some things to think about when planning a trip:

- How are you getting there? Plane, train, or automobile? Dogs aren't allowed on trains or buses. Planes cost a lot of money. A car ride may be just right.
- How flexible is your family? Does it drive your mom nuts when plans change, or does she go with the flow?
- How much extra work do you want? What sounds better—a vacation with a personal waiter who brings you ice cream and soda while you swim in a giant wave pool, or a vacation where you get up early to walk your dog and carry poop bags with you everywhere you go?
- How well behaved is your dog? Is he a perfect angel or a perfect devil? If he's left alone, will he bark and rip everything in the room to shreds or curl up for a snooze?
- Where are you going for vacation? Are you going to a rustic lakefront cabin, or are you jetting off to a fancy hotel in New York City?

Taking your dog on some trips can make it even more fun. But on others, it can be a big pain. A summer trip to a lakefront cabin is a good dog vacation. A winter trip to New York City may not be as fun. At a lakefront cabin,

Reasons to Bring Your Dog on Vacation

- It forces you to be flexible.
- It gives your dog a chance to explore new places.
- It increases the bond between you and your dog.
- It's fun for you.
- It's fun for your dog.
- You can explore places away from the tourist scene.
- You'll have a constant companion.
- You'll meet people you wouldn't have met otherwise.

Reasons Not to Bring Your Dog on Vacation

- It changes the focus of the vacation.
- It limits the places you can visit.
- It limits the restaurants you can go to.
- It can be hard to find dog-friendly hotels.
- You can't do as much without planning ahead.
- You'll have extra responsibilities.
- You'll need to find places for doggy potty breaks.

These dogs are ready to travel! Don't forget to pack your dog's suitcase with his first aid kit, extra collar and leash, and plenty of snacks.

The next time your child suggests bringing the dog on your family vacation, don't dismiss it out of hand. There is a lot to be gained by bringing your dog along. A dog helps keep things upbeat, keeps the kids happy on long car drives, gets the kids out of the cabin and into the great outdoors, and makes family hikes sound a lot more fun, even to the most committed gamer.

Yes, bringing the dog on your trip is more work and makes everything more complicated. Yes, your trip will be less spontaneous. Yes, taking a dog along means fewer four-star restaurants and more poop scooping. But the dog also means a chance for a whole new way of doing things and gives your children the opportunity to take charge of some aspects of the trip. Let them find dog-friendly hotels and tourist sites. Give them the charge of poop scooping and feeding. Bringing the dog along can help make a family vacation truly about family.

Some family friends will welcome your dog with open arms. This Poodle even got a seat at the table!

your dog will have the time of his life and will probably sleep better than he's ever slept before! Because you're in your own cabin, you won't need to worry about finding a hotel room or deal with eating out.

Your winter trip to New York is not such a good idea if you have your dog with you. Unless you want to wear a snowsuit, outdoor restaurants are out. But small lap dogs often join their people on big city trips. These pampered pups would probably prefer getting spoiled in New York to chasing ducks at the lake.

Traveling with a dog has some perks. You meet other dog people. You see places you may not see without your dog. You get the chance to have a great time with your dog. There are also downsides. It limits the things you can do. There are many places where dogs aren't allowed. You have to worry about your dog.

Visiting Friends and Family

People often bring their dogs along when they visit friends and family. This can work out great if your hosts like dogs as much as you do. It can be a big problem if they don't. Believe it or not, some people aren't dog fans.

Before bringing your dog along, consider a few things. Do your hosts like dogs? Do they like your dog? Do they have their own dogs?

Do their dogs get along with other dogs? Is anyone in the house afraid of dogs? Is your dog friendly? Is your dog well behaved? Are you sure your hosts want your dog to visit? Even if they love dogs, they may have plans that don't include dogs. They may want to take you into the city or spend the day at an amusement park.

Never, ever bring your dog without asking first! If your hosts seem unsure, don't bring your dog! There will be lots of other vacations in his future.

A dog picks out a goody from the doggy bakery case. Many cities have doggy bakeries or other dog-themed stores you can visit with your dog.

If your hosts assure you they want the entire canine and human family, be considerate. Keep your dog off the furniture, and scoop his poop. Even if your dog is well mannered, bring his crate. His crate makes him feel safe. Keep him in his crate when you go out. A crate also keeps a dog safe in the car. Offer to clean up the yard and to vacuum while you are visiting. It's not fair for your hosts to have to clean up after your dog's messes. If your dog causes any damage, offer to pay for it.

Even if your hosts have their own dogs, bring your own food, bowls, treats, and toys. Ask if there are any treats or toys that their dogs can't have. There will probably be some sharing going on.

Be a good guest to all your hosts. Your family will probably bring your human hosts a small gift. Bring one for the doggy hosts, too. Buy some fancy doggy treats for everyone!

City Vacations

You can bring your pooch on a visit to a big city. A lot of cities are actually surprisingly dog friendly. In New York City, there are tons of doggy shops and even indoor doggy playgrounds! A lot of hotels allow dogs. Some even have special pampered pet packages. Dogs are given bowls with their names on them, special treats, and doggy menus. Some fancy hotels even have people to walk your dog.

What's a vacation without a little shopping?

Bringing your dog on a city vacation gives your family a chance to get off the beaten path. Instead of eating at another tourist trap, find out where the local people eat at outdoor patios. Visit a dog park to meet other dog owners and find out the good doggy spots.

In New York, Central Park is a happening canine hot spot. It's also one of the world's most popular tourist destinations. Through the eyes of your dog, you'll see it in a whole new light! There are also many other outdoor tourist spots  that can be dog friendly. Washington, D.C.'s, National Mall; Seattle's Pike Place Market; and Los Angeles's Venice Beach boardwalk all allow leashed dogs in outdoor areas.

In San Francisco during baseball season, you can take your dog to watch the Baseball Aquatic Retrieval Korps. These are six Portuguese Water Dogs who retrieve home runs knocked out of Giants Stadium into San Francisco Bay! Pretty good entertainment for the canine set.

Walking tours of cities can also be fun. Just check to make sure the tour doesn't include any indoor stops.

One big city must for any tourist is a little shopping. Your dog can hit the stores with you. Shopping with a dog? Sounds strange, doesn't it? In fact, a lot of stores allow dogs. Dog specialty stores, of course, encourage dogs to visit. They will probably even offer your dog a tasty

This Lab loves nothing more than a trip to the water—any water!

treat while browsing. Any store that doesn't sell people food can welcome dogs. Some small stores have found that being dog friendly means better business. A sure sign of a dog-friendly store is a water bowl near the front door.

Before entering a store with your dog, poke your head in and ask if it's OK. The store keeper will appreciate how polite you are.

Country Vacations

Sometimes a vacation to the country is the best thing for kids and their dogs. If your dog loves to run, swim, hike, chase, jump, stretch, and just be plain old silly, this is the vacation for him! A vacation to a rural area is easier than going to a crowded hot spot. There's more open space for playing, fewer traffic dangers, and more chances for fun for both people and dogs!

Every season offers new things to do. During winter, your family can bring your dog on a cross-country skiing or sledding vacation. During summer, trips to the beach or lake are dog heaven.

If your family rents a cabin, you don't have worry about hotels or restaurants. Fun is just right outside the front door. Strap on your skis

RIDDLe

Where does a dog sleep
when he is camping?

In a pup tent!

A family hangs out at the campfire.

or grab your swimsuit. You and your dog are ready to go!

Make sure your family asks about dogs when making reservations. A special deposit or special rules may apply for families with dogs. Bring a crate and keep your dog off the cabin furniture, or at least cover it with a sheet before letting him up.

Some people like to go camping with their dogs—an ideal vacation for dogs who like hiking, swimming, and getting dirty. An active dog like a Lab will love it. Yorkshire Terriers? Not so much. Dogs with long silky hair end up with snarls. Small dogs won't be able to join you on hikes or swims.

This Basset isn't bothered, but not all dogs enjoy sleeping in a tent. If your dog doesn't like roughing it, leave him at home when you go camping.

Camping isn't all fun and games. In the wilderness, there are things that can hurt or scare your dog. Dogs can be dangerous to the wilderness, too. Most state and national parks require dogs to be on leash. This is important for their safety, but it also keeps the area's wildlife and plants safe from your dog. Stay on trails so you don't hurt growing plants. Loose dogs will sometimes chase small wildlife and sometimes hurt or kill little animals. Bigger wildlife, such as mountain lions, coyotes, and bears, can attack dogs as well. For everyone's sake, keep your dog with you at all times, and always keep him on leash.

Eating Out

Eating out is usually the hardest part of bringing a dog on vacation, but it doesn't have to be! If you travel during the summer, you can pretty much enjoy top-notch food and still share your dog's company. The key is to eat outdoors. That can mean a quick bite at a hot dog stand, or it can mean a four-course dinner on an oceanfront patio (grown-ups paying, of course). Many restaurants accept dogs in their outdoor dining areas.

One of the best ways to eat with your dog is to visit small neighborhood cafes, which often have outdoor tables and good, cheap food. They may pamper your pooch with a couple of dog treats as well! Look for the outdoor water bowl as a sure sign that dogs are welcome in the establishment.

There are even restaurants for dogs! Some restaurants have doggy menus. There are dog bakeries that serve only doggy delights. For good advice on dog-friendly grub, visit the neighborhood dog park, and ask the local people.

Outdoor cafes such as this are usually dog friendly. They are a great option for eating out with your pooch.

welcome dogs with open arms. A few Internet travel sites are http://www.dogfriendly.com, http://www.takeyourpet.com, and http://www.traveldog.com. Ask your family, school librarian, or teacher to help you find good doggy travel Web sites.

Use traveler resources. Organizations like the American Automobile Association (AAA) have booklets on finding dog-friendly lodgings. There are also books written especially for people who travel with their dogs. Call AAA for information at 888-874-7222. Ask your family about visiting a local bookstore to search for dog travel books. Your whole family can look through these booklets and books together.

Lodging

It can be hard to find a place to stay with your dog. A grown-up usually makes the hotel reservations, but you can help. Here are some good ways to find dog-friendly inns:

Be a techie. The Internet has great dog travel sites. These sites have dog-friendly hotels and motels across the country. Go to Web sites for discount chain motels. Some

Keep your eyes peeled. When driving, look for signs that say Dogs Welcome or Dog Friendly. These hotels hope to attract business by welcoming dogs.

Call ahead. If you know what town you'll be staying in, have an adult call local dog businesses and ask about dog-friendly hotels. Your family can make a reservation at a dog-friendly hotel so you don't run into surprises after a long drive.

These two are taking a stroll on the hotel grounds. Some hotels happily welcome dogs. Others do not.

Plan ahead. Even if you don't want to plan ahead, bring a list of dog-friendly hotels with you. That way you won't be stuck if nothing pans out.

Be considerate. Don't let dogs on furniture at hotels. If you just can't bear for your dog to be on the floor, cover the furniture with a sheet. Make sure your dog is flea free before traveling. Keep your dog in his crate when he is alone, and don't leave a barking dog alone in a hotel room. Always clean up after your dog. Hotels that have good doggy experiences will welcome dogs in the future.

Doggy Camp

Dog camps can be found all over the country. Some camps specialize in a canine sport such as agility. Others give you and your dog the chance to try all kinds of sports. There are doggy camps that focus just on giving you and dog a good time. A camp that is at a lake may have a lot of boating and swimming

A boy and his dog spend a lazy day in a hammock, which may just be the perfect summer vacation.

Top Ten Things to Bring to Doggy Camp

For You:

- Brush and comb
- Good walking shoes
- Insect repellent
- Rain gear
- Shorts
- Sleeping bag
- Sunglasses
- Sunscreen
- Sweatshirt
- Swimsuit
- Towels

For Your Dog:

- Crate
- Dog bed
- Dog food
- Food and water bowls
- Leash and collar
- Tie out or x-pen
- Towels
- Toys
- Treats (enough to use for training)

activities. A camp in the mountains may be all about hiking. Some camps, like the Dog Scouts of America, let dogs and their people earn badges or awards. Your dog can earn badges for swimming and hiking as well as for obedience and good manners.

Like all good camps, a good doggy camp isn't all hard work! There is also time for relaxing, such as at evening campfires.

Because the focus is on dogs instead of kids, some camps have an age limit. All camps require kids to have an adult with them. If a parent doesn't want to go, maybe a dog-loving aunt, uncle, or grandparent will join you.

In addition to overnight camps, there are also doggy day camps. These are places where your dog can go to play with other dogs and people while you and your family are at work and in school. Doggy day camps are basically day care centers for dogs. Some people use them because their dogs don't like to be alone. People who work really long hours may also send their dogs to doggy day camp.

How to Get to Where You Are Going

So how do you get to where you are going with a dog? Well, you can drive or you can fly. That's about it. Dogs aren't allowed on trains or buses. A few cruise ships allow dogs, but they have to stay in a kennel. Not a dog's idea of a good time!

Most people who travel with their dogs drive. Have you gone on a road trip with your family dog? Sometimes this can be fun—and sometimes not! If there isn't enough room for your dog or your dog doesn't like riding in cars, it can be a real headache.

Flying is another way that dogs and their people can get around. Flying with a dog can have its pluses and its minuses.

Flying

Flying is easiest when you have a small dog who can fit under your seat. Big dogs must fly in the cargo area—the place where your luggage goes. Some people worry about flying with their dogs because the cargo area can get very hot or very cold. Because of this, some airlines won't let any dogs

This crated pooch is ready to fly. To fly in the cabin, your dog's crate must fit underneath the seat.

travel during the hottest times of the summer and the coldest times of the winter.

Flying is the most convenient way to travel a long distance. Your dog may have to fly if you're going to a place far away or if you are moving.

Crate him. If your dog is flying in cargo, he needs a crate. The crate must be large enough for him to stand up, turn around, and lie down in. It must have air holes and a latching door. Talk to the airline about other rules when your dog flies in cargo.

If your dog is small enough to fly in the cabin, he still needs to be in a crate or what is called a Sherpa Bag. This is a soft crate that looks like a big purse.

Be alert. If your dog is in cargo, don't board the flight until you see he has been put on board. You or an adult in your family can wait at the gate until you see your dog being loaded onto the airplane. Tell everyone that your dog is on the flight—the ticket agent, the gate agent, the flight attendants, even the pilot and copilot if you see them!

Book your flight in advance. Make sure you can bring your dog on the flight before showing up! Some airlines require dog reservations. Some airlines will allow only a certain number of dogs in the cabin per flight. Your family should call to book your flight as early as possible.

Potty time. Give your dog a potty break before getting on the plane. Give him a chance

Make sure your dog travels safely in a crate or wearing a doggy seat belt.

to go potty right after picking him up, too. Some airlines have grassy spots for just this reason alone!

Keep him comfy. Your dog's crate should be a safe place for him. Put a cozy blanket on the bottom of the crate to soak up any accidents and to keep him warm. Give him one or two safe toys.

Nose warning. If your dog has a short nose, don't fly him in cargo. Dogs with short noses, such as Bulldogs and Pugs, can have problems breathing.

Be careful with medications. Don't give your dog anything that will make him sleepy. These medicines can make him have breathing problems. Talk to your vet about other ways to keep your dog calm during the flight.

Driving

Most people drive when they travel with their dogs. Driving is a lot more flexible than flying. Plus, you get to keep your dog with you at all times. A doggy road trip can actually be a lot of fun. It will give your family a chance to get off the highways and on to the byways of America! If you ever wanted to stop at a petrified forest, a dinosaur museum, or a ghost town, here's your chance. How can your family say no when your dog has to go potty!?

Driving with your dog can also be a little hectic. You have to stop more than usual, and things can get a bit crowded. If your dog doesn't like riding in cars, a road trip can be downright horrible.

Q&A

Q. My dog pukes whenever he gets in the car. What can I do?

A. Lots of dogs get car sick. It is usually because they are nervous. If your dog doesn't go for a lot of car rides, he may think he is going to the vet every time he gets into a car. The best way to cure car sickness is to teach your dog that cars are fun. Get an adult to help you out with this.

First, coax your dog into the car with a treat. Give him the treat, and let him jump out. Do this until he jumps into the car on his own.

Second, drive one-half block. Give your dog a treat and drive home. Do this several times.

Third, drive for a block. Give your dog a treat and drive home. Do this several times.

Fourth, drive to the closest park. Let him play. Make sure he has lots of fun. Drive home. Do this as many times as it takes for your dog to start wagging his tail when he sees the car!

Finally, make sure to mix up the vet car rides with the fun car rides so your dog doesn't start getting scared again.

Sometimes a road trip is the trip itself. Dogs and road trips go together like burgers and fries. There have even been books written about taking road trips with dogs. Author John Steinbeck wrote a whole book, *Travels with Charley: In Search of America*, about taking a road trip with his Poodle, Charley.

Here are some good family rules to follow on a doggy road trip:

Buckle up. We buckle up ourselves, put babies in car seats, and worry about air bags deploying. Somehow, we always forget to think about our dogs. Your dog should always be in a crate or buckled in a doggy seat belt when in the car.

Driving is probably the easiest way to travel on a vacation with your dog.

Stop every two hours. Your dog needs a chance to do his business and stretch his legs, so stop every two hours or so. It's a good rule of thumb for humans, too!

Keep your dog on leash. Don't let your dog off leash even for a quick game of Frisbee. Gas stations and rest stops are bad places for an off-leash dog. There are lots of things to spook him. If he runs away, he could get hit by a car on a busy road or freeway or he could get hopelessly lost.

Avoid puppy potty areas. Doggy potty areas can be full of germs. Instead, let your dog poop on a grassy area. Be sure to always clean up after him.

Cover it. Bring a sheet or blanket to put over the car seat. That way you can clean off hair and dirt when you get where you are going. This will also make you and your dog more comfortable.

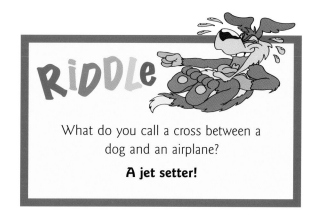

RiDDLe

What do you call a cross between a dog and an airplane?

A jet setter!

Bring plenty of water. Be sure to bring water and a portable bowl so your dog can get enough to drink on the road.

Don't overfeed. Give your dog about half of his regular meal before driving. This can help prevent tummy upset.

No Dogs Allowed!

Sometimes you won't be able to bring your dog on vacation. There are lots of options for dog care, including pet sitters and even doggy hotels.

This couple has quite a handful with four dogs to pet sit! A pet sitter can come to your home and care for your dog while you are on vacation.

Q. Is it OK to leave a dog in the car?

A. Never, ever leave your dog in a car on a hot day. Cars heat up very quickly. On a warm day, a car can reach 120 degrees in minutes. Dogs cool themselves by panting. Because panting won't work when there is only hot air to breathe, the dog's temperature rises, and he can die.

Be careful leaving your dog in a car on mild days. If the sun suddenly comes out, your dog can be in trouble. If you must leave him in the car on a mild day (under 70 degrees), make sure the car is parked in the shade. Unroll all the windows at least two inches. Don't leave him for more than a few minutes.

A Pug sits at an open car window.

You can hire a pet sitter who will come to your home, or you can take your dog to a kennel or even to a deluxe doggy hotel. You may also have friends or family who can watch your dog. To find good pet sitters and kennels, ask some dog experts for their advice. Your dog's veterinarian or groomer may have some ideas also. How about dog-owning neighbors and friends? Ask if they can recommend a good pet sitter or pet kennel.

Some dogs do better staying at home. Older, mellow dogs and dogs who don't get along with other dogs may feel stressed at a kennel. They would probably do better staying at home with a pet sitter checking in on them. However, some dogs get separation anxiety. That means that they get upset when they are left alone. Sometimes they become destructive and damage things. They may also hurt themselves by chewing or licking their paws excessively. These dogs will do better in a kennel or doggy hotel where they can be watched all the time.

A pet sitter is someone who is hired to come to your house to care for your dog. The sitter may just come to your house twice a day to feed and walk your pet. Easygoing dogs usually do fine with a pet sitter. There are also pet sitters who stay at your house. Older dogs who need to go potty a lot or dogs who like a lot of attention may do better with a pet sitter who stays with them.

You can also leave your dog at a kennel. There are boarding kennels and kennels at vet offices. Kennels make sure your dog has food and shelter while you are gone. If you have an older dog or a dog with medical problems, a vet's kennel may be best. Boarding kennels are fine for the average dog. However, they can be really noisy places, not great for very sensitive dogs.

Some lucky dogs get to have a vacation at the same time you do! These high-class hounds go to doggy hotels and pet spas, which are more like four-star resorts than your average dog kennels. Some of the things a doggy hotel may offer are extra walks and exercise, a swimming pool, one-on-one playtime with people, playtime with other dogs, special treats, mountain hikes, massages, and doggy movies. Some doggy hotels even have staff members who sleep with dogs who are afraid of the dark!

Doggy hotels are fun, but they're also expensive. They can cost more than $50 a night! That may be more than your hotel room costs. And doggy hotels not for every dog. A dog who doesn't like other dogs probably won't enjoy a doggy hotel.

A dog patiently waits for his family to return. Sometimes dogs aren't allowed in hotels, and you'll have to leave your dog at home. Find a responsible pet sitter who will make him feel comfortable while you're gone.

Chapter 20

Helping Dogs in Big and Small Ways

There are many ways to help dogs. You can help dogs every day by the decisions you make. Being kind to your dog and to the dogs around you helps dogs. Reporting people who don't treat their dogs well also helps dogs. You can volunteer to help dogs through an organization such as the Humane Society of the United States (HSUS) or through the Boy or Girl Scouts, 4-H, or your own school. You can raise money to help dogs or collect things that dogs at an animal shelter or veterinary hospital may need.

Another way to help dogs is to become a foster parent. Animal shelters and dog rescues need people to take care of dogs until they find homes. You can also be a foster parent for dogs who are being trained as service animals.

A boy and his puppy bond. Remember that helping dogs starts at home. Always treat your own dog with the love and respect she deserves.

This little girl is learning how to gently pet a dog. One of the best ways you can help dogs is by teaching younger kids the right way to treat a dog.

Everyday Ways to Help Dogs

Treating your own dog well is one of the best ways you can help dogs. Make sure she gets enough food, exercise, training, and tender loving care. This is good for her and sets a good example for other dog owners. When you walk your dog, people see you and want to walk their dogs, too. Show your friends how you care for your dog. This helps teach them to care for their own dogs. Does your class have show-and-tell? Ask your teacher if you can bring your dog to class. Tell your classmates about how you care for her.

Be a good example for how to treat other dogs. Always ask before petting a new dog. Don't run, jump, or scream around dogs. Speak up when other kids are teasing a dog. Kids usually tease dogs because they don't know any better. Help them learn that dogs have feelings.

Keep your eyes and ears open. If you see a dog who isn't getting enough food or water, doesn't have a good shelter, or is being hurt by someone, ask an adult to report it to your local animal control. If you see a dog who is wandering the streets or is in a dangerous situation, tell an adult.

Raise Money

Raising money is another way you can work to help dogs. Almost every organization that works on behalf of dogs needs money. You can be a real helper to this cause! Raise money on your own or as part of a group. Your local animal shelter probably has ideas for ways you can raise money.

Join in an animal shelter walkathon. Get people to sponsor you for every mile you walk. Volunteer to help run the walkathon. Sometimes shelters have "bath-a-thons," where they bathe community dogs for donations. Bring your own dog for a bath, or volunteer to help bathe other dogs. If

there's no walkathon or bath-a-thon for your shelter, maybe you can help start one.

Come up with your own ways to raise money. First, find a dog organization in your community that needs money. It may be an animal shelter, a rescue group, or an organization that works to fight animal cruelty. Some ways to raise money include having a bake sale, a car wash, a lemonade stand, or a garage sale. Talk to your family about doing it on your own or with a group of friends. Get your class or church group organized to help. Every little bit helps!

Some kids raise money for specific canine needs. In 1999, Stephanie Taylor, an 11-year-

Here is group of dogs and their people on a walkathon. You can help earn money for doggy causes by participating in a walkathon.

Start a Club

You can also start your own club to help dogs. Maybe you want a dog park in your town or want to help build a new animal shelter. Start a club to host fund-raising events. You can have car washes, collect recyclables, have a bake sale, maybe even have a dog-washing event. At your meetings, discuss ways to help dogs in your community. Find out what resources the different members have. Maybe someone has relatives who own a restaurant. Would they be willing to donate a percentage of a night's profits to your club? Then you can promote the event with flyers and posters.

To start your club, find an adult you trust to help you. Maybe there is a teacher at your school who loves dogs as much as you do. Would he or she be willing to help start the club? Are you a member of the Scouts or Bluebirds? Does your area have a 4-H chapter? All of these are good sources for finding interested adults.

Then, let other kids know about it. Make up flyers and distribute them at your school, community center, or church. Draw a colorful poster, and put it in your school lobby. Let teachers know about your club, and ask for their help. Pick a date, time, and place for your first meeting. Be sure to bring an agenda, a list of topics to cover. Let interested students know what to expect from the club.

You may want to work with an established organization. If there is an animal rescue organization or animal shelter in your town, maybe you can start a student chapter at your school. There are also national organizations that sponsor student clubs. One is Kids in Nature's Defense (KIND), a branch of the Humane Society of the United States (HSUS). KIND club chapters do many things to help all kinds of animals, including dogs. Visit http://www.kindnews.org to find out how you can start a club.

old girl from Oceanside, California, raised money to buy a bulletproof vest for a police dog named Tiko. Kids all over the country were inspired by her story, and they went on to do the same thing! Stephanie's organization, called Vest-A-Dog, is still working to buy vests for every police dog in the United States. You can help her raise the money she needs by visiting her Web site at http://www.vestadog.com.

You don't always have to raise money. Animal shelters and rescue groups need other things, too. Animal shelters need towels and blankets, food, pet beds, first aid supplies, and toys. Call a local shelter or rescue group, and ask what supplies it needs.

Start a food drive, a blanket drive, or a toy drive. To get the word out, make flyers and hand them out at your school, community center, church, and sports club. Put boxes at local stores, malls, churches, schools, and offices. That way, people can just drop the items off. Use your artistic skills to make the flyers and boxes colorful so they get peoples' attention. You may even want to make posters to put up. Ask an adult at your school, community center, or church to make an announcement about the drive. Be sure to have a deadline for donations! Finally, find someone with a big truck who can make the grand delivery!

A national group called Operation Santa Paws collects things for dogs and cats around the holidays. It will send you posters and flyers to help you set up a holiday animal drive. Visit http://www.santapaws.info.

Ask your parents if you can man a booth at a pet adoption fair. Maybe they'll even want to help!

Adult Alert!

Help support your children's volunteer work. Go with them to meet with a volunteer coordinator. Ask questions about work commitment, starting times, and how your children will be kept safe while they are volunteering with dogs.

Volunteer

There are lots of ways to volunteer to help dogs. Volunteering means working for free to help someone else. Volunteering can be a great way to do something good for dogs and for people. It is also a good way for you to learn skills that will prepare you for jobs in the future. Some volunteer work helps dogs, whereas other volunteer work helps dogs help people. You can volunteer to help dogs at an animal shelter or a veterinary hospital. Or you can help dogs help people by becoming a therapy dog handler.

Is there an animal shelter in your town? If so, this can be a great place to volunteer. Animal shelters need volunteers to clean out cages, walk dogs, train dogs, interview adopters, do office work, raise money, and play with dogs. Try to find an animal shelter that already has a volunteer program in place. A good volunteer program will help you figure out the best way to help and will train you in your volunteer job. Ask your vet or another dog professional you trust to recommend an animal shelter where you

Q. What is the difference between animal-assisted therapy dogs and animal-assisted activities dogs?

A. They are both therapy dogs, but they have different jobs. An animal-assisted therapy (AAT) dog is a dog who helps professional therapists do their job. An AAT dog may help a physical therapist teach people who have trouble with their hands to use their fingers again. For example, the patients can buckle and unbuckle the dog's collar or walk her. An AAT dog can also help therapists work with children learning to read. These are called "literacy dogs." It's their job to sit still and listen while a child reads aloud to them. An AAT dog needs special training.

An animal-assisted activities (AAA) dog has a more casual job, but that doesn't mean it's less important! An AAA dog visits people in nursing homes, hospitals, and other

Time for a hug break!

places. She may do tricks, or she may just visit to offer companionship. It's been proven that petting a dog can lower blood pressure and help people heal! Like AAT dogs, AAA dogs need to be trained in all their basic commands. They must be very friendly and not easily scared.

can volunteer. Call the animal shelter, and make an appointment to talk to a volunteer coordinator. Ask an adult to come with you.

The animal shelter will probably ask you what kind of work you would like to do. Be honest! If you want to work with the dogs directly, tell them. If you'd prefer to work in the office, tell them that. Ask them questions, too. How many hours per week do you have to work? Do you have to commit for a few months or even a year? What kind of work will you do? Will you have to clean out cages? Do you get to play with dogs? Will they teach you how to do the work you want to do?

Rescue the Rescuers!

The Barry Foundation is a nonprofit group that raises the St. Bernards famous for saving travelers in the Swiss Alps. The hospice of the Great St. Bernard Pass was unable to continue to raise the dogs, so the foundation took over. It is named for the most famous of the hospice's St. Bernards. Barry saved forty travelers during his career!

This is an historical photo of the hospice dogs.

Some veterinary hospitals use volunteers. Ask your own vet. Can you help care for orphaned animals? Maybe the clinic needs someone to take dogs for walks or to help care for newborn babies. If your vet doesn't use volunteers, maybe he knows a vet who does.

A child learns how to treat dogs. If you volunteer at an animal shelter, the staff will teach you how to work with the animals.

If you don't want to work with dogs but would rather work to help dogs in general, there are organizations such as the Humane Society of the United States (HSUS), the American Society for the Prevention of Cruelty to Animals (ASPCA), and the American Humane Association (AHA) that work to help dogs and other animals. They talk to people about how to treat dogs humanely. They work to pass laws to protect animals. Some of these organizations go to fairs and other events. They may also teach classes at schools and other places.

Call or e-mail a national organization to find out if there is anything you can do. Your local animal shelter may also do this kind of work. Call your local animal shelter to find out if it needs volunteers for local events. Some of the things you can do include working at a booth at a pet fair, helping out at adoption fairs, or handing out flyers at the mall or at your school.

Help Dogs Help People

Volunteering isn't just about helping dogs. You can also help dogs help people. Dogs do a lot of important work. They help blind people and deaf people. They help people in wheelchairs. Some dogs search for missing people. Other dogs work to cheer up people who are sick or are unhappy.

Service dogs are dogs who help people with physical, mental, or emotional disabilities. You can help service dogs get ready for their work! Before these dogs learn how to help people, they must learn to be good citizens. That means they need to learn manners such as getting along with other dogs, not chasing cats, and meeting new people nicely. They also need to get used to loud noises and scary situations. A service dog must be able to ride a bus, go to a movie, go to a parade, walk down a busy street, and go to a store. She can't be afraid of any of these things. That's where volunteers come in.

Foster families raise service dogs until they are about a year and a half old. If it's OK with your family, you can volunteer to foster and train a service dog. The cool thing about training a service dog is that you can take your dog everywhere you go. That means she can come to the movies, out for dinner, on the bus, maybe even to school with you! The bad thing

It's hard to imagine that this little puppy will one day be responsible for helping a person live a better life. Puppies can do it with your help!

about fostering a service dog is that she will have to leave you to begin her real work. Giving up the dog you've cared for is really hard, but foster families say it's worth it to give a great dog to a person in need. There are several organizations that will place foster dogs with kids under eighteen, as long as their guardian agrees. Canine Companions for Independence is an organization that trains dogs to help people with physical mobility problems, and kids can help their parents foster dogs. Guide Dogs

Here is a girl and her therapy dogs on a visit. Being a therapy dog handler gives you the chance to meet many different kinds of people.

neat for both of you. Your dog may make a good therapy dog if she is very gentle and loves to meet new people of every shape and size. Before beginning therapy dog training, your dog should follow your directions and know all her basic commands. After passing the therapy dog test, you can join a local therapy dog group. Many of these groups require additional training.

To become a therapy dog handler, contact the Delta Society (http://www.delta society.org) or Therapy Dogs International (http://www.tdi-dog.org). They can help you find a therapy dog group in your area. Some therapy dog groups may require that an adult work with you.

Be a Foster Parent

Shelters and rescue groups need people to take care of dogs until their forever homes are found. Animal shelters use foster homes for

for the Blind encourage kids to help raise dogs. Visit these organizations at their Web sites at http://www.caninecompanions.org and http://www.guidedogs.com.

You can also volunteer to be a therapy dog handler. Therapy dogs visit people in hospitals and nursing homes. Sometimes they are used to help people who have been through very hard times. After September 11, therapy dogs helped the victims' families.

Training your dog to be a therapy dog can be really

Is there a shortage of foster homes in your area? Your local shelter or rescue group can give you information on fostering dogs.

A young pup finds a friendly lap. Sometimes puppies need foster homes. Your family can help care for a litter until the pups are ready for their forever homes.

puppies who need special care. They also may need foster homes for dogs who get scared when they're in kennels.

To foster a dog, you must be able to take care of her. This affects your whole family, so make sure everyone is on board. If you have any pets, they must like other dogs. The hard part of fostering a dog is that you have to give her up. But you will know she is going to a good, loving home—with your help! If you want to be a foster parent, call your local animal shelter or a local rescue group.

Every family should have a plan in case of an emergency. Include your dog in your family plan. Where will she go in case of an emergency? Who is responsible for getting her out if the house is on fire or flooded? Where is the closest animal shelter? Sit down with your entire family, and work out a plan. Visit http://www.fema.gov for guidance.

Help Dogs in Disasters

Sometimes disasters such as wildfires, tornadoes, hurricanes, or earthquakes happen. You have probably talked about what to do if something like this happens. Your family may have a plan to follow in such an emergency. You know there are things you can do to keep your family safe when a disaster strikes, but what about your pets? How can you help them?

The most important thing you can do is to be prepared. What does that mean? Just as you have an evacuation plan and disaster kit for your family, you should have one for your dog. See the Doggy Disaster Kit box below for some items to put in your dog's disaster kit.

Doggy Disaster Kit

Every family needs a doggy disaster kit next to its own disaster kit. Here are some of the important items that should be in it:

- Blanket
- Can opener for wet food
- Contact information for local and out-of-area animal shelters
- Crate
- Current photo of your pet
- Dry or wet dog food (enough for one week)
- Extra flat collar in case the collar your dog is wearing gets lost
- Extra ID tags
- First aid kit (a list of all the important items that should be included in this kit can be found on page 252)
- Medication and vaccine records in a waterproof container

- Name and contact information for an out-of-area person who can take your animal in case of a disaster
- Name and contact information for out-of-area hotels or motels that accept pets
- Plastic bags
- Sturdy leash
- Toys
- Training or Elizabethan collar
- Treats
- Veterinarian name and contact information
- Water and food bowls
- Water in plastic bottles (a gallon per day for each dog)

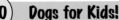

Q. **What is a microchip, and why does my dog need one?**

A. A microchip is a very small computer chip that contains a number. It is about the size of a grain of rice. The microchip is inserted between a dog's shoulder blades. Once your dog is microchipped, you register the number with a national database. The database records your dog's microchip number along with your contact information. If your dog is lost, someone at a vet clinic or an animal shelter can use a special scanner to find her number. Then that person can call the database, which will match the number with your dog's information. Your dog will be home in no time!

The problem with microchips is that more than one company makes them. Not all scanners can read all microchips. Talk to your vet about the right microchip for your dog.

Put your dog's disaster kit with your family's disaster kit. They should be in a safe place that is easy to get to. Your disaster kit should have everything you need to care for your dog for one week. It should also include things to take with you if you need to leave your house. Most Red Cross shelters do not accept pets. Where will you take your dog if you have to evacuate? Talk to a family friend or a relative who lives outside of your area. Find out if you could bring your dog there if necessary. Keep this person's contact information in your disaster kit. Keep a list of pet-friendly motels and hotels as well.

Do not leave your dog in your home if you must evacuate. Dogs left in their homes often do not survive disasters. Sometimes dogs get lost during disasters. If you can't take your dog with you, take her to a local animal shelter. If you absolutely have no other choice but to leave your dog, do what you can to make her safe. Give her lots of food and water. Put a sign outside your home saying there are pets inside. Again, don't depend on rescuers to save your dog. Take her with you!

Chapter 21

Working with Dogs

What do you dream of doing when you grow up? Do you want to be a firefighter, a doctor, an astronaut, or a teacher? Maybe you want to work with dogs. But what kind of jobs can you do with a dog?

Actually, there are hundreds of ways to work with dogs. Some of them are hands-on jobs, working with dogs day in and day out. In other jobs, you work to help dogs. Some people work with a lot of different dogs, other people

If you want to be a dog photographer when you grow up, you can start now by helping a dog photographer do his or her work, as shown here.

You can help your children prepare for a career with animals. Encourage them to sign up for appropriate science classes or even for a science camp during the summer. A love of science and a strong background in biology and chemistry will be a big help if they opt for a career in veterinary medicine.

Take them to the library, and help them check out books on animals. Give them a dog magazine subscription or a dog book on their next birthday. Visit the natural history museum, and look at the exhibits on canids.

Bring your children along when taking your dog to training classes, vet visits, and grooming appointments. This will give them a taste of what these jobs are like. If they want to volunteer with a local organization, help them talk to the right people.

Even if they ultimately decide on another career, this preparation will serve them well in many other vocations, as well as in a lifelong love of animals!

work with just one dog. You can sell products for dogs, invent toys for dogs, or even take pictures of dogs. These are all real jobs!

If you want a career with dogs, start preparing now. Taking the right classes in school will help you get ready for that dream job. You can volunteer to work with dogs, and you can read books and talk to people who work with dogs. Following are just some of the careers you can have with dogs.

This vet clearly enjoys her job. Becoming a veterinarian is a lot of work, but it is also very rewarding.

Veterinarian

When you think about a career with dogs, being a veterinarian is probably the first job that pops into your head. You may have already read some books about being a veterinarian. One famous series of books, starting with *All Creatures Great and Small*, is by James Herriott. James Herriott was a veterinarian who practiced in northern England. By reading his books, you can find out a lot about the life of a country vet. A country vet works with large and small

Search and rescue dogs like this one enjoy their work.

Search and Rescue

Dogs are used to find and save people when buildings collapse because of earthquakes, tornadoes, bombs, and other disasters. Dogs are also used to find people who get lost. Sometimes, people get lost when they are hiking. Other times, people get confused and become lost in their own neighborhoods.

There are search and rescue dogs who look for people who are caught in avalanches and are buried under the snow. Some search and rescue dogs look for people who have drowned. Sometimes a search and rescue dog is looking for a missing person who has already died. This is important so that the family of the person can bury the body and say their good-byes.

Some of the people who work with search and rescue dogs are professional emergency workers such as firefighters and ski patrollers. Most are volunteers who are not paid for their work. They do it because they love working with dogs and helping people.

You have to be eighteen to actually do search and rescue, but you can start training your dog now. You can also help search and rescue dog clubs raise money and run training sessions. You can even help out by playing a "victim." That means that you hide while a dog finds you!

animals such as horses, cows, dogs, and cats. Most vets, however, work in clinics in cities and suburbs. They work with dogs and cats as well as birds, rodents, reptiles, and even fish!

Being a vet is a hard job with long hours. It is also hard to become a vet. You must first do very well in high school and take lots of math and science classes. Then you must do well in college. In college, you will begin your courses for veterinary medicine and take science and premed classes. Once you finish college, you must apply for a veterinary college. There are fewer than thirty vet schools in the United States, so they are very hard to get into. Once you get in, you go to vet school for four years. Your education doesn't stop there. You then must do a year-long internship with another veterinarian. Finally, you must take a test in the state where you want to practice as a vet. Most states also make you stay up to date with new medical information—that means even more school!

Start preparing to be a vet now by learning as much about animals as possible. Go to the library and ask to see books about animals and animal care. It's also good to get lots of

School work is important for a career with dogs.

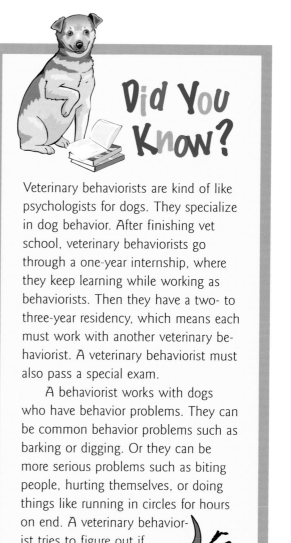

Did You Know?

Veterinary behaviorists are kind of like psychologists for dogs. They specialize in dog behavior. After finishing vet school, veterinary behaviorists go through a one-year internship, where they keep learning while working as behaviorists. Then they have a two- to three-year residency, which means each must work with another veterinary behaviorist. A veterinary behaviorist must also pass a special exam.

A behaviorist works with dogs who have behavior problems. They can be common behavior problems such as barking or digging. Or they can be more serious problems such as biting people, hurting themselves, or doing things like running in circles for hours on end. A veterinary behaviorist tries to figure out if the problems need medication or training or both.

hands-on experience with animals. Volunteer at a local animal shelter or veterinary hospital.

Being a vet is a labor of love. Good vets are kind and gentle. A good vet gets along well with animals but also gets along well with people. Being a vet can be fun. You get to meet many different animals during your day. It can also be sad.

Q. What if I want to work with dogs, but I don't want to do it for a job?

A. There are lots of great ways to work with dogs as a volunteer. You can volunteer at an animal shelter, at an animal welfare organization, or for a vet. You can be a foster parent to a dog. You can train dogs to work with people with disabilities. You can train your dog to be a therapy dog and take him to visit people in hospitals and nursing homes. There are dozens of ways to volunteer with dogs.

Vets must see animals die and sometimes need to put sick and elderly animals to sleep. Vets treat diseases and injuries, vaccinate animals, prescribe medication, and perform surgery. They also give advice about dog health, behavior, and daily care.

Some veterinarians specialize in one area of medicine. There are vets who work only with dogs who have cancers and vets who only do surgery. To become a specialist, you must become board certified. That means you will need additional education after you have become a veterinarian.

Veterinary Technician

If you want to work in a vet office but don't think you want to go through all the schooling required to be a vet, think about becoming a veterinary technician, or vet tech. A vet tech is much like a nurse for animals. Vet techs take care of sick and injured animals, draw blood, and do lab tests. They even help vets during surgery. The great thing about being a vet tech is that you get to work closely with animals. The hard thing is that you will see animals die and may have to help put sick or old animals to sleep.

Vet techs must be good in math and science. They must also get along with animals and people. You can start to prepare for a job as a vet tech now by taking math and science classes at school. You also need hands-on experience with animals. Volunteer at a local animal shelter or animal hospital. To become a vet tech, you must complete a two-year veterinary technician program. Vet tech programs are usually offered through technical colleges. Some states also make you take a test before you can work as a vet tech.

Veterinary hospitals also need veterinary assistants. These are the people at an animal hospital who take care of the animals' daily needs. They clean cages, feed animals, and walk dogs. They may work in the front of the of-

Veterinary technicians must like to work with both animals and people.

Dog Trainers

There are two dog trainer associations, the National Association of Dog Obedience Instructors (NADOI) and the Association of Pet Dog Trainers (APDT). Neither of these organizations have certification programs. There is only one organization that provides certification for pet dog trainers in the United States, the Certification Council for Pet Dog Trainers (CCPDT). The NADOI and the APDT host conferences where trainers can learn new techniques for dog training.

fice, greeting customers and checking animals in. They may also help the vet techs with their work.

Trainer

Being a dog trainer is a pretty neat job! You get to work one-on-one with dogs, and you also get to teach classes. To be a trainer, you must be very good with dogs. You must also be very good with people. In a lot of ways, training dogs is mostly about training their people.

You don't need a special degree or license to be a dog trainer. Most trainers work with another trainer to learn their craft. They may also have taken college courses in animal behavior and psychology as well as veterinary science. They keep learning about dog training through classes taught by other train-

A trainer puts her dog through his paces. Some trainers teach dogs how to act in movies and on TV.

ers. A lot of trainers start out as volunteers. They help train dogs at animal shelters and other places.

If you want to be a dog trainer when you grow up, there is a lot you can do now. The best way to learn about dog behavior is to spend time with dogs. Spend time every day training and playing with your dog. Take a class with him. Get involved in agility or Flyball. Learn about other dogs by volunteering at a local animal shelter. Your local animal shelter may even have a program for kids to help train dogs. In your spare time, read books about dogs and dog training. Try to find a mentor, a person who helps guide you and teaches you about a job. A local trainer may be willing to let you help with dog training classes.

Animal Shelter Worker

Being an animal shelter worker is a hard job. It can be very sad, and it doesn't pay much, but it is also a rewarding job because you get to help save animals' lives.

There are many jobs at animal shelters. In some jobs, you work with the dogs and the other animals at the shelter. These jobs include animal caretakers; veterinarians, vet techs, and vet assistants; and animal control officers. In other jobs, you work mostly with people. Some jobs help run the shelter. These include secretaries, marketing people, and managers. There are also adoption workers. These are the people who help match shelter dogs and cats to their new owners. At some shelters, adoption workers are volunteers.

There are two types of animal shelters—public shelters and private shelters. Public shelters are run by the city or the county. Private shelters are run by nonprofit organizations (organizations that don't make money from their work). Some nonprofit shelters work together with cities or counties to house stray dogs.

If you want to work at an animal shelter, volunteer as

This is an animal control officer. It's a hard job, but most officers do it because they want to save lives.

soon as you can! Many shelters have a minimum age requirement for volunteers, so check first. Some have special youth volunteer programs that you can enroll in with an adult. Most people who work at animal shelters start as unpaid volunteers. You may start out just cleaning kennels and end up running the whole shelter. Most shelters have lots of ways for kids to volunteer. You may even help walk or train dogs.

Q&A

Q. What's the best way to get ready for a job with dogs now?

A. Study hard in school, and spend lots and lots of time with dogs. Most jobs with dogs require you get a college degree. Some even require a master's degree or a veterinary degree. Doing well in school now will make this possible. Read as much as you can about dogs as well. There are lots of great dog books and dog magazines.

Take care of your own dog. Help give him medicines. Walk him, train him, and feed him. Take him places where he'll get to meet lots of other dogs. Volunteer at your local vet or animal shelter. Start a dog-walking business in your neighborhood. Whenever you get a chance to spend time with dogs, do it!

Animal Cop

If you've seen *Animal Precinct* or *Animal Cops* on Animal Planet on TV, you know some of what an animal cop does. But a lot of the work is less exciting than what you see on TV. Animal cops are called animal control officers or humane law enforcement officers. Their work is hard and sometimes dangerous. They have to work with aggressive animals and aggressive people! Sometimes they have to put healthy animals to sleep. They must pick up dead animals from roads, but they also get to save the lives of many animals.

Animal cops may work for public or nonprofit animal shelters. They wear uniforms and represent the animal shelter to the community. They work to protect people from animals and animals from people. They help dogs and other animals when they are injured, and they pick up stray animals. Sometimes they arrest people who abuse or neglect their animals.

To become a humane law enforcement officer, you can start now. Volunteer with an animal shelter. Ask if you can do what is called a ride-along with an animal cop. To find out if this is really the job for you, ride with an animal cop for a day. In school, take classes in social studies, law, and animal science. Later, you may take college classes in law, criminology, and animal science.

If you love dogs, a career with dogs may be just right for you.

Some animal cops start out as police officers or in the military. An animal cop must love animals, be very patient, and be able to handle a lot of tough situations.

Animal Advocate and Humane Educator

Some dog lovers don't work with animals. Instead, they work to save animals. These people are called animal advocates. They tell the public about problems that animals have. An animal advocate may work on spay and neuter laws and laws to end animal abuse. Animal advocates try to get politicians to sign laws to protect animals. They may go to local fairs or pet events to talk about these issues and make people aware of them.

There are also people who teach the public, especially kids, about caring for animals. They are called humane educators. Humane educators go to local schools and teach classes on caring for companion animals, such as dogs, cats, reptiles, birds, and even rabbits. They help kids care for the animals in their homes and neighborhoods.

Animal advocates and humane educators work for national groups such as the Humane Society of the United States (HSUS) and the American Society for the Prevention of Cruelty to Animals (ASPCA). They also work for local animal shelters and other animal groups.

To do this work, you will probably need to go to college. Most people who do this work have an Associate of Arts (AA) or a Bachelor of Arts (BA) degree. Some may have teaching credentials or a Master of Arts (MA) degree. All have a love of animals and want to help them.

To get ready for a job like this, you can start by doing well in English and social studies classes. And, of course, volunteer! You can work at a shelter walking dogs or cleaning cages, or you can help out with office work. Help send out fund-raising letters, work the booth at a pet fair, or help organize a dog walkathon in your town. You can even start a club to work on dog issues that you think are important. For example, you can work to convince people to spay and neuter their dogs. You may

This teenager is learning to be a groomer.

clients to see if there are any changes since they were last groomed. They note any new bumps or lumps they find.

Being a dog groomer isn't easy, though. Dog groomers work long hours. They have to deal with some of the icky sides of the dog world—anal glands, dirty hair, and some serious doggy odor! Some of their clients don't always have the best manners, either.

A groomer must love dogs and also like people. You don't need a degree to be a groomer. Most groomers learn their craft from other groomers. If you think you may want to be a groomer, you can start now. Help your family groom your dog. As you get better at it, take over the whole job. Ask a local groomer if you can help out. When you are older, apply for a job as an assistant at a grooming shop. This can be a good weekend or summer job once you are in high school.

start a club to work on stricter animal abuse laws. Find out what the age limit is to volunteer at your shelter. Talk to a parent or a teacher about helping you start a club. There are a lot of things kids can do!

Groomer

Dog grooming is a big business. Dog groomers get to work with dogs every day, making them look beautiful! They brush their teeth and clip their nails. Good groomers check their doggy

Many dogs, such as this Pekingese, need regular professional grooming.

Artist

Did you know there are people who make doggy art? There are dog writers, dog artists, dog photographers, and dog editors. These people use their art to celebrate the wonderful world of canines!

To be a dog artist or writer, you must first love dogs. Then, you must love your art. Most dog writers, artists, and photographers work on their art for many years before they work with animals. They may go to college or art school to learn more about their craft. In their free time, they practice a lot.

An artist's work is on display. Some artists specialize in paintings of dogs.

Most dog artists and writers work for themselves. Some writers, editors, photographers, and illustrators work for magazines or book publishers. Some of the better-known dog magazines in the United States are *Dog Fancy, Dog World,* and *Bark.* There are many books about dogs published each year. Some provide information on caring for dogs, others are stories about dogs.

Dog artists must be good with dogs because they usually have to spend a lot of time with them. Some dog writers and editors go to dog shows and animal industry conventions to get ideas. Dog artists and dog photographers must be comfortable meeting many types of dogs. They must also be good with people. Dog writers must also love to talk to people about their dogs!

If you want to be a dog artist or writer, there are many things you can do now. First, practice your craft. If you want to paint, take lessons and practice every day. If you want to write, take English classes, and keep a journal or write short stories about dogs. Plan to go to college and major in English or the visual arts. At the same time, keep learning about dogs. Read books and magazines about dogs. Spend time with your own dog. Make new dog friends by volunteering at a shelter. Make a point of meeting people who have dogs. Being able to talk to people about their dogs may be a great help in your future career!

Police officers who work with dogs, such as this one, place their lives in their dogs' paws.

Canine Caretaker

If you really just want to work with dogs day in and day out, consider becoming a canine caretaker. Dog kennels and pet spas need people to walk and play with dogs, to give doggy massages, and to generally make dogs happy. It's a fun job because you get to hang out with dogs all day long! The downside is that you spend a lot of time cleaning up after dogs— mucking out of a lot of cages and scooping a lot of poop.

You can work as a dog walker or as a dog sitter. These are usually one-person businesses and are great jobs for dog lovers who want flexible schedules. You won't get rich, but you'll probably have a lot of fun. A dog walker may just walk dogs. She may also feed the dogs and other family animals, give medications, and clean up after the dogs. A dog sitter may stay overnight when a family is away as well as water the plants and pick up mail.

To become a canine caretaker, get to know dogs—big dogs, little dogs, fast dogs, slow dogs, old dogs, and young dogs. The more dogs you know and the more comfortable you are with them, the better canine caretaker you will be. This is one doggy job you can even start now with help from an adult. Do you have neighbors who go out of town? Offer to walk and feed their dogs while they're gone. Ask for a small payment. As you get more experience, you can raise your rate. In a couple of years, apply for a job at a kennel or a doggy spa. This can be a fun job during the summer.

Dog Handler

Some people work with dogs as part of their jobs. Some police officers have doggy partners. Their dogs help them find and capture people breaking the law and look for people who are missing. Police dogs may sniff out illegal things like drugs and guns.

Police dog handlers must first become police officers. Most police officers have a two- or four-year college degree. They must go through police officer training and take tests. Once you become a police officer, you must do an excellent job. Then you may get the chance to become a police dog handler.

There are other jobs where dogs and humans are partners. Under the Department of

This handler works with Beagles who sniff out illegal food brought with tourists on airplanes.

Homeland Security (DHS), U.S. Customs and Border Patrol uses dogs to search people crossing the border into the United States for drugs and explosives. People called canine enforcement officers (CEOs) train and handle these special sniffer dogs. Most CEOs have a four-year college degree. They may have worked as police officers or have been in the military. Once they are hired by DHS, they have to go through fifteen weeks of training.

The DHS also uses dogs to search for food. Some fruits, vegetables, and meat products from other countries carry germs that can affect the food we grow in the United States. These dogs search passengers when they get off airplanes, and they search cars crossing the border into the United States from Mexico and Canada. The people who work with these dogs are called Plant Protection and Quarantine (PPQ) canine officers. PPQ officers also work with a special group of dogs called the Beagle Brigade made up of, you guessed it, Beagles! The Beagle Brigade works in air- and sea ports and at border crossings into the United States, sniffing out illegal food items.

If you're interested in a job as PPQ officer, it's important to work hard in school. Good grades and a degree are very important. PPQ officers must have a four-year degree in science or agriculture. Many PPQ officers also take extra classes after college. Once hired by the DHS, they have nine weeks of officer training and ten weeks of dog training (training to train dogs!). A background with dogs also helps. A love of dogs is a

RIDDLE

What do you call a canine scientist?
A Lab-rador!

must! After all, you are working with a dog eight hours a day, seven days a week! Customs and PPQ dogs do not live with their handlers. However, when the dogs retire, their handlers usually bring them home to live with them.

There are also people who handle show dogs. These people usually train, groom, and care for the dogs when they are not in the show ring and show the dogs when they are. There are also handlers who only show dogs in the ring. A show dog handler is someone who is able to make a dog look as good as possible in front of the judges. If you are interested in becoming a handler, start showing

Dog Walker

You've found your first dog walking customer! Here is a sample list of information to get from the doggy parents:

- Owner's contact info, emergency number
- Dog's name, breed, age
- Dog's personality
- Date and time you're needed
- How many times a day you are expected to walk the dog
- What to do in case of an emergency

- What to feed the dog and how many times a day to feed him
- Whether the dog takes any medication
- Your fee
- Where stuff is—food, leash, poop bags, treats, water bowl
- How to get into the house

Maybe you can work at a doggy toy company, inventing new toys such as this dog's stuffed ducky.

dogs now! Get involved in junior handlers through the AKC or 4-H.

Barking Businesses

Some of the other jobs in the doggy world include dog toy inventor, dog food salesperson, and dog food baker. Many businesses now cater to dogs and their people. Big stores such as Petco and PetSmart need salespeople and managers. Companies that sell products such as dog food, dog toys, and dog beds need managers, salespeople, and public relations people. Small dog businesses such as dog bakeries and dog boutiques need bak-

ers and managers. Maybe you can start a business yourself.

The love of dogs is what ties all these jobs together. You'll find that people who work for dog-related companies love all things canine. Some dog product companies even let their employees bring their dogs to work. That's a real perk!

Very few people get rich working with dogs. If you want to live in a mansion when you grow up, working in the dog business is probably not the job for you! But if you love dogs and want to work with them or work to help them, it can be the best job ever.

As much work as dogs are, they are even more fun. Once you have experienced life with a dog, you'll never want to live without one. Enjoy your dog! Teach her, play with her, love her, and guide her. Try to be the best dog companion you can be. She'll reward you in a million ways. You'll remember your first dog the rest of your life, and you'll never know another dog like her.

Breed Pronunciation Guide

Affenpinscher (AFF-un-pin-shur)
Afghan Hound (AFF-gan hound)
Airedale Terrier (AIR-dale terrier)
Akita (ah-KEE-tah)
Alaskan Malamute (Alaskan MAL-uh-myoot)
Anatolian Shepherd Dog
   (an-ah-TOLL-ee-yun shepherd dog)
Appenzeller (APP-un-zell-er)
Basenji (buh-SEN-gee)
Beauceron (BO-sir-on)
Belgian Laekenois (BELL-juhn LA-kin-wa)
Belgian Malinois (BELL-juhn MA-lin-wa)
Belgian Turveren (BELL-juhn tur-VUR-en)
Bernese Mountain Dog (bur-NEEZ mountain dog)
Bichon Frise (BEE-shawn freez or fri-zay)
Borzoi (BORE-zoy)
Bouvier des Flandres (BOO-vee-yay day FLAN-durz)
Briard (BREE-yard)
Brittany (BRIT-uh-nee)
Brussels Griffon (BRUSS-sells GRIFF-on)
Bullmastiff (bull-MASS-tiff)
Cairn Terrier (KAY-rn terrier)
Canaan Dog (KAY-nun dog)
Cardigan Welsh Corgi (Kar-duh-gun welsh KOR-ghee)
Cavalier King Charles Spaniel (kav-uh-LEER king charles
   spaniel)
Chesapeake Bay Retriever (CHESS-uh-peek bay retriever)
Chihuahua (chi-WA-wa)
Chinese Shar-Pei (Chinese shar-PAY)
Dachshund (DOX-hoont or hoond)
Doberman Pinscher (DOH-ber-man PIN-shur)
Entlebucher (ENT-lay-boo-cur)
German Pinscher (german PIN-shur)
Giant Schnauzer (giant sh-NOW-shur)
Glen of Imaal Terrier (glen of EE-mahl terrier)
Great Pyrenees (great PEER-uh-neez)

Harrier (HAIR-ee-ur)
Havanese (HAH-vuh-neez)
Ibizan Hound (ih-BEE-zun)
Keeshond (KAYZ-hawnd)
Komondor (KAH-mon-dore)
Kuvasz (KOO-vahz)
Lhasa Apso (LAH-sah AHP-so)
Löwchen (LEUV-chun)
Maltese (mahl-TEEZ)
Mastiff (MASS-tiff)
Newfoundland (noo-fun-LUND or -LAND)
Nova Scotia Duck Tolling Retriever
   (NO-vah SKO-sha duck TOLE-ing retriever)
Papillon (PAPPY-yawn)
Pekingese (PEEK-in-eez)
Petit Basset Griffon Vendéen
   (Puh-TEE Bah-SAY Gree-FOHN VON-day-uhn—
   or PVBG, for short!)
Pharaoh Hound (FARE-oh hound)
Pomeranian (pom-er-AY-nee-un)
Puli (POO-lee)
Pumi (POO-mee)
Rhodesian Ridgeback (Ro-DEE-szuhn ridgeback)
Rottweiler (ROTT-why-ler)
Saint Bernard (saint ber-NARD)
Saluki (sah-LOO-kee)
Samoyed (SAM-oh-yed or SAM-uh-yed)
Schipperke (SKIP-er-kee)
Sealyham Terrier (SEE-lee-ham terrier)
Shiba Inu (SHEE-bah INN-you)
Shih Tzu (SHEET-soo)
Spinone Italiano (spih-NO-nee or spuh-NO-nay ee-tahl-
   ee-AH-no)
Swedish Vallhund (Swedish VAHL-hoond)
Vizsla (VEESH-lah)
Weimaraner (VIE-mer-on-er or WHY-mer-on-er)

Glossary

Here is a list of terms you may be unfamiliar with that appear in the book.

The descriptions of coat colors and ear and tail types are in the charts on pages 60–61.

abscess: an infected pocket under the skin that is filled with pus

agility: a dog sport in which dogs and handlers run an obstacle course

AKC: American Kennel Club, the nation's largest dog registry

allergy: a body's overreaction to something that is not harmful to most people (such as dog and cat dander)

aggressive: a dog who acts as though he will, or actually will, bite or attack

alter: spay or neuter

anal glands: glands located on either side of a dog's anus

ancestors: a dog's family history

ASPCA: American Society for the Prevention of Cruelty to Animals, the nation's oldest animal welfare group

assistance dog: a dog who helps a human with physical, mental, or emotional problems

breed: the type of dog; also to mate two dogs to have puppies

breeder: a person who breeds dogs

breed registry: an organization, such as the AKC, that keeps a record of purebred dogs

breed standard: a description of the way the ideal dog of a breed should look and act

canid: a member of the Canidae family, which includes dogs, wolves, and coyotes

canine: doglike

canine disc: competitive Frisbee for dogs

canine freestyle: a doggy sport in which dogs move and perform dancelike moves to music

carting: a doggy activity in which dogs pull carts

cataract: a clouding of the lens of the eye, usually due to age

cattle driver/drover: a dog who moves cattle from one place to another

clicker: a training tool that makes a clicking noise

coat: a dog's hair or fur

companion dog: a dog who is a pet; also an AKC category

competition: a game or sport that is played against other dogs and people with the goal of winning

conformation: a category in which dogs compete against other dogs to see which is closest to the breed ideal; see *dog show*

congenital: something a dog is born with

Glossary

coprophagia: eating poop

crop: to surgically change a dog's ears so they will stand up

cyst: a pocket under the skin that is filled with fluid

dam: a mama dog

dander: tiny hair and skin scales (often the cause of pet allergies)

dehydrated: a loss of water or body fluids; a condition that results when an animal (or person) doesn't get enough water

designer dog: a term used to describe mixed breed dogs that are bred on purpose

dew claw: a fifth claw that is located on the inside ankle of a dog's front legs

deworm: to use medicine to flush out parasites living in a dog's digestive system

dingo: a wild dog that lives in Australia

dock: to surgically shorten a dog's tail

dog show: a conformation event

dogsledding: a sport in which dogs pull a sled

domesticated: a description of an animal that depends on humans to survive

dominant: a dog that is, or acts as if he is, the boss of other dogs

double coat: a coat type with both an outer coat and an undercoat

drafting: a doggy sport in which dogs compete to see which dog can pull the most weight

fancier: a person who is interested in a particular breed of dog

feral: a description of an animal that was once domesticated but no longer lives with people

field trial: a doggy sport in which dogs compete against other dogs to see which have the best hunting skills

fix: see *alter*

Flyball: a doggy sport in which dogs run, jump over hurdles, and catch a ball in a relay race

freestyle: see *canine freestyle*

genetic disease: a disease or condition that is passed down from the parents

guide dog: a dog who helps a person who has problems seeing

gun dog: a term for dogs who were originally bred to help hunters

handler: a person who works with a dog to get a job done, such as a police dog handler

hemolytic anemia: anemia (low red blood cell count) caused by the destruction of red blood cells

herder: a dog who herds, or moves, livestock

hereditary: something that is passed down from the parents

hound: a dog who is part of the AKC hound group; a general term for a dog

Glossary

HSUS: the Humane Society of the United States, one of the nation's largest animal welfare groups

hunt test: a doggy sport in which a dog tries to prove his hunting skills

junior handler: a kid who participates in doggy sports

K9: common slang for a dog

kibble: dry commercial dog food

lenticular sclerosis: a condition in which an older dog's eyes look blue and cloudy but sight is not affected

littermate: a dog's sibling from the same pregnancy

livestock guardian: a dog who guards livestock

lure coursing: a doggy sport in which dogs, usually sighthounds, race against one another while chasing a fake rabbit

malnourished: a condition that results when an animal (or person) doesn't get enough of the right food to eat

mixed breed: a dog whose parents are more than one breed

mucus: snot

musher: the person who drives a dogsled

neuter: to surgically alter a male dog so he cannot reproduce

nurse: to drink milk from the mother

obese: very overweight

olfactory: relating to smell

outer coat: the outer layer of fur of a dog's coat (the part of a double-coated dog's fur that we see)

parasite: a bug that lives in or on a dog

pit bull: a group of pit bull–type dogs that have similar backgrounds and looks, including the American Pit Bull Terrier, the American Staffordshire Terrier, the Staffordshire Bull Terrier, and mixes of these breeds

protective: referring to dogs who will act aggressively when their people or homes are threatened

random bred: a dog who is of more than one breed

ratters: dogs who were originally bred to hunt and kill rats on farms and in homes

retina: the tissue at the back of the eye that focuses light

saliva: spit

scenthound: a dog originally bred to hunt by smell

schutzhund: a German doggy sport that tests a dog's working skills

show dog: a dog who competes in dog shows

sighthound: a dog originally bred to hunt by sight

single coat: a coat type having only an outer coat

sire: a doggy dad

skijoring: a doggy sport in which dogs pull cross-country skiers

socialization: the process of introducing dogs to scary situations

spay: to surgically alter a female dog so she cannot have puppies

standard: see *breed standard*

submissive: referring to a dog who lets other dogs (or people) be the boss

tapetum lucidum: tissue in dogs' (and cats') eyes that reflects light onto the retina to help the animals see at night

terrier: a group of dogs first bred in Great Britain to hunt small animals such as rats

toy dog: a group of dogs bred to be small companion dogs

tracking: a doggy sport in which dogs try to find a person or thing by smell

tumor: a lump in the skin

undercoat: the fuzzy soft hair that grows close to the skin in double-coated dogs

vaccine: a small amount of a virus that is given to help dogs fight off the real virus

watchdogs: usually refers to dogs who will bark when strangers come near their houses or people

whelp: to give birth to puppies

working dog: a dog who has a job; also an AKC group

Recommended Readings

Books

Books for Learning More

American Kennel Club. *The Complete Dog Book for Kids.* Howell Book House, 1996.

Choron, Sandra, and Choron, Harry. *Planet Dog: A Doglopedia.* Houghton Mifflin, 2005.

Coren, Stanley. *Why Do Dogs Have Wet Noses?* Kids Can Press, Ltd., 2006.

Crisp, Marty. *Everything Dog: What Kids Really Want to Know About Dogs.* Northwood Press, 2003.

Evans, Mark. *Puppy: A Practical Guide to Caring for Your Puppy.* DK Children, 2001.

George, Jean Craighead. *How to Talk to Your Dog.* HarperTrophy, 2003.

Gorrell, Gena K. *Working Like a Dog: The Story of Working Dogs Through History.* Tundra Press, 2003.

Jackson, Donna M. *Hero Dogs: Courageous Canines in Action.* Megan Tingley, 2003.

Mehus-Roe, Kristin, ed. *The Original Dog Bible.* BowTie Press, 2005.

Mehus-Roe, Kristin. *Working Dogs: True Stories of Dogs and Their Handlers.* BowTie Press, 2003.

Rock, Maxine. *Totally Fun Things to Do with Your Dog.* Jossey-Bass, 1998.

Whitehead, Sarah. *Puppy Training for Kids.* Barron's Educational Series, 2001.

Books Just for Fun

Armstrong, William H. *Sounder.* Harper Perennial Modern Classics, 2001 (reprint).

Cleary, Beverly. *Ribsy.* HarperTrophy, 1990 (reprint).

DiCamillo, Kate. *Because of Winn-Dixie.* Candlewick, 2001 (reprint).

Gardiner, John Reynolds. *Stone Fox.* HarperTrophy, 1983 (reissue).

Gipson, Fred. *Old Yeller.* Harper Perennial Modern Classics, 2001 (reprint).

London, Jack. *The Call of the Wild.* Aladdin Classics, 2003 (reprint).

Miller, Sara Swan. *Three More Stories You Can Read to Your Dog.* Houghton Mifflin, 2000.

Miller, Sara Swan. *Three Stories You Can Read to Your Dog.* Houghton Mifflin, 1997.

Naylor, Phyllis. *Shiloh.* Aladdin, 2000 (reprint).

Rawls, Wilson. *Where the Red Fern Grows.* Yearling, 1996 (reprint).

Wallace, Bill. *A Dog Called Kitty.* Aladdin, 1992 (reprint).

Recommended Readings

Web Sites

http://www.akc.org/kids_juniors/
AKC junior handler information

http://www.animalnetwork.com
General information about animals and dogs

http://www.dogchannel.com
General information about dogs

http://www.dogfriendly.com
Dog-friendly travel tips

http://www.dogsforkids.com
Kids' site about dogs

http://www.fbi.gov/kids/dogs/doghome.htm
FBI Working Dogs

http://www.fema.gov/kids/
FEMA for Kids

http://www.hikewithyourdog.com
Hiking information

http://www.kidsrunning.com
Running site for kids

http://www.kindnews.org
Kind News Online

http://www.loveyourdog.com/
How to Love Your Dog

http://www.nhm.org/exhibitions/dogs/
Dogs: Wolf, Myth, Hero & Friend

http://www.pbs.org/wgbh/nova/dogs/
NOVA: Dogs and More Dogs

http://www.pbs.org/wgbh/woof/
Woof! It's a Dog's Life

http://www.petswelcome.com
Dog-friendly travel tips

http://www.workingdogweb.com/Kids&Dogs.htm
Kids' site about working dogs

Periodicals

Dogs for Kids
http://www.dogchannel.com/dogsforkids
888-644-8387

KIND News
http://www.nahee.org
nahee@nahee.org
860-434-8666

National Geographic: Kids
http://www.nationalgeographic.com/ngkids/
800-NGS-LINE

Photo Credits

Front Cover: **(main image):** Faith Uridel. **left (top to bottom):** Diane Lewis, Fotopup, Diane Lewis, Creatas.

Back cover: **(left to right):** Barbara Kimmel, Close Encounters of the Furry Kind, Diane Lewis.

Acknowledgments
6: Alice Su.

Introduction
7: Diane Lewis.

Chapter 1
8: Ron Kimball. **10:** Laurie O'Keefe. **11:** photos.com. **12:** Alice Su. **14-15:** Courtesy of Kennel Club Books. **16:** Courtesy of Kennel Club Books/Bernd Brinkmann.

Chapter 2
17: Laurie O'Keefe. **18 (top):** Ron Kimball. **18 (bottom):** Bonnie Nance. **19, 32:** Courtesy of the National Disaster Search Dog Foundation. **20:** Courtesy of NASA. **21, 22, 24, 29:** Courtesy of Kennel Club Books/Isabelle Francais. **21:** Diane Calkins. **22:** Tara Darling. **23, 24, 25, 26 (bottom left), 27, 28 (left and right):** Courtesy of the Library of Congress. **26 (top):** photos.com. **26 (bottom right):** Courtesy of Kennel Club Books/Isabelle Francais. **30 (top):** Dreamstime. **30 (bottom):** Courtesy of NASA. **31:** Courtesy of the John F. Kennedy Presidential Library and Museum/Cecil Stoughton.

Chapter 3
33, 46 (second and third): Close Encounters of the Furry Kind. **34:** Bonnie Nance. **34, 35, 36, 37, 38, 42, 44, 45:** Laurie O'Keefe. **39:** Diane Calkins. **41:** photos.com. **43:** Dreamstime. **46 (first):** Ron Kimball. **46 (fifth):** Cindy K. Rogers. **46 (fourth):** Tara Darling.

Chapter 4
47 (top): Laurie O'Keefe. **47 (bottom):** Connie Summers. **48 (top), 51, 52, 55:** Bonnie Nance. **48 (bottom), 50 (bottom):** Norvia Behling. **49:** Close Encounters of the Furry Kind. **50 (top):** Ron Kimball. **53 (top):** Pam Marks. **53 (bottom):** Cris Kelly.

Chapter 5
56: Ron Kimball. **57:** Pets by Paulette. **58, 59:** Tara Darling. **62 (top left and top right), 65 (right), 68 (left), 74 (left), 78 (left), 83 (left), 87 (top left), 109 (right), 111 (left), 120 (right):** Courtesy of Kennel Club Books. **62 (bottom), 67 (bottom), 69 (left), 102 (left), 103 (left), 104 (left), 107 (right), 115 (left), 116 (left), 117 (top right), 118 (right), 124 (right), 127 (left and right):** Courtesy of Kennel Club Books/Bernd Brinkmann. **63 (top, middle, and bottom), 64, 65 (left), 66 (top), 67 (top), 69 (right), 70 (left and right), 71 (top left, top right, and bottom), 72 (left and right), 73 (top left and right), 75 (left and right), 76 (left and right), 77 (top left and right), 79 (top left, bottom left, and right), 80 (left and right), 81 (top and bottom left), 82 (left), 83 (top right), 84 (right), 85 (top left, bottom left, and right), 86 (left and right), 87 (bottom left), 88 (left and top right), 89 (right), 90 (left and right), 91 (top left, bottom left, and right), 93 (left, top right, and bottom right), 94 (left and right), 95 (left and right), 96 (left and right), 97 (bottom left and right), 98 (left and right), 99 (left and right), 100 (top left, bottom left, and right), 101 (left and right), 102 (top right and bottom right), 103 (right), 104 (top and bottom right), 105 (bottom left), 106 (left and right), 107 (left), 108 (top left, bottom left, and right), 110 (left and right), 111 (right), 112 (right), 115 (top and bottom right), 117 (left and bottom right), 118 (left), 119 (left and right), 120 (left), 121 (left and right), 122 (top left, bottom left, and right), 123 (left), 125 (left and right), 126 (left and right):** Courtesy of Kennel Club Books/ Cheryl Ertelt. **64 (right), 109 (left):** Courtesy of Kennel Club Books /Isabelle Francais. **66 (bottom), 78 (right), 82 (right), 105 (top left), 123 (right), 124 (left):** Courtesy of Kennel Club Books/Carol Ann Johnson. **68 (right), 81 (bottom right), 84 (left), 105 (right), 116 (right):** Courtesy of Kennel Club Books/Alice van Kempen. **73 (bottom left), 74 (right), 77 (bottom left):** Courtesy of Kennel Club Books/Slinsky. **87 (right), 89 (left), 108 (left):** Isabelle Francais. **88 (bottom right):** Courtesy of Kennel Club Books/Marc Hand. **92 (left):** Courtesy of Kennel Club Books/David Dalton. **92 (right):** Ron Kimball. **97 (top left):** Dwight Dyke. **112 (left):** Courtesy of Kennel Club Books/Karen Taylor. **113** Norvia Behling. **114 (left):** Close Encounters of the Furry Kind.

Chapter 6
128: Ron Kimball. **129:** Diane Lewis. **130, 137:** Bonnie Nance. **131:** Keith May. **131, 134:** Norvia Behling. **132:** Cris Kelly. **135:** Tara Darling. **136:** Judith Strom.

Chapter 7
139: Norvia Behling. **140:** Ron Kimball. **141:** Fotopup. **142:** Dale Spartas. **143, 150:** Bonnie Nance. **144:** Jean

Photo Credits

Fogle. **145, 146:** Tara Darling. **147:** Shirley Fernandez. **148 (top):** Rosemary Shelton. **148 (bottom), 152:** Diane Lewis. **149:** Nancy McCallum. **151:** Cheryl Ertelt.

Chapter 8
153: Pets by Paulette. **154, 157:** Cindy K. Rogers. **155:** photos.com. **156:** Nancy McCallum. **158:** Diane Lewis. **159:** Jean Fogle. **161:** Bonnie Nance.

Chapter 9
162, 166: Ron Kimball. **163 (top):** Bonnie Nance. **163 (bottom):** Pam Marks. **165, 168 (bottom), 170:** Norvia Behling. **168 (top):** D. Johnson. **169:** Pets by Paulette.

Chapter 10
171, 172, 177: Pets by Paulette. **173:** Ron Kimball. **175, 182, 189 (bottom):** Jean Fogle. **176, 180, 187:** Bonnie Nance. **178, 189 (top):** Pam Marks. **179 (top, middle, and bottom):** Norvia Behling. **181 (top, middle, and bottom):** Tara Darling. **183 (left), 184:** Mark Raycroft. **183 (right):** Close Encounters of the Furry Kind. **190 (bottom):** D. Johnson. **190 (top):** Cris Kelly.

Chapter 11
191: Connie Summers. **193:** Diane Lewis. **195:** Pets by Paulette. **196:** Jean Fogle. **197:** Pam Marks. **198:** Ron Kimball. **199:** Bonnie Nance. **200:** Rosemary Shelton.

Chapter 12
201, 207: D. Johnson. **202, 203, 205:** Norvia Behling. **206:** Courtesy of USDA. **208:** Pets by Paulette. **209:** Alice Su. **210 (top):** Bonnie Nance. **210 (bottom):** Dwight Dyke.

Chapter 13
211, 214, 217, 219: Norvia Behling. **212, 213 (bottom), 215, 224:** Bonnie Nance. **213 (top):** Cris Kelly. **216:** Laurie O'Keefe. **221:** D. Johnson. **223:** Close Encounters of the Furry Kind.

Chapter 14
225, 226 (left and right), 228: Keith May. **227:** Norvia Behling. **230:** Dale Spartas. **232:** Cris Kelly. **233:** Close Encounters of the Furry Kind. **234:** Bonnie Nance.

Chapter 15
235, 237, 243, 245, 249, 253: Norvia Behling. **236, 251, 255:** Dwight Dyke. **238:** Pam Marks. **239, 241 (top), 248:** Bonnie Nance. **241 (bottom):** Tara Darling. **242:** Rosemary Shelton. **244, 254:** Cris Kelly. **247:** Pets by

Paulette. **250 (top):** Cindy K. Rogers. **256:** Dreamstime. **257:** Ron Kimball.

Chapter 16
260, 268, 276: Norvia Behling. **262, 271:** photos.com. **263, 266 (top):** Pam Marks. **264:** Alice Su. **265:** Cris Kelly. **266 (bottom):** Laurie O'Keefe. **267:** Mark Raycroft. **269, 272:** Diane Calkins. **273:** Tara Darling. **274:** Ron Kimball. **275:** Dale Spartas.

Chapter 17
277, 291: Shirley Fernandez. **278, 279 (top), 288:** Fotopup. **279 (bottom), 282:** Diane Lewis. **280:** Jean Fogle. **281:** Tara Darling. **283, 284, 287:** Bonnie Nance. **285:** Ron Kimball. **286, 294:** Judith Strom. **289:** Cris Kelly. **292:** Pam Marks. **293:** Bill Love. **295:** Mark Raycroft. **297:** Cheryl Ertelt.

Chapter 18
298: Diane Calkins. **299, 305, 316:** Norvia Behling. **300:** Close Encounters of the Furry Kind. **302, 306:** Tara Darling. **303 (top):** Fotopup. **303 (bottom):** Marmaduke copyright United Features Syndicate, Inc. **304, 307, 322:** Bonnie Nance. **308–309, 312, 314:** Keith May. **311, 313, 315:** Ron Kimball. **317 (top), 318:** Cris Kelly. **317 (bottom):** Pets by Paulette. **320:** Jean Fogle.

Chapter 19
323: Mark Raycroft. **324, 338:** Dreamstime. **325:** Keith May. **326, 336:** Tara Darling. **327, 328:** Diane Lewis. **329, 330 (top):** Bonnie Nance. **330 (bottom):** Cris Kelly. **331:** Norvia Behling. **332 (top), 334:** Pam Marks. **332 (bottom):** Rosemary Shelton. **335:** Jean Fogle. **337:** photos.com. **339:** Cindy K. Rogers.

Chapter 20
340, 341, 348 (top), 349: Bonnie Nance. **342, 344, 346 (bottom):** Cris Kelly. **345:** Fotopup. **346 (top):** Courtesy of the Library of Congress. **347:** Pets by Paulette. **348 (bottom):** Norvia Behling.

Chapter 21
352: D. Johnson. **353:** Norvia Behling. **354, 360, 367:** Bonnie Nance. **355:** photos.com. **356:** Pets by Paulette. **357, 363, 364:** Keith May. **358:** Rosemary Shelton. **361 (top), 362:** Cris Kelly. **361 (bottom):** Alice Su. **366:** Dreamstime.

Index

A

AAA (animal-assisted activity) dogs, 345
AAT (animal-assisted therapy) dogs, 345, 348
abscesses, 247
abuse, 260–62, 268
acclimating your new dog
    to family cats, 166–67
    to family dogs, 163, 164–67
    first day, 164, 167–69
    first month, 169–70
    socialization timeline, 194, 197
acting like a dog, 153–54
adult alerts
    canine sports, 275
    children's volunteer work, 344
    dog bites, 227
    emergency planning, 350
    food aggression, 203
    grooming, 217
    history and kids, 31
    preparing children for career
        with animals, 353
    puppy-proofing, 154
    supervising children, 142, 300,
        310
    training puppies, 173, 174
    vacations with dogs, 325
    veterinary care, 236
adult dogs, 53, 147–49, 152, 188
Affenpinscher, 62
Afghan Hound, 62
African wild dogs (Lycaon pictus), 10, 11
age, selecting dogs based on, 141–43
aggressive behavior, 198, 225–26
agility trials, 278–79
aging, signs of, 53–55
Airedale Terrier, 62

AKC (American Kennel Club), 59, 186, 279, 284
Akita, 63
Alaskan Malamute, 63
alcohol, harm from, 206
allergies of dogs, 246–47
allergy to dogs, 218
American Civil War, 27
American Eskimo Dog, 63
American Foxhound, 64
American Kennel Club (AKC), 59, 186, 279, 284
American Pit Bull Terrier, 64
American Revolution, 25
American Staffordshire Terrier, 64
American Water Spaniel, 65
anal glands, 41, 42
Anatolian Shepherd Dog, 65
anatomy, 34–40
ancient dogs, 12
animal advocates, 360–61
animal-assisted activity (AAA) dogs, 345
animal-assisted therapy (AAT) dogs, 345, 348
animal cops, 359–60
animal cruelty laws, 260–62
animal shelters and rescue groups
    about, 272–73
    adopting adult dogs, 147–49, 152
    breed rescue groups, 148
    fostering puppies for, 348–49
    questions for, 146, 163
    volunteering at, 344–45, 346
    working at, 358–59
animal welfare organizations, 272–73
antifreeze, 157
Appenzeller, 66
artists, 362–63
attention command, 179

Australian Cattle Dog, 66
Australian Kelpie, 67
Australian Shepherd, 48, 67
Australian Terrier, 68

B

bad breath, 46
bad habits, 187–90, 263, 355. See also biters and biting
barking prevention, 187, 188, 263
Basenji, 68
Basset Hound, 69, 330
bathing, 219–20
Beagle Brigade, 364, 365
Beagle, 49, 69, 148
Bearded Collie, 69
Beauceron, 70
Bedlington Terrier, 70
begging prevention, 187, 190
behavior problems, 187–90, 263, 355. See also biters and biting
Belgian Shepherd Dog, 71
Bernese Mountain Dog, 71
Bichon Frise, 72
biking with dogs, 276
biters and biting
    breed characteristics, 264–68
    laws against, 262–63
    signs of impending bite, 198, 229, 233–34, 311
    training to prevent, 189–90, 225–26, 229, 230–34, 242
bites, dog vs. human, 41
Black and Tan Coonhound, 72
Black Russian Terrier, 72
Bloodhound, 73
Border Collie, 57, 73
Border Terrier, 74
Borzoi, 74
Boston Terrier, 75
Bouvier des Flandres, 75
bow trick, 314–15

Index

Boxer, 75

breathing problems, 249–50

breeders, 57, 149–51, 163, 267, 268–69

breed guide, 59, 64–137

breed rescue groups, 148. *See also* animal shelters and rescue groups

breeds
about, 11–13, 33–34, 59, 62–127, 141
characteristics of, 264–68
by continent, 14–16
pronunciation guide, 368
rare breeds, 57–58
selecting puppies based on, 141

Briard, 76

Brittany, 76

brushing and combing, 215, 218–19

Brussels Griffon, 77

Bulldog, 77

Bullmastiff, 78

Bull Terrier, 78

butts
passing gas, 45, 250, 258
problems with, 41–43
sniffing, 44

C

Cairn Terrier, 78

camp for dogs, 332–33

Canaan Dog, 79

cancer, 254

canine caretakers, 362–63

canine enforcement officers, 364–65

canine freestyle dancing, 280–81

Canine Good Citizen test, 186

Cardigan Welsh Corgi, 79

carnivores, 204

cars, not leaving dogs in, 338

cartoon dogs, 29, 30, 167, 303

cat poop, 43–44

cats in the home, 166–67

Cavalier King Charles Spaniel, 80

chase instinct, 233

Chase Me game, 304

chasing your dog, 301

Chesapeake Bay Retriever, 80

chewing prevention, 187, 188–89

Chihuahua, 13, 57, 80

Chinese Crested, 81

Chinese Shar-Pei, 81

chocolate, harm from, 206

choosing your dog
about, 139–41, 152
adopting adult dogs, 147–49
from breeders, 149–51, 152
desirable characteristics, 141–47

Chow Chow, 82

clicker training, 178

Clumber Spaniel, 82

coats
at birth, 51
brushing and combing, 215, 218–19
colors of, 60
health problems, 246–48
signs of aging, 53
types of, 144–45, 212–16

Cocker Spaniel, 83

coffee, harm from, 206

collars, 177–78, 325

Collie, 29, 83, 217

colors, names of, 60

Columbus, Christopher, 25

combing and brushing, 215, 218–19

come command, 181, 182–84, 300–301, 304

commands, basic, 178–86

common names, 9, 11–13

conformation dog shows, 27, 282–84, 365

congenital disorders, 242, 244, 253

congestive heart failure, 248–49

constellations, 26–28

Coonhound, 72

Corgi, 48, 79, 107, 201

coughing, 258

crates, utilizing, 159, 163, 168, 327, 334–36

crate-training, 172–75

Crufts Dog Show, 27, 283–84

Curly-Coated Retriever, 83

cysts, 245, 247, 248

D

Dachshund, 84

Dalmatian, 57, 84

dancing dogs, 280–81

Dandie Dinmont Terrier, 85

deaf dogs, training, 176

Department of Homeland Security dogs, 364–65

designer dogs, 58–59

dewclaws, 224

diarrhea, 259

digestive system, 35, 250–52

digging and digging spots, 187–88

disaster kits, 350–51

disc dogs, 281–82

diseases, 254–55

DNA, 9, 11–13, 32

Doberman Pinscher, 85

dog artists, 362–63

dog duty roster for families, 133, 134, 135–37

dog etiquette, 226–30, 321–22

dog handlers, 364–66

dog licenses, 263

Index

dog parks, 318–21
dogs (*Canis familiaris*)
    growing up, 47–55, 49
    history of, 8–10, 17–18, 20–25
    in mythology, 25–28
    in religion, 28–32
    taxonomy of, 9–12
dogs already at home, 158, 163, 164–65
dogs chasing animals, 263, 301
dog shows
    conformation, 27, 282–84, 365
    organized sports, 277–82, 284–86
Dog Star, 27
dog trainer, becoming a, 357
domestication of dogs, 17–18
down command, 179, 180–81
drooling behavior, 43, 258

E
ears
    at birth, 51
    health problems, 242–43
    sense of hearing, 36, 55, 192
    smelly, 46, 243, 259
    types of, 61
eating. *See* food and feeding
eating grass or poop, 43–45
emergencies, 239, 240, 244
energy level, food and, 209
English Cocker Spaniel, 86
English Foxhound, 86
English Setter, 86
English Springer Spaniel, 87
Entlebucher, 87
euthanization of excess dogs, 268, 271
exercise for puppies, 51–52
exercise-type games, 303–4. *See also* games for dogs; sports for dogs

eyes
    anatomy of, 38
    at birth, 51
    crustiness around, 44
    health problems, 242
    signs of aging, 53–54
    vision capability, 38–39

F
fanciers, 57
farting, 45, 250, 258
fearful puppies and dogs, 191–93, 195–98, 229, 231
feral dogs, 17–18
fetch games, 303
first aid kits, 252, 325
Flat-Coated Retriever, 88
fleas, 246, 256, 332
flyball team relays, 279–80
food and feeding
    about, 201–3
    bowls for, 159
    dog kibble ingredients, 203–5
    homemade foods, 206–7
    snacks, 210
    special diets, 208–10
    toxic foods, 206
Foxhound, 64, 86
Fox Terrier, 25, 88
French Bulldog, 88
Frisbee (canine disc), 281–82
fund-raising for doggy causes, 342–44

G
games for dogs
    about, 298
    with action toys, 318
    exercise-type, 303–4
    learning games, 298–302
    mind-strengthening, 304–6

paw painting and sculpting, 308–10
photo shoots, 306–8
tricks, 311–16
See also sports for dogs
garlic, harm from, 206
genetic diseases, 257
genetics, 9, 11–13, 32
German Pinscher, 89
German Shepherd Dog, 89
German Shorthaired Pointer, 90
German Wirehaired Pointer, 90
gestation period, 34, 47
Giant Schnauzer, 90
Glen of Imaal Terrier, 91
Golden Retriever, 91, 142, 230, 254
Gordon Setter, 92
grapes, harm from, 206
Great Dane, 92, 143, 200, 208
Greater Swiss Mountain Dog, 92
Great Pyrenees, 93
greeting a dog, 226, 228–30
Greyhound, 93, 97, 215, 273
groomer, becoming a, 361
grooming, 211–19
grooming tools, 159, 212, 215, 218
guard dogs, 12, 13, 18
guide dogs, 22, 263, 265, 347–48

H
hackles, raising, 229
hairless dogs, grooming, 216
harnesses, 177
Harrier, 94
Havanese, 94
health problems
    about, 241, 258–59
    digestive system, 250–52
    diseases, 254–55
    ears, 242–43

eyes, 242
heart, 248–49
lungs and breathing, 249–50
mouth and throat, 245–46
musculoskeletal system, 253–54
nervous system, 252–53
nose, 243–44
parasites, 256–57
paws, 248
skin and coat, 246–48
hearing, sense of, 36, 55, 192.
heart problems, 248–49
heartworms, 257
herbivores, 204
herding dogs, 12, 13, 19
hide and seek, 304
hiking, 293–95
hot spots, 246
house-training, 175–77
humane educators, 360–61
hunting dogs, 12, 13, 18

I
Ibizan Hound, 95
Inca Empire, 244
in-line skating with dogs, 276
Irish Setter, 50, 95
Irish Terrier, 96
Irish Water Spaniel, 96
Irish Wolfhound, 13, 96
Italian Greyhound, 97

J
Jack Russell Terrier, 97
Japanese Chin, 98
jumping up prevention, 187, 188

K
Keeshond, 98
kennels, 339
Kerry Blue Terrier, 98

kibble ingredients, 203–5
Kids in Nature's Defense (KIND), 343
KIND (Kids in Nature's Defense), 343
kiss on command, 315–16
Komondor, 99, 214–15
Korean War, 30
Kuvasz, 99

L
Labradoodle, 59
Labrador Retriever, 100
Lassie, 29
laws for dog owners
    against abuse, 260–62, 268
    owners' requirements, 262–63
    working dogs, 263, 265
learning games, 298–304
leashes, 177–78, 325, 337
leash laws, 262, 263
leash training, 177–78, 184, 185–86
leave it command, 184–85
Lewis and Clark expedition, 26
Lhasa Apso, 100
licenses, 263
lick granulomas, 246–47, 248
licking behavior, 41–43
lost dogs, finding, 351
Löwchen, 101
low-shedding dogs, 213–14, 218
Lundehund, 33, 58
lung problems, 249–50

M
Macadamia nuts, harm from, 206
malnourishment, 210, 257
Maltese, 101
mammals, 12, 13
Manchester Terrier, 101
massaging your dog, 310–11

Mastiff, 22, 78, 102, 103, 123, 146
meeting a new dog, 226, 228–30
memory games, 304–6
microchips, 351
Miniature Pinscher, 102
Miniature Poodle, 111
Miniature Rat Terrier, 113
Miniature Schnauzer, 103
mites, 242–43, 256
mouth and throat health problems, 245–46
movie dogs, 29
musculoskeletal system, 34, 253–54
mutts, 33, 58–59
muzzles, 242
mythology, 25–28

N
nail trimming, 222–24
naming your puppy, 160–61
Neapolitan Mastiff, 103
nervous system, 34, 252–53
Newfoundland, 26, 103
nipping. *See* biters and biting
Norfolk Terrier, 104
Norwegian Elkhound, 104
Norwich Terrier, 104
nose, 37, 243–44
Nova Scotia Duck Trolling Retriever, 105

O
obstacle course games, 278–79, 301–2
Old English Sheepdog, 105
omnivores, 204
onions, harm from, 206
organized sports. *See* sports for dogs
Otterhound, 106

Index

outside dangers, 154–57
overpopulation, 268–71

P
Papillon, 106
parasites
fleas, 246, 256, 332
mites, 242–43, 256
worms, 41, 42, 237, 256, 257
Parson Russell Terrier, 97
parties for dogs, 320, 321–22
passing gas, 45, 250, 258
Pavlov, 42
paws
health problems, 248
painting and sculpting, 308–10
snowballs in, 297
Pearl Harbor, 29
pee, 35, 175–77, 259
Pekingese, 29, 30–31, 107
Pembroke Welsh Corgi, 107
personality, selecting puppies
based on, 145–47, 152
Peruvian Inca Orchid, 58, 107
Petit Basset Griffon Vendéen,
108
pet sitters and doggy hotels,
337–39
Pharaoh Hound, 108
pit bull-type dogs, 64, 265–66,
267
Plant Protection and Quarantine
(PPQ) officers, 365
play dead, 313
Plott, 109
Pluto, 29
Pointer, 109
police dogs, 19, 363, 364
Polish Lowland Sheepdog, 110
Pomeranian, 110
Poodle, 111, 191, 214
poop, 35, 43–44, 175–77, 259

poop dogs, 20
poop scoop laws, 262, 263
Portuguese Water Dog, 111, 328
potty areas for dogs, 337
PPQ (Plant Protection and
Quarantine) officers, 365
pregnant dogs, 34, 47
pros and cons list, 130, 131
Pug, 22, 112, 203, 227
Puli, 112
Pumi, 113
puppies
at birth, 47–48, 49
gestation period, 34, 47
socializing, 48, 50, 191–200,
230–33
puppy paraphernalia
collars, 177–78, 325
collars and leashes, 177–78
grooming tools, 159, 212, 215,
218
leashes, 177–78, 325, 337
licenses, 263
shopping for, 157–59
toys, 159, 167–68, 169,
316–18, 366
puppy proofing home and yard,
153–61

Q
questions to ask
during adoption process, 146,
151, 163, 166
main caretaker and family, 130,
131, 132, 135–37
veterinarians, 238, 240

R
races with dogs, 303
raisins, harm from, 206
rare breeds, 57–58
Rat Terrier, 113

recommended reading, 373–74
religion, 28–32
Renaissance in Europe, 24
rescuers. *See* animal shelters and
rescue groups
responsibilities of humans
basics, 128–30
dog duty roster, 133, 134,
135–37
family involvement, 129,
130–32, 137
loving your dog, 128, 129,
136–37, 340–41
researching breed and care
issues, 132–34
responsibility contracts, 137–38
Rhodesian Ridgeback, 114
roll over trick, 314
Roman Empire, 22
Rottweiler, 43, 114, 267
rough games, 301
running, 289–91

S
Saint Bernard, 115, 208, 346
Saluki, 115
Samoyed, 116
scent discrimination, 287
Schipperke, 116
Schnauzer, 103, 121
scientific names, 9–12
scooting behavior, 40–41
Scottish Deerhound, 116
Scottish Terrier, 117
Sealyham Terrier, 117
search and rescue dogs
about, 24–25
after Sept. 11, 2001, terrorist
attacks, 19, 25, 32
training your dog for, 305–6,
354
at work, 18

Index

senses, 36–40

service dogs, 22, 263, 265, 347–48

shake and give me five tricks, 311–12

Shar-Pei, 81

shed cycles, 213–14

shedding, 46

Sheepdog, 105, 110, 118

shelters. *See* animal shelters and rescue groups

Shetland Sheepdog, 118

Shiba Inu, 16, 118

Shih Tzu, 119, 214

shopping. *See* puppy paraphernalia

shopping with dogs, 158, 328–29

Siberian Husky, 119, 145

silky coats, grooming, 215–16

Silky Terrier, 119

sit command, 179–80

size, selecting puppies based on, 143–44

skateboarding with dogs, 276

skijoring, 286

skin and coat problems, 246–48

Skye Terrier, 120

sled dogs, 28, 29, 284–86

slicker burn, 219

smell, sense of, 36–38, 243–44

smelling butts, 44

smelly dogs, 45–46, 243, 259

smoking (tobacco) households, 238

snacks, 210, 325

snakebites, 293

sneezing, 259

snow sports, 284–86, 295

socializing puppies and dogs, 48, 50, 191–200, 230–33

Soft Coated Wheaten Terrier, 120, 213

Space Age dogs, 30

spaying and neutering
  facts and fiction, 269–71
  reasons for, 233, 240–41, 268–69

spinal cord injuries, 252–53

spin trick, 312

sports for dogs
  about, 274–77, 286–87
  agility trials, 278–79
  canine disc competitions, 281–82
  canine freestyle dancing, 280–81
  conformation dog shows, 27, 282–84, 365
  every day sports, 289–97
  flyball team relays, 279–80
  hiking, 293–95
  organized sports, 277–86
  rules for, 288
  running, 289–91
  safety ideas, 296–97
  snow sports, 28, 29, 284–86, 295
  swimming, 295–96
  walking, 292
  warm-up with stretching, 290

Staffordshire Bull Terrier, 121

Staffordshire Terrier, 64

Standard Poodle, 111

Standard Rat Terrier, 113

Standard Schnauzer, 121

stay command, 181–82

stretching, 290

styptic powder, 224

sunscreen, 216, 246

Sussex Spaniel, 122

Swedish Vallhund, 24, 122

swimming, 295–96

T

tails, types of, 61

tails, wagging, 230

teasing (not), 192, 225, 226, 232

teeth
  bared, 198, 229
  brushing, 46, 220–22
  development of, 48
  mouth and throat problems, 245–46
  number of, 34

terminology, 369–72

therapy dogs, 345, 348

thunderstorms, fear of, 192

Tibetan Mastiff, 123

Tibetan Spaniel, 123

Tibetan Terrier, 124

ticks, 256, 293

tobacco smoking households, 238

toothpaste, 220. *See also* teeth

touch, sense of, 39–40

toxins, 154–57, 206

Toy Poodle, 111

toys, 159, 167–68, 169, 316–18, 366

training classes for new dogs, 170

training puppies
  about food, 167, 168
  about grooming, 211–12
  basic commands, 178–85
  clicker training, 178
  crate-training, 172–75
  house-training, 175–77
  leash training, 177–78, 184, 185–86
  overcoming bad habits, 187–90
  overcoming fear, 193–93, 195–98
  reasons for, 171–72, 178

traveling with your dog
  about, 323, 333–34

Index

doggy camp, 332–33
driving, 162–63, 335–37
flying, 334–35
on vacation, 323–32
tricks, 311–16
tug (not tug-of-war), 299–300, 301
tumors, 245

u

undercoats, 212, 213, 216
U.S. state dogs, 66

v

vaccinations, 236–37, 255
veterinarian, becoming a, 353, 355–56
veterinary behaviorists, 355
veterinary care
about veterinarians, 238–40
adopting sick dogs and, 152
for crustiness around the eyes, 44
emergencies, 239, 240, 244
maintenance visits, 52, 53, 55, 128, 235
microchips, 351
for new puppy/dog, 170, 236–38, 255
snakebites, 293
special diets, 208–10

See also health problems; spaying and neutering
veterinary technicians, 356–57
Vietnam War, 31
viruses, 255
vision, sense of, 38–39
Vizsla, 124
volunteering to help dogs
about, 340–41, 344–46, 356
fostering puppies for shelters, 348–49
fund-raisers, 342–44
vomiting, 258

w

walking, 292
war dogs, 25, 27, 28, 30, 31, 32
water, drinking excessively, 258
water, exercise and, 291, 297
wave trick, 312–13
Weimaraner, 125, 130
Welsh Corgi, 48, 79, 107, 201
Welsh Springer Spaniel, 125
Welsh Terrier, 125
West Highland White Terrier, 126
Westminster Kennel Club Dog Show, 27, 283–84
Whippet, 127
whiskers, 40
wiry coats, grooming, 215
wolves, 9–10, 18

working dog organizations
adopting from, 148–49
fostering puppies for, 347–48
working dogs
AAA and AAT dogs, 345
about, 18–23
service dogs, 22, 263, 265, 347–48
working with dogs
about, 352–53
animal advocates and humane educators, 360–61
animal cops, 359–60
at animal shelters, 358–59
canine caretakers, 362–63
dog artists, 362–63
dog handlers, 364–66
dog trainers, 357
groomers, 361
veterinarians, 353, 355–56
veterinary technicians, 356–57
World Trade Center search and rescue dogs, 19, 25, 32
World War I, 28
worms, 41, 42, 237, 257

y

years, dog-to-human, 54
Yorkshire Terrier, 127

About the Author

Kristin Mehus-Roe is the editor of *The Original Dog Bible*, the author of *Working Dogs: True Stories of Dogs and Their Handlers*, former managing editor of *Popular Pets* dog magazines, and a frequent contributor to several other companion animal magazines. She is especially interested in issues of animal welfare. She lives in Seattle, Washington, with her husband, son, and two dogs.